Study Guide

UNDERSTANDING ABNORMAL BEHAVIOR

Study Guide

UNDERSTANDING ABNORMAL BEHAVIOR

Fourth Edition

Richard L. Leavy
Ohio Wesleyan University

David Sue
Western Washington University

Derald Sue
California State University, Hayward

Stanley Sue
University of California, Los Angeles

HOUGHTON MIFFLIN COMPANY BOSTON TORONTO
Geneva, Illinois Palo Alto Princeton, New Jersey

Senior Sponsoring Editor: Michael DeRocco
Development Editor: Susan Yanchus
Editorial Assistant: Stefanie Jacobs
Production Coordinator: LuAnn Belmonte Paladino
Senior Manufacturing Coordinator: Marie Barnes
Marketing Manager: Rebecca J. Dudley

Printed in the U.S.A.

Library of Congress Catalog Card Number: 93-78705

ISBN: 0-395-69104-4

123456789-PO-97 96 95 94 93

CONTENTS

PREFACE

TO THE STUDENT

This Study Guide was designed to help you master the material in the Fourth Edition of *Understanding Abnormal Behavior* by Sue/Sue/Sue. The Study Guide supplements the text but does not replace it. If used properly, it should help you to understand and master key facts, concepts, and - issues discussed in the text.

ORGANIZATION OF THE STUDY GUIDE

Each Study Guide chapter corresponds to a text chapter and is divided into the following sections: Learning Objectives, Chapter Outlines, Key Terms, and Multiple-Choice questions (fact and concept questions and application questions).

- *Learning Objectives* The learning objectives guide your mastery of the material by focusing your attention on the key ideas and concepts in each chapter. Page numbers corresponding to the objectives have been identified to encourage you to use the text and Study Guide interactively for maximum benefit.

- *Chapter Outlines* The outlines present the major ideas and topics in each chapter. Key terms are defined and page numbers corresponding to the outline material are provided. The outlines are condensed overviews of chapter material and are excellent review mechanisms. But they cannot and should not be used as substitutes for reading the chapter.

- *Key Terms* Key terms appearing at the end of each chapter in the text are also defined in the chapter outlines. To further reinforce your mastery of these terms, we provide fill-in-the-blank quizzes. This three-pronged approach to learning should strengthen your command of the terminology common to abnormal psychology.

- *Multiple-Choice Questions* Once you have read the text and worked your way through the first three sections of the Study Guide, you will be ready to test your knowlege of the material covered. Thirty multiple-choice questions have been constructed for this purpose. Twenty fact-and-concept questions test your understanding of facts, principles, definitions, and the relationships among them. Ten application questions test your ability to apply the information you are learning. At the end of these tests, we provide the correct answers and explain why each answer is correct or incorrect. Page numbers identify where in the text answers can be found.

A FINAL WORD

We hope you find this Study Guide useful in mastering the often complex and at times conflicting material confronting you. Our goal in designing this Guide has been to provide a structured approach to learning that will maximize your ability to successfully complete your course in abnormal psychology. Good luck!

Study Guide

UNDERSTANDING ABNORMAL BEHAVIOR

PART 1
The Study of Abnormal Behavior

CHAPTER 1
Abnormal Behavior

LEARNING OBJECTIVES

When you have mastered the material in Chapter 1, you should be able to:

1. List and describe the concerns of abnormal psychology, including description, explanation, prediction, and control of abnormal behavior. (pp. 3–5)
2. Discuss the assumptions of and problems with the statistical, ideal mental health, and traditional criteria used to define abnormality. Explain the multicultural approach to understanding abnormal behavior, and define the terms *cultural universality* and *cultural relativism.* (pp. 5–9)
3. Discuss the components of the practical criteria for defining abnormality. Give illustrations of discomfort, bizarreness, disorientation, and inefficiency. (pp. 9–11)
4. Describe the concept of multiple perspectives and the text authors' definition of abnormal behavior. Discuss Wakefield's (1992) linking of biological facts and social values.(pp. 11–12)
5. Discuss the scope of mental disorders in the United States. Describe the most prevalent disorders and the role played by age and gender. (pp. 12–14)
6. Describe recent trends in mental health problems and the use of professional care. Describe the beliefs that underlie current enthusiasm for therapy. (Focus 1.1; pp. 14-15)
7. Discuss common myths concerning abnormal behavior and the facts that refute them. (pp. 14–17)
8. Describe the training and typical work roles of clinical psychologists, counseling psychologists, psychiatrists, psychoanalysts, psychiatric social workers, and marriage and family counselors. (Table 1.1; pp. 17–18)
9. Describe the different explanations of abnormal behavior from prehistoric times to the Middle Ages. (pp. 18–21)
10. Describe the changes that occurred in the treatment of abnormal behavior during the era of witchcraft, humanism, and the reform movement until the present. (pp. 21–23)
11. Discuss the main assumptions of the organic and psychological viewpoints on abnormal behavior. Discuss the contributions of mesmerism and hypnosis to the psychoanalytic viewpoint. (pp. 23–26)
12. Describe and discuss the biopsychosocial approach to abnormal behavior. (pp. 26–27)
13. Describe medical student syndrome and reactions to it. (p. 28; Focus 1.2)

CHAPTER OUTLINE

1. **The Case of Steven V.** (pp. 1–3) Steven V. (a hypothetical composite case) is threatening to kill his ex-girlfriend. He has a long psychiatric history and current problems that include depression and a violent, sexually oriented fantasy life.

2. **The concerns of abnormal psychology** (pp. 3–5) *Abnormal psychology* seeks to describe, explain, predict, and control those behaviors that are considered strange. In describing disorders, psychologists develop a *psychodiagnosis.* Diagnosis is a useful first step in treatment but, because of labeling, may be harmful. Explanations of abnormal behavior depend on the psychologist's theoretical orientation. The prediction of future behavior is difficult; for instance, psychologists tend to overpredict future violent behavior. The *Tarasoff* legal decision, which says that therapists can be sued if they fail to warn people who are later harmed by clients, points out the ethical and legal problems with incorrect prediction of future behavior. *Therapy* is the method by which psychologists try to control behavior.

3. **Defining abnormal behavior** (pp. 5–11) Statistical criteria define abnormality as those behaviors that are infrequent. One problem with this standard is that it provides no means for deciding what is rare and what is undesirable.

   Ideal mental health criteria define abnormality as deviation from some positive behavior. Unfortunately, there is little agreement on the positive behavior psychologists should choose.

   Multicultural criteria strive for a middle ground between two opposite views. One approach is *cultural universality,* the traditional viewpoint on abnormality, which states that there are universal symptoms. The opposite is *cultural relativism,* which says that deviance reflects cultural values. A combination of the two approaches seems appropriate.

   Practical criteria for judging abnormality include discomfort, bizarreness, disorientation, and inefficiency. Discomfort involves both physical and psychological pain. Bizarreness refers to odd behaviors, such as *hallucinations* (false sensory impressions) and *delusions* (false beliefs). One problem with the bizarreness criterion is that as cultures change, so do judgments about what is odd. *Disorientation* is confusion concerning identity, place, or time. Inefficiency is exhibited when a person's performance falls well short of his or her potential.

4. **The concept of multiple perspectives** (pp. 11–12) Since all criteria have some shortcomings, a combination of criteria may be most effective. Strupp and Hadley (1977) suggest that judgments concerning abnormality use three vantage points: the individual, the mental health professional, and society. Wakefield (1992) proposes that mental disorder be defined as a harmful dysfunction, where "harmful" is defined by society and "dysfunction" is based on biological sciences.

5. **A definition of abnormal behavior** (p. 12) The authors define *abnormal behavior* as "behavior that departs from some norm and is detrimental to the affected individual or to others."

6. **The incidence of abnormal behavior** (pp. 12–14) The goals of psychiatric epidemiology are to determine how frequent disorders are in the population, how such factors as age and gender affect their prevalence, and whether trends are changing. About 29 to 38 percent of the U.S. population have experienced at least one DSM-III disorder. The most common mental disorder is alcohol abuse or alcohol dependence. Although, overall, men and women are equally likely to suffer from disorders, men are more likely to have alcohol problems, and women are more likely to become depressed or anxious. Older people are vulnerable to cognitive impairments.

7. **The psychologically oriented society** (pp. 14, 15; Focus 1.1) Americans, in general, spend a great deal of money on the growing business of psychological care. From 1974 to 1985, the number of practicing psychologists increased by over 100 percent. College -educated people tend to use psychotherapy a good deal, as do mental health professionals themselves.

8. **Stereotypes about the mentally disturbed** (pp. 14–17) One myth is that mentally disturbed people can be readily spotted. This is not true because there are no sharp dividing lines between normality and abnormality and because some forms of deviance can be hidden. Another myth is that mental disorder is always inherited. Genetics can play a role in some disorders, but environmental stress is a crucial influence. Other myths are that people with mental disorders cannot be cured, that their problems stem from a lack of will power, that those who suffer disorders contribute nothing to society, and that they are more dangerous than other people.

9. **The mental health professions** (Table 1.1; pp. 17–18) There are an increasing number of mental health professionals in the United States. Clinical psychologists have Ph.D. or Psy.D. degrees and are trained to assess and treat people with serious disorders. Counseling psychologists are trained in much the same way as clinical psychologists, but they traditionally emphasize less serious problems. Psychiatrists have medical degrees and can prescribe medication. Psychoanalysts are trained in psychoanalytic institutes and complete a personal analysis. Psychiatric social workers usually get a master's degree and often work in family or community agencies. Marriage and family counseling is a new field with a wide range of training and work-setting options, but most counselors have a master's degree and many hours of supervised clinical experience.

10. **Historical perspectives on abnormal behavior** (pp. 18–23) How people view mental disorders is related to the beliefs of their culture and time. During prehistoric times, people believed in *demonology*. Treatments included *trephining* (chipping open the skull) and exorcism (prayers, noise making, and even starvation to drive out spirits). During the Greco-Roman era, disorders were seen as being due to organic factors such as brain pathology.

    During the Middle Ages, the Catholic Church dominated all thought and explained mental disorder in supernatural terms. Whole populations were sometimes affected by such forms of mass madness as tarantism (a dance mania) and lycanthropy (in which people believe themselves to be wolves).

    Witchcraft became a common explanation for mental disorder during the 1500s and 1600s, when the Catholic Church was under attack. Some mentally ill people were considered witches and received brutal punishment, but most witches were sane.

    In the mid-1500s, *humanism* stressed human welfare and rejected the supernatural aspects of witchcraft. Johann Weyer asserted that people who had been thought to be witches were actually mentally disturbed.

    Around 1800, a reform movement called the *moral treatment movement* began in France (Philippe Pinel) and England (William Tuke). In America (Benjamin Rush), mental patients were also treated more humanely. Dorothea Dix pushed for the improvement of mental hospitals. Clifford Beers exposed the cruel treatment he and other patients experienced in mental institutions.

11. **Causes: Early viewpoints** (pp. 23–26) From Hippocrates' day to our own, organic explanations of abnormality have existed. During the late 1800s, there was a strong increase in this *biogenic view.* The discovery that general paresis had an organic cause supported this idea. When certain symptoms occur in clusters, they are called *syndromes.* It was believed that each syndrome had a unique cause.

The *psychogenic view* (that emotions can cause disorder) is an alternative view. Anton Mesmer used trances (mesmerism) to treat people with hysteria, sometimes successfully. Although he was declared a fraud, these treatments underscored the power of suggestion for curing disorder. *Hypnotism* was studied and used by several French physicians (Liebeault, Bernheim, and Charcot) to treat hysteria during the late 1800s. Breuer found that reliving past experiences (the *cathartic method*) removed symptoms, too. Sigmund Freud built upon this foundation.

12. **The contemporary viewpoint: A biopsychosocial approach** (pp. 26–27) Contemporary psychologists appreciate the contribution of drug treatment and research on abnormal psychology, and have come to believe that multiple factors combine to cause most forms of abnormal behavior. This viewpoint involving biological, cognitive, and environmental factors is called the *biopsychosocial* perspective.

13. **What lies ahead in this text** (pp. 27–28) The first part of the book acquaints the reader with explanations for abnormal psychology, diagnosis, and research methods. The major portion of the text examines disorders that involve a wide range of problems. Finally, the text examines therapies and prevention efforts, as well as the legal and ethical issues raised in the study of abnormal behavior.

    The Case of Steven V. is used in future chapters to emphasize the fact that abnormal behavior is nonetheless human behavior. Steve's case will be used to illustrate different disorders, ways of explaining those disorders, and methods of treating them.

    Readers may experience "medical student syndrome"—the tendency to think one has a disorder described in the text. Discussing such concerns with friends or the professor of the course is advised.

KEY TERMS

Fill-in-the-Blanks Quiz

1. The therapeutic use of verbal expression to release pent-up unconscious conflicts is called the ____________.

2. The belief that mental disorders are caused by psychological or emotional factors is called the ____________.

3. The ancient surgical technique in which part of the skull is chipped away to provide an escape for evil spirits is called ____________.

4. The belief that problems are caused by evil spirits that invade the victim is called ____________.

5. False beliefs that are not altered by evidence are called ____________.

6. Begun by Philippe Pinel, this movement was a shift toward more humane treatment for mentally disturbed patients. It was called the ____________.

7. A cluster of symptoms that tends to occur together and is believed to be indicative of a particular disorder is called a(n) ____________.

8. A program of systematic intervention whose purpose is to modify a client's behavior, emotions, or thoughts is called ___________.

9. Confusion about one's identity or where one is or the time during which events are occurring is called ___________.

10. The scientific discipline that seeks to describe, explain, predict, and control behaviors that are considered unusual is called ___________.

11. A false sensory impression such as hearing voices that are not present is called a(n) ___________.

12. This movement challenged supernatural explanations and emphasized the uniqueness of the individual and human welfare. It was called ___________.

13. The belief that mental disorders have a physical or physiological basis is called the ___________.

14. The belief that many behavior disorders cut across lifestyles, cultural norms, and world views is called ___________.

15. The belief that lifestyles, cultural values, and world views affect the expression and determination of deviant behavior is called ___________.

16. An attempt to describe, assess, and systematically draw inferences about an individual's psychological disorder is called a(n) ___________.

17. The contemporary approach that sees the cause of most disorders as a combination of biological, psychological, and social factors is called the ___________.

18. The trance-inducing technique that has been used to unlock unconscious experiences is called ___________.

19. Behavior that departs from some norm and harms the affected individual or others is called ___________.

Answers to Fill-in-the-Blanks Quiz

1. cathartic method
2. psychogenic view
3. trephining
4. demonology
5. delusions
6. moral treatment movement
7. syndrome
8. therapy
9. disorientation
10. abnormal psychology
11. hallucination
12. humanism
13. biogenic view
14. cultural universality
15. cultural relativism
16. psychodiagnosis
17. biopsychosocial perspective
18. hypnotism
19. abnormal behavior

FACT AND CONCEPT QUESTIONS

1. When a psychologist attempts to change or control abnormal behavior, this is done through the process of
   a. psychodiagnosis.
   b. therapy.
   c. research.
   d. clinical assessment.

2. Which of the following is a drawback to using statistical criteria for defining abnormal behavior?
   a. They fail to distinguish rare behaviors that are desirable from those that are undesirable.
   b. They fail to examine how frequently a behavior occurs.
   c. They fail to show a relationship between prediction and control of behavior.
   d. They fail to use objective, empirical information about deviant behavior.

3. The ideal mental health criteria
   a. are based on discomfort, bizarreness, and inefficiency.
   b. have few drawbacks.
   c. look at deviations from a positive goal.
   d. are based on the frequency of deviant actions.

4. How does cultural relativism respond to Kraepelin's traditional approach to abnormality?
   a. It rejects the idea that behaviors defined as abnormal in western culture are abnormal everywhere else.
   b. It agrees with the idea that abnormality is defined in terms of deviation from some ideal of mental health.
   c. It takes no stand on the traditional approach.
   d. It supports the idea that abnormality is based on biological differences.

5. According to the practical criteria for abnormality, when a person complains of asthma, fatigue, and nausea, this is evidence of
   a. disorientation.
   b. discomfort.
   c. bizarreness.
   d. inefficiency.

6. False sensory impressions are called ____________; false beliefs that are held despite contradictory evidence are called ____________.
   a. disorientations; delusions
   b. hallucinations; delusions
   c. hallucinations; disorientations
   d. delusions; hallucinations

7. Wakefield (1992) suggests that mental disorder be seen as
   a. a biologically caused phenomenon which is unchanged by society.
   b. having three components: rarity, deviation from ideal, and cultural norms.
   c. a functional deficiency based on biological science that is seen as harmful by society.
   d. the result of poor parenting, inadequate social resources, and unavailable treatment.

8. Based on the National Institute of Mental Health epidemiological study of mental disorders in three major cities,
   a. the rate of mental disorders has steadily decreased over the past twenty years.
   b. approximately one in fifty Americans suffers from an emotional disorder.
   c. depression is among the least common disorders in the United States.
   d. alcohol problems and phobic disorders are the most common disorders in the United States.

9. Which of the following is an accurate statement concerning heredity and mental disorder?
   a. Heredity has such a powerful influence on the occurrence of some disorders that environmental factors play no role.
   b. Heredity has been found to play no role in even the most serious mental disorders.
   c. Because most mental disorders are inherited, they cannot be cured.
   d. Although heredity plays an important role in some disorders, the environment plays a major role in all of them.

10. A clinical psychologist's education includes
   a. training in the assessment and treatment of abnormal behaviors.
   b. original research in an area of specialization.
   c. getting a Ph.D. or Psy.D. degree.
   d. all of the above.

11. Among all the mental health professionals, only the ___________ can prescribe medicine.
   a. psychiatrist
   b. clinical psychologist
   c. psychiatric social worker
   d. counseling psychologist

12. Which of the following treatments for abnormal behavior is correctly paired with its period in history?
   a. Exorcism—Middle Ages
   b. Trephining—Renaissance
   c. Exorcism—moral treatment era
   d. Cathartic method—moral treatment era

13. Tarantism and lycanthropy are examples of ___________, which occurred during the ___________.
   a. mesmerism; 1200s
   b. mass madness; 1200s
   c. exorcism; 1800s
   d. mass madness; time of ancient Greece and Rome

14. Modern interpretations of witchcraft suggest that
   a. people who were seen as voluntary witches were treated with sympathy and kindness.
   b. witches were often not insane.
   c. the church actually tried to stop the hunting of witches.
   d. the church believed that witches were suffering from brain pathology.

15. Clifford Beers, Dorothea Dix, and Benjamin Rush were all
    a. Americans who supported Freud's psychoanalytic theory.
    b. researchers on hypnosis and hysteria.
    c. involved in improving the treatment offered in mental institutions.
    d. supporters of the idea that mental disorder stems from organic causes.

16. A person who discusses mental disorders in terms of syndromes and believes that they are caused solely by brain disease, heredity, or metabolic disturbances supports the
    a. psychogenic viewpoint.
    b. idea of demonology.
    c. organic viewpoint.
    d. biopsychosocial orientation.

17. The technique of mesmerism was a forerunner of
    a. hypnotism.
    b. drug therapy.
    c. exorcism.
    d. trephining.

18. Charcot and Bernheim were to ____________ as Breuer was to ____________.
    a. freeing mental patients; hypnosis
    b. schizophrenia; hysteria
    c. freeing mental patients; the cathartic method
    d. hypnosis; the cathartic method

19. What was a major contribution of the physicians of the Nancy school?
    a. They showed that the symptoms of hysteria could be produced and removed using hypnosis.
    b. They showed that mental patients could be unchained without endangering the treatment staff.
    c. They showed that Mesmer's "treatment" was a fraud.
    d. They showed that general paresis was due to brain damage caused by syphilis.

20. According to your textbook authors, *most* psychologists believe that mental disorders are caused by
    a. psychological factors only.
    b. heredity and brain deficits.
    c. cultural factors only.
    d. a combination of biological, psychological, and societal influences.

APPLICATION QUESTIONS

1. Dr. Eberhardt has already collected information on a person through observations and psychological tests, and is now formulating a psychodiagnosis. Dr. Eberhardt is involved in which objective of abnormal psychology?
    a. Prediction
    b. Control
    c. Research
    d. Definition

2. Dr. Smith says, "Abnormality is simply based on how rare a particular behavior is." Dr. Wright says, "Abnormality is defined by the values of the society in which it takes place." Dr. Smith's ideas reflect the ____________ criteria; Dr. Wright's ideas reflect the ____________ criteria.
   a. practical; traditional
   b. ideal mental health; cultural relativist
   c. ideal mental health; traditional
   d. statistical; cultural relativist

3. Martin is hearing voices, and he firmly believes that Martians are poisoning his oatmeal. Martin's behavior illustrates the ____________ component of the practical criteria for defining abnormality.
   a. disorientation
   b. bizarreness
   c. inefficiency
   d. discomfort

4. Dr. Rivers says, "We should look at abnormality from three vantage points: the individual's, society's, and the mental health professional's." Dr. Rivers would be in agreement with the ____________ criteria for abnormality.
   a. cultural relativism
   b. multiple perspectives
   c. practical
   d. statistical

5. Imagine that you work in the admissions service for a large mental health center. Most of your clients suffer from the most common mental disorder in the United States today. What are the age and gender characteristics of these clients?
   a. Older females
   b. Younger males
   c. Younger females
   d. Older males

6. Dr. Kramer is not permitted to prescribe medicine. She works with severely disturbed people in a mental hospital. During her training, she completed a piece of research called a dissertation. Dr. Kramer is most likely a
   a. marriage and family counselor.
   b. clinical psychologist.
   c. psychiatrist.
   d. counseling psychologist.

7. Strabismus lives in ancient Greece. He goes to see his physician, Hippocrates, about his problem with sadness and fatigue. What is Hippocrates likely to say to Strabismus?
   a. "You need to have a portion of your skull removed; let me get my trephining gear."
   b. "Satan has possessed you; you need to go through an exorcism."
   c. "Your body fluids, and perhaps your brain, are disturbed; you need rest and good food."
   d. "Emotionally charged events from your past are affecting you; you need the cathartic method."

8. Johann Weyer and Philippe Pinel would have probably agreed that
   a. witches need to be starved and burned in order to save their souls.
   b. abnormal behavior is best treated with hypnosis.
   c. most people with behavior disorders have a form of brain pathology.
   d. witchcraft is not an acceptable explanation for mental disturbance.

9. Suzanne undergoes a process whereby, in a trance, she relives forgotten, emotionally charged events. Suzanne's treatment is called
   a. the cathartic method.
   b. mesmerism.
   c. exorcism.
   d. moral treatment.

10. Julie says, "Every time I read about a psychological disorder, I think I'm reading about myself." What is this reaction called?
   a. Catharsis
   b. Medical student syndrome
   c. Cultural relativism
   d. None of the above

ANSWERS TO FACT AND CONCEPT QUESTIONS

1. a. Psychodiagnosis is an aspect of defining a person's abnormality.
   *b. Therapy is a means of controlling maladaptive behavior and helping people change. (p. 5)
   c. Research increases knowledge but does not exercise control over people.
   d. Clinical assessment is another way of defining a person's abnormality.

2. *a. The statistical criteria do not decide whether a rare behavior is desirable or not; they equate rare with abnormal. (p. 6)
   b. The only factor the statistical criteria use is frequency.
   c. Statistical criteria are interested in defining abnormality, not predicting or controlling behavior.
   d. Statistics are considered to be objective and empirical.

3. a. Discomfort, bizarreness, and inefficiency are components of the practical criteria.
   b. There are several drawbacks to the ideal mental health criteria, such as uncertainty over what the goals of treatment should be.
   *c. The ideal mental health criteria require setting a positive goal (an ideal) and judging how far from that goal an individual is. (p. 6)
   d. Frequency of deviant actions is important in the statistical criteria.

4. *a. Cultural relativism focuses on the diversity of symptoms as they relate to social values. Proponents of cultural relativism do not believe that symptoms are universal across cultures. (p. 7)
   b. Cultural relativism does not use the ideal mental health criteria.
   c. Cultural relativism rejects the traditional approach.
   d. Cultural relativism emphasizes social values, not biological differences.

5. a. Disorientation involves confusion about who you are or where you are.
   *b. Discomfort includes such physical reactions as asthma, fatigue, and nausea. (p. 10)
   c. Bizarreness takes the form of delusions, hallucinations, or other rare behaviors.
   d. Inefficiency refers to a discrepancy between one's potential and one's performance.

6. a. Disorientation involves not knowing who you are or where you are.
   *b. Hallucinations are false perceptions involving the senses; delusions are beliefs held by people despite contradictory evidence. (p. 10)
   c. Disorientation involves not knowing who you are or where you are.
   d. The terms are reversed here.

7. a. Wakefield does not take a pure biogenic view and accepts the importance of cultural factors.
   b. These are separate criteria for defining "abnormal" and are unrelated to Wakefield's argument.
   *c. Wakefield sees mental disorder as a "harmful dysfunction," where *harmful* is defined by society and *dysfunction* is defined by the biological sciences. (p. 12)
   d. Wakefield's view stresses biological factors as the cause of mental disorders.

8. a. The rate of disorder has seemed to stay fairly constant over the past twenty years.
   b. Between 29 and 38 percent of the samples reported a disorder.
   c. In some studies, depressive symptoms are estimated to occur in 44 million Americans; it is a common emotional disorder.
   *d. Alcohol abuse and dependence was most prevalent (11–16 percent); phobic disorders (8–23 percent) was second. (p. 14)

9. a. Environmental factors are influential in all forms of disorder.
   b. Heredity plays a critical role in schizophrenia, bipolar disorder, and alcoholism.
   c. Most mental disorders are *not* inherited, and most people can be cured.
   *d. In some cases heredity gives a person a predisposition toward a disorder, but, in all cases, the environment determines whether any predisposition is expressed in behavior. (p. 16)

10. a. This is only part of the answer. It cannot be the best choice.
    b. This is only part of the answer. It cannot be the best choice.
    c. This is only part of the answer. It cannot be the best choice.
    *d. Clinical psychologists are trained in the assessment and treatment of disturbed people. They also do original research work, which is the reason they are awarded the Ph.D. degree. (p. 17)

11. *a. Psychiatrists are trained in medicine and, as M.D.s, may prescribe medicine. None of the other types of mental health professionals is always trained in medicine. (Table 1.1; p. 18)
    b. Clinical psychologists are not trained in medicine. It is against the law for them to prescribe medication.
    c. Psychiatric social workers are not trained in medicine. It is against the law for them to prescribe medication.
    d. Counseling psychologists have the same type of training as clinical psychologists; they cannot prescribe medicine.

12. *a. During the Middle Ages, abnormality was explained in terms of demonic possession. The treatment for possession was exorcism. (p. 21)
    b. Trephining was principally used during prehistoric times.
    c. Moral treatment included discussions with a physician, work, and rest; exorcism was done by a clergyman.
    d. The cathartic method was developed around the turn of the 20th century, fifty to seventy-five years after the moral treatment era.

13. a. Mesmerism occurred in the late 1700s and was not a form of mass madness.
    *b. Tarantism and lycanthropy are examples of mass madness that occurred in the 1200s. (p. 21)
    c. Tarantism and lycanthropy involved disorder on a mass scale; exorcism is a form of treatment for individuals.
    d. Tarantism and lycanthropy were reported during the Middle Ages (the 1200s).

14. a. Voluntary witches were treated with brutality.
    *b. A comprehensive review of the period by Spanos shows that many witches were not insane. (p. 22)
    c. The church led the fight to hunt down witches.
    d. The church explained abnormal behavior in terms of the supernatural, not the biological.

15. a. Beers, Dix, and Rush all lived before Freud's ideas were known in the United States.
    b. Charcot, Liebeault, and Bernheim were researchers who looked at hypnosis and its relation to hysteria.
    *c. Beers, Dix, and Rush worked to humanize the treatment of the mentally ill in the United States. (pp. 22–23)
    d. Dix and Beers took no distinct stand on whether mental disorder was biogenic or not.

16. a. A psychogenic approach argues that disorders are caused by parenting, environmental factors, and other forces outside the body.
    b. Demonology involves a belief that individuals are possessed by agents of the devil.
    *c. The organic or biogenic viewpoint sees disorders in terms of clusters of symptoms (syndromes) and believes that the causes are biological. (p. 24)
    d. The biopsychosocial approach accepts the importance of biology, but also argues that psychological and social forces outside the person influence the development and course of disorders.

17. *a. Mesmerism involved a trance-like state, much like hypnotism, during which the subject was highly suggestible. (p. 25)
    b. Mesmerism made no use of drugs.
    c. Mesmerism was not a religiously oriented treatment, as exorcism is.
    d. Mesmerism did not involve the kind of skull surgery seen in trephining.

18. a. Pinel was the one who freed mental patients from their chains.
    b. Charcot and Bernheim did not study schizophrenia.
    c. Pinel was the one who freed mental patients from their chains.
    *d. Charcot and Bernheim were physicians who investigated hypnosis and its relation to hysteria. Breuer was an Austrian physician who used the cathartic method to treat hysterics. (p. 25)

19. *a. Liebeault and Bernheim demonstrated that hypnotic states (psychological factors) could produce or remove hysterical symptoms. (p. 25)
    b. Pinel unchained mental patients; he was not associated with the Nancy school.
    c. Mesmer was declared a fraud by a committee of scientists including Benjamin Franklin. This took place fifty years before the Nancy school.
    d. Several German physicians made the link between syphilis and general paresis.

20. a. Most contemporary psychologists do not hold a purely psychogenic viewpoint.
    b. Most contemporary psychologists do not hold a purely biogenic viewpoint.
    c. Most contemporary psychologists do not hold a purely sociocultural viewpoint.
    *d. Most contemporary psychologists endorse a biopsychosocial perspective due to evidence from psychopharmacology, as well as research on how family upbringing and social forces affect mental health (pp. 26–27).

ANSWERS TO APPLICATION QUESTIONS

1. a. Prediction involves anticipation of future events; psychodiagnosis refers to current description.
   b. Control involves treatment, not description.
   c. Research can be done on any of the objectives of abnormal psychology.
   *d. Psychodiagnosis involves description and definition of just what a person is experiencing. (p. 3)

2. a. Rare behavior is the main component of the statistical criteria, not the practical criteria.
   b. The ideal mental health criteria do not base judgments on the rarity of behavior.
   c. The ideal mental health criteria do not base judgments on the rarity of behavior.
   *d. The statistical criteria are based on the rarity of behavior; cultural relativism assumes that social values determine what is abnormal. (pp. 6, 7)

3. a. There is no information indicating that Martin does not know his own name or what day of the week it is. These are examples of disorientation.
   *b. Martin is exhibiting auditory hallucinations and delusions (about Martians), which are forms of bizarre behavior. (p. 10)
   c. There is no information indicating that Martin is unable to live up to his potential, which would indicate inefficiency.
   d. If Martin complained about physical or psychological pain, that would be an indication of discomfort.

4. a. Cultural relativism emphasizes social values only.
   *b. The statement reflects Strupp and Hadley's proposal for a multiple perspectives approach to defining abnormality. (p. 11)
   c. The practical criteria include discomfort, bizarreness, disorientation, and inefficiency.
   d. The statistical criteria put their emphasis on the frequency of behavior only.

5. a. Older people are more likely to suffer from organic brain problems, not alcohol abuse, which is the most common form of disorder.
*b. Alcohol problems are the most common forms of disorder; they are most likely in younger people and males. (p. 14)
c. Although alcohol problems are common in the young, females are not as likely as males to develop them.
d. Older people are more likely to suffer from organic brain problems, not alcohol problems.

6. a. Marriage and family counselors usually have a master's degree. They are not called "doctor" and are not trained in research.
*b. Clinical psychologists have doctorates (Ph.D.s or Psy.D.s) and are trained in both research and treatment. Because they are not physicians, they are not qualified to prescribe medicine. (p. 17)
c. Psychiatrists are physicians, so they can prescribe medicine.
d. Counseling psychologists usually work in educational settings with people who have less severe problems.

7. a. Trephining was most common in prehistoric times, not in ancient Greece.
b. What made ancient Greece and Rome unique was that their physicians did *not* believe that demons caused disorder.
*c. Hippocrates' theory of abnormality assumed that the body's fluids were out of balance and that there was brain pathology. (p. 19)
d. Ideas about catharsis and emotional memories were developed around the turn of the 20th century.

8. a. Neither Weyer nor Pinel believed that witchcraft existed.
b. Both Weyer and Pinel lived before hypnosis was first used.
c. Neither Weyer nor Pinel took a biogenic view of abnormal behavior.
*d. Weyer was the first to challenge witchcraft; Pinel lived more than 100 years after witchcraft faded as a common explanation. (p. 22)

9. *a. The cathartic method, hypnosis, and other techniques seek to bring to consciousness painful, forgotten memories. This is the method that Breuer, and later Freud, used to cure patients. (p. 25)
b. Mesmerism involved trances, but there was no goal of reviving memories.
c. Exorcism was a religious practice with the goal of driving out demons.
d. Moral treatment relied on work, rest, and prayer for cures.

10. a. Catharsis is the painful reliving of past memories. This is usually induced by therapy.
*b. Medical students often see themselves described as they read about each disorder; something similar is probably happening to Julie. (Focus 1.2; p. 28)
c. Cultural relativism means that abnormality is defined by the social values that have influenced a person.
d. Because b is correct, this cannot be the best choice.

CHAPTER 2
Biogenic and Psychogenic Models of Abnormal Behavior

LEARNING OBJECTIVES

When you have mastered the material in Chapter 2, you should be able to:

1. Define *psychopathology* and describe what a model is. Discuss how the model a clinician chooses influences thought and action toward abnormal behavior. Define and discuss the strengths and weaknesses of an eclectic approach (pp. 31–34)
2. Describe the biogenic model. Discuss the action of neurons and the major structures of the human brain. Describe and discuss the components of neurons and the role neurotransmitters play in specific mental disorders. Explain how knowledge of biochemistry can be used in treatment (pp. 34–37)
3. Discuss the relationship between genetics and psychopathology; give evidence from twin studies that inheritance contributes to abnormal behavior. (pp. 37–40)
4. Assess the strengths and weaknesses of the biogenic model. Apply the biogenic view to the Case of Steven V. (pp. 40–42)
5. Describe the basic concepts of psychoanalytic theory, including the components of personality structure, instincts, and the five stages of psychosexual development. Explain the effect of unresolved conflicts in each stage. (pp. 42–45)
6. Discuss the relationship between anxiety and psychopathology. Give an example of each of the following defense mechanisms: repression, reaction formation, projection, rationalization, displacement, undoing, and regression. (pp. 45–48)
7. Describe how psychoanalysts get access to information in the unconscious for use in therapy. Discuss how neo-Freudians are similar to and different from traditional psychoanalytic theorists. Identify the major contributions of Adler, Jung, Hartmann, Anna Freud, and Erikson to psychoanalytic thinking. (pp. 44–48)
8. Identify the major contributions of Fromm, Horney, and Sullivan to psychoanalytic thought. Discuss Fromm's ideas in light of research on cults. Define the object relations theorists and their main ideas. (pp. 50–53)
9. Describe what happens in psychoanalytic therapy and the type of patients for which it was intended. Discuss the psychoanalytic model's degree of scientific rigor. (pp. 53–54).
10. Discuss the problems in applying psychoanalytic thinking to women. Discuss feminist psychology and psychopathology. Discuss the usefulness of psychoanalytic therapy with poor people or those with lower verbal skills. Apply psychoanalytic concepts to the Case of Steven V. (pp. 54–56)

11. Describe how humanistic approaches differ from psychodynamic theories. Describe the basic concepts of Carl Rogers and Abraham Maslow. List the seven traits of the healthy personality. Describe how abnormal behavior develops according to the humanistic approach. (pp. 56–59).
12. Describe Rogers's person-centered therapy. (pp. 59–60).
13. Describe the roots of the existential approach. Describe the main concepts of existentialist theorists, including being, nonbeing, and being-in-the-world. Discuss the causes of behavior disorders from an existentialist approach. (p. 61)
14. Describe the goals and characteristics of existential therapy. Critically analyze the humanistic and existential approaches. Apply humanistic-existential concepts to the Case of Steven V. (pp. 61–64)

CHAPTER OUTLINE

1. **Models in the study of *psychopathology*** (pp. 32–33) *Models* are analogies that scientists use to describe things they cannot directly observe. Models are useful but limited. Most clinicians take an *eclectic approach*—they use a mixture of models—although this, too, has its disadvantages.

2. **The biogenic model—the human brain** (p. 35) The biogenic model suggests that abnormal behavior is caused by biological factors, especially involving the brain. The brain is composed of billions of *neurons* (nerve cells) that receive and transmit information. The brain is divided into two hemispheres, each controlling the opposite side of the body. The brain structures most relevant to abnormal behavior include the thalamus, hypothalamus, reticular activating system, limbic system, and cerebrum. Other structures, in the midbrain and hindbrain, manufacture chemicals that are implicated in mental disorders.

3. **The biogenic model—biochemical theories** (pp. 35–37) Neurons are composed of *dendrites,* which receive signals from other neurons, and *axons*, which send the signals to other neurons. At the end of the axon is a gap called the *synapse,* into which chemicals called *neurotransmitters* are released. Imbalances in neurotransmitters are associated with many mental disorders. Certain medications can reduce symptoms of abnormal behavior by blocking or facilitating neurotransmitter activity. Excessive dopamine activity is associated with schizophrenia, drugs to treat depression affect norepinephrine and serotonin, while anxiety is related to the neurotransmitter GABA.

4. **The biogenic model—genetic explanations** (pp. 37–40) Genetics also plays an important part in explaining the development of disorders. A person's *genotype* (genetic makeup) interacts with the environment to produce physical or behavioral characteristics (their *phenotype*). *Monozygotic (MZ) twins* have identical genotypes; *dizygotic (DZ) twins* do not. In accordance with the biogenic model, correlations exist between genotype similarity and mental disorders, but cause-and-effect relationships cannot be established.

5. **Criticisms of the biogenic model** (pp. 40–41) The biogenic model overemphasizes internal causes, equates organic dysfunction with mental dysfunction, and assumes that biochemical differences are the *cause* of disorder when they may be the *result. Diathesis-stress theory* argues that people can inherit a vulnerability to develop an illness, but this must be activated by environmental forces for the disorder to occur.

6. **A biogenic view of Steven V.** (pp. 41–42) Steven's early behavior indicates bipolar (manic-depressive) disorder, which has a strong biological component. Medication would be the best treatment.

7. **The psychoanalytic model** (pp. 42–48) Freud's *psychoanalytic model* emphasizes early childhood experiences. Anxiety remains unconscious and threatens us; in dealing with those threats, we develop symptoms.

   Personality is composed of three components: the id, the ego, and the superego. The id exists from birth and operates on the *pleasure principle*—a need for immediate gratification. The ego represents the realistic part of the mind—the *reality principle*. The superego is composed of the conscience and the ego ideal.

   We are driven by unconscious instincts that determine our actions, but we are taught by society to inhibit these instincts. According to Freud, humans develop through five *psychosexual stages*. Trauma during any of the stages leads to fixation. During the *oral* stage, the first year of life, pleasure centers on the mouth. The *anal* stage lasts from the end of the first year to the third year of life. During this stage, the anal region becomes the focus of pleasure. The genitals are the focus of the third, the *phallic*, stage. For boys, the *oedipal complex* produces intense feelings for the opposite-sexed parent that must be resolved. The boy has *castration anxiety* that the father will punish these forbidden desires. Freud believed that girls experience *penis envy*. According to Freud, from ages 6 to 12 (the *latency* stage) there is no sexual motivation. At puberty, sexual urges return in the *genital* stage.

   Anxiety takes three forms. Realistic anxiety comes from the external environment. Moralistic anxiety stems from a failure to live up to moral standards. Neurotic anxiety results when id impulses threaten to burst through ego controls. Ego *defense mechanisms* against anxiety include *repression* (when painful thoughts are blocked from consciousness), *reaction formation* (the conversion of dangerous impulses into their opposite), *projection* (the attribution of personally threatening desires to others, which may form a *delusional system*), *rationalization* (giving socially acceptable reasons for behavior), *displacement* (directing emotions toward a substitute target), *undoing* (repetitive acts done to negate a disapproved thought), and *regression* (retreating to an earlier developmental level).

   In *psychoanalysis,* therapists induce ego weakness so that unconscious material can be brought to the surface. These insights help patients understand their inner motives.

8. **Neo-Freudian perspectives** (pp. 48–53) *Neo-Freudians* continued to believe in the power of the unconscious and the three-part structure of personality but differed from Freud in several ways. Alfred Adler stressed social drives and goal-directedness. Carl Jung proposed the *collective unconscious,* the storehouse of religious and aesthetic values derived from the human species' cumulative experience.

   Heinz Hartmann, Anna Freud, and Erik Erikson (known as ego psychologists) argued that the ego operates independently from the id. Erikson also proposed that personality development continues throughout the lifespan.

   Erich Fromm, Karen Horney, and Harry Stack Sullivan argued that interpersonal relationships are critical for personality development. Fromm emphasized the potential conflict between freedom and loneliness. Horney suggested that neurotic behavior stems from a need to reduce basic anxiety. She also rejected Freud's notion of penis envy. Sullivan saw all disorders as related to social relations.

   Object relations theory emphasizes how the incorporation of important figures from childhood (particularly mother) affects adult behavior. Margaret Mahler concentrated on individuation of the child from the mother. Otto Kernberg and Heinz Kohut studied the borderline personality and parental emotional support, respectively.

Recent trends have extended psychoanalysis to more disturbed individuals who might otherwise be unable to understand psychoanalytic interpretations of behavior.

9. **Criticisms of the psychoanalytic model** (pp. 53–55) Psychoanalysis has been criticized for basing its evidence on case studies, which are subject to distortion. Psychoanalytic theory is also imprecise and lacking in the ability to predict future behavior. Freudian theory is seen as biased against women, particularly the concept of penis envy. Studies of nonwestern cultures indicate that "masculine" and "feminine" characteristics are not as much a biological certainty as they are culturally defined.

10. **A psychoanalytic view of Steven V.** (pp. 55–56) Steven's problems stem from early childhood rejection, a sexually tinged relationship with his mother, and unresolved oedipal issues.

11. **The humanistic perspective** (pp. 56–60) The *humanistic* and the *existential approaches* emphasize the need to appreciate the world from the individual's vantage point. They also highlight freedom of choice and the wholeness of the individual. Humanistic psychologists Carl Rogers and Abraham Maslow suggested that people are motivated by the actualizing tendency to enhance the self *(self-actualization)*. When society imposes conditions of worth on people, their *self-concept* and actualizing tendency can become incongruent. This incongruence produces behavior disorders.

    In Rogers's person-centered therapy, people are free to grow toward their potential. The therapist uses reflection of feelings and acceptance rather than advice to help the client actively evaluate his or her experience.

12. **The existential perspective** (pp. 60–61) The existential perspective differs from the humanistic perspective by being less optimistic, viewing the individual within the human condition, and focusing on individual struggles and responsibility to others. Viktor Frankl emphasized the need to find a spiritual meaning in life. Rollo May stressed the confusion and strain related to modern technology.

13. **Existential concepts** (pp. 61–62) Humans are aware of being alive (being) and aware that they will die (nonbeing). This generates existential anxiety. Our being exists within a structure of relationships: being-in-the-world.

14. **Existential theory on abnormal behavior and therapy** (p. 62) Anxiety that stems from the threat of nonbeing and an inability to relate to the world results in symptoms. Therapy helps the individual find meaning in life. Specific therapeutic techniques are deemphasized by existentialists.

15. **Criticisms of the humanistic and existential approaches** (pp. 62–63) Both approaches lack scientific grounding, are vague, and have therapies that are ineffective with severely disturbed clients.

16. **A humanistic-existential view of Steven V.** (pp. 63–64) Steven is seen as a whole person, not just a "schizophrenic" or "manic-depressive" case. Steven feels trapped, lonely, and angry. Therapy would stress awareness of this and the need for Steven to take greater responsibility for his actions.

KEY TERMS

Fill-in-the-Blanks Quiz

1. The optimistic viewpoint that people are born with the ability to fulfill their potential is called the ___________.

2. In psychoanalytic theory, the ego is protected from anxiety-provoking conflicts through an unconscious and automatic process called a(n) ___________.

3. A psychologist who is open to all models of abnormal behavior and selectively uses techniques from various models to help his or her clients is using the ___________.

4. The therapy based on Freud's view that unconscious conflicts must be aired and understood by the patient is called ___________.

5. The theory that every mental disorder has an organic basis and cure is called the ___________.

6. The theory that a predisposition to mental illness is inherited and that this predisposition is activated by environmental factors is called the ___________.

7. Another name for abnormal behavior is ___________.

8. The belief that contemporary society has a dehumanizing effect and that mental disorders result from a conflict between essential human nature and social demands is called the ___________.

9. An analogy most often used to describe something that cannot be directly observed is called a(n) ___________.

10. Psychologists who were strongly influenced by Freud's psychoanalytic model but who modified that model in various ways are called ___________.

11. The view that adult disorders arise from the unconscious operation of repressed anxieties originally experienced in childhood is called the ___________.

12. A term devised by Jung that refers to ancient, primordial memories common to all humanity is called the ___________.

13. The genetic component of a trait or characteristic is called the ___________.

14. The observable result of the interaction of the genotype and the environment is called the ___________.

15. Genetically identical twins who developed from one fertilized egg are called ___________.

16. Twins from two separate eggs who share about 50 percent of the same genes are called ___________.

17. In psychoanalytic theory, past interpersonal relations that shape and affect the individual's current interactions with people are called ___________.

18. The impulsive, pleasure-seeking aspect of our being, usually associated with the id, that seeks immediate gratification is called the ___________.

19. In Freudian theory, awareness of the demands of the environment and adjustment of behavior to meet these demands is called the ___________.

20. An inherent tendency for people to strive toward the realization of their full potential is called ___________.

21. An individual's assessment of his or her own value and worth is called the ___________.

22. In psychoanalytic theory, humans develop through a sequence of stages (oral, anal, phallic, latency, and genital), which collectively are called ___________.

23. The space between neurons is called the ___________.

24. The first of Freud's psychosexual stages is called the ___________ stage.

25. The defense mechanism in which undesirable thoughts and emotions are blocked from consciousness is called ___________.

26. The part of the neuron that receives information is called the ___________.

27. According to Freudian theory, the emotional involvement of 3- to 5-year-old boys with their mothers is called the ___________.

28. The defense mechanism in which personal undesirable thoughts or emotions are attributed to other people is called ___________.

29. The second of Freud's psychosexual stages of development is called the ___________ stage.

30. The part of the neuron that sends a signal to a distant neuron is called the ___________.

31. In Freud's theory, the stage during which children from 6 to 12 are believed not to have sexual motivations is called ___________.

32. In Freud's theory, the psychosexual stage from 3 to 5 years of age when children are believed to have sexual feelings for their opposite sex parent is called the ___________ stage.

33. In Freudian theory, the concept of boys fearing that their fathers will punish them for having sexual feelings towards their mothers is called ___________.

34. Nerve cells are also called ___________.

35. The defense mechanism in which people express their undesirable emotions toward substitute targets is called ___________.

36. The defense mechanism in which people provide socially appropriate but incorrect explanations for their behavior is called ___________.

37. Chemicals that are released into the synapse so that neural messages are facilitated or blocked are called ___________.

38. The defense mechanism in which people revert to an earlier level of development is called ___________.

39. In Freudian theory, the concept of girls wishing they had the genital equipment of boys is called ___________.

40. The defense mechanism in which people repetitively act in ways to correct some unacceptable thought or behavior is called ___________.

41. The last of the psychosexual stages is called the ___________ stage.

42. The defense mechanism in which people convert unacceptable impulses into their opposite is called ___________.

43. In extreme cases, a person who employs projection may develop a set of erroneous beliefs called a(n) ___________.

Answers to Fill-in-the-Blanks Quiz

1. humanistic perspective
2. defense mechanism
3. eclectic approach
4. psychoanalysis
5. biogenic model
6. diathesis-stress theory
7. psychopathology
8. existential approach
9. model
10. neo-Freudians
11. psychoanalytic model
12. collective unconscious
13. genotype
14. phenotype
15. monozygotic (or identical) twins
16. dizygotic (or fraternal) twins
17. object relations
18. pleasure principle
19. reality principle
20. self-actualization
21. self-concept
22. psychosexual stages
23. synapse
24. oral
25. repression
26. dendrites
27. oedipal complex
28. projection
29. anal
30. axon
31. latency
32. phallic
33. castration anxiety
34. neurons
35. displacement
36. rationalization
37. neurotransmitters
38. regression
39. penis envy
40. undoing
41. genital
42. reaction formation
43. delusional system

FACT AND CONCEPT QUESTIONS

1. An eclectic psychologist
   a. uses one theoretical perspective to describe, explain, and treat disorders.
   b. has not been formally trained in treatment.
   c. does not make use of any theories when describing, explaining, or treating disorders.
   d. uses a variety of perspectives to describe, explain, and treat disorders.

2. A psychologist who believes that genetics, brain chemistry, and damage to the nervous system are the major causes of mental disorder subscribes to the ___________ model.
   a. psychoanalytic
   b. existential
   c. biogenic
   d. multicultural

3. Chemicals called neurotransmitters are released into the spaces between neurons called
   a. axons.
   b. synapses.
   c. dendrites.
   d. hemispheres.

4. The biogenic model of schizophrenia would be supported if researchers found that
   a. it occurs most frequently among those from the lower socioeconomic groups.
   b. pairs of dizygotic (DZ) twins are more likely to share the disorder than pairs of monozygotic (MZ) twins.
   c. pairs of monozygotic (MZ) twins are more likely to share the disorder than pairs of dizygotic (DZ) twins.
   d. people who suffer from the disorder came from families with great marital conflict.

5. One of the weaknesses of the biogenic model is that it
   a. does not acknowledge the importance of social forces.
   b. exaggerates the importance of unconscious sexual and aggressive urges.
   c. does not rely on science for its data.
   d. exaggerates the importance of the individual's subjective view of the world.

6. According to Freud, ___________ is present at birth and impulsively seeks immediate gratification of pleasure needs.
   a. the id
   b. the ego
   c. the superego
   d. the oedipal complex

7. Which perspective most emphasizes the importance of early childhood experiences for behavior problems in adulthood?
   a. Existential
   b. Biogenic
   c. Humanistic
   d. Psychoanalytic

8. According to Freud, the more fixation a person experiences in childhood,
   a. the more likely the person is to develop mental disorders.
   b. the more likely the person is to develop a strong sense of conscience.
   c. the less likely the person is to have an id as an adult.
   d. the more likely the person is to develop a healthy personality.

9. According to psychoanalytic theory, the oedipal complex
   a. occurs during the first two years of life.
   b. is much stronger for girls than for boys.
   c. is a conflict between wanting sexual possession and fearing punishment.
   d. occurs during the latency stage, when children are believed to have no sexual motivations.

10. According to Freud, when id impulses threaten to break through ego controls, we experience
   a. anxiety.
   b. nonbeing.
   c. instincts.
   d. object relations.

11. People who blame others for their mistakes and people who believe that others are out to get them both use the same defense mechanism to excess. It is called
   a. rationalization.
   b. repression.
   c. projection.
   d. reaction formation.

12. ___________ was an ego psychologist who suggested that personality development goes on throughout the lifespan.
   a. Erik Erikson
   b. Carl Jung
   c. Harry Stack Sullivan
   d. Viktor Frankl

13. Margaret Mahler, Otto Kernberg, and Heinz Kohut are all psychoanalysts who
   a. believed in the collective unconscious.
   b. rejected the idea of the unconscious.
   c. believed that childhood relationships were unimportant in understanding adult psychological problems.
   d. contributed to object relations theory.

14. Which statement about the humanistic and existential theories is accurate?
   a. They believe that biological and instinctual forces determine each individual's behaviors.
   b. They argue that the individual's subjective view of events is more important than the events themselves.
   c. They emphasize the need to break down personality into its component parts.
   d. They reject the idea of an actualizing tendency.

15. Conditions of worth, conditional positive regard, and incongruence are all associated with ___________ approach to abnormal behavior.
    a. Rogers's humanistic
    b. the diathesis-stress
    c. Frankl's existential
    d. the ego-analytic

16. According to the existential perspective, abnormal behavior results from
    a. hereditary factors combined with social stress.
    b. fixation at early psychosexual stages.
    c. incongruence between a person's self and his or her actualizing tendency.
    d. conflict between people's essential nature and the demands placed on them by others.

17. The ___________ approach is really not a systematized school of thought but a set of attitudes that stresses the quest for meaning and individual responsibility in a technological world.
    a. existential
    b. object relations
    c. biopsychosocial
    d. ego-analytic

18. According to existential theory, ___________ stems from the threat of nonbeing and the inability to relate to all the ways of our world.
    a. unconditioned positive regard
    b. fixation
    c. anxiety
    d. being

19. Which of the following is a characteristic of existential therapy?
    a. Patients learn to alter their behavior to meet the requirements of society.
    b. Therapists focus almost exclusively on the past experiences and feelings of clients.
    c. Therapists actively teach and reward clients for appropriate behavior.
    d. Patients are urged to become aware of their current encounter with the therapist.

20. Which of the following is a sound criticism of the humanistic and existential approaches?
    a. They do not work well with severely disturbed clients.
    b. They rely too heavily on research data from nonhuman subjects.
    c. They tend to discount the phenomenology of the client.
    d. All of the above.

APPLICATION QUESTIONS

1. Dr. Chapman thinks of the brain as a kind of computer that takes in data, processes it, stores it, and retrieves it at a later date. Dr. Chapman is
    a. an eclectic thinker.
    b. taking a humanistic view of the brain.
    c. a supporter of the biogenic approach.
    d. using a model to think about the brain.

2. Suppose Norton is involved in a car accident that injures the right side of his brain. We can expect that he will
   a. show many of the symptoms of schizophrenia.
   b. be unable to regulate such body drives as hunger and sex.
   c. have trouble seeing and breathing.
   d. lose the ability to control the left side of his body.

3. Dr. Mandler says, "We know that this patient has a high genetic vulnerability to the disorder. Given the current difficulties in his life, it is logical that he would develop a severe case of the disorder." Which perspective does Dr. Mandler's statement illustrate?
   a. Eclectic
   b. Diathesis-stress
   c. Psychogenic
   d. Neurochemical

4. Harry is feeling a great deal of guilt. According to Freud, this feeling stems from
   a. unfulfilled id needs.
   b. the superego.
   c. a lack of defense mechanisms.
   d. the ego.

5. Dr. Jimenez, a psychoanalyst, says, "This patient was traumatized in infancy by not being given adequate time to suck on the breast. This accounts for her current eating and smoking problems." Dr. Jimenez's analysis
   a. suggests that the ego controls all adult behavior.
   b. fails to look at the effects of oral fixation.
   c. links oral fixation to adult symptoms.
   d. ignores the importance of early childhood experience.

6. Marilyn spends her first four years as an only child. When her baby brother is born, she returns to sucking her thumb and wetting her bed. Marilyn's behavior illustrates the defense mechanism of
   a. projection.
   b. reaction formation.
   c. rationalization.
   d. regression.

7. Dr. Layton says, "I cannot agree with you. I think that social forces are much more important than primitive sexual impulses in determining behavior." With whom is Dr. Layton disagreeing?
   a. A humanistic psychologist
   b. A Freudian psychologist
   c. A neo-Freudian such as Erich Fromm
   d. An existential psychologist

8. Kate is an outspoken feminist. With which perspective is she likely to have the most disagreements?
   a. Eclectic
   b. Biopsychosocial
   c. Humanistic
   d. Psychoanalytic

9. Paula R. says, "I cannot decide on anything! I am drifting, and I have no direction." Dr. Pratt responds, "You feel you have no goal to help you decide things." What form of therapy does this interchange illustrate best?
   a. Psychoanalytic therapy
   b. Rogers' person-centered therapy
   c. May's object relations therapy
   d. Biogenic-oriented psychotherapy

10. Dr. Bach says, "Your anxiety stems from your awareness that, in the end, we all die. Many of your symptoms are connected to such anxieties." Dr. Bach is
   a. an existential psychologist talking about nonbeing.
   b. a humanistic psychologist talking about the actualizing tendency.
   c. a psychoanalytic psychologist talking about fixation at the oral stage.
   d. an object relations psychologist talking about separation fears.

ANSWERS TO FACT AND CONCEPT QUESTIONS

1. a. Eclectic psychologists use a range of theories.
   b. Psychologists are formally trained in treatment.
   c. Eclectic psychologists use a range of theories.
   *d. Eclectic psychologists use a range of theories, and use them selectively with clients. (p. 34)

2. a. Psychoanalysts subscribe to a version of the psychogenic view.
   b. Existentialists subscribe to a version of the psychogenic view.
   *c. The biogenic model assumes that biological factors such as genetics, brain chemistry, and nervous system damage account for abnormal behavior. (p. 34)
   d. The multicultural model emphasizes social factors, and is, therefore, a variant of the psychogenic view.

3. a. Axons are the portion of the neuron that sends the message to other neurons.
   *b. Synapses are the very small spaces that separate neurons and into which neurotransmitters are released. (p. 36)
   c. Dendrites are the portion of the neuron that receives messages.
   d. Hemispheres are what the two sides of the brain are called.

4. a. The influence of social class on disorder would support a socio-cultural viewpoint.
   b. Since DZ twins have dissimilar genetic material, if their behavior were more similar than that of MZ twins, factors other than heredity or biology would have to be important.
   *c. Since MZ twins have identical genetic material, greater similarity in the behavior of MZ twins than DZ twins would point to a strong hereditary factor in schizophrenia. (pp. 38–39)
   d. Marital conflict is an environmental and psychological factor that is not included in a purely biogenic perspective.

5. *a. The biogenic model tends to ignore interpersonal and social causes in both the explanation and treatment of disorder. (p. 40)
   b. The psychoanalytic perspective, not the biogenic model, stresses the unconscious.
   c. The biogenic model relies heavily on the biological sciences for data.
   d. The humanistic and existential perspectives, not the biogenic model, stress the individual's subjective view of the world.

6. *a. The id is the portion of personality that psychoanalysts describe as pleasure-seeking, impulsive, and unable to delay gratification. We can see this sort of behavior in newborns. (pp. 42–43)
   b. The ego develops out of the id and is reality oriented.
   c. The superego develops at age 5 or 6 and is oriented toward morality.
   d. The libido is the manifestation of sexual instincts.

7. a. Existential psychology stresses alienation and conflict between being and nonbeing.
   b. Biogenic theory stresses brain damage, neurochemistry, and genetics.
   c. Humanistic psychology stresses perceptions of the world in the "here-and-now."
   *d. Psychoanalytic theorists stress how fixation and anxiety from early childhood experiences produce symptoms in adults. (p. 39)

8. *a. Fixation is an arresting of psychological development. According to psychoanalysts, greater fixation means less maturation of personality and more behavior problems in adulthood. (p. 43)
   b. Conscience is an outgrowth of successfully resolving phallic stage conflicts.
   c. All people have ids, both as infants and as adults.
   d. Fixation leads to disorder, not health.

9. a. The oral stage occurs in the first year of life; the anal stage occurs in the second and third.
   b Because girls cannot experience castration anxiety, psychoanalysts propose that girls experience a reduced conflict; oedipal complex is a term reserved for males.
   *c. In the oedipal complex, the 3-to-5-year-old sexually desires his mother but fears castration by the punishing father. (p. 44)
   d. The oedipal complex involves a great deal of sexual motivation and occurs during the phallic stage.

10. *a. Neurotic anxiety occurs when unacceptable id impulses threaten to overwhelm ego control. (pp. 45–46)
    b. Nonbeing is an existential concept related to awareness of death.
    c. Instincts, according to psychoanalysts, are always at work and consist of sexual, aggressive, and other biological needs.
    d. Object relations refers to a psychoanalytic school of thought that focuses on child-parent relationships.

11. a. Rationalization is finding plausible but inaccurate reasons for one's behavior.
    b. Repression is banishing unwanted thoughts and memories into unconsciousness.
    *c. Projection is attributing to others threatening aspects of one's self. In the extreme, this can take the form of delusions of grandeur or persecution. (p. 47)
    d. Reaction formation is the defense of converting dangerous impulses into their opposite; for example, hate into superficial love.

12. *a. Erik Erikson is the most influential of the ego psychologists because, unlike Freud, he suggested that personality development continues throughout life. (pp. 49–50)
    b. Carl Jung's chief contribution was the idea of the collective unconscious.
    c. Harry Stack Sullivan suggested that psychological disorders stem from interpersonal relationships.
    d. Viktor Frankl was an existential psychologist.

13. a. Of the neo-Freudians, only Carl Jung believed in the collective unconscious.
    b. No psychoanalyst would wholly reject the idea of the unconscious.
    c. Kernberg, Kohut, and especially Mahler put very strong emphasis on the role of child-mother relationships in causing adult psychological problems.
    *d. Mahler, Kernberg, and Kohut are all object relations theorists. (p. 51–53)

14. a. Humanistic and existential thinkers suggest that people are free to make life choices; they reject the ideas of biological destiny and instinctual forces.
    *b. Central to both humanistic and existential theories is the importance placed on how the individual subjectively views the world. (p. 56)
    c. Humanistic and existential thinkers value the integrity of the human personality and argue against breaking it down into components or formulas.
    d. The actualizing tendency is a core idea in humanistic theory.

15. *a. All three are important concepts in Rogers's theory. When there are conditions of worth, incongruence is likely—resulting in behavior disorders. (p. 59)
    b. Diathesis-stress theory combines genetic vulnerability and environmental factors to explain abnormal behavior.
    c. Frankl's theory stresses the need to find meaning in one's life.
    d. Ego analysts stress the ego's autonomy from the id.

16. a. Diathesis-stress theory focuses on the combination of biological and environmental stress factors.
    b. Fixation in earlier psychosexual stages is a psychoanalytic explanation.
    c. Incongruence is a humanistic (Rogerian) explanation.
    *d. Existentialists believe that the human drive to reach full potential and develop a spiritual life can be thwarted by social demands that produce alienation and loneliness. (p. 60)

17. *a. The existential perspective places more emphasis on meaning (Frankl) and alienation (May) than any other. (p. 61)
    b. Object relations is a neo-Freudian perspective that focuses on the early mother-infant relationship.
    c. Diathesis-stress theory involves genetic vulnerability coupled with environmental stressors.
    d. Psychoanalytic theory puts emphasis on unconscious processes; meaning and alienation are more conscious.

18. a. Unconditional positive regard is a growth-enhancing situation in which one is accepted and respected as a person.
    b. Fixation is a psychoanalytic term for arrested personality development.
    *c. Existentialists suggest that unresolved conflict between nonbeing and being-in-the-world produces crippling anxiety. (pp. 61–62)
    d. Being is a distinctive characteristic of humans to be aware of themselves and experience their existence at a particular moment.

19. a. Humanistic and existential theorists stress freedom and authenticity in society rather than accommodation to social control.
    b. Humanistic and existential therapists focus on the client's present subjective experience.
    c. Humanistic and existential theorists reject the behavioral approach of controlling behavior through reward and punishment.
    *d. Humanistic and existential theorists emphasize the individual's subjective experience and interactions with others. (p. 58)

20. *a. Humanistic and existential therapies seem to be most effective with well-educated, relatively "normal" individuals. (p. 63)
    b. Neither humanistic nor existential theory relies on nonhuman data.
    c. Phenomenology is central to both theories and therapies.
    d. Because b and c are incorrect, this cannot be the best answer.

ANSWERS TO APPLICATION QUESTIONS

1. a. An eclectic approach uses ideas from different theories to find whatever works best to explain and treat a condition.
   b. Humanistic thinkers do not consider the human mind to be like a machine.
   c. Nothing indicates whether Dr. Chapman believes that biological factors cause disorders, so it is unclear whether he/she supports the biogenic view.
   *d. A model is an analogy; the analogy between computer and brain may help Dr. Chapman understand the brain better. (p. 32)

2. a. Schizophrenia is associated with excessive dopamine activity, not damage to the right side of the brain.
   b. Regulation of body drives is principally located in the hypothalamus, not the right side of the brain.
   c. The right side of the brain does not control vision or breathing.
   *d. Each hemisphere of the brain controls movement on the opposite side of the body; right brain injury would impair control over the left side of the body. (p. 35)

3. a. Eclectic psychologists make use of a variety of perspectives, but do not necessarily stress heredity and stress.
   *b. Diathesis-stress theory emphasizes just these ideas: that inherited vulnerability combines with environmental stress to cause disorders. (p. 40)
   c. Psychogenic perspectives emphasize factors other than inheritance.
   d. The neurochemical perspective might be interested in genetic vulnerability, but would be less likely to discuss environmental stress.

4. a. When id needs go unfulfilled, there may be frustration, but not guilt.
   *b. The superego is the seat of conscience and morality, so guilt originates there. (p. 43)
   c. A lack of defense mechanisms may make a person vulnerable to id impulses; a complete lack of defenses leads to a break with reality, not guilt.
   d. The ego is driven by the reality principle, not a moral code.

5. a. The doctor is emphasizing primitive urges that stem from the id, not the ego.
   b. The doctor's analysis centers on oral deprivation.
   *c. The analysis links a lack of gratification at a particular psychosexual stage (fixation) to current, adult problems. (p. 43)
   d. The doctor places great emphasis on early childhood experience.

6. a. In projection, people attribute to others characteristics they cannot accept in themselves.
   b. Reaction formation involves total contradiction of an unacceptable impulse by endorsing its opposites; for example, hate becomes superficial love.
   c. Rationalization is the defense of giving plausible, but inaccurate, explanations for behavior.
   *d. Regression is characterized by a return to more primitive behavior when a person is faced with severe stresses and anxiety. (p. 48)

7. a. Humanistic psychologists do not suggest that sexual impulses determine behavior. In fact, they do not believe that any unconscious or outside forces determine behavior.
   *b. The chief criticism of Freud by neo-Freudians is his emphasis on sexual motivation for all behavior. (p. 48)
   c. Erich Fromm and other neo-Freudians diminished the importance of sexual motivation. The quotation might have *come* from a neo-Freudian, rather than being targeted at one.
   d. Existential psychologists are much like humanistic psychologists. They, too, deemphasize the idea of unconscious forces determining our behavior.

8. a. Eclectic professionals borrow from a variety of theories, so it is hard to know if an outspoken feminist would be in disagreement.
   b. The biopsychosocial perspective accepts the importance of sociocultural factors as well as biological and psychological ones.
   c. The humanistic approach has not proposed any concepts inconsistent with a feminist approach.
   *d. Psychoanalytic theory has been criticized by feminists for taking a biased view of women, particularly in using the concept of penis envy. (p. 54)

9. a. A psychoanalyst might emphasize the unconscious needs of this person, his or her dependency on others to give direction.
   *b. The therapist is using reflection of feelings, a major technique in Rogers's person-centered therapy. The aim is for the therapist to understand the client's inner experience. (p. 59)
   c. May is an existential psychologist, not an object relations theorist.
   d. Biogenic models do not make great use of psychotherapy. To an extent, "biogenic" and "psychotherapy" are contradictory terms.

10. *a. Existentialists emphasize anxiety over death, an awareness of nonbeing, as a source of psychopathology. (p. 61)
   b. Humanistic psychologists tend to be more optimistic than existential psychologists. They rarely deal with anxiety over impending death.
   c. Psychoanalysts talking about fixation at the oral stage would emphasize infancy.
   d. The separation that object relations theorists discuss has to do with early mother-infant bonds.

CHAPTER 3
Behavioral, Cognitive, and Family Systems Models of Psychopathology

LEARNING OBJECTIVES

When you have mastered the material in Chapter 3, you should be able to:

1. Discuss how the behavioral, cognitive, and family systems models place greater emphasis on environmental influences than the biogenic and other psychogenic models. (pp. 69–70)
2. Describe the origins of the behavioral model. List and explain the components of classical conditioning, as well as extinction, generalization, and stimulus discrimination. (pp. 70–72)
3. Discuss how classical conditioning principles explain the development of psychopathology. Describe how counterconditioning can be used therapeutically. (pp. 72–73)
4. Compare and contrast operant and classical conditioning. Describe and give examples of the following operant principles: positive reinforcer, negative reinforcer, punishment, extinction, discriminative stimulus, and shaping. (pp. 73–75)
5. Discuss how operant conditioning principles explain the development and maintenance of psychopathology. (pp. 75–76)
6. Describe the observational learning model and differentiate vicarious classical conditioning from vicarious operant conditioning. Discuss how observational learning is related to the development of psychopathology and its treatment. (pp. 76–77)
7. Describe and discuss the criticisms of the behavioral models. Apply the behavioral models to the Case of Steven V. (pp. 77–79)
8. Describe the assumptions of the cognitive model. Discuss the role of irrational/maladaptive thoughts and Beck's three levels of cognitive content. List the major irrational beliefs, according to Ellis, and their role in sustaining negative emotions. Describe the method and outcome of rational emotive therapy. (pp. 79–81; Focus 3.1)
9. Discuss how cognitive distortions account for psychopathology. List and give examples of Beck's six types of faulty thinking processes. (pp. 81–83)
10. Describe the cognitive approaches to therapy, including cognitive restructuring and Meichenbaum's coping strategies and stress inoculation training. (pp. 83–85)
11. Discuss the criticisms of the cognitive model. Apply the cognitive model to the Case of Steven V. (pp. 85–87)
12. Identify the three distinct characteristics of the family systems approach. Discuss the possibility that psychopathology can serve a family function. (pp. 87–88; Critical Thinking 3.1)

13. Using the Case of Jonathan R. and the concepts of Sullivan and Erikson, discuss how personality and identity develop within the family. Discuss what is meant by "family dynamics." (pp. 88–90)
14. Describe and discuss Satir's communication approach, including the five groups of communication patterns. Describe and discuss strategic and structural approaches to families. (pp. 90–92)
15. Discuss the criticisms of the family systems model. Apply the family systems model to the Case of Steven V. (pp. 92–95; Focus 3.2)
16. Using Table 3.3, compare and contrast the biogenic, psychoanalytic, humanistic, existential, behavioral, cognitive, and family systems models of psychopathology. (pp. 95–97)

CHAPTER OUTLINE

1. **Behavioral, cognitive, and family systems models of psychopathology** (pp. 69–70) *Behavioral* and *cognitive models* suggest that all behavior is learned through interaction between the person and the environment. Therapy is directed toward replacing inappropriate behaviors or thoughts and learning appropriate ones. The *family systems model* focuses on the quality of family relationships.

2. **Environmental determinants of abnormal behavior** (p. 70) Models previously discussed in the text emphasize internal factors. Those in this chapter stress environmental or sociocultural conditions and interactions in the interpersonal and sociocultural environments. These models incorporate internal mechanisms, such as our processes of thought, by which we interpret the outside environment.

3. **Behavioral models of psychopathology** (pp. 70–71) John B. Watson, a founder of behaviorism, argued that psychology could not be a science if it attempted to study subjective events such as thoughts and emotions. Watson emphasized the prediction and control of behavior.

4. **The classical conditioning model** (pp. 71–73) *Classical (respondent) conditioning* involves the pairing of a neutral *(conditioned) stimulus* with an *unconditioned stimulus* which automatically produces certain responses, called the *unconditioned response*. After repeated pairing, the conditioned stimulus alone can produce a weakened version of the response, called the *conditioned response.* If the conditioned stimulus is presented many times without following it with the unconditioned stimulus, there is a reduction in the conditioned response, a process called *extinction*. Responding to similar stimuli *(generalization)* and *not* responding to different stimuli *(stimulus discrimination)* are important concepts. These concepts can be used to explain the development of phobias and deviant sexual behavior.

   Classical conditioning principles are used to understand psychopathology. Watson demonstrated the development of a *phobia* (an exaggerated fear) in a child called Little Albert. Mary Cover Jones showed that classical conditioning could be used to reduce fears, too. However, the passive nature of associative learning makes it a limited explanatory tool.

5. **The operant conditioning model** (pp. 73–76) *Operant conditioning* stresses the consequences of voluntary and controllable behaviors called *operant behaviors.* According to Thorndike's *law of effect,* these behaviors are more likely when they produce positive consequences and less likely when they produce negative consequences. A *positive reinforcer* is any positive consequence that increases a behavior's frequency or magnitude. A *negative*

reinforcer is a consequence that increases the frequency of a behavior by removing an unpleasant situation. *Punishment* and *extinction* reduce behavior. A cue that is present when reinforcement occurs is known as a *discriminative stimulus.* When successive steps toward a complex behavior are reinforced, *shaping* occurs.

Operant conditioning principles help explain such forms of psychopathology as self-injurious behavior. Principles of positive and negative reinforcement can be applied to treatment, as well.

6. **The observational learning model** (pp. 76–77) Also called vicarious learning or *modeling, observational learning theory* emphasizes learning by watching. Observing others going through classical and operant conditioning can influence the observer's behavior in processes called vicarious classical and vicarious operant conditioning. These processes are also used in the treatment of psychopathology.

7. **Criticisms of the behavioral models** (pp. 77–78) Behavioral models are an important force in psychology today. They stress nonorganic explanations, scientific verification, and external factors. Some have criticized the noncognitive behavioral models for disregarding thought processes. However, recent writings indicate that behaviorism is integrating contrasting views to become more eclectic.

8. **A behavioral view of Steven V.** (pp. 78–79) A behavioral therapist would see many of Steve's troubles as stemming from a lack of social skills and would examine the situations in which he had difficulty. Modeling and operant conditioning methods would be used to teach improved skills. Steve's heterosexual anxiety would be treated using classical conditioning principles. Extinction would reduce his concerns with Satanism.

9. **Cognitive models of psychopathology** (pp. 79–83) The cognitive model suggests that how we think about events influences our feelings and actions. Interpretations stem from *schemas,* or underlying assumptions. Albert Ellis calls maladaptive thoughts "irrational," Aaron Beck considers them dysfunctional "automatic thoughts," and Donald Meichenbaum refers to them as counterproductive "self-statements." Ellis focuses on the absolutistic nature of irrational thoughts ("shoulds" and "musts"). In therapy, clients learn to be aware of and challenge their irrational beliefs. Ellis describes an "A-B-C theory of personality" in which A is an event, B is a belief, and C is a consequent behavior or emotion. Beck's work on depression helped him identify six types of faulty thinking: arbitrary inference, selective abstraction, overgeneralization, magnification, personalization, and all-or-nothing thinking.

10. **Cognitive approaches to therapy** (pp. 83–85) All cognitive therapies have clients monitor their thoughts; recognize the connections between thoughts, emotions, and behaviors; examine the evidence for their assumptions; and substitute more reality-oriented interpretations. *Cognitive restructuring* and Ellis's *rational-emotive therapy* are two such therapies. Meichenbaum developed another therapy that emphasizes coping strategies where irrational self-statements are replaced with more productive ones.

11. **Criticisms of the cognitive models** (pp. 85–86) Some behaviorists warn that cognitions cannot be observed and therefore are not the stuff of science. Humanistically oriented psychologists object to reducing human beings to the sum of their cognitions. Others object to confrontative cognitive therapy methods.

12. **A cognitive view of Steven V.** (pp. 86–87) Treatment would help Steve become aware of his unrealistic standards and irrational beliefs. He would need to replace maladaptive ideas with productive self-statements.

13. **The family systems model of psychopathology** (pp. 87–90) Unlike the biogenic, psychogenic, and behavior models, which stress the individual, the *family systems model* emphasizes the influence of the family on individual behavior. Abnormality is seen as a symptom of unhealthy family dynamics. Family systems thinking sees causality as more cyclic than linear. It also argues that individuals' pathological symptoms can serve functions for the family and therefore be unwittingly sustained by the family system.

    Harry Stack Sullivan and Erik Erikson focused on parent-child relationships and laid the groundwork for the family systems model.

14. **Family dynamics** (p. 90) *Family dynamics* are the day-to-day communication patterns of the family. Contradictory communication, such as the double bind, where one message is negated by another, may result in psychopathology.

15. **Communication, strategic, and structural approaches** (pp. 90–92) Virginia Satir has developed conjoint family therapy that stresses the importance of message-sending and message-receiving skills. Communications consist of messages at two levels: literal and affective (metacommunicative). Only one of five communication patterns is seen as healthy. The strategic approach highlights the roles of power and control, and owes much of its techniques to Milton Erickson. Salvatore Minuchin's structural approach holds that, when family members are either too involved or too little involved with one another, there will be problems.

16. **Criticisms of the family systems model** (pp. 92, 94) The family systems model has added an important social dimension to our understanding of abnormal behavior. However, the model's concepts are difficult to study; it fails to explain how some children in families are abnormal whereas others are not, and it may blame parents for disorders over which they have no control. The most credible attack comes from the feminist perspective, which objects to seeing an abused wife or child as a contributor to a sick system.

17. **A family systems view of Steven V.** (pp. 94–95) A family systems psychologist would examine Steve's relationship with his father, his relationship with his mother, and the relationship between the husband and wife. The therapist would want to include the entire family in treatment.

KEY TERMS

Fill-in-the-Blanks Quiz

1. The theory that people create their own problems by the way they interpret events is called the ____________.

2. In classical and operant conditioning, the process by which a response is gradually eliminated by not being reinforced is called ____________.

3. In operant conditioning, a positive consequence that increases the frequency or strength of a response is called a(n) ____________.

4. The theory of learning that holds that individuals learn new behaviors by watching other people perform those behaviors is called ___________.

5. The theory of learning in which involuntary responses to new stimuli are learned through association is called ___________.

6. In operant conditioning, any consequence that increases the frequency of the behavior it follows is called ___________.

7. The model of psychopathology that emphasizes the influence of the family on individual behavior is called the ___________.

8. A theory of learning, applying primarily to voluntary behaviors, that holds that these behaviors are controlled by the consequences that follow them is called ___________.

9. Models that are based on the idea that both normal and abnormal behaviors are learned through interaction between the person and the environment are called ___________.

10. In classical conditioning, the response made to a previously neutral stimulus is called the ___________.

11. In classical conditioning, a previously neutral stimulus is called a(n) ___________.

12. An excessive fear, which may develop because of classical conditioning, is called a(n) ___________.

13. An attempt to alter problematic cognitions by replacing them with more rational and positive thoughts is called ___________.

14. A cue that is usually present when reinforcement occurs is called a(n) ___________.

15. The process of producing similar behavior in response to different stimuli is called ___________.

16. The idea that increases in behavior are associated with positive consequences and that reductions in behavior are associated with unpleasant ones is called ___________.

17. The process of learning by observing others is called ___________.

18. The systematic but incremental method of rewarding behavior with the purpose of attaining a desired but more complex goal behavior is called ___________.

19. The underlying assumptions held by a person that influence how he or she interprets events are called ___________.

20. The ability to differentiate differences between similar stimuli is called ___________.

21. In classical conditioning, the response first made to the unconditioned stimulus is called the ___________.

22. In classical conditioning, the stimulus that elicits the unconditioned response is called the ___________.

23. The system of therapy developed by Albert Ellis that stresses changing irrational thought patterns is called ___________.

24. The day-to-day operation of the family system is called ___________.

25. A consequence that increases the frequency of a behavior by removing an aversive event is called a(n) ___________.

26. A voluntary and controllable behavior that "operates" on an individual's environment is called a(n) ___________.

27. The removal of a positive reinforcer or the presentation of an aversive stimulus that reduces the probability of a response is called ___________.

Answers to Fill-in-the-Blanks Quiz

1. cognitive model
2. extinction
3. positive reinforcer
4. observational learning theory
5. classical conditioning
6. reinforcement
7. family systems model
8. operant conditioning
9. behavioral models
10. conditioned response
11. conditioned stimulus
12. phobia
13. cognitive restructuring
14. discriminative stimulus
15. generalization
16. the law of effect
17. modeling
18. shaping
19. schemas
20. stimulus discrimination
21. unconditioned response
22. unconditioned stimulus
23. rational-emotive therapy (RET)
24. family dynamics
25. negative reinforcer
26. operant behavior
27. punishment

FACT AND CONCEPT QUESTIONS

1. In classical conditioning, the ___________ is initially neutral, but can evoke a response if it is paired with the ___________.
   a. unconditioned stimulus; conditioned response
   b. operant stimulus; classical stimulus
   c. unconditioned response; conditioned stimulus
   d. conditioned stimulus; unconditioned stimulus

2. The classical conditioning case studies by Watson and Rayner and Mary Cover Jones showed that
   a. phobias are caused by classical conditioning, but only operant conditioning can be used to treat them.
   b. phobias are actually learned through observation of a model.
   c. children cannot learn generalization or discrimination the way animals can.
   d. classical conditioning priniciples can explain both the cause and treatment of phobias.

3. Which of the following is probably best explained by classical conditioning?
   a. Learning how to use chopsticks in a Chinese restaurant
   b. Becoming silent when your friend continually interrupts anything you say
   c. Two people getting the same grade on a test, but only one of them feeling proud of it
   d. Developing a fear of cars after being in a traffic accident

4. One form of therapy for alcoholism involves pairing nausea and vomiting with the smell and taste of alcoholic beverages. This treatment is based on
   a. classical conditioning.
   b. observational learning.
   c. shaping.
   d. cognitive therapy.

5. Because they are voluntary behaviors, social skills are learned through
   a. classical conditioning.
   b. operant conditioning.
   c. extinction.
   d. the pairing of conditioned and unconditioned stimuli.

6. In ___________, behavior is controlled by preceding stimuli; in ___________, learning is based on the consequences of behavior.
   a. modeling; cognitive-behavioral theory
   b. classical conditioning; operant conditioning
   c. operant conditioning; modeling
   d. classical conditioning; cognitive-behavioral theory

7. If an action increases the frequency of a behavior by removing an unpleasant situation, the action is considered a
   a. positive reinforcer.
   b. negative reinforcer.
   c. shaping agent.
   d. form of vicarious operant conditioning.

8. Punishment differs from extinction in that punishment
   a. decreases the frequency of the behavior, whereas extinction increases it.
   b. adds an aversive consequence after the behavior, whereas extinction does not.
   c. increases the frequency of the behavior, whereas extinction decreases it.
   d. involves a mediating thought process, whereas extinction does not.

9. When teaching table manners, parents praise young children when they are able to pick up a spoon and put half of their applesauce inside their mouth. Later, however, a child must become neater before praise is forthcoming. What operant conditioning process does this illustrate?
   a. Stimulus generalization
   b. Extinction
   c. Shaping
   d. A conditioned response

10. Research indicates that, when children watch television violence, they often imitate the aggressive actions in their own lives. This illustrates
    a. classically conditioned shaping.
    b. vicarious operant conditioning.
    c. discrimination learning.
    d. vicarious respondent conditioning.

11. According to Albert Ellis, negative emotions are the result of
    a. irrational beliefs about events that occur in our lives.
    b. modeling inappropriate behaviors.
    c. pairing certain conditioned stimuli with negative unconditioned responses.
    d. faulty communications in which verbal messages contradict nonverbal messages.

12. Selective abstraction, overgeneralization, and magnification are all
    a. forms of maladaptive communication, according to family systems thinkers.
    b. observational learning methods.
    c. types of faulty thinking processes that Beck believes operate in most disorders.
    d. irrational beliefs, according to Albert Ellis.

13. The therapy in which clients are taught to use specific self-statements and coping skills to deal with threatening situations is called
    a. vicarious respondent conditioning.
    b. systematic desensitization.
    c. stress inoculation training.
    d. biofeedback.

14. Which of the following is true about criticisms of the cognitive model?
    a. Most critics say it cannot be integrated with behavioral models.
    b. Some behaviorists think it is not scientific enough; some humanistic psychologists think it is too mechanistic.
    c. Most critics argue that it does not provide clients with enough guidance on how to change.
    d. Some psychoanalysts say it puts too much emphasis on biological factors such as heredity and brain function.

15. Which statement is *true* concerning the family systems model?
    a. It suggests that all phenomena can be understood in terms of linear, cause-and-effect relationships.
    b. It suggests that abnormal behavior in an individual reflects unhealthy dynamics in the family.
    c. It does not believe that family dynamics can be changed once they have been established.
    d. It assumes that genetics explains why some families have certain behavior problems generation after generation.

16. According to the family systems model, if a teenage boy addicted to drugs were successfully treated, his parents might unconsciously force him back into a "sick role" because
    a. of genetics.
    b. all behavior is presumed to be based on modeling.
    c. family equilibrium was disturbed when the son got better.
    d. families need to metacommunicate.

17. Research on families from different cultural backgrounds shows that
    a. regardless of culture, the family is defined as the mother, father, and children.
    b. the rules governing non-European American ethnic minorities are similar to each other and different from those in European American families.
    c. most ethnic minorities give greatest control to mothers and the youngest children in the family.
    d. ethnic minority families have communication patterns that are less free and open than in traditional European American familes.

18. In ___________ therapy, problems are seen in terms of power struggles, control, and the need to reestablish boundaries.
    a. strategic family
    b. conjoint family
    c. rational-emotive
    d. cognitive restructuring

19. Salvatore Minuchin's structural approach to family therapy stresses
    a. the degree to which family members are over- or underinvolved in one another's lives.
    b. the ways in which messages are sent and received by family members.
    c. the cross-cultural differences in communication patterns.
    d. the need for the therapist to take over power from the father of the family.

20. Which of the following is a sound criticism of the family systems model?
    a. It puts too much emphasis on the genetic origins of psychopathology.
    b. It gives women too much control and power in the family.
    c. Both a and b.
    d. Neither a nor b.

APPLICATION QUESTIONS

1. Jim once developed nausea and vomited after eating spaghetti at Marco's Italian Villa. Now, he feels sick not only when he is served spaghetti, but also when he is served other Italian dishes or walks into Marco's. This illustrates
    a. generalization in classical conditioning.
    b. punishment in operant conditioning.
    c. negative reinforcement in operant conditioning.
    d. discrimination learning in classical conditioning.

2. In the Case of Steven V., Steven becomes sexually aroused when watching violent movies. From a classical conditioning viewpoint, a violent movie is a ___________ for Steven.
    a. conditioned response
    b. conditioned stimulus
    c. positive reinforcer
    d. negative reinforcer

3. When little Janie cries for a cookie, her mother tries not to give in, but, after listening to five minutes of crying, she gives Janie the cookie she wants. From an operant conditioning point of view, what kind of reinforcement maintains the *mother's* habit of cookie giving?
   a. Shaping
   b. Negative reinforcement
   c. Extinction
   d. Positive reinforcement

4. In order to stop Brad from borrowing class notes (a strong and obnoxious habit of Brad's), all his acquaintances pretend not to hear him when he asks for notes. Sure enough, Brad stops his annoying habit. According to operant conditioning, the reason was
   a. extinction.
   b. modeling.
   c. punishment.
   d. negative reinforcement.

5. Mrs. Kelly did not talk for the first three weeks she was at the nursing home. The staff began to give her food as a reinforcer whenever she made any sound at all. Then they gave reinforcement when she spoke words, and then sentences. What form of therapy did the staff use?
   a. Systematic desensitization
   b. Covert sensitization
   c. Shaping
   d. Cognitive restructuring

6. Dr. Lawrence says to a client, "Your phobia of spiders came about because your mother set an example by jumping on a chair and shrieking any time a spider was within twenty yards of her." Dr. Lawrence's explanation follows the ____________ model.
   a. metacommunication
   b. classical conditioning
   c. operant conditioning
   d. observational learning

7. Dr. McNally says to a depressed client, "You are not depressed because of bad events; you are depressed because you have the irrational belief that any bad event is a catastrophe that is totally unfair and inhumane." Dr. McNally's statement reflects ____________ approach to depression.
   a. Albert Ellis's rational-emotive
   b. John B. Watson's classical conditioning
   c. Erik Erikson's psychodynamic
   d. Virginia Satir's stress inoculation

8. Dr. Sall says, "The family systems model holds that all members of families are enmeshed in interdependent roles. Problems in one person are a reflection of poor communications in the family. One of the earliest psychiatrists to state these ideas was J. B. Watson." What statement by Dr. Sall is incorrect?
   a. The idea that family members are enmeshed
   b. The idea that there are interdependent roles
   c. The idea that communications are important
   d. The idea that J. B. Watson was a family theorist

9. Mr. and Mrs. Appley are very concerned about their daughter's performance in school. They see her as "sick," but their therapist thinks they are diverting attention from their own troubled marriage. What kind of therapist are the Appleys probably seeing?
   a. A cognitive therapist
   b. A behavior therapist
   c. A family systems therapist
   d. An operant conditioning therapist

10. When analyzing the Case of Steven V., a(n) ___________ therapist would be most likely to focus on the lack of boundaries that existed in Mr. and Mrs. V.'s relationship.
   a. structural family
   b. conjoint family
   c. cognitive restructuring
   d. operantly oriented

ANSWERS TO FACT AND CONCEPT QUESTIONS

1. a. The unconditioned stimulus is not neutral; it automatically elicits the unconditioned response.
   b. *Operant* is a word used to describe behavior in the operant conditioning model.
   c. Stimuli are paired in classical conditioning, not responses and stimuli.
   *d. The conditioned stimulus is neutral with respect to a response until it has been paired with the unconditioned stimulus that can elicit the response in question. (p. 71)

2. a. Jones's work showed that classical conditioning principles could be used to reduce or eliminate a phobia in treatment.
   b. Both cases focused on classical conditioning and did not look at observational learning.
   c. Little Albert learned to generalize—from the rat to other furry objects.
   *d. The Case of Little Albert showed how acquiring a phobia could be explained by classical conditioning; Jones showed how a child's fears could be reduced using the same principles. (p. 72)

3. a. Chopsticks use is a voluntary behavior, and is therefore more related to operant or modeling approaches.
   b. Reduced behavior after an aversive event illustrates punishment.
   c. This illustrates how individuals interpret events—a component of the cognitive behavioral approach.
   *d. Classical conditioning involves an involuntary response (fear) that is paired with previously neutral stimuli (cars). (p. 74)

4. *a. Pairing an aversive event with stimuli that are associated with an undesirable response is a treatment method based on classical conditioning. (pp. 74–75)
   b. Observational learning therapies involve modeling others.
   c. Shaping is an operant conditioning method that reinforces approximations toward a complex behavior.
   d. Cognitive therapy would examine the thoughts that alcoholics use to interpret events.

5. a. Classical conditioning involves the learning of involuntary behaviors.
*b. Operant conditioning involves the learning of voluntary behaviors. (p. 74)
c. Extinction decreases the frequency of a behavior.
d. The pairing of stimuli is a part of classical conditioning.

6. a. Modeling is part of observational learning; cognitive-behavioral theory stresses thinking.
*b. Behaviors learned through classical conditioning are controlled by stimuli preceding the response. In operant conditioning, behaviors are controlled by events that follow them. (p. 74)
c. Operant conditioning is based on consequences; modeling is a part of observational learning.
d. Stimuli that precede responses do control classical conditioning, but cognitive behavioral theory stresses thinking.

7. a. Positive reinforcers are pleasant consequences for actions and do not involve the removal of an unpleasant situation.
*b. Negative reinforcers increase behavior by removing unpleasant situations. (p. 74)
c. Shaping is the use of reinforcement for successive approximations of some goal behavior.
d. Vicarious operant conditioning occurs when one watches the reinforcement of another person and learns through modeling.

8. a. Punishment and extinction both decrease the frequency of a behavior.
*b. Punishment occurs when a behavior is followed by an aversive event, such as a yell or a slap; in extinction, the behavior's frequency is reduced by stopping reinforcement. (p. 75)
c. Punishment and extinction both decrease a response's frequency.
d. Punishment is a part of strict operant theory and therefore does not require a mediating (cognitive) component.

9. a. Stimulus generalization is the process of making the same response to a range of stimuli.
b. Extinction occurs when a behavior decreases in frequency because reinforcement is stopped.
*c. Shaping is an operant procedure in which successive behaviors that approximate a goal behavior are reinforced. (p. 75)
d. A conditioned response is a result of classical conditioning.

10. a. Shaping is an operant conditioning process.
*b. These children are imitating operant behaviors (aggressive acts); this is called vicarious operant conditioning. (p. 77)
c. Discrimination learning involves "turning on" a behavior in the presence of some stimuli and "turning off" the behavior in the presence of others.
d. Vicarious respondent conditioning involves involuntary behaviors such as fear or sexual arousal.

11. *a. Ellis's rational-emotive therapy says that negative emotions are the result of irrational beliefs. (p. 80)
b. Observational learning stresses modeling.
c. The pairing of stimuli is the essence of classical conditioning.
d. Virginia Satir stresses faulty communications in families.

12. a. Maladaptive communication patterns (according to Satir) involve literal messages that differ from emotional (affective) messages.
  b. Observational learning involves attention and remembering, not logical reasoning.
  *c. Beck has six types of faulty logic, of which selective abstraction, overgeneralization, and magnification are three. (p. 83)
  d. Ellis's irrational beliefs involve "shoulds" and "musts" that do not necessarily involve these kinds of faulty thinking.

13. a. Vicarious respondent conditioning involves learning by observing classical conditioning in another person.
  b. Systematic desensitization is a classical conditioning therapy in which relaxation is paired with anxiety-provoking stimuli.
  *c. Meichenbaum's stress inoculation training teaches coping self-statements and stress-reduction strategies. (p. 84)
  d. Biofeedback is an operant therapy that helps people change such internal responses as heart rate and muscle tension.

14. a. Cognitive therapies are often integrated with behavior therapies.
  *b. Skinner, a behaviorist, argued that emphasizing non-observable thinking weakens the scientific foundation of psychology; humanistic psychologists see personality as more than the sum of our thoughts. (p. 86)
  c. The opposite is argued: that cognitive therapists control treatment too much.
  d. Cognitive therapists give no weighting to heredity or brain functioning.

15. a. Classical conditioning emphasizes the pairing of stimuli.
  *b. Family systems theory suggests that symptoms in an individual reflect unhealthy family dynamics. (p. 90)
  c. Although family systems theory recognizes that change that threatens homeostasis is unwelcome, the whole thrust of therapy is to produce change toward healthy dynamics.
  d. The biogenic model stresses genetics; the family systems approach would emphasize parents' rules and behavior patterns.

16. a. The family systems model places no emphasis on genetics.
  b. The observational learning model places greatest emphasis on modeling.
  *c. The family systems model proposes that major changes in one family member upset the family's homeostasis; equilibrium is maintained by reverting to familiar roles. (p. 80)
  d. Although metacommunication is a part of the family systems model, it is not relevant to why a member returns to a sick role.

17. a. Non-European American cultures define families to include godparents, aunts, uncles, and other extended family members.
  b. Non-European American ethnic minorities can be quite different from one another; African American fathers are less dominant in their families than Asian American or Hispanic fathers.
  c. Ethnic minorities tend to give fathers and oldest children more control than is seen in European American, traditional families.
  *d. Communications between parent and child are more equal in European American, traditional families than in most ethnic minority families, where children are not to initiate conversations (p. 93).

18. *a. Strategic family therapy attempts to change the power relationships and boundaries in distressed families. (p. 91)
    b. Conjoint family therapy tries to change the communication patterns in distressed families.
    c. Rational-emotive therapy focuses on the irrational thoughts of individuals.
    d. Cognitive restructuring helps clients identify and change their thought processes.

19. *a. Minuchin's structural approach stresses systems of relationships that may be overly involved or overly separate. (p. 91)
    b. Satir's communications approach stresses how messages are sent and received.
    c. Minuchin's approach does not emphasize communications.
    d. Power is an issue in the strategic family therapy of Haley and Erikson.

20. a. The family systems model places no emphasis on genetics.
    b. A strong objection to family systems thinking comes from feminists who attack the idea that abused women can be seen as contributing to the problem.
    c. Because both a and b are incorrect, this cannot be the best choice.
    *d. Because both a and b are incorrect, this is the best choice. (p. 94)

ANSWERS TO APPLICATION QUESTIONS

1. *a. In classical conditioning, generalization is showing a conditioned response to stimuli similar to the original conditioning stimulus—in this case, nausea in the presence of similar foods or settings. (p. 71)
   b. Punishment involves aversive consequences after behaviors, which leads to a decrease in response frequency.
   c. Negative reinforcement produces an increase in behavior frequency when the behavior eliminates or reduces an aversive stimulus; in this case, if Jim avoided all Italian foods when the thought of them produced distress, that would illustrate negative reinforcement.
   d. Discrimination learning is the opposite of generalization; Jim has failed to show discrimination learning.

2. a. Sexual arousal would be an example of a conditioned response.
   *b. The movies were probably initially neutral (with respect to sex), but were paired with situations for sexual arousal and came to be a conditioned stimulus for arousal. (p. 71)
   c. Positive reinforcers follow a response.
   d. Negative reinforcers increase behavior because they eliminate or reduce some aversive situation.

3. a. Shaping involves reinforcement for step-by-step approximations of some complex behavior.
   *b. By giving a cookie, the mother stops Janie's screaming; in negative reinforcement, a response that stops or reduces an aversive situation is strengthened. Little Janie is being positively reinforced for crying. (p. 74)
   c. Extinction occurs when reinforcement stops and a behavior decreases.
   d. Janie is positively reinforced, not her mother.

4. *a. Extinction occurs when behavior that had been reinforced is no longer reinforced and decreases. (p. 75)
   b. Modeling involves the observation of others' behavior.
   c. Punishment would occur if an aversive consequence happened after Brad's behavior, such as someone yelling at him.
   d. Negative reinforcement increases the likelihood of a behavior.

5. a. Systematic desensitization is a therapy based on classical conditioning that is primarily used to reduce anxiety.
   b. Covert sensitization is a therapy based on classical conditioning that reduces the likelihood of unwanted behaviors.
   *c Shaping is the process of reinforcing behaviors that, step by step, approximate a complex goal—in this case, reinforcing sounds and words until full sentences are produced. (p. 75)
   d. Cognitive restructuring involves reevaluating how events are interpreted.

6. a. Metacommunication relates to the message about a message; it is not a model at all.
   b. Classical conditioning involves direct learning, not observation.
   c. Operant conditioning involves direct learning, not observation.
   *d. Observational learning involves learning through modeling; in this case, it is vicarious respondent conditioning. (p. 76)

7. *a. Ellis's rational-emotive therapy holds that depression is a result of irrational beliefs that catastrophize unpleasant events. (p. 84)
   b. Watson's approach did not consider the role of thought.
   c. Erikson's approach focuses on unconscious motives that stem from parent-child relationships.
   d. Satir is the originator of conjoint family therapy; Meichenbaum developed stress inoculation training.

8. a. Family systems psychologists focus on the interlocking nature of family relationships.
   b. Family systems are just that, *systems;* they involve interdependent members who affect one another.
   c. Communications are a key factor in psychopathology, according to family systems thinking.
   *d. Sullivan was a major contributor to family systems thinking; J. B. Watson was a founding father of behaviorism. (pp. 86–87)

9. a. A cognitive therapist would help them examine their thinking about their daughter's performance and develop more realistic expecations.
   b. A behavior therapist would stress the environmental factors that reduce their daughter's school performance.
   *c. Family systems therapists would see the daughter as serving as a diversion from a marital problem and thereby relieving the entire system. (Critical Thinking, p. 89)
   d. Operantly oriented therapists are behavior therapists interested in behaviors and their consequences.

10. *a. Structural family therapists believe that enmeshed or disengaged families—where boundaries are rigid or unclear—produce psychopathology. (p. 91)
    b. Conjoint family therapy stresses communications and would examine Mr. and Mrs. V.'s ways of communicating.
    c. Cognitive restructuring would entail Mr. and Mrs. V.'s monitoring their irrational thoughts, challenging them, and replacing them with more productive thoughts.
    d. Operantly oriented therapists would emphasize the importance of social skills to individuals in the V. family.

CHAPTER 4
Assessment and Classification of Abnormal Behavior

LEARNING OBJECTIVES

When you have mastered the material in Chapter 4, you should be able to:

1. Describe the functions of a psychodiagnosis. Define reliability, and differentiate among test-retest, internal, and interrater reliability. Define validity, and differentiate between criterion and construct validity. (pp. 101–102)
2. Define assessment, and discuss the role of assessment and the choice of assessment tools in clinical psychology. Discuss the problems of assessment in different cultural groups and the means by which assessment data are interpreted. (pp. 102–105; Critical Thinking 4.1)
3. Describe and discuss observations of behavior and problems related to them. Describe and discuss clinical interviews and issues of standardization and interviewer errors. (pp. 103–106)
4. Describe the common features of psychological tests. Describe the nature and purposes of projective personality tests, including the Rorschach, Thematic Apperception Test (TAT), sentence-completion test, and draw-a-person test. Discuss the strengths and weaknesses of projective tests. (pp. 106–107)
5. Describe the nature and purposes of objective personality tests, including the Minnesota Multiphasic Personality Inventory (MMPI-2). Discuss the strengths and weaknesses of personality inventories. (pp. 109–111)
6. Describe the purposes and procedures of the Wechsler and Stanford-Binet intelligence tests. Describe research relating IQ scores to brain function. Discuss the criticisms of these tests and new tests that respond to those criticisms. (pp. 111–113)
7. Describe methods for assessing brain damage, including the WAIS-R, Bender-Gestalt Visual-Motor Test, Halstead-Reitan Neuropsychological Test Battery, and Luria-Nebraska Neuropsychological Battery. Describe neurological procedures for detecting brain damage, including CAT and PET scans, EEGs, and MRIs. (pp. 113–115)
8. Discuss the ethical issues in assessment. Discuss the likelihood of computer assessment. Review research on cultural differences in clinical judgments. (pp. 116–117; Focus 4.1)
9. Explain the goals of classifying abnormal behaviors and review the history of classification systems. Discuss how validity problems have been raised and dealt with. (pp. 116–118)
10. Describe the features of the DSM-IV, including its five axes. Review the broad categories of mental disorders. Discuss what are expected to be the major improvements in the DSM-IV. (pp. 119–127; Table 4.1)

11. List and discuss the objections to the DSM classification system, including accusations of gender bias and the findings from the Rosenhan study. Describe the arguments supporting the DSM system. (pp. 127–128; Focus 4.3)
12. Describe the five-category behavioral classification approach. Compare its usefulness with the DSM system. (pp. 128–130; Table 4.4)
13. Describe three problems associated with labeling and the research related to these problems. Discuss how the findings of Rosenhan (1973) relate to the impact of labeling. (pp. 130–131; Focus 4.4)

CHAPTER OUTLINE

1. **Reliability and validity** (p. 102) Evaluation of information about an individual leads to a *psychodiagnosis*, which involves describing and drawing inferences about the person's psychological state. The psychodiagnosis clarifies the picture of that state, may lead to a treatment program, provides an efficient way of referring to disorders, and serves to standardize assessment procedures. To be useful, assessment tools must show *reliability*, the ability to get the same results across time or across different observers. Measures that are reliable can also demonstrate *validity*. There are two types of validity: criterion-related and construct.

2. **The assessment of abnormal behavior: Observations and interviews** (pp. 101–106) *Assessment* requires obtaining information from many sources, including tests, interviews, observations, and reports from the patient and his or her relatives and friends. An array of measures, sometimes in the form of a *test battery*, produces a more comprehensive assessment. However, measurement accuracy is affected by cultural differences and the way the clinician interprets findings. *Clinical observations* in either controlled or naturalistic settings are usually made in conjunction with an interview and can have diagnostic significance. The content and process of communications are important to analyze. Interviews stress different information depending on the interviewer's theoretical orientation. Standardized interviews are structured and produce fewer errors but may not yield usable information.

3. **The assessment of abnormal behavior: Psychological tests** (pp. 106–111) Psychological tests have a wide range of application. They provide a standard situation for responses and allow comparison of results with normative samples. *Projective personality tests* present ambiguous stimuli and ask for responses that "project" the person's motives. The *Rorschach technique* is a series of cards displaying inkblots. What people see where in the blots and why they see what they do are interpreted in terms of psychoanalytic symbolism. The *Thematic Apperception Test (TAT)* uses pictures of people and asks the person to tell a story about each picture. The style and themes of the stories are used to gain insight into conflicts and personality. The sentence-completion test and the Draw-a-Person test are other examples of projective tests. Projectives tend to have low reliability and validity.

   Objective personality inventories supply the test taker with a list of alternative answers. The *Minnesota Multiphasic Personality Inventory (MMPI)* consists of 567 statements that are answered "true," "false," or "cannot say," and was recently revised to become the MMPI-2. MMPI-2 responses are scored on ten clinical and three validity scales. Profiles of scale results indicate personality styles. Inventories have been criticized for being restrictive, pathology oriented, and easily faked. Still, inventories are widely used, and some show both reliability and validity since the techniques used in making mental measurement—psychometrics—are becoming increasingly sophisticated.

4. **The assessment of abnormal behavior: Intelligence tests** (pp. 111–113) Intelligence tests are designed to measure cognitive functioning, called the *intelligence quotient* (IQ), and to detect organic disorders. The *Wechsler Adult Intelligence Scale* (revised to become the WAIS-R), and two other forms for children (WISC-III) and preschoolers (WPPSI-R) are widely used. Also used is the *Stanford-Binet Scale*. Ethnic groups have attacked IQ tests for being culturally biased, and it is clear that reliance on IQ has led to discrimination. Social competency cannot be adquately assessed with IQ tests. The *System of Multicultural Pluralistic Assessment (SOMPA)* and the *Kaufman Assessment Battery for Children (K-ABC)* are tests that address this and other criticisms.

5. **The assessment of abnormal behavior: Tests for brain damage and neurological tests** (pp. 113–115) Tests to detect and assess brain damage to the central nervous system (organicity) include the WAIS-R, the *Bender-Gestalt Visual-Motor Test*, the *Halstead-Reitan Neuropsychological Test Battery*, and the *Luria-Nebraska Neuropsychological Battery*. Neurological medical procedures such as *computerized axial tomography* (CAT scan), *positron emission tomography* (PET scan), the *electroencephalograph* (EEG), and *magnetic resonance imaging* (MRI) are also used to assess brain conditions.

6. **The ethics of assessment** (p. 116) There is a strong antitesting movement in the United States. Criticisms include the undesirable social consequences of using test results and problems of using tests on people from nonwestern cultures. Computer assessment has been viewed as a potential substitute for some testing.

7. **The classification of abnormal behavior** (pp. 116–119) The goal of a *classification system* is to provide distinct categories for different behavior problems. Classification systems should provide distinct categories that are used consistently but that still accommodate imperfect cases. Kraepelin's system and the original DSM were based on medical model principles and the hope that similar disorders would have a common *etiology* (cause). The *Diagnostic and Statistical Manual of Mental Disorder (DSM)* was first published in 1952 and is now revised *(DSM-IV)*. Interrater reliability of recent editions of the DSM has been good. Older editions of the DSM were criticized for having poor reliability and validity.

8. **The current system: DSM-IV** (Table 4.3; pp. 119–124) This newest version (1993) evaluates an individual on five dimensions or axes: Axis I, clinical syndromes; Axis II, personality or specific developmental disorders; Axis III, general medical conditions; Axis IV, psychosocial problems; and Axis V, global assessment of the highest level of adaptive functioning. The reliability of DSM-IV is being studied.

9. **DSM-IV mental disorders** (pp. 124–127) The broad categories of mental disorders discussed in the text are: disorders usually first diagnosed in infancy, childhood, or adolescence; delirium, demential, amnestic, and other cognitive disorders; mental disorders due to a general medical condition; substance-related disorders; schizophrenia and other psychotic disorders; mood disorders; anxiety disorders; somatoform disorders; factitious disorders; dissociative disorders; sexual and gender identity disorders; eating disorders, sleep disorders, impulse control disorders not elsewhere classified; adjustment disorders; and personality disorders. The DSM-IV emphasizes cross-cultural assessment more than previous DSM versions.

10. **Evaluation of the DSM classification system** (pp. 127–128) It is too soon to provide an evaluation of DSM-IV; however, critics of past DSMs argue it is biased toward the medical model, will not adequately classify psychopathology in nonwestern cultures, and classifies

people into categories rather than seeing them as having more or less of certain characteristics. Supporters suggest that its weaknesses reflect current gaps in knowledge.

11. **An alternative approach: Behavioral classification** (pp. 128–130) Behaviorists have proposed an alternative to the DSM system that uses five categories of classification: stimulus control, deficient behavioral repertoire, aversive behaviors, incentive systems, and aversive self-reinforcement.

12. **Objections to classification and labeling** (Focus 4.4; pp. 130–131) Classification can exaggerate the differences between normal and abnormal. It can also lead people to misinterpret normal behavior as pathological, affect the way people treat those who are labeled, and change the behavior of people who are labeled (self-fulfilling prophecies). Rosenhan's study with pseudopatients illustrates these problems.

KEY TERMS

Fill-in-the-Blanks Quiz

1. The degree to which a procedure or test yields the same result repeatedly under the same circumstances is called ___________.

2. An inventory of personality attributes in which the test-taker either agrees or disagrees with specific self-descriptive statements is called a(n) ___________.

3. Any test instrument used to assess personality, maladaptive behavior, social skills, intellectual abilities, vocational interests, or brain damage is called a(n) ___________.

4. The process of gathering information about an individual's traits, skills, abilities, emotional functioning, and psychological problems is called ___________.

5. The cause or origin of a disorder is called the disorder's ___________.

6. A personality assessment technique in which the test-taker is presented with ambiguous stimuli to which he or she is asked to respond is called a(n) ___________.

7. A psychological test made up of designs that must be copied by the test-taker and which is used to assess brain damage is called the ___________.

8. The degree to which a procedure or test actually performs the function that it was designed to perform is called ___________.

9. With regard to psychopathology, a system of distinct categories, indicators, and nomenclature for different patterns of behavior, thought processes, and emotional disturbances is called a(n) ___________.

10. The objective personality test comprised of 567 statements that yields ten clinical scales is called the ___________.

11. The group of tests that takes a great deal of time to complete and is used to assess brain damage is called the ___________.

12. The technique for diagnosing brain damage that uses radioactive substances in the bloodstream is called ___________.

13. The measure of mental facility that is the result of intelligence testing is called the ___________.

14. The intelligence test for children that is believed to be low in cultural bias is called the ___________.

15. The technique for diagnosing brain damage that uses magnetic fields is called ___________.

16. The assessment method that uses multiple psychological tests to give a comprehensive picture of a person is called a(n) ___________.

17. The most frequently used intelligence test for adults is called the ___________.

18. In the DSM-IV, the five dimensions on which individuals are assessed are called ___________.

19. The projective personality test that uses pictures of individuals and asks the test-taker to make up a story about these individuals is called the ___________.

20. The group of psychological tests used to assess brain damage that is briefer than the Halstead-Reitan Neuropsychological Test Battery is called the ___________.

21. The result of an assessment that involves drawing inferences about a person's psychological state and which is the basis for formulating a treatment program is called a(n) ___________.

22. The intelligence test that is used for both children and adults and which requires considerable testing skill is called the ___________.

23. The method for assessing brain function that records brain wave activity is called the ___________.

24. Looking at the behavior of individuals in controlled or naturalistic situations for the purpose of assessing their psychological condition is called ___________.

25. The method of assessing brain function that uses multiple x-ray scans is called ___________.

26. The projective personality test that uses ten cards on which inkblots are displayed is called the ___________.

Answers to Fill-in-the-Blanks Quiz

1. reliability
2. objective personality test
3. psychological test
4. assessment
5. etiology
6. projective personality test
7. Bender-Gestalt Visual-Motor Test
8. validity
9. classification system
10. MMPI or MMPI-2

11. Halstead-Reitan Neuropsychological Test Battery
12. positron emission tomography (PET) scan
13. intelligence quotient (IQ)
14. Kaufman Assessment Battery for Children (K-ABC)
15. magnetic resonance imaging
16. test battery
17. Wechsler Adult Intelligence Scale, Revised (WAIS-R)
18. axes
19. Thematic Apperception Test (TAT)
20. Luria-Nebraska Neuropsychological Battery
21. psychodiagnosis
22. Stanford-Binet Scale
23. electroencephalograph
24. clinical observation
25. computerized axial tomography (CAT) scan
26. Rorschach technique

FACT AND CONCEPT QUESTIONS

1. Which of the following statements about assessment is *true*?
   a. Assessment uses a wide range of information sources to get a clearer picture of a client's problem.
   b. Assessment occurs when information is boiled down to a particular category.
   c. Assessment must use psychological tests in order to be valid.
   d. Assessment methods are not affected by the psychologist's theoretical perspective.

2. A test that gives the same results repeatedly is considered
   a. an objective personality test.
   b. a test with high validity.
   c. a structured test.
   d. a test with high reliability.

3. What did Kraepelin's and the original DSM classification system have in common?
   a. High reliability
   b. An eclectic approach that described disorders rather than proposing specific causes for them
   c. Reliance on the behavioral perspective
   d. Reliance on the medical model

4. The poor reliability of the original DSM was mostly due to
   a. the poor training of the people who used it.
   b. its excessive use of specific behavior to define categories.
   c. inadequacies in the system itself.
   d. faking in the clients who were examined.

5. If a classification system provided useful information about the etiology and prognosis of disorders, it would be
   a. based on the behavioral model of abnormality.
   b. low in reliability but high in validity.
   c. considered a standardized instrument.
   d. telling about the cause and future course of disorders.

6. What information is revealed on Axis II of DSM-IV?
   a. Level of functioning now and in the past year
   b. Any personality or specific developmental disorder
   c. Level of stress experienced in the past year
   d. The clinical syndrome

7. Anxiety disorders, mood disorders, and substance-related disorders are all categories of behavior that appear on which axis of the DSM-IV?
   a. Axis I
   b. Axis III
   c. Axis V
   d. None; these categories have been omitted from the DSM-IV

8. Stimulus control and aversive self-reinforcement are factors that are important in
   a. the DSM-IV's definition of self-defeating personality disorder.
   b. scoring a WAIS or WISC.
   c. the behavioral classification system.
   d. making an assessment based on objective personality tests.

9. What did the Rosenhan study with pseudopatients illustrate?
   a. The high reliability of the new DSM-IV
   b. The ability of professionals to detect faking
   c. How self-fulfilling prophecies can make normal people act "insane"
   d. How labels influence us to see abnormality even when people act normally

10. Reactivity is a major problem for which of the following assessment methods?
    a. Observation
    b. Neurological procedures to detect brain damage
    c. Projective intelligence testing
    d. Structured interviews

11. Which method of assessing brain function records brain wave patterns?
    a. Electroencephalograph
    b. Bender-Gestalt Visual-Motor Test
    c. Computerized axial tomography (CAT) scan
    d. Magnetic resonance imaging (MRI)

12. Which of the following statements about clinical interviews is *true*?
    a. Despite differences in theoretical orientations, psychologists all interview clients in the same way.
    b. Clinical interviews do not make use of observations.
    c. The quality of the relationship between interviewer and interviewee has a strong effect on the value of the interview.
    d. Interviews are most likely to be highly structured if performed by psychoanalytically oriented psychologists.

13. Which of the following is characteristic of psychological tests?
    a. They typically measure intellectual functioning.
    b. They rely on norms for making assessments of individuals.
    c. They allow the tester to use his or her own judgment about how to administer and score the test.
    d. They are typically used for research purposes only.

14. The Rorschach inkblot technique
    a. is most commonly used to detect brain damage.
    b. examines responses to color and the use of detail areas, as well as what is seen.
    c. requires the test-taker to tell a story about people who are portrayed in pictures.
    d. sometimes uses the completion of sentence fragments to reveal underlying conflicts and motives.

15. Projective personality tests are most likely to be used by psychologists who agree with the
    a. psychoanalytic perspective.
    b. medical model.
    c. behavioral perspective.
    d. family systems model.

16. Which personality test has more than 550 items and reports results on ten clinical scales and three validity scales?
    a. The TAT
    b. The Wechsler scales
    c. The MMPI
    d. The Bender-Gestalt

17. Unlike the Stanford-Binet, the WAIS-R
    a. gives separate verbal IQ and performance IQ scores.
    b. is a structured interview as well.
    c. is used to assess children's intelligence.
    d. does not examine verbal IQ.

18. The System of Multicultural Pluralistic Assessment was developed in order to
    a. address the criticism that males were unfairly getting higher IQ scores than females.
    b. address the criticism that IQ tests are culturally biased.
    c. widen the range of abnormal behaviors that could be detected through intelligence testing.
    d. prevent people from faking their intelligence.

19. ___________ requires the test-taker to copy designs that are drawn on a set of cards. It is used to detect brain damage.
    a. The Rorschach inkblot technique
    b. The MMPI
    c. The DSM-IV
    d. The Bender-Gestalt

20. The good news about this psychological test is that it can detect organic brain damage; the bad news is that it can take more than six hours to administer. The method being described is the
    a. WAIS.
    b. Bender-Gestalt Visual-Motor Test.
    c. Halstead-Reitan Neuropsychological Test Battery.
    d. positron emission tomography (PET) scan.

APPLICATION QUESTIONS

1. Ross has a phobia about going out in public. He was recently and unexpectedly divorced by his wife, and he has a heart condition. How would this information about Ross's life show up on the DSM-IV?
    a. His phobia would be given on Axis II.
    b. His heart condition would be considered a form of "stimulus control."
    c. His divorce would add to his stress rating on Axis IV.
    d. The phobia would not show up since it is not a disorder.

2. Dr. Shaw says, "This classification system may focus on stimulus control and incentive systems, but it fails to convey useful information about the prognosis of disorders." What can be said of the doctor's complaint?
    a. The target of the complaint is the DSM-IV.
    b. It has no basis in truth.
    c. The target of the complaint is the behavioral classification system.
    d. It represents the existential perspective.

3. After Ellen is diagnosed as "schizophrenic," she begins to act so bizarrely that she seems more schizophrenic than before. This illustrates the problem of
    a. self-fulfilling prophecies.
    b. poor reliability in the DSM-IV.
    c. diagnosis without the use of norms.
    d. reactivity in controlled observations.

4. A psychologist records the posture, facial expressions, and language patterns of adolescents in a local bowling alley. This represents assessment based on
    a. controlled observation.
    b. structured interviews.
    c. projective personality testing.
    d. naturalistic observation.

5. A psychologist gives Larry two tests. In one test, Larry draws a picture of a person. In the other, he tells what he sees in ten symmetrical inkblots. The psychologist is assessing Larry by using
    a. objective personality tests.
    b. intelligence tests.
    c. projective personality techniques.
    d. one intelligence and one projective test.

6. Gary thinks that projective tests are excellent because they reveal underlying conflicts and motives. Gary is probably in agreement with the ___________ perspective on abnormal behavior.
   a. behavioral
   b. neuropsychological
   c. humanistic
   d. psychoanalytic

7. Alan is given the Luria-Nebraska Neuropsychological Battery and an MRI. We can assume that
   a. Alan is being assessed for brain damage.
   b. Alan is a young child.
   c. Alan's clinical psychologist is a behaviorist.
   d. Alan's clinical psychologist is a psychoanalyst.

8. ___________ will probably be less costly because it does not need person-to-person contact, and research seems to show that people are willing to be assessed with it. However, we are a long way from knowing whether it increases assessment validity.
   a. The Rorschach inkblot technique
   b. Computerized assessment
   c. The behavioral classification system
   d. The Halstead-Reitan Neuropsychological Test Battery

9. Dr. Ireland asks, "Who will use the test results you ask for; for what purpose is this assessment requested?" These questions highlight ___________ concerns about testing.
   a. standardization
   b. psychometric
   c. ethical
   d. biomedical

10. Oscar says, "The IQ testing of minority groups is always a discriminatory act. No test exists that acknowledges cultural differences." Oscar is wrong because he apparently does not know about
    a. the changes that have been made in the DSM-IV.
    b. the System of Multicultural Pluralistic Assessment.
    c. the use of projective tests for intelligence assessment.
    d. the recent improvements in the reliability of the MMPI.

ANSWERS TO FACT AND CONCEPT QUESTIONS

1. *a. Assessment involves collecting as much information as possible so that the clinician gains a better understanding of the client. (p. 101)
   b. When assessment information is "boiled down," classification or psychodiagnosis is being done.
   c. Tests are a possible source of information, but they are not required.
   d. The psychologist's orientation has a major effect on the assessment method chosen and how information is used.

2. a. A variety of tests besides objective personality tests can give results that remain stable.
   b. Validity is the degree to which the test measures what it is supposed to measure; meaningfulness is not the same as consistency.
   c. Interviews can be considered structured or unstructured, not tests.
   *d. Reliability is the degree to which an assessment method gives consistent results. (p. 102)

3. a. The failing of both the original DSM and Kraepelin's system was poor reliability.
   b. Both systems relied on the medical model, not a broad range of ideas as occurs with an eclectic approach.
   c. Neither system relied on a behavioral approach; behaviorists are the prime movers of the alternative system.
   *d. Both the original DSM and Kraepelin's system were based on the biogenic idea that common symptoms have the same cause. (pp. 117–118)

4. a. In the Ward et al. (1962) study of the DSM, poor training was not a major reason for poor reliability.
   b. The DSM's poor reliability was traced to a *lack* of specific behavioral guidelines for diagnosis.
   *c. In the Ward et al. (1962) study, 62.5 percent of the errors came from inadequacies in the system itself. (p. 118)
   d. Faking has not been found to be a major source of errors.

5. a. The behavioral classification system emphasizes the description of behavior problems and the factors that immediately precede or follow them.
   b. One cannot have high validity without also having high reliability.
   c. Standardization requires giving a test in the same manner each time and using data from a large comparison group (a set of norms).
   *d. *Etiology* is the cause of a disorder; *prognosis* refers to the future course of the disorder. (pp. 117, 118)

6. a. Functioning level is indicated on Axis V.
   *b. Axis II indicates personality disorders or, in the case of children, developmental disorders. (p. 119)
   c. Stress level is indicated on Axis IV.
   d. The clinical syndrome—the main mental disorder—is listed on Axis I.

7. *a. The principal mental disorders are listed on Axis I. (p. 119)
   b. Axis III lists physical illnesses or disorders that relate to the clinical syndrome (for example, a thyroid condition).
   c. Axis V rates the person's level of functioning currently and in the past year.
   d. The categories listed are included in DSM-IV.

8. a. Self-defeating personality disorder is a proposed category in the DSM-IV that stresses a pattern of relationships that leads to suffering.
   b. Scoring of the WAIS or WISC is based on overt responses to test items.
   *c. The behavioral classification system is interested in five factors, among them the triggers for behavior (stimulus control) and the negative thoughts (aversive self-reinforcement) that influence problem behavior. (pp. 128–129)
   d. Objective personality tests are based on responses to test items, not environmental stimuli or negative thoughts.

9. a. Rosenhan's study undercut the field's faith in the DSM's reliability because professionals could not detect faked symptoms.
   b. The results were the reverse of this: Patients on the ward could tell that the pseudopatients were faking, whereas professionals could not.
   c. The pseudopatients never acted insane; they continued to act normally while in the hospital.
   *d. Hospital staff started to see abnormal behavior ("excessive note-taking") in those labeled as schizophrenic. (Focus 4.4; p. 131)

10. *a. Observation can lead to reactivity—the problem of people changing the way they act because they know someone is watching. (p. 103)
   b. Neurological procedures do not change the way people act, or at least they don't change the way people's *brains* act.
   c. Projective techniques are used in personality testing, not in intelligence testing.
   d. Structured interviews ask very specific questions, so although people may fake their answers, they do not change their actual behavior in response to the interviewer.

11. *a. An electroencephalograph involves attaching electrodes to the scalp so that brain wave activity patterns can be recorded. (p. 115)
   b. The Bender-Gestalt involves copying a number of designs.
   c. CAT scans involve the use of multiple x-rays of the brain; they produce images of the brain, not recordings of brain wave activity.
   d. MRI produces a clear picture of the brain (or other structure) by surrounding the area with powerful magnetic fields.

12. a. Different perspectives lead to different interview strategies: psychoanalysts use less structured formats than behaviorists.
   b. Interviews rely on the combination of observation and verbal information.
   *c. According to Kleinmuntz, the relationship between interviewer and interviewee is one of three main reasons for interviewing errors. (p. 106)
   d. Psychoanalysts are least likely to use structured interviews.

13. a. Psychological tests usually look for underlying traits, not intellectual functioning.
   *b. Tests commonly have these two characteristics: a standard situation in which they are given, and the use of norms for making comparisons. (p. 106)
   c. Tests are usually standardized, so that they are given in a uniform manner.
   d. Tests are used for both research and clinical purposes.

14. a. The Rorschach is designed to reveal unconscious modes of functioning that relate to personality in general.
   *b. The Rorschach is scored on the basis of what people see, where they see it, and the influences of color and movement, among other factors. (p. 107)
   c. Stories are told based on TAT pictures.
   d. The Rorschach uses inkblots as the ambiguous stimuli, not incomplete sentences.

15. *a. Because they reveal unconscious conflicts and symbolic behaviors, projective tests are favored by psychoanalysts. (p. 108)
   b. The medical model would emphasize neurophysiological functioning.
   c. The behavioral perspective would favor observations of behavior and its consequences.
   d. The family systems model would examine actual communications in family settings.

16. a. The TAT uses pictures of people and asks the test-taker to tell a story about them.
 b. The Wechsler scales are intelligence tests.
 *c. The MMPI consists of 567 statements and yields scores on ten scales to indicate abnormal behavior and three scales to see whether the test-taker gave accurate answers. (p. 109)
 d. The Bender-Gestalt asks test takers to copy designs.

17. *a. The Wechsler Adult Intelligence Scale, Revised (WAIS-R), like all Wechsler scales, yields both verbal and performance IQ scores. (p. 111)
 b. The WAIS is an IQ test, not a diagnostic interview.
 c. The Stanford-Binet can be given to children, but the WAIS is usually given to people over age 15.
 d. The WAIS, like all Wechsler scales, has a verbal and a performance component.

18. a. There is no evidence of sexism in IQ testing.
 *b. The SOMPA compares groups with similar cultural backgrounds so that there is less minority discrimination. (p. 113)
 c. Intelligence testing is not designed to detect abnormal behavior.
 d. The SOMPA is no more able to detect faking than earlier tests.

19. a. In the Rorschach, test-takers say what, where, and why they see what they do in ten symmetrical inkblots.
 b. In the MMPI, 567 statements are answered "true," "false," or "cannot say."
 c. The DSM-IV is a classification system, not a test.
 *d. The Bender-Gestalt consists of cards with designs on them that the test-taker copies; it is used to assess organicity. (p. 114)

20. a. The WAIS can detect organicity, but it does not take six hours to administer.
 b. The Bender-Gestalt may detect organicity, but it only requires the copying of nine geometric designs.
 *c. The Halstead-Reitan is a complex method involving a number of tests, and takes six or more hours to complete. (p. 114)
 d. A PET scan can detect organicity, but it is a neurological procedure, not a psychological test.

ANSWERS TO APPLICATION QUESTIONS

1. a. Axis II lists personality and developmental disorders, not the clinical syndrome (in this case, phobia).
 b. The behavioral classification system, not the DSM-IV, examines stimulus controls.
 *c. The divorce is a strong stressor and would contribute to a high stress level rating on Axis IV. (p. 119)
 d. Phobias are considered disorders and are shown on Axis I.

2. a. The DSM-IV does not use stimulus control or incentive systems in making diagnoses.
 b. Behavioral classification does not predict the prognosis of disorders.
 *c. The behavioral classification system uses five factors in assessing disorder; stimulus control and incentive (reward) systems are two of them. (p. 128)
 d. No one perspective challenges the usefulness of the behavioral classification system.

3. *a. Labels can change people's behavior in a process called self-fulfilling prophecy. (p. 130)
   b. We would see poor reliability if one doctor diagnosed Ellen as schizophrenic and another considered her depressed.
   c. Diagnosis without norms would occur if Ellen were considered schizophrenic without being compared with other schizophrenics.
   d. Reactivity would occur if, knowing she was being observed, Ellen began to act differently.

4. a. Although this illustrates observation, it is not being done in a controlled setting such as a laboratory or clinic.
   b. A structured interview would involve a predetermined list of questions and a limited set of responses.
   c. Projective tests present test-takers with ambiguous stimuli, as in the case of the Rorschach or TAT.
   *d. A bowling alley is a "real world" place where natural behavior can be observed. (p. 103)

5. a. Objective tests offer set responses ("true" or "false") to predetermined, written items.
   b. Intelligence tests also offer structured problems with a limited range of alternative responses.
   *c. Larry is completing the Draw-a-Person test and the Rorschach test; both are projective because the stimuli presented to him are ambiguous. (p. 106)
   d. Because both tests Larry is completing are projective, this cannot be the best answer.

6. a. Behaviorists do not emphasize underlying conflicts, so they are less likely to use projective tests.
   b. Neuropsychologists focus on brain function, so they would be more likely to use the Luria-Nebraska or a medical test.
   c. Humanists are interested in the current, conscious, subjective world of clients more than in their underlying conflicts.
   *d. Psychoanalysts have developed and used projective tests to get a general picture of functioning, underlying motives, and conflicts. (p. 106)

7. *a. The Luria-Nebraska is a test battery used to assess brain damage; an MRI is also able to detect brain lesions, tumors, and other problems associated with brain damage. (pp. 114, 115)
   b. Neither the Luria-Nebraska nor MRI is limited to being used with children.
   c. A behaviorist would be interested in observable behaviors; Alan's clinical psychologist is probably a specialist in brain disorders with a biogenic orientation.
   d. A psychoanalyst would be interested in unconscious conflicts; Alan's clinical psychologist is probably a specialist in brain disorders with a biogenic orientation.

8. a. The Rorschach involves person-to-person contact.
   *b. Computerized assessment can be done without personal contact, and Farrell et al.'s (1987) study says clients accept it. (Focus 4.1; p. 117)
   c. The behavioral classification system involves person-to-person contact.
   d. The Halstead-Reitan involves person-to-person contact.

9. a. When tests are standardized, the questions are asked and responses are scored in a consistent manner.
   b. Psychometric concerns involve reliability and validity.
   *c. These questions reflect the ethical concerns that many have about psychological tests. (p. 116)
   d. Biomedical concerns would highlight the impact of tests on the human body.

10. a. Changes in the DSM-IV have *not* addressed IQ testing methods.
   *b. The SOMPA uses the WISC-R in ways that prevent minorities from being unfairly compared with other groups; it has reduced inaccurate diagnoses of mental retardation. (p. 113)
   c. Projective tests are used for personality assessment, not IQ.
   d. The MMPI is used for personality assessment, not IQ.

CHAPTER 5
The Scientific Method in Abnormal Psychology

LEARNING OBJECTIVES

When you have mastered the material in Chapter 5, you should be able to:

1. Describe the primary goals of scientists in the field of abnormal psychology and the reason scientists are skeptics. Discuss the initial report of a gene for alcoholism and subsequent scientific investigation on the matter. (pp. 135–137; Focus 5.1)
2. Discuss the characteristics of the scientific method in clinical research, including how hypotheses must be stated, definitions, and the reliability and validity of measures and observations. (pp. 137–139)
3. Describe and discuss the research concepts of base rates. Describe and differentiate statistical and clinical significance. (pp. 139–140)
4. List the components of an experiment. Describe the experimental group and compare this to the control group. Explain why a placebo group may be important. Discuss the need for blind and double-blind research designs. (pp. 140–142)
5. Describe and discuss the characteristics and limitations of correlational studies. Use the Sanders and Giolas (1991) study to discuss how correlational research can be improved. (pp. 142–145)
6. Describe and discuss the characteristics and limitations of analogue and field studies. Discuss the methods and findings of the Adams and Adams (1984) study of the effects of the Mt. St. Helens volcano eruption on abnormal behavior. (Focus 5.2; pp. 145–147)
7. Define the nomothetic and idiographic orientations toward research. Describe and discuss the characteristics and limitations of case studies, including ways to make case studies more precise. Describe and differentiate the reversal design single-subject experiment from the multiple-baseline design. List the advantages and limitations of the single-case experiment. (pp. 147–150)
8. List and discuss the following types of research: survey, longitudinal, historical, treatment outcome, treatment process, and program evaluation studies. Discuss the history of research on minorities and pathology. (pp. 150–153; Focus 5.3)
9. Describe epidemiological research. Define and differentiate prevalence and incidence. Discuss the implications of the study of mental disorders in China (1986). (Focus 5.4; pp. 150–154)
10. Describe and discuss the biological research strategies including genetic linkage studies, biological markers, iatrogenic effects, genetic penetrance, pathognomonic symptoms, and biological challenge tests. (pp. 152–155)
11. Discuss the ethical issues in conducting research and the American Psychological Association's guiding principles on ethics, including the use of animals and research with culturally diverse populations. (pp. 155–157)

CHAPTER OUTLINE

1. **Reasons for skepticism** (pp. 135–137) News articles frequently describe research findings as "conclusive," but, when there is a failure to replicate results, these claims are proven unfounded. Firm scientific information requires good research methods and a skeptical attitude.

2. **The scientific method in clinical research** (pp. 137–140) The most general characteristic of science is its potential for self-correction. *Hypotheses* must be clearly stated and variables given definitions. Recent studies of child sexual abuse illustrate the range of definitions used. Measures must show reliability and validity. Appropriate comparison frequencies for a phenomenon (*base rates*) should be provided. For instance, if eating problems and child abuse are both commonly occurring events but one is unaware of this, one could mistakenly conclude that abuse causes eating problems. Finally, results should be evaluated in terms of both statistical significance (results were due to a factor other than chance) and clinical significance (results have clinical value). In large-sample studies, statistically significant differences are sometimes clinically meaningless.

3. **The experiment** (pp. 140–142) Experiments include experimental and control groups. Only the experimental group subjects are exposed to the *independent variable* (the possible cause of behavior the experimenter manipulates). Measures of the *dependent variable* (the behavior believed to be controlled by the independent variable) are taken for subjects in both groups. *Placebo groups* can be included to rule out the possibility that subjects' expectations alter their behavior in the experimental group. Experimenter expectations can also be controlled by making the clinicians in a study *blind* (uninformed) as to the experimenter's hypothesis. To reduce the impact of both experimenter and subject expectations, there are *double-blind* designs where neither the individual working directly with the subject nor the subject is aware of who is in the experimental group.

4. **Correlations** (p. 142) Correlations measure the degree to which changes in one variable are associated with changes in another variable. Statistically, these associations are symbolized by *r*, which ranges from –1.00 to +1.00. Even if a correlational study shows a strong association, it is often difficult to determine whether Variable A caused changes in Variable B, Variable B caused changes in Variable A, or some third variable affected the other two.

5. **Analogue studies and field studies** (pp. 145–147; Focus 5.2) When the study of real-life situations is impractical or unethical, *analogue studies* are conducted in simulated, but controlled, circumstances. When analogue studies are too contrived, observations can be made in the real-life situation in what is called a *field study*. Adams and Adams's (1984) study of the effects of the Mt. St. Helens volcano eruption on the people of Othello, Washington, is an example of a field study.

6. **Single-subject studies** (pp. 147–150) Although most research methods use groups of people (the *nomothetic* orientation), in-depth studies are sometimes done on individuals (the *idiographic* orientation). The *case study* is used extensively by clinicians, and, although it lacks control and objectivity, it examines and analyzes conditions over a period of time. The scientific value of case studies is increased when clients are described in detail, concepts are operationally defined, descriptions of techniques used are described fully, pre-and post-measures of outcome are given, and study results are replicated.

   The *single-subject experiment* measures an individual's behavior over time. It observes changes that occur after some behavior modification has been applied. In the multiple-baseline design, several related behaviors are measured. In some cases, an intervention on the same behavior is done in different settings. In the reversal (ABAB) design, a return to baseline conditions confirms that the change in behavior was due to the modification introduced.

7. **Epidemiological and other forms of research** (Focus 5.3; pp. 150–152) A variety of research types can use experimental, correlational, or single-subject methods including: survey research, longitudinal research, historical research, twin studies, treatment outcome and treatment process studies, and program evaluation. An important type of research is *epidemiological research,* which examines the rate and distribution of mental disorders. It can reveal the rate of new cases (*incidence*) and the total rate of cases (*prevalence*) as well as risk factors associated with the disorder. Cross-cultural research shows that such rates vary.

8. **Biological research strategies** (pp. 152–155) *Genetic linkage studies* determine if a disorder follows a genetic pattern by identifying the family members of a person with a disorder (proband) who also suffer from it. *Biological marker studies* identify a biological characteristic (for example, blood flow patterns or brain size) that are associated with a disorder in family members of a proband.

   Researchers must be on guard for *iatrogenic* effects—those brought on by treatment. For example, traumatic events recalled during hypnosis may be a function of hypnotic suggestion more than accurate recollection. When a person carries a gene for a characteristic but fails to show the characteristic, there is incomplete *penetrance*. Symptoms that are distinctive for a disorder are considered *pathognomonic*. Finally, when clinical researchers use *biological challenge tests,* they observe for changes in behavior when chemicals (foods, allergens, or drugs) are introduced and for those behaviors to disappear when the chemical is absent.

9. **Ethical issues in research** (pp. 155–157) The scientific method can be abused and misused. The American Psychological Association has adopted the principle that the likely benefits of research must outweigh the risk or discomfort to its subjects. Deception should be used only when alternatives are not possible. Only when alternatives are unavailable should animals be used as subjects, and then they should be treated in humane ways. Guidelines for research sensitive to minority ethnic and religious groups are also in place.

KEY TERMS

Fill-in-the-Blanks Quiz

1. The degree to which two variables are associated with each other is called a(n) ___________.

2. The research technique in which behaviors are observed or recorded in the natural environment is called a(n) ___________.

3. The method of inquiry that involves systematic collection of data through controlled observation and provides for the testing of hypotheses based on those data is called the ___________.

4. An investigation that attempts to replicate, as closely as possible, under controlled conditions a situation that occurs in real life is called a(n) ___________.

5. The biological research method that compares the rate at which a disorder occurs in relatives of a person who has the disorder is called a(n) ___________.

6. The degree to which the presence of a gene determines whether an individual displays a trait believed to be genetic is called ___________.

7. The research approach that does in-depth studies of individual subjects is called the ___________ orientation.

8. A technique of scientific inquiry in which an independent variable is manipulated by having experimental and control groups and the changes in a dependent variable are measured is called a(n) ___________.

9. Frequencies of phenomena that occur without treatment and which are used for comparing populations are called ___________.

10. Research that studies the rate and distribution of mental disorders in a population is called ___________.

11. In a psychological experiment, the attitudes or behaviors that are expected to change as a result of the manipulation of an independent variable are called ___________.

12. When a symptom is distinctive of a specific disorder it is said to be ___________ for the disorder.

13. The variable or condition that is manipulated by the experimenter and tested for its effects on the dependent variable is called the ___________.

14. A description of concepts in terms of the operations used to measure them is called a(n) ___________.

15. A single-subject experiment in which behaviors are measured before and after an independent variable is introduced, after the independent variable is withdrawn, and again after the independent variable is reintroduced is called a(n) ___________.

16. The intensive study of one individual that relies on observation, psychological tests, and historical data is called a(n) ___________.

17. Behavioral effects that are caused by treatment are considered ___________ effects.

18. An experiment performed on a single individual in which the individual's own behavior is used as the control is called a(n) ___________.

19. The research method that examines changes in behavior when chemicals are introduced into a subject's body and when the chemicals are absent is called a(n) ___________.

20. Studies that control for expectation effects by not informing clinicians or interviewers of the researcher's hypothesis are considered to be a(n) ___________ design.

21. A biological research method that assesses the family members of a person with a disorder for the presence of a particular biological characteristic believed to be associated with the disorder is called a(n) ___________.

22. The research approach that uses large numbers of subjects to find general psychological principles is called the ___________ orientation.

23. Experiments that control for expectation effects may have a group that appears to be getting the independent variable but is not; this is called a(n) ___________ group.

24. Studies in which neither the subjects nor the people who come in direct contact with the subjects know the experimental hypothesis or who is in the experimental or control groups are considered ___________ studies.

Answers to Fill-in-the-Blanks Quiz

1. correlation
2. field study
3. scientific method
4. analogue study
5. genetic linkage study
6. penetrance
7. idiographic
8. experiment
9. base rates
10. epidemiological research
11. dependent variables
12. pathognomonic
13. independent variable
14. definition
15. reversal (ABAB) design
16. case study
17. iatrogenic
18. single-subject experiment
19. biological challenge test
20. blind
21. biological marker study
22. nomothetic
23. placebo
24. double-blind

FACT AND CONCEPT QUESTIONS

1. It now seems premature to say that alcoholism is caused by the A1 allele on a specific chromosome. Why?
   a. The relationship between the gene and alcoholism was iatrogenic.
   b. The A1 allele proved to be pathognomonic for alcoholism.
   c. The A1 allele finding was replicated in other populations of alcoholics.
   d. Later studies showed no difference in the likelihood of the A1 allele in control and alcoholic samples.

2. What are the main characteristics of the scientific method?
   a. Acceptance and faith
   b. Personal belief and emotion
   c. Skepticism and self-correction
   d. Subjectivity and personal values

3. A researcher interested in thumb sucking and later adult personality would need to know how common thumb sucking is among children. The researcher would need to know
   a. if thumb sucking is genetic.
   b. the base rate for thumb sucking.
   c. whether there is a biological marker for thumb sucking.
   d. what is a placebo for thumb sucking.

4. In very large samples, you can have statistically significant results without having
   a. any variables being measured.
   b. employed the nomothetic approach.
   c. clinically significant results.
   d. any of the above.

5. A study examining the level of certain neurotransmitters in people with a disorder and a control group without the disorder is attempting to identify
   a. biological markers.
   b. iatrogenic effects.
   c. double-blind effects.
   d. the base rate of the disorder.

6. The ____________ is the best research method for making cause-and-effect inferences.
   a. correlation
   b. historical research method
   c. case study
   d. experiment

7. In an experiment, which group is exposed to the independent variable?
   a. The control group
   b. The experimental group
   c. Both the control group and the experimental group
   d. The placebo group

8. Placebo control groups are necessary
   a. to overcome the impact of the clinician or interviewer's expectations.
   b. to account for the effect of subjects' expectations.
   c. when no pretest has been done on the experimental group.
   d. when correlational studies have included an independent variable.

9. In a double-blind study,
   a. it is impossible to tell whether Variable A causes Variable B or the other way around.
   b. single subjects' behaviors are measured before the presentation of an intervention and afterwards.
   c. the results are expressed by the statistic *r*, which ranges between +1.00 and –1.00.
   d. neither the subjects nor the person working directly with the subjects is aware of the experimental conditions.

10. If the results of a correlation study showed that $r = -0.73$, what could be said?
    a. There is a strong inverse relationship between the factors that were studied.
    b. The association between the two factors is so weak that the study was a failure.
    c. In 73 percent of the cases, one variable causes the other.
    d. As the scores on one of the factors go up, scores on the other factor go up, too.

11. Unlike experiments, correlations do not
    a. make use of the scientific method.
    b. explain the cause of a relationship between variables.
    c. involve the use of statistics.
    d. examine human behavior.

12. ___________ are the research methods most often used to study rare conditions or when ethical standards only allow research in simulated, controlled situations.
    a. Longitudinal studies
    b. Correlations
    c. Case studies
    d. Analogue studies

13. When researchers go into a real-life situation and observe people's behavior, they are using the research method called the
    a. analogue study.
    b. correlation.
    c. field study.
    d. historical study.

14. Adams and Adams's (1984) research on the effects of the Mt. St. Helens volcano eruption on mental disorder
    a. was an example of a field study.
    b. showed that mental disorder increased by more than 200 percent after the eruption.
    c. showed both a and b.
    d. showed neither a nor b.

15. Correlations and experiments are to the ___________ orientation as case studies and single-subject experiments are to the ___________ orientation.
    a. common-sense; scientific
    b. scientific; nomothetic
    c. idiographic; nomothetic
    d. nomothetic; idiographic

16. A single-subject experiment that measures changes in several behaviors before and after a particular modification is applied can be called a(n)
    a. multiple-baseline experiment.
    b. longitudinal field study experiment.
    c. epidemiological study.
    d. a reversal design analogue study.

17. Prevalence and incidence rates are two concepts related to
    a. epidemiology.
    b. analogue studies.
    c. single-subject experiments.
    d. idiographic research.

18. Which statement is *true* concerning the rates of mental disorder in the United States and China?
    a. A far larger percentage of the Chinese have some form of mental disorder.
    b. There are no cultural differences when it comes to demonstrating symptoms.
    c. A larger percentage of Americans is identified as having a form of mental disorder.
    d. Any differences that exist can be explained by the Americans' cultural need to hide symptoms.

19. Which of the following types of research methods would be used to learn how the pioneers of the American West dealt with psychosis?
    a. Longitudinal study
    b. Historical research
    c. Analogue study
    d. Treatment process studies

20. Which statement below accurately sums up the American Psychological Association's guidelines for ethical research?
    a. "Any research effort that might hurt a person or animal cannot be allowed."
    b. "Most of human behavior is best left as a mystery."
    c. "The value of any research effort must outweigh its potential risks."
    d. "Animals may be treated in any manner as long as scientific truths are the result."

APPLICATION QUESTIONS

1. Jenny reads in the paper that scientists have found unusually high levels of a hormone in women who develop cancer. What information does Jenny need before she can believe the hormone increases the risk of cancer?
   a. Evidence that high levels are *not* found in women who do not develop cancer.
   b. Replication of the results by other scientists.
   c. Evidence that the hormone is pathognomonic for cancer.
   d. All of the above

2. In a research study, "alcoholism" is defined as a score of five or more on the Michigan Alcoholism Screening Test. This illustrates
   a. the use of a definition.
   b. a low-reliability measure.
   c. an iatrogenic effect.
   d. a low base rate.

3. In an experiment to see whether diet influences depression, subjects are randomly selected to eat either a high-protein-low-carbohydrate diet or their usual diet. At the end of six weeks on the diets, the experimental group is significantly less depressed. What is missing in this experiment?
   a. A control group
   b. A dependent variable
   c. An independent variable
   d. A pretest of depression

4. In a study of the effects of a drug on anxiety, some subjects are told they are receiving the drug when they are actually getting an inert (nonactive) pill. This group is called the
   a. experimental group.
   b. placebo control group.
   c. analogue group.
   d. double-blind group.

5. Researchers interested in phobias identify 100 people who have a fear of animals. They assess the presence of a similar phobia in the parents and grandparents of all 100 people. This is an example of a(n) ____________ study.
   a. longitudinal study
   b. analogue study
   c. biological challenge
   d. genetic linkage

6. The longer Stephanie stays awake at night, the less efficient her study becomes. Which of the following best expresses the relationship between hours staying awake and study efficiency?
   a. $r = +1.00$
   b. A negative correlation
   c. A positive correlation
   d. $r = -1.00$

7. If a research study shows that life stress correlates positively with alcohol consumption, what can we conclude about the cause-and-effect relationship between these two variables?
   a. That stress causes drinking
   b. That drinking causes stress
   c. That genetics cause both stress and drinking
   d. Nothing

8. Dr. Keys reports that one of her patients has sixteen distinct personalities. There are both male and female personalities. She reports that, through hypnosis, she has helped the personalities fuse into one competent individual. This report illustrates
   a. a correlation between sex-role typing and hypnosis.
   b. an analogue study, because the person did not receive hypnosis in the "real world."
   c. a case study.
   d. an experiment, because Dr. Keys was not sure the hypnosis would work.

9. To treat Jimmy's hyperactivity, his therapist-researcher asks his teacher to keep track of how often he is out of his chair for five straight school days. Then, over the next twenty days, Jimmy is rewarded when he stays in his chair. His behavior improves. When the teacher stops the rewards, Jimmy gets worse, so rewards are returned, and his behavior improves again. This illustrates
   a. a positive correlation between reward and hyperactivity.
   b. an analogue study.
   c. a multiple-baseline correlation.
   d. a reversal design single-subject experiment.

10. Dr. Szezch is interested in the rate of new cases of childhood autism in Poland. Dr. Szezch is
    a. doing an analogue experiment.
    b. interested in the prevalence of childhood autism.
    c. doing epidemiological research.
    d. interested in the r between age and autism.

ANSWERS TO FACT AND CONCEPT QUESTIONS

1. a. An iatrogenic effect is one caused by treatment; there was no treatment and genes cannot be changed that way.
   b. If the gene were pathognomonic (specific to the disorder) it would support the idea that it causes alcoholism.
   c. If the finding were replicated in other alcoholic populations, the genetic cause of alcoholism would have been supported.
   *d. Lack of replication has led to reduced confidence that the A1 allele is a marker for alcoholism. (Focus 5.1; pp. 136–137)

2. a. Scientists do not accept results on faith.
   b. Scientists seek ways to reduce the influence of personal belief and emotion on their search for answers.
   *c. The hallmarks of the scientific method are skepticism (cautiousness) and self-correction (replication and efforts directed at ruling out alternative explanations). (p. 136)
   d. Scientists try to be as free from subjectivity and personal values as possible.

3. a. Genetics would have no relevance to this study.
   *b. Base rates are the frequencies of phenomena and are used to compare groups; if thumb sucking is very common, it may mean that there is little relationship between it and adult personality. (p. 139)
   c. Since the researcher is using thumb sucking as a predictor, it is unnecessary to find a biological marker for it.
   d. Placebos are only necessary in experiments; this is not an experiment.

4. a. There can be no statistical analyses unless there are variables that have been measured.
   b. The nomothetic approach uses groups of people as subjects.
   *c. In very large samples, statistically significant differences can have no clinical or real-world significance. (p. 140)
   d. Because statistically significant differences can have no clinical or real-world significance in very large samples, "any of the above" is an impossible choice.

5. *a. A biological characteristic such as neurotransmitter level is a biological marker that might identify those who are at risk for developing a disorder. (p. 153)
   b. Iatrogenic effects are the side effects of treatment; there is no treatment in this study.
   c. Double-blind refers to a study design where neither the subjects nor the individuals who work directly with them know who is in the experimental or control groups.
   d. A study concerned with base rates would not care about neurotransmitters and would simple count the number of individuals with the disorder.

6. a. Correlational studies can only show an association between two variables, not what caused what.
   b. Historical research cannot create the experimental and control groups necessary to infer cause.
   c. Case studies examine individuals, provide no control groups, and make causal inferences impossible.
   *d. The greatest strength of the experiment is the manipulation of one factor by the experimenter and the consequent ability to make causal inferences. (p. 140)

7. a. The control group experiences the same factors as the experimental group *except* for the independent variable.
   *b. The definition of an experimental group is that it is exposed to the independent variable. (p. 140)
   c. If both groups were exposed to the independent variable, there would be no basis for comparing the two groups.
   d. The placebo group is led to believe it gets the independent variable but does not.

8. a. Placebo control groups control for the *subjects'* expectations.
   *b. Placebo groups control for the effects of subjects' expectations, as when people receive a drug or other treatment. (p. 141)
   c. A lack of a pretest will make it impossible to tell whether a treatment made a difference; placebos cannot help with this problem.
   d. Correlational studies do not have independent variables.

9. a. Correlational studies leave one unable to make these judgments; double-blind designs occur in experiments.
   b. When single subjects are measured before and after an intervention, they are participating in a reversal design study.
   c. Results of correlational studies are expressed statistically in terms of r.
   *d. Double-blind studies prevent the expectations of both the subjects and research assistants from affecting behavior. (p. 141)

10. *a. When $r = -0.73$, there is a strong negative correlation, which indicates that as scores on one variable increase, scores on the other decrease—an inverse relationship. (p. 142)
   b. A weak association would be indicated by an r around 0.00.
   c. The correlation coefficient r is not a percentage, it is a measure of association.
   d. This kind of positive correlation would yield a positive r, such as $r = +0.66$.

11. a. Both experiments and correlations are part of the scientific method.
   *b. Because they do not control for extraneous variables nor have an independent variable, correlations cannot determine cause-and-effect relationships. (p. 142)
   c. Correlations use the statistic r.
   d. Experiments and correlations both look at human behavior.

12. a. Longitudinal studies follow individuals across time; they do not involve simulated situations.
   b. Correlations involve an examination of how two factors are associated.
   c. Case studies involve an examination of one person or situation.
   *d. Analogue studies are used when it is impractical to study behavior in real-life situations, either because the behavior is rare or because control over the situation is impossible. (p. 145)

13. a. Analogue studies are done when researchers *cannot* go into a real-life situation.
   b. Correlations involve an examination of how two factors are associated.
   *c. Field studies involve "going into the field" to examine behavior in "the real world." (p. 145)
   d. Historical research involves the collection of documents to shed light on behavior in a prior period.

14. a. Since Adams and Adams went out to Othello, Washington, to interview and collect documents on actual changes in behavior, it was a field study.
    b. The rate of mental disorder was 236 percent higher in a seven-month period after the eruption compared with a similar period before.
    *c. Because both a and b are correct, this is the best answer. (Focus 5.2; pp. 146–147)
    d. Because both a and b are correct, this cannot be the answer.

15. a. Correlations and experiments are part of the scientific method; they do not necessarily rely on common sense.
    b. Case studies and single-subject experiments use one person and are therefore the opposite of the nomothetic orientation, which looks for universal behavior from many subjects.
    c. These are reversed.
    *d. Correlations and experiments use groups of people (a nomothetic approach); case studies and single-subject experiments focus on the individual (idiographic orientation). (p. 147)

16. *a. Multiple-baseline studies examine several behaviors over time as they are exhibited by individuals. (p. 149)
    b. Longitudinal field studies would look at behavior in groups of people across a period of time without introducing any modifications.
    c. Epidemiological studies use large groups of subjects to identify the frequency of disorders.
    d. Reversal designs involve stopping the modification and reinstating it; also, they do not look at several behaviors at once.

17. *a. Epidemiology is research that examines the distribution of cases, including new ones (incidence) and the total number (prevalence). (p. 151)
    b. Analogue studies involve the simulation of real-life situations under more controlled circumstances.
    c. Single-subject experiments look at one person's behavior, not that of many.
    d. The idiographic approach involves the in-depth study of individuals.

18. a. The research shows that the Chinese report a lower prevalence rate of disorder.
    b. In Chinese culture, people are reluctant to outwardly show symptoms.
    *c. Prevalence rates are much higher in the United States; for schizophrenia, there are twice the cases reported in China. (Focus 5.4; p. 154)
    d. If anything, Americans are *more* likely to show symptoms than are the Chinese.

19. a. Longitudinal research looks at a group of people in the present and "follows them" over an extended period of time.
    *b. Historical research uses documents and records to examine behavior in times past. (p. 150)
    c. Analogue studies use simulated situations.
    d. Treatment process studies examine the reasons why individuals are successfully or unsuccessfully treated.

20. a. APA guidelines accept the fact that some studies may induce embarrassment or pain in some subjects.
    b. APA guidelines encourage the pursuit of complete knowledge.
    *c. APA guidelines try to strike a balance between the need to learn and the need to protect subjects; they suggest that any risk to the subject must be overshadowed by potential benefits. (p. 157)
    d. APA guidelines have policies for the humane care of animal subjects.

ANSWERS TO APPLICATION QUESTIONS

1. a. Unless we know the base rate of the hormone levels, we cannot say that these are unusual levels for normal individuals.
   b. Unless the study is replicated, we should remain skeptical about the "truth" of the finding.
   c. Unless the hormone is specifically associated with cancer and not many other conditions (is pathognomonic), it will not tell us it is a causal agent.
   *d. Because a, b, and c are all true, this is the best answer. (p. 136)

2. *a. Operational definitions define concepts in terms of how they are measured; in this case, alcoholism is defined in terms of a score on a questionnaire. (p. 138)
   b. Reliability refers to the consistency of a measure; the Michigan Alcoholism Screening Test has very strong reliability.
   c. An iatrogenic effect is caused by treatment; no treatment exists in this study.
   d. Base rates involve the frequency of a phenomenon; if the study looked at how often people score 5 on the MAST, that would entail base rates.

3. a. All experiments include control groups; in this case, it is the group that eats its normal diet.
   b. All experiments include a measure of behavior (the dependent variable); in this case, it is depressive symptoms.
   c. All experiments include an independent variable; in this case, it is the high-protein-low-carbohydrate diet.
   *d. Without knowing what the depression scores were before the diet began, the experi menter cannot know whether there was a change in depressive symptoms. (p. 140)

4. a. Experimental groups receive the independent variable (the drug).
   *b. Placebo groups are led to believe that they are getting the independent variable (the drug) to control for expectations. (p. 141)
   c. Analogue studies look at behavior in simulated situations.
   d. Double-blind studies keep both the subjects and those who work directly with them in the dark about experimental conditions.

5. a. A longitudinal study would repeatedly observe the same 100 people over time.
   b. An analogue study would put individuals in a simulated situation so that an independent variable could be introduced.
   c. A biological challenge test would introduce some chemical into the bodies of individuals to see if behavior changed.
   *d. Genetic linkage studies examine the frequency of a disorder in the family members of those who have the disorder. (pp. 152–153)

6. a. An r of +1.00 would be a perfect positive correlation; it would mean that every minute she was awake, her studying would get a certain unit *better*.
   *b. As her time awake increases, study efficiency decreases; that is a negative correlation. (p. 142)
   c. A positive correlation would mean that as she stays awake longer, her efficiency increases.
   d. A perfect negative correlation ($r = -1.00$) would mean that for every minute of staying awake, her efficiency would decrease by a set amount.

7. a. With correlational studies, no direction of causality can be determined.
   b. With correlational studies, no direction of causality can be determined.
   c. Correlational studies cannot determine whether a third variable causes the relationship in the other two.
   *d. Correlations tell nothing about causality. (p. 142)

8. a. Since only one person is being examined, a correlation is impossible.
   b. An analogue study would look at therapy in some simulated environment, not an actual therapy.
   *c. Since only one person is being examined, it is a case study. (p. 148)
   d. An experiment requires a control group or the use of a person's own behavior as a control (in the case of single-subject experiments).

9. a. Since hyperactivity seems to go down with rewards, the correlation would be a negative one.
   b. This work is taking place in an actual classroom, so it is not an analogue study; those use simulated settings.
   c. Multiple-baseline studies examine more than one behavior and do not return to conditions before the manipulation was made.
   *d. Reversal designs look at one behavior and return to conditions before its manipulation before reinstating the conditions that changed the original behavior. (p. 149)

10. a. An analogue study puts subjects in simulated situations.
    b. Prevalence is the total number of cases (new and old).
    *c. Studies of the distribution of cases of disorder are called epidemiological research. (p. 151)
    d. There is no evidence that the doctor is doing a correlational study, although that could be done through epidemiological work.

PART 2
Anxiety and Stress

CHAPTER 6
Anxiety Disorders

LEARNING OBJECTIVES

When you have mastered the material in Chapter 6, you should be able to:

1. Describe and discuss the nature and manifestations of anxiety in anxiety disorders. Explain when fear is valuable. Discuss the controversies in classifying anxiety disorders and the criteria for diagnosing an anxiety disorder.(Focus 6.1; pp. 161–165)
2. Describe the symptoms and frequency of panic disorder and the three types of panic attacks. Describe the symptoms and frequency of generalized anxiety disorder. Compare symptoms of generalized anxiety disorder with other anxiety disorders. (pp. 165–169)
3. Discuss the psychoanalytic, behavioral, cognitive-behavioral, and biogenic theories of cause for panic disorder and generalized anxiety disorder. (pp. 165–169)
4. Describe, discuss, and compare the biochemical and behavioral treatment of panic disorder and generalized anxiety disorder. (pp. 170–171)
5. Describe the symptoms and frequency of agoraphobia and social phobias. Differentiate the types of social phobias and discuss the difficulties in differentiating social phobias from normal social fears. (Focus 6.2; pp. 171–174)
6. Describe the symptoms and frequency of specific phobias. Differentiate the types of specific phobias and discuss evidence and reasons for gender differences in phobias. (Focus 6.3; pp. 174–175)
7. Discuss the psychoanalytic, classical conditioning, observational learning, operant conditioning, and biogenic causes of agoraphobia, social phobias, and specific phobias. (pp. 175–179)
8. Describe and discuss the biochemical and behavioral treatment of agoraphobia, social phobias, and specific phobias. (pp. 179–182)
9. Describe the symptoms and prevalence of obsessive-compulsive disorder. Discuss the factors associated with obsessions and compulsions. (pp. 182–185)
10. Discuss the psychoanalytic, behavioral, and biogenic causes of obsessive-compulsive disorder. (pp. 185–187)
11. Describe and discuss the biological, behavioral, and cognitive treatment of obsessive-compulsive disorder. (pp. 187–189)
12. Describe the symptoms, diagnostic problems, and frequency of posttraumatic stress disorder (PTSD). (pp. 189–192)
13. Discuss the causes and treatment of PTSD, including prolonged exposure, eye movement desensitization, and cognitive-behavioral approaches. (pp. 192–194)

CHAPTER OUTLINE

1. **Manifestations of anxiety** (Focus 6.1; pp. 161–165) Anxiety is a fundamental human emotion that has an adaptive function. *Anxiety disorders* are characterized by feelings of fear that produce seemingly illogical patterns of behavior, almost always involving avoidance. *Anxiety* is manifested cognitively, behaviorally, and somatically. Although anxiety can be disabling, it can also be beneficial, and many people report anxiety at work and home. Only when anxiety disrupts functioning or produces significant distress is an anxiety disorder diagnosed. In the current diagnostic system, anxiety disorders consist of *panic disorder, generalized anxiety disorder (GAD), phobias,* and *obsessive-compulsive disorder*. There are diagnostic controversies, but, in the anxiety disorder, either anxiety itself is a major symptom or attempts to master it are. *Posttraumatic stress disorder (PTSD)* is a related problem.

2. **Panic disorder and generalized anxiety disorder** (pp. 165–169) In panic disorder, severe attacks of terror and impending doom may last from a few minutes to several hours. Sweating, choking, and heart palpitations are often reported; four such attacks must occur within a 4-week period for a diagnosis of panic disorder to be made. There are three types of attacks: (1) situationally bound (occurring in response to a stimulus); (2) situationally predisposed (usually occurring in response to a stimulus); and (3) unexpected attacks. Most attacks are of the first two types. While attacks are fairly common, the disorder is not. Generalized anxiety disorder is characterized by persistent anxiety, heart palpitations, tension, and restlessness. People with GAD worry over major and minor events and have more persistent but less severe physical symptoms than people with panic disorder. Estimated lifetime prevalence of GAD in the United States is 8.4 percent, making it the second most common anxiety disorder after phobias.

   Psychoanalysts suggest that internal (sexual) conflicts are expressed in outward anxiety. The effectiveness of defenses used determines whether the person develops panic disorder or generalized anxiety disorder. The behavioral perspective emphasizes classical conditioning. Conditioning to words or other cues may increase the risk for panic attacks; stimuli that are omnipresent may produce the pervasive anxiety seen in GAD. Cognitive behavioral thinkers argue that catastrophic thoughts and overattention to internal signals maintain and inflate anxiety symptoms. The biogenic perspective focuses on panic disorder and notes that such factors as oxygen-monitoring receptors and response to sodium lactate influence panic attacks. Dysfunction in the locus ceruleus, a part of the central anxiety system in the brain, may account for panic disorders. Genetics also seem to play a role, particularly in panic disorder.

3. **Treatment of panic disorder and generalized anxiety disorder** (pp. 170–171) Medication, particularly the antidepressants, has proven useful in treating panic disorder, although relapse rates after ceasing the drugs is high. Benzodiazepines (Valium and Librium) have been used successfully to treat generalized anxiety disorder, but psychological treatment is also necessary. Behavior therapies, including relaxation training and cognitive restructuring, show promise. Treatment for panic disorder can include new thoughts, facing the symptoms, and developing coping strategies. Cognitive therapy seems particularly effective for generalized anxiety disorder.

4. **Phobias: Agoraphobia, social phobias, and specific phobias** (pp. 171–175) A *phobia* is an intense, persistent, and unwarranted fear of an object or situation. The lifetime prevalence for phobias in the United States is 12.5 percent, affecting over 15 million Americans. *Agoraphobia* is a fear of being in public places without the availability of help. The disorder, more common in females than males, often has a precipitating event, and thoughts play a key role. People with agoraphobia tend to react more intensely to anxiety symptoms than people with

other anxiety problems. *Social phobia* is an intense fear of being watched and humiliated. There are three types of social phobias: performance (involving such activities as public speaking), limited interactional (involving such interactions as going out on a date), and generalized (where extreme anxiety occurs in most social situations). The last category has been criticized for being too similar to avoidant personality disorder. Except for public speaking, social phobias are somewhat rare. Despite knowing that their fears are irrational, people with social phobias curtail many activities. The distinction between social phobias and normal social fears is a difficult one to make. *Specific phobias* are fears of specific objects and include a long list of disorders. In DSM-IV there are four types: natural environmental (for example, animals); blood/injections or injury; situational (for example, heights); and other (a range of situations that may lead to choking or illness). The most common phobias involve animals, heights, the dark, and lightning. They are more prevalent in women than men and are rarely incapacitating.

5. **Etiology and treatment of phobias** (pp. 175–182) Psychoanalysts see phobias as symbolic of unconscious sexual or aggressive conflicts. The case of little Hans is used to explain a youth's fear of horses. Classical conditioning explains the development of some phobias. Observational learning and operant conditioning principles may explain some phobias. Retrospective reports indicate that conditioning experiences play a major causative role. However, in one study, 36 percent of phobics could not remember how their fear was acquired. Genetic evidence indicates that phobias may stem from a predisposition to excessive autonomic reaction to stress, but genetic vulnerability has only a modest relationship to specific phobias. The notion of preparedness is also related to the existence of certain phobias and the nonexistence of others.

   Biochemical treatment of the phobias usually involves antidepressants, but behavioral treatment seems necessary in addition when treating agoraphobia. *Exposure therapy* (the gradual presentation of the feared situation) has been helpful in reducing fears and panic attacks in agoraphobic individuals and those with specific phobias. Multimodal treatment that includes cognitive, behavioral, and physiological components is increasingly used. *Systematic desensitization* is often used to treat social and simple phobias. *Modeling therapy* and cognitive-behavioral approaches are also highly effective with certain phobias.

6. **Obsessive-compulsive disorder** (pp. 182–185) Obsessive-compulsive disorder is an anxiety disorder characterized by intrusive thoughts and the need to perform ritualistic actions. The symptoms are "ego-dystonic"—they are involuntary and are perceived as alien. Once thought to be rare, obsessive-compulsive disorder has an estimated lifetime prevalence of between 2 and 3 percent. About half of those with the disorder report obsessions, half report compulsions, and only 9 percent report both. Four factors are associated with *obsessions*: (1) impaired control over mental processes, (2) worries over loss of motor control, (3) worries over contamination, and (4) checking behaviors. *Compulsions* are behaviors performed in a stereotyped way to reduce anxiety. To the compulsive, these actions have the magical ability to ward off danger.

7. **Etiology and treatment of obsessive-compulsive disorder** (pp. 185–189) The causes of obsessive-compulsive disorder are unclear. One theory, favored by psychoanalysts, suggests that obsessions substitute for unconscious conflicts and that compulsions are based on defense mechanisms such as undoing and reaction formation. The behavioral perspective emphasizes the anxiety-reducing functions of compulsions. The superstition hypothesis, based on operant conditioning, suggests that rituals occur because of chance reinforcement. Biogenic models emphasize differences in brain function, genetic vulnerability, and effects of medication

on individuals with obsessive-compulsive disorder. Recent research shows that people with obsessive-compulsive disorder have higher levels of glucose metabolism in the frontal lobes.

Antidepressant medication is the chief biological treatment for obsessive-compulsive disorder, but only 60 to 80 percent of obsessive-compulsives respond to these drugs; relief is only partial, and relapse is a problem. Behavioral treatments, including systematic desensitization, *flooding,* and response prevention have been effective. Cognitive approaches identify and challenge the irrational thoughts of obsessive-compulsives.

8. **Posttraumatic stress disorder (PTSD): Diagnosis, etiology, and treatment** (pp. 189–194) PTSD is an anxiety disorder involving delayed reactions to extraordinarily distressing events. Symptoms include reexperiencing the event, intrusive memories and dreams, emotional numbing, and heightened autonomic arousal. Diagnosis is subjective and difficult because it is dependent on the definition of the stressor. Recent research suggests that some extreme stressors may produce PTSD in almost everyone. Women seem to be more likely than men to suffer from PTSD. Classical conditioning combined with poor coping styles seems a good explanation for the development of this disorder. Preexisting anxiety disorder or a family history of anxiety occurs in many with PTSD. A range of treatments for PTSD exists, but a four-step model is recommended: building rapport, allowing the individual to express emotions, helping the individual give up the "sick" role, and solving current problems. Extinction through prolonged exposure has helped individuals with PTSD. A new, promising treatment is called *eye movement desensitization,* in which the individual visualizes the disturbing situation and then visually tracks back and forth the clinician's finger while keeping the head immobile. It is not clear how this treatment has its therapeutic effects. Cognitive behavioral approaches are also effective.

KEY TERMS

Fill-in-the-Blanks Quiz

1. An involuntary impulse to perform a particular act repeatedly is called a(n) ___________.

2. Formerly a category of mental disorders including those now called the anxiety, dissociative, and somatoform disorders, this category, called ___________, is now generally used to denote a less severe mental disorder.

3. A strong, persistent, and unwarranted fear of a specific object or situation is called a(n) ___________.

4. The therapy similar to flooding that may involve gradual exposure to the feared situation is called ___________.

5. An irrational and strong fear of social situations is called a(n) ___________.

6. Feelings of fear and apprehension are also called ___________.

7. The disorder characterized by persistent high levels of anxiety in situations where no real danger is present is called ___________.

8. The anxiety disorder characterized by intrusive memories of a traumatic event, emotional withdrawal, and increased arousal levels is called ___________.

9. The therapy technique of gradually exposing the client to a feared situation is called ___________.

10. An extreme fear of a specific object that is not classified as agoraphobia or a social phobia is called a(n) ___________.

11. Disorders such as phobias and panic disorder that are characterized by irrational feelings of fear and apprehension are called ___________.

12. The therapy technique that involves continued actual or imagined exposure to a situation involving high anxiety is called ___________.

13. The anxiety disorder that involves intrusive and uncontrollable thoughts, the need to perform specific acts repeatedly, or both is called ___________.

14. The anxiety disorder characterized by severe attacks of apprehension and feelings of impending doom is called ___________.

15. An intrusive, uncontrollable, and persistent thought is called a(n) ___________.

16. The disorder involving an intense fear of open spaces or of being alone where help may not be available is called ___________.

17. The therapeutic approach to phobias in which the phobic client observes a fearless individual coping with the fear-producing situation is called ___________.

18. The therapy in which relaxation is used to eliminate the anxiety associated with phobias and other fear-evoking situations is called ___________.

Answers to Fill-in-the-Blanks Quiz

1. compulsion
2. neurosis
3. phobia
4. exposure therapy
5. social phobia
6. anxiety
7. generalized anxiety disorder
8. posttraumatic stress disorder
9. graduated exposure
10. specific phobia
11. anxiety disorders
12. flooding
13. obsessive-compulsive disorder
14. panic disorder
15. obsession
16. agoraphobia
17. modeling therapy
18. systematic desensitization

FACT AND CONCEPT QUESTIONS

1. When anxiety produces changes in breathing, perspiration, and muscle tension, these changes reflect ___________ manifestations of anxiety.
   a. behavioral
   b. somatic
   c. cognitive
   d. neurological

2. Four episodes of sweating, choking, and heart palpitations within a 4-week period is the criterion for diagnosing
   a. agoraphobia.
   b. panic disorder.
   c. generalized anxiety disorder.
   d. posttraumatic stress disorder.

3. Constant worry over several life situations, hypervigilance, and physiological symptoms that last more than six months are the chief characteristics of
   a. psychogenic amnesia.
   b. panic disorder.
   c. obsessive-compulsive disorder.
   d. generalized anxiety disorder.

4. Which statement below concerning panic attacks is *true*?
   a. They always occur in specific situations and have warning signs of their occurrence.
   b. They are fairly common.
   c. They occur only in people who suffer from panic disorder.
   d. They involve behavioral aspects of anxiety but not cognitive or somatic ones.

5. Learning theorists suggest that generalized anxiety disorder develops when
   a. intense unconditioned stimuli are associated with anxiety in the absence of distinct environmental stimuli.
   b. the consequence of a fear response is punishment or extinction.
   c. early childhood experiences are pushed into the unconscious.
   d. a biological predisposition to excessive autonomic responses is coupled with a lack of interpersonal support for coping.

6. The chemical that seems capable of inducing panic attacks in clients with panic disorder is
   a. imipramine.
   b. serotonin.
   c. alcohol.
   d. sodium lactate.

7. Which statement about the biological treatment of generalized anxiety disorder is *true*?
   a. The first effective treatment was a form of brain surgery called leucotomy.
   b. Medication helps reduce anxiety, but psychological treatment is also necessary for successful treatment.
   c. Drugs as different as sodium lactate, antidepressants, and benzodiazepines are effective on a long-range basis.
   d. The most effective medication is sodium lactate.

8. Agoraphobia is
   a. much more common in men than in women.
   b. characterized by persistent unwanted thoughts and rituals.
   c. an intense fear of being in public places without available help.
   d. so similar to generalized anxiety disorder that the two have been merged in the DSM-IV.

9. What makes it difficult to diagnose the generalized type of social phobia?
   a. The phobic individual is only frightened in the presence of a specific situation.
   b. The phobic individual does not believe that his or her fears are irrational.
   c. The symptoms overlap with many other disorders.
   d. The lifetime prevalence rate is so high (about 20 percent) that it seems as if everyone has the disorder.

10. A psychoanalytic explanation for specific phobias stresses
    a. the preparedness of the individual.
    b. the reinforcement the individual receives for being fearful.
    c. how symptoms are a compromise between the ego and the id's need to gratify sexual impulses.
    d. how parents provide modeling for the fears that develop in early childhood.

11. Research on the genetic cause of agoraphobia
    a. suggests that both heredity and modeling may account for it being prevalent in first-degree relatives of agoraphobics.
    b. has shown no higher vulnerability in parents or siblings of agoraphobic patients than in control groups.
    c. indicates that what is inherited is an underactive autonomic nervous system.
    d. suggests that the neurotransmitter imipramine is deficient in these clients.

12. If preparedness were *not* an issue in the development of phobias,
    a. it would be unlikely that we would find any phobias for cars or airplanes.
    b. we would find that any object was as likely as any other to be a source of terror.
    c. genetics would be the sole reason for phobias.
    d. classical conditioning could no longer be considered a reason for phobias.

13. The behavior therapy that teaches clients to relax while imagining a feared stimulus is called
    a. systematic desensitization.
    b. cognitive restructuring.
    c. flooding.
    d. *in vivo* response prevention.

14. An effective multimodal approach for treating agoraphobia might include
    a. cognitive restructuring to increase positive coping statements.
    b. imipramine and exposure to public places.
    c. both a and b.
    d. neither a nor b.

15. A persistent and unwanted fear of being contaminated by dirt and germs illustrates ___________ and is often associated with the ___________ of handwashing.
    a. a phobia; obsession
    b. an obsession; compulsion
    c. a compulsion; phobia
    d. preparedness; compulsion

16. Which of the following is *true* about the psychoanalytic theory of obsessive-compulsive disorder?
    a. It is based on observational learning.
    b. It adequately explains the majority of cases of obsessive-compulsive disorder.
    c. It is essentially the same thing as the superstition hypothesis.
    d. It assumes that symptoms originate out of defenses against unconscious conflicts.

17. The anxiety reduction hypothesis for compulsive handwashing
    a. adequately explains why compulsive actions are continued.
    b. adequately explains why compulsive actions originate.
    c. includes both a and b.
    d. includes neither a nor b.

18. The preferred behavioral treatment for obsessive-compulsive disorder is
    a. relaxation training and biofeedback.
    b. biofeedback and response prevention.
    c. cognitive restructuring and positive reinforcement.
    d. flooding and response prevention.

19. Anxiety disorders that stem from extraordinarily distressing events such as tornadoes, concentration camp experiences, and incest or rape are considered
    a. forms of social phobia.
    b. forms of generalized anxiety disorder.
    c. forms of obsessive-compulsive disorder.
    d. posttraumatic stress disorder.

20. A new treatment for posttraumatic stress disorder involves
    a. the use of the tranquilizer imipramine.
    b. visually tracking the clinician's finger back and forth.
    c. repeated exposure and response prevention.
    d. avoidance of the distressing situation.

APPLICATION QUESTIONS

1. Dr. Thomas says, "They can occur in response to a specific feared stimulus or come on unexpectedly. When you have one, you think you might be dying of a heart attack. They are fairly common: Between one-quarter and one-third of college students report having had one in the past year." What is Dr. Thomas referring to?
    a. Obsessions
    b. Compulsions
    c. Posttraumatic stress reactions
    d. Panic attacks

2. Gene is diagnosed as suffering from generalized anxiety disorder, whereas Paul is diagnosed with panic disorder. What is the main difference between the two diagnoses?
   a. In panic disorder, the person shows relatively low anxiety levels between panic episodes.
   b. In panic disorder, the person is constantly worried about a range of life situations.
   c. In generalized anxiety disorder, the person experiences the somatic aspects of anxiety.
   d. In generalized anxiety disorder, the person performs rituals as a way of reducing anxiety.

3. Ben is being treated for panic disorder. His therapist tells him, "You need to change from thinking 'I'll pass out if I walk into that store' to 'I can control my anxiety.' " What perspective on anxiety disorders does this illustrate?
   a. Classical conditioning
   b. Psychoanalytic
   c. Cognitive-behavioral
   d. Biological

4. Charlene is receiving biological treatment for her panic disorder. It is most likely that she is getting
   a. electroshock treatments.
   b. antidepressants.
   c. biofeedback.
   d. sodium lactate.

5. Laurie is terribly afraid of being seen in restaurants or movie theaters because she fears she will make a complete fool of herself in some way. She recognizes that her fear is irrational, but the fear completely controls her. Laurie's problem best illustrates
   a. a social phobia.
   b. agoraphobia.
   c. phobophobia.
   d. generalized anxiety disorder.

6. A psychologist says, "The case of little Hans (and his 'widdler') illustrates that classical conditioning might cause phobias. Unfortunately, other attempts to replicate that study have failed." What part of the psychologist's statement is inaccurate?
   a. The case that he is referring to involved modeling and operant conditioning.
   b. The case of little Hans was one that Freud used to explain phobias.
   c. The case that he is referring to has been replicated many times.
   d. The case of little Hans has nothing to do with phobias.

7. Suppose we found that, of 100 people with phobias, 80 percent had a fear of animals, 10 percent had a fear of germs and dirt, and the remainder feared enclosed places. None of the people had phobias about machinery. This finding would support the ___________ approach to phobias.
   a. cognitive-behavioral
   b. psychoanalytic
   c. exposure
   d. preparedness

8. A psychiatrist says, "Even in normal populations, there are people who are fearful of contamination and of being out of control. They check everything to lessen their worries." What kind of problem is the psychiatrist describing?
   a. Posttraumatic stress disorder
   b. Obsessions
   c. Panic disorder
   d. Reaction formation

9. After being unsuccessfully treated with antidepressants for an intense phobia, Wayne is looking for a treatment technique that both is effective and takes little time. You might suggest ____________ to Wayne.
   a. biofeedback
   b. psychoanalytic psychotherapy
   c. flooding and response prevention
   d. systematic desensitization

10. Greg was in Lebanon when his marine buddies were killed in a terrorist raid. He still has nightmares about it and has emotionally withdrawn from his family. The only thing that has helped is joining a support group of other veterans with the same disorder. What is the disorder?
   a. Obsessive-compulsive disorder
   b. Generalized anxiety disorder
   c. Social phobia
   d. Posttraumatic stress disorder

ANSWERS TO FACT AND CONCEPT QUESTIONS

1. a. Behavioral aspects of anxiety involve avoidance of places where anxiety has occurred in the past.
   *b. Sweating, muscular tension, heart palpitations, cold hands and feet, perspiration, and diarrhea are all somatic manifestations of anxiety. (p. 163)
   c. Cognitive manifestations of anxiety include worrying, indecisiveness, and confusion.
   d. There are no neurological manifestations of anxiety, but, if there were, they would involve changes in nervous system structures.

2. a. Agoraphobia involves intense fear of going out in public without assistance.
   *b. Panic disorder is diagnosed when there are four or more panic attacks in a 4-week period. (p. 165)
   c. Generalized anxiety disorder is characterized by constant worry and anxiety symptoms that are less intense than those in panic disorder.
   d. Posttraumatic stress disorder is diagnosed when symptoms occur after an event outside the normal range of life stressors (for example, a tornado or terrorist raid)

3. a. Psychogenic amnesia is a dissociative disorder characterized by memory loss.
   b. Panic disorder is characterized by intermittent yet terrifying episodes, but relatively low anxiety levels otherwise.
   c. Obsessive-compulsive disorder is diagnosed when a person has worrisome thoughts that lead to ritualistic actions such as handwashing or repetitive checking.
   *d. Generalized anxiety disorder is characterized by constant worry and physiological and cognitive manifestations of anxiety such as sweating and hypervigilance. (p. 167)

4. a. Panic attacks are particularly frightening because they come on without warning.
   *b. Although panic disorder (four attacks in a short period of time) is uncommon, many people report having had at least one panic attack. (p. 166)
   c. Panic disorder is defined by four or more panic attacks in 4 weeks, but many "normal" people have one or two such attacks over a lifetime.
   d. Panic attacks are so distressful because they affect behavior, thought, and physical functioning.

5. *a. Classical conditioning involves unconditioned stimuli; the disorder is generalized anxiety because there is no specific situation in which the conditioned response occurs. (p. 167)
   b. Consequences are the focus of operant conditioning principles.
   c. Early childhood experiences are the focus of psychoanalytic explanations.
   d. The biological explanation would focus on excessive autonomic reactivity.

6. a. Imipramine is an antidepressant drug that reduces symptoms of anxiety.
   b. Serotonin is a neurotransmitter that appears to regulate emotional experience.
   c. Alcohol does not increase anxiety; it tends to reduce it.
   *d. Sensitivity to sodium lactate appears to be a biological difference between those who are vulnerable to panic disorder and those who are not. (p. 169)

7. a. Leucotomy was originally used as a surgical treatment for obsessive-compulsive disorder.
   *b. Medication such as benzodiazepines helps reduce symptoms, but anxiety management training seems necessary to alter avoidance responses. (p. 170)
   c. A variety of drugs have been useful with panic attacks, but not generalized anxiety disorder; still, individuals have dependence problems, and relapse occurs when one ceases taking the drugs.
   d. Sodium lactate increases the likelihood of panic attacks, rather than reducing it.

8. a. Agoraphobia is two or three times more likely in women.
   b. Persistent thoughts and rituals are symptoms of obsessive-compulsive disorder.
   *c. Agoraphobia is an intense fear of being in public without support or assistance, and leads to avoidance of such situations. (p. 171)
   d. Agoraphobia does not involve the constant worry that is seen in generalized anxiety disorder.

9. a. The generalized type does *not* respond with anxiety to a specific situation.
   b. All phobic individuals know that their fears are irrational, but they are controlled by them anyway.
   *c. Several researchers report complete overlap in the symptoms of generalized anxiety disorder and avoidant personality disorder. (p. 166)
   d. Altogether social phobias are quite rare; one study gives a six-month prevalence of less than 2 percent. Generalized social phobia is much less common.

10. a. Preparedness is a biological concept.
    b. Reinforcement is an operant conditioning concept.
    *c. Psychoanalytic explanations stress unconscious conflicts. (p. 167)
    d. Modeling is a social learning concept.

11. *a. Just because a disorder runs in families does not mean that inheritance is the cause; imitation of parents is just as likely an explanation. (p. 179)
    b. First-degree relatives do show higher percentages of cases.
    c. If anything is inherited, it is an *over*active autonomic nervous system.
    d. Imipramine is an antidepressant medication, not a neurotransmitter.

12. a. Preparedness suggests that posttechnical-age objects (such as cars) do not easily become conditioned stimuli.
    *b. If preparedness did not enter into the equation, every object would have an equal chance of being a source of phobia if it were paired with anxiety. (p. 179)
    c. Preparedness only suggests that certain categories of objects are easily associated with anxiety; no prediction is made as to the importance of genetics as the cause.
    d. Classical conditioning could still be the explanation; all that changes is the *object* that induces terror.

13. *a. Systematic desensitization involves teaching relaxation skills and then pairing relaxation with imagined or real anxiety-producing situations on a gradual basis. (p. 181)
    b. Cognitive restructuring focuses on how we think about situations and our behavior in them.
    c. Flooding represents "cold turkey" extinction and high levels of anxiety; it is the opposite of systematic desensitization.
    d. *In vivo* response prevention would involve placing the feared object before the patient and preventing him or her from running away.

14. a. Successful treatment of agoraphobia appears to require changing the way patients think about entering public places. (p. 180)
    b. Successful treatment of agoraphobia appears to require methods for reducing anxiety (medication) and ways to stop avoidance responses. (p. 180)
    *c. Because both a and b are correct, this is the best answer.
    d. Because both a and b are correct, this cannot be the best answer.

15. a. A phobia is an intense, irrational fear of an object, not an unwanted thought.
    *b. An obsession is an unwanted and unstoppable thought; a compulsion is a ritualistic behavior to ward off the worry. (p. 182)
    c. A phobia is an intense, irrational fear, not a ritualistic action.
    d. Preparedness deals with the likelihood of certain phobic stimuli, not with persistent thoughts.

16. a. Substitution, not observation, is a psychoanalytic explanation.
    b. Although psychoanalytic explanations have clinical appeal, they do not explain the majority of cases.
    c. The superstition hypothesis is derived from operant conditioning principles.
    *d. As a psychoanalytic explanation, substitution says that symptoms at the surface substitute for conflicts below the surface. (pp. 185–186)

17. a. Anxiety reduction does not explain why ritualistic actions begin.
    *b. Anxiety reduction explains ritualistic behavior in terms of lowering arousal if the ritual is not performed. However, it cannot explain why the compulsion began in the first place. (p. 186)
    c. Because a is incorrect, this cannot be the best answer.
    d. Because b is correct, this cannot be the best answer.

18. a. Relaxation training may be helpful, but biofeedback will have little effect on reducing ritualistic actions.
    b. Biofeedback will have little effect on reducing ritualistic actions.
    c. Positive reinforcement will not reduce the likelihood of ritualistic actions.
    *d. It is necessary to extinguish both anxiety (through flooding) and ritualistic actions (through response prevention). (p. 188)

19. a. Social phobias involve intense fears of activity in public (such as using public toilets) and are not related to severe traumatic events.
    b. Generalized anxiety disorder rarely develops out of a particular traumatic event.
    c. Obsessive-compulsive disorder is characterized by unwanted thoughts and ritualistic actions.
    *d. Posttraumatic stress disorder is a delayed reaction to a stressful event outside the normal range of human experience. (p. 189)

20. a. Imipramine is an antidepressant that is most effective in treating panic disorder and agoraphobia.
    *b. Eye movement desensitization, which involves visualizing the disturbing situation and tracking the clinician's finger or pencil as it moves from side to side, is a new and promising treatment for PTSD. (p. 193)
    c. Repeated exposure may reduce the anxiety of the remembered situation, but there is no ritualistic action that must be prevented.
    d. Continued avoidance of disturbing situations maintains an anxiety disorder rather than effectively treating it.

ANSWERS TO APPLICATION QUESTIONS

1. a. Obsessions are unwanted, persistent anxiety-arousing thoughts. They do not come on without warning.
   b. Compulsions are stereotyped, ritualistic actions that reduce anxiety.
   c. Posttraumatic stress disorder occurs in response to a specific, highly stressful event.
   *d. Panic attacks involve heart palpitations and can occur in response to a specific situation or be unexpected; college students report they are fairly common. (pp. 165, 166)

2. *a. In between panic attacks, those with panic disorder are relatively low in anxiety; those with generalized anxiety disorder are *never* low in anxiety. (p. 166)
   b. It is in generalized anxiety disorder that worry is constant.
   c. In both disorders, anxiety produces somatic complaints; in panic disorder, the anxiety is so great the patient may think he or she will die.
   d. Rituals are associated with obsessive-compulsive disorder.

3. a. Classical conditioning focuses on the external stimuli that are associated with fear responses.
   b. Psychoanalytic explanations look for the unconscious conflicts that surface in symbolic symptoms.
   *c. Cognitive-behavioral theorists stress how thinking influences the experience of anxiety. (p. 168)
   d. Biological explanations stress the genetics of patients and their sensitivity to such chemicals as sodium lactate.

4. a. Electroshock treatments may be helpful in depression, but not in panic disorder.
   *b. Antidepressants such as imipramine have been helpful in reducing the frequency and intensity of panic attacks. (p. 170)
   c. Biofeedback has not been an effective treatment for panic attacks.
   d. Sodium lactate seems to increase panic attacks in patients, but not in controls.

5. *a. Social phobias are characterized by irrational fears of performing actions in public that will be evaluated. (p. 173)
   b. Agoraphobia is an intense fear of being in public (in general) without available help.
   c. Phobophobia is a fear of having a phobia.
   d. Generalized anxiety disorder involves worry about almost everything, not a specific target as in phobias.

6. a. The case of little Hans underscored psychoanalytic explanations, not learning or social learning ones.
   *b. The case of little Hans was used by Freud to explain how the surface symptoms of a phobia stemmed from unconscious (oedipal) conflicts. (pp. 175–176)
   c. The Watson and Raymer study that showed how conditioning could produce a phobia has *not* been replicated.
   d. The case of little Hans was Freud's principal means of explaining phobias.

7. a. Cognitive-behavioral explanations focus on thoughts.
   b. Psychoanalytic explanations focus on unconscious conflicts.
   c. Exposure is the treatment technique of extinguishing anxiety through habituation.
   *d. Preparedness is the concept that pretechnical objects related to evolution are more likely to be objects of phobic fear than technical ones such as cars and machinery. (p. 179)

8. a. Posttraumatic stress disorder involves events, not thoughts.
   *b. Contamination worries and checking behaviors are seen in the obsessional activities of many people. (p. 183)
   c. Panic disorder involves fears of attacks, not worries over contamination.
   d. Reaction formation is a defense mechanism, not a disorder.

9. a. Biofeedback has not been helpful in treating phobias.
   b. Psychoanalytic therapy takes a long time.
   *c. Flooding (arousal of intense fear) and response prevention (stopping avoidance of the object) is a quick and effective treatment. (p. 188)
   d. Systematic desensitization may be helpful (in about 50 percent of cases), but it is more time-consuming than flooding.

10. a. Obsessive-compulsive disorder involves unwanted thoughts and rituals.
   b. Generalized anxiety disorder is rarely triggered by one event.
   c. Social phobias involve fears of specific public activities.
   *d. Posttraumatic stress disorder (PTSD) stems from a horrifying event and is frequently treated with support from others who have survived similar events. (p. 192)

CHAPTER 7
Dissociative Disorders and Somatoform Disorders

LEARNING OBJECTIVES

When you have mastered the material in Chapter 7, you should be able to:

1. Describe the basic characteristics of dissociative disorders. Discuss the characteristics of the four types of dissociative amnesia and the process by which they occur. (pp. 197–200)
2. Describe the characteristics of dissociative fugue and depersonalization disorder. (pp. 200–203)
3. Describe the characteristics of multiple personality and its prevalence. (pp. 203–204)
4. Discuss the diagnostic controversies concerning multiple personality and the degree to which therapists may contribute to its existence. (Focus 7.1; pp. 204–207)
5. Discuss the causes of dissociative disorders from the psychoanalytic and behavioral perspectives. (pp. 207–208)
6. Discuss the treatment of dissociative disorders using psychoanalytic, behavioral, and family systems therapies. (pp. 208–211)
7. Describe the basic characteristics of somatoform disorders and list the five subtypes. Discuss cross-cultural differences in somatic complaints. Discuss how somatoform disorders differ from factitious disorders. (Focus 7.2; pp. 211–213)
8. Describe the characteristics of somatization disorder. (pp. 213–214)
9. Describe the characteristics of conversion disorder. (pp. 214–215)
10. Describe the characteristics of somatoform pain disorder, hypochondriasis, and body dysmorphic disorder. Discuss the diagnostic issues related to body dysmorphic disorder. (pp. 215–217)
11. Describe and discuss the causes of somatoform disorders from the psychoanalytic, behavioral, sociocultural, and biological perspectives. (pp. 217–220)
12. Describe and discuss the treatment of somatoform disorders with psychoanalytic, behavioral, and family systems therapies. (pp. 220–222)

CHAPTER OUTLINE

1. **Dissociative and somatoform disorders** (pp. 197–199) The *dissociative disorders* and the *somatoform disorders* involve the symptoms related to psychological conflict or need. The dissociative disorders show altered or disrupted memory or consciousness; the somatoform disorders involve physical symptoms that have no physiological basis. Both disorders rely on

self-reports, and so are subject to faking, but their existence can be substantiated. Reports of one dissociative disorder—multiple personality—have increased dramatically.

2. **Dissociative amnesia** (pp. 199–200) *Amnesia* is memory loss due to either organic or psychological causes. *Dissociative amnesia* is psychologically based and is usually associated with a traumatic event. *Localized amnesia* is characterized by total memory loss for a particular time period. In *selective amnesia,* the memory loss is for details about an incident. Total loss of memory for one's past life is the criterion for *generalized amnesia*, and total loss of memory from one point in time to another occurs in *continuous amnesia*. Repression seems to be the main reason for psychogenic amnesia; a similar process occurs in *posthypnotic amnesia.*

3. **Dissociative fugue and depersonalization disorder** (pp. 200–203) In *dissociative fugue*, memory loss is accompanied by flight to another area and establishment of a new identity. Recovery from this and from psychogenic amnesia is usually abrupt and spontaneous.

   Depersonalization disorder is characterized by feelings of unreality or distorted perceptions of the body or environment. It is more common than the other dissociative disorders and can be precipitated by stress.

4. **Dissociative identity disorder (multiple-personality disorder)** (Focus 7.1; pp. 203–207) In *multiple personality,* two or more (often many more) distinct personalities exist in one individual. Not all personalities are aware of one another. Objective testing indicates that the personalities are "real" and separate. Although this condition was once thought to be rare, there has been a dramatic increase in reported cases, perhaps because of the influence of therapists while clients are under hypnosis. People with multiple personality often report a history of childhood abuse. Diagnosis in childhood is possible, but misdiagnosis is common, both by seeing the disorder in people who have other problems and by failing to see multiple personality in people diagnosed with other disorders.

5. **Etiology and treatment of dissociative disorders** (pp. 207–211) The causes of dissociative disorders are subject to a good deal of conjecture because faking is always a possibility. Even electroencephalogram readings may not be reliable measures of multiple personalities. The psychoanalytic perspective sees repression of unpleasant emotions as the cause of dissociative disorders. Splits in consciousness protect the individual from anxiety and pain. Behavioral theorists suggest that avoidance of stress is the main causative factor. Role playing also helps explain multiple personality.

   Recovery from dissociative amnesia, dissociative fugue, and depersonalization disorder often occurs spontaneously; therefore, treatment often aims at reducing the depression or anxiety these conditions produce. Multiple personality is usually treated with psychotherapy and hypnosis, but not with notable success. Behavior therapists use contingent reinforcement for the "healthy personality" and extinction for the others. Family therapy is also used, particularly with children suffering from multiple personality.

6. **Somatoform disorders** (Focus 7.2; pp. 211–213) The principal symptoms of *somatoform disorders* are complaints of physical symptoms that have no apparent physiological cause. Faking is possible, but when symptoms such as fever are consciously induced, they are considered *factitious disorders* rather than *malingering*. Somatic complaints are far more common in nonwestern cultures where a somatopsychic view (physical problems produce emotional symptoms) is more prevalent than the western psychosomatic (internal conflicts are expressed as physical symptoms) view.

7. **Somatization disorders and conversion disorder** (pp. 213–215) In *somatization disorder,* individuals have physical complaints in four or more different sites in the body, symptoms for which there are no physiological explanations. Patients shop around for doctors and often have unneeded surgery. Somatization disorder, formerly called hysteria, is rarely diagnosed in men although over one-third of males referred for unexplained somatic complaints meet the criteria for the disorder.

   In *conversion disorder,* there is a significant physical impairment, such as paralysis in a limb or sensory problems, without physical basis. When neurological or other processes prove the symptoms impossible, diagnosis is readily made; otherwise, it is quite hard to differentiate conversion disorder from actual illnesses or faking.

8. **Pain disorder, hypochondriasis, and body dysmorphic disorder** (pp. 215–217) Pain that is excessive, lingers too long, or is unrelated to a physiological cause is characteristic of *somatoform pain disorder*. As with ordinary pain, there is a complex interaction between perception, thinking, and behavior.

   In *hypochondriasis,* there is a consistent preoccupation with illness in the face of doctors' repeated assurances of health. Those with hypochondriasis often have a history of illness and parents who focused on illness. Fear, anxiety, and depression are common complaints.

   Body dysmorphic disorder involves an excessive concern with an imagined or slight physical defect such as facial features, excessive hair, or the shape of genitals. Individuals with this disorder frequently check their appearance in the mirror and fear that others are looking at the defect. They make frequent requests for plastic surgery regardless of the treatment's outcome. Because the disorder involves obsessive thinking and delusions, its placement in the diagnostic category of somatoform disorders can be questioned.

9. **Etiology and treatment of somatoform disorders** (pp. 217–222) A diathesis-stress view of somatoform disorders suggests that individuals are hypersensitive to bodily sensations and are predisposed to react strongly to somatic sensations. In the event of a stressor, they develop intense bodily complaints and symptoms. Psychoanalysts believe that repression accounts for the process of converting unconscious conflicts into physical symptoms. There is primary gain in the reduction of anxiety and secondary gain in the sympathy the individual receives. Behavioral theorists contend that a "sick role" is reinforced by others and helps the person escape from responsibilities. The sociocultural perspective stresses that, historically, social norms did not provide women with appropriate channels for the expression of aggressive or sexual needs. As a result, women developed hysterical symptoms. The biological perspective notes that individuals differ in pain sensitivity, with those having somatoform disorders at the extreme end of the scale. However, there is little evidence for a significant genetic contribution to the disorder per se.

   Psychoanalytic treatment emphasizes the need to relive unpleasant experiences so that they can be mastered rather than converted into symptoms. Behavioral therapists advise extinction for complaints and reinforcement for healthy behavior. Cognitive-behavioral treatments focus on changing the conscious thoughts and expectations of clients. Family therapists teach family members to support one another without resorting to physical symptoms and to anticipate such problems.

KEY TERMS

Fill-in-the-Blanks Quiz

1. The somatoform disorder characterized by a persistent preoccupation with one's health is called ____________.

2. The dissociative disorder in which psychogenic amnesia is accompanied by flight from familiar surroundings is called ____________.

3. The dissociative disorder in which there are feelings of unreality or distortions of self and the environment is called ____________.

4. The disorder that involves chronic complaints about a number of physical symptoms for which there is no physical basis is called ____________.

5. The somatoform disorder in which there is a significant impairment of physical function without an underlying organic cause is called ____________.

6. Mental disorders characterized by disruption or alteration of one's identity or consciousness are called ____________.

7. Mental disorders involving complaints of physical symptoms that mimic authentic medical conditions but have no physical basis are called ____________.

8. The somatoform disorder characterized by pain that has a psychological, rather than a physical, basis is called ____________.

9. The dissociative disorder characterized by an inability to recall information of personal significance, usually after a traumatic event, is called ____________.

10. The dissociative disorder in which two or more relatively distinct personalities exist in one individual is called ____________.

11. The somatoform disorder that involves preoccupation with an imagined physical defect is called ____________.

12. The inability to recall past and present events where each new event is forgotten after it occurs is called ____________.

13. The inability to recall the entire past, due to some psychosocial crisis, is called ____________.

14. The inability to recall all events during a specific period is the most common type of amnesia and is called ____________.

15. The inability to recall information as a result of a suggestion made during a hypnotic state is called ____________.

16. The inability to recall only some aspects of a situation as a result of some psychosocial stress is called ____________.

17. The partial or total loss of memory due to either organic or psychological causes is called ___________.

18. Deliberately self-induced or simulated physical or mental conditions are called ___________.

19. Faking an illness to obtain a goal is called ___________.

Answers to Fill-in-the-Blanks Quiz

1. hypochondriasis
2. dissociative fugue (or fugue state)
3. depersonalization disorder
4. somatization disorder
5. conversion disorder
6. dissociative disorders
7. somatoform disorders
8. somatoform pain disorder
9. dissociative amnesia
10. multiple personality
11. body dysmorphic disorder
12. continuous amnesia
13. generalized amnesia
14. localized amnesia
15. posthypnotic amnesia
16. selective amnesia
17. amnesia
18. factitious disorders
19. malingering

FACT AND CONCEPT QUESTIONS

1. Dissociative amnesia, multiple personality, and depersonalization disorder are all examples of
   a. somatoform disorders.
   b. anxiety disorders.
   c. dissociative disorders.
   d. phobic disorders.

2. In localized amnesia, the memory loss is
   a. total; nothing can be remembered about one's past life.
   b. always due to a biological cause.
   c. only for specific details of a specific event.
   d. complete for a specific period in one's life.

3. When people develop amnesia and then travel to a new area where they establish a new identity, the problem is called
   a. dissociative fugue.
   b. generalized amnesia.
   c. multiple personality.
   d. dissociative phobia.

4. It is the most common dissociative disorder and involves feelings of unreality about one's body or the environment. These intense experiences may lead sufferers to wonder whether they are losing their minds. The disorder being described is called
   a. multiple personality.
   b. dissociative fugue.
   c. somatoform disorder.
   d. depersonalization disorder.

5. How can we tell that the distinct personalities in multiple personality are not the result of faking?
   a. They usually *are* the result of faking.
   b. Physiological records such as GSR and EEG readings differ for each personality.
   c. Multiple personalities have abnormal genetic material.
   d. They can be easily detected in personal interviews.

6. In multiple-personality disorder, it is rare to find
   a. more than three distinct personalities.
   b. that the personalities are distinct from one another.
   c. that every personality is aware of every other one.
   d. evidence that there is dissociation.

7. The majority of people with multiple personality report a history of
   a. vague physical complaints.
   b. excessively permissive upbringing.
   c. physical and sexual abuse.
   d. having one traumatic incident in adulthood.

8. In recent years, the number of ___________ cases reported by mental health professionals has increased.
   a. conversion disorder
   b. dissociative fugue
   c. hypochondriasis
   d. multiple-personality

9. Among the dissociative disorders, the development of ___________ is thought to be partially iatrogenic (induced by certain treatment methods).
   a. multiple personality
   b. depersonalization disorder
   c. dissociative amnesia
   d. body dysmorphic disorder

10. Avoidance of stress is the main factor in the ___________ theorist's explanation of dissociative disorders.
    a. family systems
    b. biological
    c. learning
    d. psychoanalytic

11. Long-term psychotherapy is usually not necessary for ___________ because it usually stops spontaneously.
    a. dissociative amnesia
    b. multiple personality
    c. hypochondriasis
    d. factitious disorders

12. In somatoform disorders, the fundamental symptom is
    a. the involuntary separation of consciousness in response to traumatic events.
    b. irrational fears of specific objects.
    c. physical symptoms, such as ulcers and diabetes, that develop in response to stress.
    d. involuntarily produced physical symptoms that occur in the absence of organic causes.

13. Unlike somatoform disorders, factitious disorders
    a. are complicated by depression and anxiety.
    b. are under voluntary control.
    c. involve a separation of consciousness.
    d. stem from repression of psychological conflicts.

14. Which statement about somatization disorder is *true*?
    a. The disorder is defined in terms of numerous physical complaints.
    b. The disorder's main symptom is exaggerated or lingering pain.
    c. The disorder is related to physical and sexual abuse during childhood.
    d. The disorder is more common in men than in women.

15. Somatization disorder was previously called
    a. hysteria.
    b. phobia.
    c. dementia praecox.
    d. manic depression.

16. Because it involves symptoms that mimic physical disorders, it is difficult to differentiate ___________ from faking and from organic problems.
    a. depersonalization disorder
    b. body dysmorphic disorder
    c. conversion disorder
    d. dissociative amnesia

17. A history of physical illness, a low pain threshold, and parents who focused on the symptoms of illness are all believed to be factors related to
    a. body dysmorphic disorder.
    b. hypochondriasis.
    c. multiple personality.
    d. factitious disorder.

18. Primary gain and secondary gain are concepts that ___________ theorists use to explain the adaptive qualities of somatoform disorders.
    a. psychoanalytic
    b. biological
    c. learning
    d. humanistic

19. Hypnotherapy is used to treat somatoform disorders because
    a. it prevents others from reinforcing the patient's symptom complaints.
    b. it helps the patient understand the physical causes of his or her complaints.
    c. it raises the patient's pain threshold.
    d. it helps the patient relive feelings associated with a traumatic event.

20. Family therapists would see somatoform complaints as a way of
    a. avoiding family responsibilities.
    b. crying for help.
    c. responding to childhood abuse and neglect.
    d. repressing unpleasant emotions related to an earlier trauma.

APPLICATION QUESTIONS

1. Nora has no recollection of the events just before her house burned down, although she recalls running to a neighbor's house to call for the fire department. Nora's amnesia illustrates
   a. dissociative fugue.
   b. continuous amnesia.
   c. selective amnesia.
   d. depersonalization disorder.

2. Paula is diagnosed as having multiple personality. One personality, Mark, protects her from trouble, while another personality, Kim, is sexually promiscuous. All three personalities are aware of one another. What is unusual about Paula's case of multiple personality?
   a. There are rarely three separate personalities.
   b. Rarely are all personalities aware of one another.
   c. A male personality is rarely found in a female patient.
   d. Sexually promiscuous personalities are rare.

3. "Multiple personality is an adaptive response to unbearable psychological torture: the repression is so complete that distinct personalities are protected from any memory of the trauma." What kind of psychologist would say this?
   a. A behavior therapist
   b. A biologically oriented psychologist
   c. A therapist who does not believe in multiple personality
   d. A psychoanalyst

4. Dr. Greise says to a patient's husband, "Whenever she says she is feeling as though she or the world is getting distorted and unreal, you should ignore her. Make sure you show attention, though, when she is in control." The disorder being treated is ____________ , and Dr. Greise is a ____________ theorist.
   a. depersonalization disorder; learning
   b. multiple-personality disorder; psychoanalytic
   c. somatoform pain disorder; learning
   d. depersonalization disorder; biological

5. Dr. O'Neil says, "These disorders involving physical symptoms are diagnosed by what they *aren't:* they aren't under voluntary control, they aren't faked, and they aren't due to physiological causes." What is Dr. O'Neil talking about?
   a. Dissociative disorders
   b. Anxiety disorders
   c. Factitious disorders
   d. Somatoform disorders

6. Sharon has complained about more than fifteen physical problems over the past year and has had surgery four times even though there is no evidence of physiological causes. She constantly "shops around" for doctors. Sharon suffers from
   a. conversion disorder.
   b. dissociative amnesia.
   c. somatization disorder.
   d. hypochondriasis.

7. Milton began complaining of leg paralysis after he lost his job. There is no evidence of a physical cause. He shows no muscle atrophy, but it is also clear that he is not faking the problem. Milton suffers from
   a. conversion disorder.
   b. malingering.
   c. somatization disorder.
   d. hypochondriasis.

8. Dr. Wimsey says, "There is no doubt that this patient is preoccupied with health concerns, and that there are no physiological reasons behind the complaints. However, the insistence on one complaint (upset stomach) means that the diagnosis should be ___________ rather than ___________."
   a. hysteria; Briquet's syndrome
   b. conversion disorder; somatization disorder
   c. hypochondriasis; somatization disorder
   d. malingering; factitious disorder

9. Dr. Blue thinks that somatoform symptoms are triggered by memories of traumatic events and conflicts. It is likely that Dr. Blue is a ___________ theorist.
   a. sociocultural
   b. humanistic
   c. biological
   d. psychoanalytic

10. "Physicians, nurses, and, eventually, spouses are trained to respond to complaints of pain. Unless attention to (and reinforcement for) such complaints is ended, you cannot expect the somatoform pain patient to improve." Who might say this?
   a. A psychoanalyst
   b. A psychiatrist who treats disorders with medication
   c. A behavior therapist
   d. A humanistic psychotherapist

ANSWERS TO FACT AND CONCEPT QUESTIONS

1. a. Somatoform disorders involve physical complaints; they include such problems as hypochondriasis and conversion disorder.
   b. Anxiety disorders do not produce memory problems; they include phobias and panic disorder.
   *c. Dissociative disorders involve a division of consciousness, usually producing memory problems, as is seen in amnesia and multiple personality (p. 198)
   d. Phobic disorders are a part of anxiety disorder; they do not produce memory problems.

2. a. Complete loss of previous experience occurs in generalized dissociative amnesia.
   b. Localized amnesia can be caused by psychosocial stressors.
   c. Selective amnesia involves loss of memory of specific aspects of a traumatic incident, such as amnesia for some events related to a devastating tornado.
   *d. Localized amnesia is complete memory loss for a specific time; for example, one may not remember being robbed and threatened. (p. 199)

3. *a. The central characteristic of fugue is dissociative amnesia together with travel to a new region to establish a new identity. (p. 200)
   b. Generalized amnesia involves complete loss of memory of previous experience.
   c. Multiple personality is characterized by distinct personalities, not by travel to another area.
   d. Dissociative phobia is a made-up term; dissociative is usually associated with amnesia or fugue, and phobia is a disorder on its own.

4. a. Multiple personality is characterized by distinct personalities, not a sense of unreality.
   b. Dissociative fugue is characterized by travel to a new region and establishment of a new identity.
   c. Somatoform disorders involve physical complaints such as anesthesia, paralysis, or dizziness.
   *d. Depersonalization disorder is characterized by feeling unreal, seeing distortions in the environment or one's body parts, and fear of going crazy. (p. 209)

5. a. Although faking is possible, research by Coons et al. and others shows that separate personalities are not consciously created or portrayed.
   *b. Research by Coons et al. showed GSR and EEG differences in different personalities. (p. 208)
   c. Genes would not change as personalities did.
   d. Interviews are too subjective to easily detect faking.

6. a. Many more than three personalities have been reported: Chris Sizemore (the real "Eve") had more than twenty, and one clinician says the average is thirteen to fourteen!
   b. The diagnosis of multiple personality rests on the notion that the personalities are distinct.
   *c. Usually one personality has limited or no awareness of the others; this is the basic dissociation of consciousness. (p. 208)
   d. Multiple personality is a form of dissociative disorder because one part of the person (along with memories for that part) dissociates itself from the rest.

7. a. Vague physical complaints are more likely to be related to hypochondriasis than to multiple personality.
   b. Multiple personality is not associated with permissive upbringing.
   *c. Most cases of multiple personality seem to develop out of childhood abuse, as in the cases of Billy Milligan and Sybil. (p. 208)
   d. Single traumatic events are more likely to be associated with dissociative amnesia; multiple personality usually involves a childhood full of trauma.

8. a. There is no evidence that conversion disorder has increased recently.
   b. There is no evidence that dissociative fugue has increased recently.
   c. There is no evidence that hypochondriasis has increased recently.
   *d. There has been an enormous upsurge in reported cases of multiple personality recently; one clinician alone reported 130 cases. (p. 204)

9. *a. Research indicates that the suggestion of a therapist can influence the reporting of multiple-personality-like symptoms. (Focus 7.1; pp. 206–207)
   b. Depersonalization disorder does not seem to be induced by therapy.
   c. Dissociative amnesia is triggered by traumatic events, not by therapy.
   d. Body dysmorphic disorder does not seem to be induced by therapy.

10. a. Family systems theory stresses how the patient's disorder may be functional to the family's needs.
    b. Biological theory does not emphasize avoidance; it emphasizes genetics and body processes.
    *c. Learning theory looks at dissociative symptoms in terms of rewards and punishments, the rewards being attention and avoidance of stressful situations. (p. 208)
    d. Psychoanalytic theory emphasizes repression of traumatic events.

11. *a. Dissociative amnesia often ends as abruptly as it begins. (p. 209)
    b. Multiple personality is often a lifelong problem; it is difficult to treat even with extensive psychotherapy.
    c. Hypochondriasis is usually a lifelong problem; it is as much a lifestyle as a psychological disorder.
    d. Factitious disorders are poorly understood but are believed to be linked to deep-seated and enduring problems.

12. a. The separation of consciousness is a fundamental symptom of the dissociative disorders.
    b. Irrational fears of objects are associated with phobias.
    c. Actual physical damage associated with stress is called stress-related illness or psychophysiological illness.
    *d. When physical symptoms are not caused by organic factors and do not seem to be voluntarily induced (as they are in factitious disorders), the diagnosis is somatoform disorder. (p. 211)

13. a. It is not believed that factitious disorders are complicated by depression and anxiety.
    *b. In factitious disorders the person may either inject himself/herself with agents that produce fever or consciously mimic physical disorders. (Focus 7.2; pp. 211–212)
    c. Dissociative disorders involve the division of consciousness.
    d. Factitious disorders are poorly understood, but repression is more involved in somatoform disorders.

14. *a. In the DSM-III-R, somatization disorder is diagnosed when thirteen or more separate physical complaints are reported; the number of complaints is a prime way of differentiating this disorder from hypochondriasis. (p. 214)
    b. Lingering and exaggerated pain are symptoms of somatoform pain disorder.
    c. Childhood abuse is more related to multiple personality than to somatization disorder.
    d. Somatization disorder is more common in women than in men.

15. *a. An older name for somatization disorder was *hysteria;* another term still used is *Briquet's syndrome.* (pp. 214, 223)
    b. *Phobia* is a term for an anxiety disorder, not a somatoform disorder.
    c. *Dementia praecox* is the older term for schizophrenia.
    d. *Manic depression* is the older term for the mood disorder called bipolar disorder.

16. a. Depersonalization is a dissociative disorder, not a somatoform disorder, which would involve physical complaints.
    b. Body dysmorphic disorder involves exaggerated concern about a body part, such as too much hair or too long a nose.
    *c. Conversion disorder involves somatic complaints that might be due to organic causes or sheer fakery. (p. 214)
    d. Dissociative amnesia is a memory problem, not one connected with somatic complaints.

17. a. Too little is known about body dysmorphic disorder to speculate on preexisting factors.
*b. Hypochondriasis is a preoccupation with illness that stems from actual illness and parental modeling. (p. 217)
c. The major preexisting factors in multiple personality seem to be child abuse and an ability to dissociate.
d. Too little is known about factitious disorders to speculate on preexisting factors.

18. *a. Psychoanalysts consider the primary gain in somatoform disorders to be relief from unconscious conflicts and the secondary gain to be attention from others, which meets dependency needs. (p. 218)
b. Biological theory stresses the pain and sensory thresholds of people with somatoform disorders.
c. Learning theory highlights the positive consequences of making physical complaints.
d. Humanistic theorists do not address the adaptive aspects of somatoform disorders.

19. a. The learning concept of extinction is more likely to prevent reinforcement from being given to the patient.
b. Since there are few, if any, physical causes for the complaints, hypnotherapy is not used to explain these.
c. Although biological theorists suggest that hypochondriacs have low pain thresholds, hypnotherapy is not used to raise the threshold.
*d. Hypnotherapy is usually used as a way of bringing unconscious feelings to consciousness. (p. 221)

20. *a. The impact of these complaints is to disrupt family functioning by taking the patient "off the hook" for his or her responsibilities. (p. 219)
b. Family therapists do not see these physical complaints as cries for help.
c. Family therapists tend to focus on current relationships, not childhood issues; also, abuse is more related to dissociative disorder.
d. Psychoanalysts, not family therapists, would stress the repression of emotions.

ANSWERS TO APPLICATION QUESTIONS

1. a. Dissociative fugue is characterized by amnesia, travel to a new place, and the establishment of a new identity.
b. Continuous amnesia is a rare form of dissociative disorder in which there is complete memory loss for the past until a specific point in time.
*c. Selective amnesia involves partial memory loss for a specific traumatic event. (p. 199)
d. Depersonalization disorder is characterized by feelings of body distortion and unreality.

2. a. Three separate personalities are commonly found in multiple personality.
*b. Typically, one or more of the separate personalities are unaware of the existence of the others. (p. 203)
c. In many cases, male personalities are found in females (as in the case of Sybil) and female personalities are found in males (as in the case of Billy Milligan).
d. Often, one of the personalities is sexually promiscuous or aggressive (taking on id qualities).

3. a. Behavior therapists stress how dissociation is a coping strategy for daily stress.
   b. Biological theorists have rarely commented on multiple personality, but would emphasize brain function or genetics if they did.
   c. Those who do not believe in multiple personality would argue that these people role-play or fake differences in personality.
   *d. Psychoanalysts emphasize the function of repression in all dissociative disorders. (p. 208)

4. *a. Depersonalization disorder involves complaints of feeling unreal; behaviorists would treat the problem through extinction of the complaints and rewards for "healthy talk." (p. 209)
   b. Multiple personality does not involve feelings of unreality; psychoanalysts would try to unlock unconscious factors.
   c. Somatoform pain disorder is about pain, not body distortions or feelings of unreality.
   d. The biological viewpoint would use medication for treatment.

5. a. Dissociative disorders involve a split in consciousness, usually involving memory loss, not physical symptoms.
   b. Anxiety disorders are not thought to be faked and involve only physical complaints that are secondary to the anxiety.
   c. Factitious disorders *are* under voluntary control.
   *d. Part of the problem of diagnosing somatoform disorders (particularly conversion) is that there are these other possible explanations for the complaints. (p. 214)

6. a. Conversion disorder usually involves paralysis or sensory problems (blurred vision, for instance), and there is rarely much "doctor shopping."
   b. Dissociative amnesia is characterized by memory loss, not physical complaints.
   *c. Somatization disorder (Briquet's syndrome) involves multiple (thirteen or more) physical complaints that often lead to unnecessary surgery. (p. 214)
   d. Hypochondriasis involves a preoccupation with health problems and often centers on one vague complaint.

7. *a. Conversion disorder often involves paralysis in an extremity without the accompanying atrophy of muscle tissue that occurs in physically caused paralysis. (p. 214)
   b. *Malingering* is when a person consciously fakes his or her symptoms.
   c. Somatization disorder involves multiple complaints.
   d. Hypochondriasis is characterized by a preoccupation with illness; rarely is the complaint about a specific dysfunction like leg paralysis.

8. a. *Hysteria* is an older name for somatization disorder; *Briquet's syndrome* is a synonym for somatization disorder.
   b. Conversion disorder usually involves one complaint (extremity paralysis or sensory loss), not the multiple complaints seen in somatization disorder.
   *c. Upset stomach is the kind of complaint registered by those with hypochondriasis; in somatization disorder, thirteen or more complaints would be made. (p. 215)
   d. Both malingering and factitious disorders rarely involve more than one problem.

9. a. Sociocultural theorists rarely deal with somatoform disorders, but might stress current conditions if they did.
   b. Humanistic theorists rarely deal with somatoform disorders, but might stress current experience if they did.
   c. Biological theorists stress the lower pain tolerance and heightened internal awareness of somatoform patients.
   *d. Psychoanalysts relate the physical complaints to repressed unpleasant memories and conflicts. (p. 218)

10. a. Psychoanalysts would stress the repression behind such complaints and the need for unconscious feelings to become conscious.
   b. Psychiatrists (medical doctors) are likely to be attentive to pain complaints rather than to suggest that they be ignored.
   *c. Behavior therapists want to extinguish pain complaints by reducing the attention patients receive for them. (p. 219)
   d. Humanistic therapists would accept as valid the subjective experience of the patient and would not encourage this kind of selective attention.

CHAPTER 8
Psychological Factors Affecting Medical Conditions

LEARNING OBJECTIVES

When you have mastered the material in Chapter 8, you should be able to:

1. Describe the sudden death syndrome and discuss it in relation to "culture shock" experienced by Hmong immigrants. Explain changes in terminology from "psychosomatic" to "psychophysiological." Discuss what behavioral medicine entails. (Focus 8.1; pp. 225–228)
2. Discuss the evidence presented and the questions raised in the Critical Thinking box "Should We Fear Our Birthdays?" (p. 226)
3. Describe the stages of the general adaptation model. Explain how stress can lead to life-threatening diseases such as heart attack. Discuss how psychological responses to crisis compare with Selye's general adaptation syndrome. (pp. 228–230)
4. Describe the life change model and the research evidence that life events cause illness. Discuss Lazarus's transaction model. (pp. 230–232)
5. Discuss how psychological and biological factors interact and affect the human immune system. Discuss how stress influences the development of Acquired Immune Deficiency Syndrome (AIDS). Describe the components of the immune system and evidence that stress decreases its functioning. (pp. 233–235)
6. Describe the mediating effects of control and hardiness on stress. Discuss the evidence concerning personality and mood influences on cancer development and cancer recovery, including current controversies over these issues in medical circles. (Focus 8.2; pp. 235–239)
7. Describe coronary heart disease and the influence of the Type A personality. Discuss current questions about the risk factor in Type A. (pp. 239–240)
8. Describe essential hypertension and peptic ulcers and the psychological factors that are related to both. Discuss gender and ethnic differences in hypertension. (pp. 240–243)
9. Describe the nature of migraine, tension, and cluster headaches. Describe asthma and the psychological factors related to it. (pp. 243–245)
10. Discuss the psychodynamic and biological perspectives on psychophysiological disorders, including the somatic weakness, autonomic response specificity, and general adaptation hypotheses. (pp. 245–247)
11. Discuss the behavioral perspective on psychophysiological disorders, including the influence of classical conditioning and operant conditioning. Describe how sociocultural factors influence coronary heart disease. (pp. 247–248)
12. Describe how treatment of psychophysiological disorders combines medicine with relaxation training and biofeedback. (pp. 248–249)

13. Describe cognitive-behavioral interventions for psychophysiological disorders. (pp. 249–250)

CHAPTER OUTLINE

1. **Psychological factors affecting medical conditions** (Focus 8.1; pp. 225–228) Anxiety can be great enough to kill people. *Sudden death syndrome,* incidents in which fright is the sole cause of death, may explain deaths among displaced peoples such as the Hmong in the United States. More commonly, death results from impaired heart function.

   In earlier versions of the DSM, certain disorders (psychosomatic disorders) were seen as stemming from psychological problems. Now, psychological problems are believed to be potential factors in almost any physical problem. Disorders that include both psychological and physical problems are called *psychophysiological disorders*. Unlike in conversion disorders, the tissue damage is real.

   The new field of *behavioral medicine* examines the psychological causes and mechanisms involved in disease as well as the behaviors and interventions that induce and prevent illness.

2. **Models for understanding stress** (pp. 228–232) *Stress* is an internal response to an external event or *stressor*. Stressors can be biological, psychological, or social. In the *general adaptation syndrome,* formulated by Selye, the body automatically reacts to prolonged stress in three stages: alarm, resistance, and exhaustion. Sustained stress may not only reduce resistance to disease, but also alter its course. In the case of heart attack, stress increases blood pressure and blood clotting, increasing the chances that clots or loose fat deposits will close off coronary arteries; stress can also lead to heart arrhythmias. Psychological responses to crisis, including *decompensation,* may follow Selye's three-part model, too.

   The *life change model* emphasizes the frequency and characteristics of the stressors. Cumulative changes, both positive and negative, are measured on the Social Readjustment Rating Scale (Holmes and Rahe) in life change units. The more units, the greater the likelihood and severity of illness, although it is too soon to say if stressors are the cause of illness.

   Lazarus's *transaction model* suggests that both the situation and the person's reaction to it explain stress-related illnesses. Perceptions of events are critical; those who deny any negative effect of a disease do more poorly than those who cope.

3. **Stress and the immune system** (pp. 233–235) Viral conditions such as herpes infections and even Acquired Immune Deficiency Syndrome (AIDS) may be influenced by emotional factors. Stress may reduce resistance to infections, trigger the expression of existing pathogens, or contribute to the disease process. Over short periods of time, depression seems to have no influence on the development of AIDS in infected individuals, but, over longer time periods, depression is associated with weaker immune function. Stress reactions release chemicals that suppress such immune system components as lymphocytes, phagocytes, and natural killer cells. Divorce, bereavement, and other stressors can impair immune functioning directly or indirectly through such poor health practices as sleeping less or drinking more.

4. **Mediating the effects of stressors** (pp. 235–236) Perception of control over the environment seems to reduce stress effects, as evidenced by rats' ability to reject cancer cells and by reduced mortality rates in nursing home patients given additional responsibilities. *Hardiness*, a personality trait characterized by openness to change, commitment, and a sense of personal control, appears to protect individuals against stress-related illness.

5. **Personality, mood states, and cancer** (Focus 8.2; pp. 236–238) Positive emotions and the expression of such negative ones as anger may be involved in the development, course, and recurrence of cancer. Several research method problems make these propositions controversial. Even well-designed studies linking anger expression and breast cancer have alternative explanations. However, in one prospective study, MMPI depression scores predicted cancer even when lifestyle and family history factors were taken into account.

6. **Psychological involvement in specific physical disorders** (pp. 239–245) *Coronary heart disease*, a narrowing of arteries to or in the heart, kills more than 600,000 Americans each year. In addition to biological factors, the Type A personality pattern is involved in its occurrence. Type A's are time-pressured, hostile, and competitive. Hostility seems to be the most significant risk factor, although depression and anxiety are also important.

   Essential hypertension (high blood pressure) can lead to heart attacks and other fatal disorders. Higher stress levels correlate with higher blood pressure. Anger, expressed and unexpressed, may be related to chronic hypertension, particularly for men. Hypertension is a greater problem for blacks than for whites, perhaps because of differences in psychosocial resources.

   Peptic ulcers, sores in the digestive system, afflict one in ten Americans at some point in their lives. They may be caused by excessive pepsinogen (a digestive system chemical) and other biological abnormalities, along with psychological conflicts.

   Stress contributes to all three types of headaches: *migraine headaches*, *tension headaches*, and *cluster headaches*. The classic migraine headache has neurological warning signs, such as distorted vision or numbness in the body, followed by intense, throbbing pain. In the common migraine, there may be no neurological symptoms. Although the name implies it, tension headaches are not necessarily caused by muscular tension; psychological factors are often the precipitants. Cluster headaches are excruciating and center on the area around the eye. Relaxation, biofeedback, and cognitive therapy show promise in treating headaches.

   Asthma is a respiratory disorder that makes breathing difficult, and has led to an increasing number of deaths. Most sufferers are adolescents or younger children who have allergies. However, psychological factors involving family dynamics can also be involved.

7. **Perspectives on etiology** (pp. 245–248) According to Alexander, a psychoanalyst, each type of psychophysiological disorder is caused by a specific unconscious conflict. Research support for this is not strong.

   There is some evidence that genetics influences the rate of psychophysiological disorder. Somatic weakness theory proposes that certain organs are weakened by earlier experience and are vulnerable to disease under stress. The autonomic response specificity hypothesis argues that each person has a unique way of responding to stressors. The *general adaptation syndrome* may be combined with the previous two theories to understand illness as a disease of adaptation.

   Classical conditioning may explain how certain stress reactions can generalize to a wide range of stressful stimuli. However, this perspective cannot account for the original reaction. Operant approaches note that internal processes originally thought to be involuntary can be influenced by external reinforcement and biofeedback.

   Japanese who retain close social and emotional ties and maintain traditional values seem to have lower coronary heart disease levels than acculturated Japanese Americans.

8. **Treatment of psychophysiological disorders: Relaxation training, biofeedback, and cognitive-behavioral interventions** (pp. 248–250) In *relaxation training*, individuals are taught to alternately tense and relax muscle groups in the body. In *biofeedback* training, clients are informed about small internal changes (such as in blood pressure and heart rate). They

learn to control these internal processes and eventually do not need the monitoring devices. Essentially an operant technique, biofeedback has been used to treat a range of psychophysiological disorders, from headache to asthma. Stress management programs often include self-instructional techniques and cognitive restructuring.

9. **Critical Thinking: Should We Fear Our Birthdays?** (p. 226) Recent research on the timing of the deaths of nearly 3 million people shows that women are more likely to die the week following their birthdays than any other week; men are more likely to die the week before their birthdays.

KEY TERMS

Fill-in-the-Blanks Quiz

1. A number of disciplines that study social, psychological, and lifestyle influences are collectively called ___________.

2. The concept developed by Kobasa and Maddi that refers to an individual's ability to deal well with stress is called ___________.

3. Severe headaches that result from the dilation of cerebral blood vessels after an initial contraction are called ___________.

4. The respiratory disorder characterized by attacks in which breathing becomes extremely difficult as a result of constriction of lung airways is called ___________.

5. The therapeutic technique in which the individual acquires the ability to relax the muscles of the body is called ___________.

6. The cardiovascular disease in which the flow of blood and oxygen to the heart is restricted because of narrowed arteries in or near the heart is called ___________.

7. An open sore within the digestive system is called a(n) ___________.

8. Unexpected death that may be brought on by stress and in most cases is also due to an underlying coronary condition is called ___________.

9. A physical or psychological demand placed on an individual by some external situation is called a(n) ___________.

10. The therapeutic technique in which the individual receives information about internal physiological functions and learns to control them is called ___________.

11. A headache that may be produced by prolonged contraction of scalp and neck muscles is called a(n) ___________.

12. High blood pressure with no known organic cause is called ___________.

13. A model that assumes that the body's physical and psychological reaction to biological stressors involves three stages of response is called the ___________.

14. A physical disorder that has a strong psychological basis or component is called a(n) ___________.

15. An individual's internal reaction to the physical or psychological demands placed on him or her by the environment is called ___________.

16. The loss of the ability to successfully deal with stress, resulting in more primitive coping methods, is called ___________.

17. The hypothesis that all life changes can act as stressors is called the ___________.

18. The hypothesis that stress is a transaction between the person and the situation is called the ___________.

Answers to Fill-in-the-Blanks Quiz

1. behavioral medicine
2. hardiness
3. migraine headaches
4. asthma
5. relaxation training
6. coronary heart disease
7. peptic ulcer
8. sudden death syndrome
9. stressor
10. biofeedback training
11. tension headache
12. essential hypertension
13. general adaptation syndrome
14. psychophysiological disorder
15. stress
16. decompensation
17. life change model
18. transaction model of stress

FACT AND CONCEPT QUESTIONS

1. It is an extreme example of the effects of psychological stress on illness because it leads to death. It has occurred with disturbing frequency in Hmong immigrants to the United States. What is "it"?
   a. Essential hypertension
   b. Peptic ulcers
   c. Sudden death syndrome
   d. Coronary heart disease

2. Because any physical disorder can have a psychological component, the term now being used by psychologists to describe stress-related illnesses is
   a. *psychosomatic.*
   b. *adaptive.*
   c. *neuropsychological.*
   d. *psychophysiological.*

3. *Alarm, resistance,* and *exhaustion* are terms associated with the ___________ model of stress-related illness.
   a. general adaptation
   b. life change
   c. classical conditioning
   d. operant conditioning

4. In the stages of crisis decompensation, the first stage is characterized by ____________, whereas the second features ____________.
   a. increases in catecholamine levels; an increase in NK cells
   b. dependency on others for support; panic and confusion
   c. panic and confusion; attempted resolution of the problem
   d. panic and confusion; tissue damage and illness

5. According to the life change model of psychophysiological disorders,
   a. only positive life changes produce stress.
   b. the accumulation of even small changes increases the likelihood of illness.
   c. the way a person interprets the stressfulness of an event determines the likelihood of illness.
   d. after a stage of resistance, the body "gives out," and tissue damage results.

6. The greater the number of life change units experienced in a year's time,
   a. the lower the likelihood of illness.
   b. the more serious the illness that is experienced.
   c. the hardier the personality as a result.
   d. the stronger the immune system as a result.

7. The transaction model of stress argues that
   a. a person's upbringing determines how he or she will respond to stressors.
   b. the greater the number of negative life events, the greater the risk of serious illness.
   c. biology plays little or no role in the development of psychophysiological disorders.
   d. stressors negatively affect people because of the way people perceive and cope with them.

8. As a result of marital separation or bereavement, people often experience
   a. an increase in NK cells.
   b. impairments in the immune system.
   c. an increase in phagocytes and lymphocytes.
   d. a lowering of their life change units.

9. Research on nursing home residents indicates that those who live the longest
   a. have the highest catecholamine levels.
   b. relinquish most of their decision-making power to the nursing home staff.
   c. tend to suppress their anger.
   d. are allowed to make certain decisions that increase their sense of control.

10. Openness to change, commitment, and a sense of personal control are all components of the personality pattern called
    a. hardiness.
    b. Type A.
    c. general adaptation.
    d. Type B.

11. The majority of psychologists and physicians believe that psychological moods
    a. have absolutely no effect on the progression of cancer.
    b. completely determine whether or not a person develops cancer.
    c. are an important factor in the development of cancer only for women.
    d. may have an impact on cancer, but research is too inconclusive to be sure.

12. Recent research examining depression before cancer was diagnosed found that
    a. the cancer death rate was two times greater for people with high depression scores than for those with low depression scores.
    b. cancer was unrelated to depression scores.
    c. the cancer death rate was two times lower for people with high depression scores than for those with low depression scores.
    d. high depression scores predicted cancer death, but only when people were also anger suppressors.

13. The key element in the relationship between Type A and heart disease seems to be
    a. the Type A's tendency to do everything quickly.
    b. the Type A's tendency to relax too much.
    c. the fact that Type A behavior reduces catecholamine levels.
    d. the Type A's tendency to be hostile.

14. When a person has high blood pressure without physiological reason, the disorder is called
    a. coronary heart disease.
    b. essential hypertension.
    c. angina pectoris.
    d. psychosomatic blood pressure.

15. An African American who is excessively angry and deficient in psychosocial resources is believed to be at particularly high risk for developing
    a. peptic ulcer.
    b. asthma.
    c. high blood pressure.
    d. defective NK cells.

16. Coronary heart disease is related to Type A personality; peptic ulcer is
    a. related to Type B personality.
    b. related to high depression scores.
    c. not related to any one personality pattern.
    d. related to hardiness.

17. Headaches that are preceded by neurological symptoms such as blurred vision and that are caused by uncontrolled blood flow to the brain are called
    a. essential headaches.
    b. classic migraine headaches.
    c. cluster headaches.
    d. common tension headaches.

18. The concept of ____________ explains how bronchial irritation can become associated with stressors and other stimuli so that conflicts produce asthma attacks.
    a. operant conditioning
    b. the hardy personality
    c. general adaptation
    d. classical conditioning

19. The autonomic response specificity hypothesis suggests that
    a. if a stressor goes on long enough, any person's body will become exhausted.
    b. each individual has a unique way of reacting to stressors.
    c. each type of psychophysiological disorder has a specific conflict associated with it.
    d. certain body parts respond to certain levels of life change.

20. The voluntary control of a physiological response such as heart rate can be demonstrated by using
    a. biofeedback.
    b. progressive relaxation.
    c. classical conditioning.
    d. modeling.

APPLICATION QUESTIONS

1. Dr. Morgan conducts research investigating how personality style may increase one's ability to withstand stress, and she teaches large groups about healthy lifestyles. Dr. Morgan's interests are in the new field of
    a. behavioral medicine.
    b. neuropsychology.
    c. somatic medicine.
    d. cardiology.

2. Gina's reactions to a snarling dog are a rapid heartbeat and the secretion of hormones by her adrenal glands that temporarily reduce the efficiency of her immune system. These reactions are
    a. an illustration of the somatic weakness hypothesis.
    b. the exhaustion stage of the general adaptation syndrome.
    c. an illustration of the hardy personality.
    d. the alarm stage of the general adaptation syndrome.

3. In the past three months, Vera has changed jobs twice, has learned that her parents plan to divorce, and has gone on a vacation. The life change model of stress suggests that
    a. only the vacation is a stressor.
    b. the way she interprets these events will determine whether or not she becomes ill.
    c. all these changes increase her chances of becoming ill.
    d. she is now in the alarm stage of adapting to stressors.

4. Mr. Panzano, upon learning that he has lung cancer, considers his life to be a failure. He gives up all hope of being successfully treated and becomes depressed. Mr. Panzano's reaction illustrates what the ____________ perspective on stress emphasizes.
    a. life change
    b. transaction
    c. classical conditioning
    d. somatic weakness

5. Jill is being transferred to Tokyo. She sees this as a challenge and an opportunity. She believes that she is in control of her life and that she must remain open to change. Jill illustrates
   a. the Type A personality.
   b. learned helplessness.
   c. the hardy personality.
   d. classically conditioned adaptation.

6. Barbara has never outwardly expressed anger in her life. On the MMPI, she shows a very high depression score. What physical illness is she at higher risk for developing?
   a. Peptic ulcer
   b. Coronary heart disease
   c. Cancer
   d. Asthma

7. John, age 36, is a poor black man with a Type A personality. He is almost always angry and upset. John is at highest risk for developing which disorders?
   a. Asthma and migraine headaches
   b. Essential hypertension and coronary heart disease
   c. Cancer and migraine headaches
   d. Peptic ulcer and asthma

8. Dr. George says, "Peptic ulcer is related to excessive gastric activity, which is often preceded by stressful events. Type B personalities are particularly at risk. The most common site for the ulcer is in the small intestine." What part of Dr. George's statement is inaccurate?
   a. Type B personality is unrelated to ulcers.
   b. The most common site is the stomach.
   c. Ulcers are unrelated to gastric activity.
   d. Gastric activity and stressful events are unrelated.

9. Don says, "When I was small, I was exposed to severe air pollution that damaged my lungs. Now, whenever I am under stress, I develop a bad cough and wheezing." Don's explanation reflects the ____________ hypothesis on psychophysiological illnesses.
   a. operant conditioning
   b. psychoanalytic
   c. neurotransmitter
   d. autonomic weakness

10. To treat his hypertension, Carl is hooked up to a machine that shows small changes in his blood pressure. The information that he is lowering his blood pressure acts as reinforcement. Carl's treatment is
    a. progressive relaxation.
    b. cognitive restructuring.
    c. biofeedback.
    d. implosive therapy.

ANSWERS TO FACT AND CONCEPT QUESTIONS

1. a. Essential hypertension is a common disorder involving high blood pressure without obvious reasons for that condition.
   b. Peptic ulcer is another common disorder involving open sores in the gastrointestinal tract.
   *c. A disturbing number of Hmong immigrants have died in their sleep for no other reason than fright. (Focus 8.1; p. 227)
   d. Coronary heart disease is the most common reason for death in all groups in the United States.

2. a. "Psychosomatic" is the old term that implied that only some disorders were related to psychological states.
   b. "Adaptive" may be related to the general adaptation syndrome view of psychophysiological illnesses, but this represents only one viewpoint.
   c. "Neuropsychological" is a term reserved for conditions involving brain damage; psychophysiological disorders can affect any system in the body.
   *d. In order to convey the idea that any physical condition can be related to psychological states, the new term used is "psychophysiological." (p. 227)

3. *a. There are three stages in the general adaptation syndrome: alarm, resistance, and exhaustion. (p. 229)
   b. The life change model stresses the role of small and large life events; it simply predicts that higher life change scores lead to greater illness.
   c. Classical conditioning explains how different stressful situations may elicit the same physiological reaction.
   d. Operant conditioning examines the reinforcements that exist for developing an illness.

4. a. Catecholamines and NK (natural killer) cells are related to biological processes in stress; NK cells decrease during stress.
   b. Panic and confusion are early responses to stress in decompensation theory.
   *c. Decompensation theory suggests that panic and confusion are first responses, followed by attempts at resolution and, if these are unsuccessful, a stage of apathy and withdrawal. (p. 230)
   d. Decompensation deals with psychological consequences, not physical ones such as tissue damage.

5. a. The life change model originally looked at both positive and negative changes as stressors; more recent work considers negative events as the sole influence.
   *b. Life changes, regardless of type, are seen as piling together to reduce the person's coping ability (p. 230)
   c. The transaction model stresses the cognitive aspects of coping, such as interpretation.
   d. The general adaptation model consists of alarm, resistance, and exhaustion stages.

6. a. The correlation is positive between life change units and likelihood of illness.
   *b. The correlation is positive between life change units and severity of illness. (p. 232)
   c. Life change theory does not examine such personality variables as hardiness.
   d. As the number of life changes increases, the immune system is weakened.

7. a. Psychoanalytic theory would stress early childhood experiences, although it is conceivable that individual differences in coping could be related to such experiences.
   b. Life change theory emphasizes the role of negative life events.
   c. The transaction model accepts the importance of biology, but adds the influence of cognitions and coping strategies.
   *d. Perceptions and methods of coping are central to the transaction model of stress. (p. 232)

8. a. When people are under stress, their NK cells are less responsive.
   *b. A variety of impairments in the immune system, including decreased NK cell responsiveness, are found during stress. (p. 234)
   c. Phagocytes and lymphocytes are components of the immune system; they are weakened by stress.
   d. Separation and bereavement are life events associated with high numbers of life change units.

9. a. High catecholamine levels are a sign of stress and may lead to early death rather than long life.
   b. Reduced personal control is associated with shortened life span in nursing homes.
   c. Suppression of anger is, if anything, related to an increased likelihood of essential hypertension.
   *d. Research by Rodin and Langer indicates that personal control in nursing home residents is associated with longer life. (p. 235)

10. *a. The hardy personality features an openness to change, a commitment to a life course, and a sense of being able to control future events. (p. 236)
   b. The Type A personality is characterized by hostility, time pressure, and competitiveness.
   c. *General adaptation* is a term used to describe a generic response to stress that involves the stages of alarm, resistance, and exhaustion.
   d. The Type B personality is characterized by the ability to sequence tasks and relax between work efforts.

11. a. There is too much evidence linking personality and cancer to dismiss the entire topic.
   b. Cancer is related to diet, pollution, genetics, and many other nonpersonality dimensions.
   c. There is no evidence that women alone develop cancer because of emotions.
   *d. There are too many methodological problems in the current research to permit definite conclusions about the role of moods in cancer. (Focus 8.2; p. 238)

12. *a. Research shows that high depression scores on the MMPI predict future mortality due to cancer. (p. 237)
   b. Cancer is related to high scores on the depression scale of the MMPI.
   c. The reverse of this is true: As depression scores increase, so does the risk of later cancer (at least in one study).
   d. The research reports no interaction between depression and anger suppression.

13. a. Although Type A's work fast, this is not the key element in the personality's relationship to heart disease.
   b. The Type A is unable to relax.
   c. Type A behavior seems to increase catecholamine levels, a biological sign of the stress response.
   *d. Hostility is the component of the Type A personality that is most closely associated with heart disease. (p. 240)

14. a. *Coronary heart disease* is a more general term for conditions that reduce the efficiency and longevity of the heart.
*b. Essential hypertension exists when blood pressure is high, but this cannot be traced to a direct cause. (p. 241)
c. *Angina pectoris* is a term for pains in the chest caused by heart disease.
d. *Psychosomatic blood pressure* is a made-up term.

15. a. Peptic ulcer is not clearly related to any personality pattern or ethnicity.
b. Asthma is primarily a problem in youths, and is not related to any particular personality pattern or ethnicity.
*c. Poor blacks (who have fewer psychosocial resources) and those who are either excessive anger expressors or suppressors are most likely to have essential hypertension. (p. 242)
d. There is no evidence that defective NK cells are related to ethnicity or personality.

16. a. Peptic ulcer does not seem to be related to any one personality.
b. High depression scores seem related to cancer, not peptic ulcer.
*c. No particular personality pattern is associated with peptic ulcer. (p. 243)
d. Hardiness is associated with resistance to physical disorders, not with a condition such as peptic ulcer.

17. a. *Essential headache* is a made-up term.
*b. Classic migraines have such neurological signs as blurred vision and tingling sensations prior to the headache itself. (p. 243)
c. Cluster headaches are not believed to be related to blood flow; they involve excruciating pain around the eye.
d. Common tension headaches are not believed to be related to blood flow.

18. a. Operant conditioning stresses the consequences of responses; it would examine the rewards for having an attack.
b. Hardiness is associated with reduced risk of illness in the face of stressors.
c. General adaptation is a model that proposes a generic response to stressors.
*d. Classical conditioning focuses on the pairing of stimuli and would explain the generalization of attacks to a variety of stimuli. (p. 245).

19. a. The general adaptation model predicts that exhaustion occurs after a stressor has gone on long enough.
*b. Autonomic response specificity argues that each person has a unique way of reacting to stressors. (p. 247).
c. Psychoanalytic theory (Alexander) suggests that each disorder is associated with a particular unconscious conflict.
d. There is no theory that suggests that body parts react differently to different levels of stress.

20. *a. Biofeedback is an operant procedure that gives one control over autonomic responses such as heart rate and skin temperature. (p. 249)
b. Progressive relaxation (Jacobson) involves tensing and relaxing muscle groups throughout the body.
c. Classical conditioning is a passive process, unlike the operant conditioning that occurs in biofeedback.
d. Modeling entails the imitation of others; none of this occurs in biofeedback.

ANSWERS TO APPLICATION QUESTIONS

1. *a. Behavioral medicine is a field that examines how personal behavior and thought affect the development of and recovery from illness. (p. 228)
   b. Neuropsychology is exclusively concerned with the workings of the central nervous system.
   c. *Somatic medicine,* a made-up term, would focus solely on the physiological side of illness.
   d. Cardiology is a subdiscipline of medicine that studies the heart.

2. a. The somatic weakness hypothesis would be illustrated by Gina having heart trouble after this episode.
   b. The exhaustion stage is illustrated by the breakdown of tissues that have experienced prolonged resistance.
   c. The hardy personality is one that shows openness to change, commitment, and a sense of personal control.
   *d. The first stage of the general adaptation syndrome (alarm) involves a general mobilization of body functions that reduces immune system strength. (p. 229)

3. a. The life change model would consider all the events as examples of stressors.
   b. The interpretation of events is a key component of the transaction model.
   *c. The life change model suggests that all events—negative and positive, large and small—increase the likelihood of illness. (p. 230)
   d. The general adaptation syndrome suggests that alarm occurs soon after a stressor.

4. a. The life change perspective emphasizes the external environment.
   *b. The transaction perspective suggests that the way we interpret life events affects how stressed we become and how we cope with those reactions. (p. 232)
   c. Classical conditioning explains how a range of stimuli can produce the same stress reactions.
   d. Somatic weakness theory proposes that, after an earlier illness, certain body parts are vulnerable to impairment during stress.

5. a. The Type A personality is hostile and time-pressured.
   b. Learned helplessness involves a sense that personal control is lost.
   *c. According to Maddi and Kobasa, people like Jill are hardy in that they seem less vulnerable to stress-related illness than others. (p. 236)
   d. Classical conditioning may explain stress responses to various stimuli, but it has nothing to do with the cognitive factors described here.

6. a. There is no evidence that peptic ulcer is related to a particular personality pattern.
   b. Coronary heart disease is related to hostility, but not to suppressed anger.
   *c. Cancer has been found to be more common both in people who are extreme anger suppressors and in those with high depression scores on the MMPI. (p. 237)
   d. Asthma is primarily a biological disorder, although fear of separation from others is related to some attacks.

7. a. Ethnicity and personality are unrelated to asthma and migraines.
   *b. Essential hypertension is related to race and anger expression; coronary heart disease is related to Type A personality. (pp. 240, 242)
   c. Cancer may be related to depression and anger suppression, but migraines are not related to any of the factors listed in John's case.
   d. Ethnicity and personality are unrelated to peptic ulcer and asthma.

8. *a. Type B's who are able to relax are not especially prone to ulcers. (p. 240)
   b. Most ulcers are found in the small intestine and are called duodenal ulcers.
   c. The greater the gastric activity (and acid secretion), the greater the likelihood of ulcer.
   d. Soon after stressful events occur, gastric activity often increases.

9. a. Operant conditioning would focus on the consequences of a wheezing attack, such as increased attention.
   b. Psychoanalytic thinking would examine the unconscious conflicts underlying a wheezing attack.
   c. Neurotransmitters play no role in the development of a cough.
   *d. Autonomic weakness theory suggests that each person has a unique physiological reaction to all types of stressful situations. (p. 247)

10. a. Progressive relaxation involves the tensing and relaxing of muscle groups.
   b. Cognitive restructuring features changing the way people think about stressors and their ability to cope.
   *c. Biofeedback is an operant procedure that uses machinery to give information that leads to the voluntary altering of internal processes. (p. 249)
   d. Implosive therapy is used to extinguish fears by having people experience high levels of anxiety.

PART 3
Disorders Involving Conduct

CHAPTER 9
Personality Disorders and Impulse Control Disorders

LEARNING OBJECTIVES

When you have mastered the material in Chapter 9, you should be able to:

1. Discuss the general characteristics of personality disorders and the difficulties in diagnosing them. List the three clusters of personality disorders and the proposed disorders of depressive, negativistic, self-defeating, and sadistic personality disorder. (Focus 9.1; pp. 253–255)
2. Describe and differentiate among the characteristics of paranoid, schizoid, and schizotypal personality disorders. Discuss how schizoid and schizotypal personality disorders are differentiated from schizophrenia. (pp. 255–258)
3. Describe and differentiate among the characteristics of histrionic, narcissistic, antisocial, and borderline personality disorders. (pp. 258–261)
4. Discuss the causal explanations for borderline personality disorder and its estimated prevalence. (pp. 261–263)
5. Describe and differentiate among the characteristics of avoidant, dependent, and obsessive-compulsive personality disorders. (pp. 263–265)
6. Describe the characteristics and incidence of antisocial personality disorder and how it is differentiated from criminal behavior. Explain why it is a difficult population to study (pp. 265–268)
7. Describe and discuss the psychoanalytic, family learning/socialization, and genetic etiological theories of antisocial personality. (pp. 268–269)
8. Discuss the effects that central nervous system and autonomic nervous system abnormalities have on antisocial personality. Discuss the role of fearlessness, lack of anxiety, underarousal, learning deficits, and thrill seeking in the disorder. (Focus 9.2; pp. 269–274)
9. Describe treatments for antisocial personality and their success. (pp. 274–275)
10. Describe and discuss the etiological and treatment considerations of personality disorders in general. (pp. 275–278)
11. Describe and differentiate among the following impulse control disorders: intermittent explosive disorder, kleptomania, pathological gambling, pyromania, and trichotillomania. (pp. 278–282)
12. Discuss the various etiological explanations for impulse control disorders. Compare the two explanatory "camps" for these disorders. Review the treatments for impulse control disorders and their success. (pp. 282–283)

CHAPTER OUTLINE

1. **The personality disorders** (Focus 9.1; pp. 253–255) *Personality disorders* involve inflexible and maladaptive behavior patterns that produce personal and social difficulties, distress, or problems in functioning in society. Diagnosis is difficult because symptoms represent extremes of normal personality traits, are rarely stable across situations, and may overlap with other disorders. Further, clinicians often render diagnoses inconsistent with DSM criteria. Personality disorders reflect long-term patterns that start in adolescence. In the DSM-IV, personality disorders are recorded on Axis II.

   DSM-IV lists ten personality disorders in three clusters: odd or eccentric behaviors; dramatic, emotional, or erratic behaviors; and anxious or fearful behaviors.

   Four new categories of personality disorder have been proposed. Depressive personality disorder is characterized by low self-esteem and unhappiness. Symptoms of negativistic personality disorder are passive resistance to demands for social or occupational performance and a critical attitude toward others. Individuals with self-defeating personality disorder avoid or undermine pleasurable encounters and are drawn to experiences of suffering. Critics feel that this category will be unfairly applied to battered women. Sadistic personality disorder is characterized by cruelty toward family members and subordinates but rarely toward people in authority positions.

2. **Disorders characterized by odd or eccentric behaviors** (pp. 255–258) *Paranoid personality disorder* is characterized by suspiciousness, hypersensitivity, and lack of emotion. *Schizoid personality disorder* is marked by voluntary social isolation. In order to avoid conflicts and emotional involvements, these people withdraw from others or comply superficially with requests from others. *Schizotypal personality disorder* involves odd thoughts and actions, such as speech oddities or beliefs in personal magical powers. However, individuals with this disorder are confused by their odd thoughts. Both schizoid and schizotypal personality disorders may have a genetic link to schizophrenia.

3. **Disorders characterized by dramatic, emotional, or erratic behaviors** (pp. 258–263) *Histrionic personality disorder* is marked by self-dramatization, exaggerated emotional expression, and attention-seeking behaviors. *Narcissistic personality disorder* involves an exaggerated sense of self-importance. *Antisocial personality disorder* involves exploitation of others, irresponsibility, and guiltlessness. *Borderline personality disorder* is characterized by extreme fluctuations in mood: borderline personalities may be friendly one day and hostile the next. They also feel lost and empty; they engage in self-destructive behaviors. The core aspects seem to be difficulty regulating emotions and intense, unstable relationships. Prevalence figures are not available, but some researchers feel it affects between 1 and 4 percent of the population.

4. **Disorders characterized by anxious or fearful behaviors** (pp. 263–265) Individuals with *avoidant personality disorder* desire interpersonal contact but demand uncritical acceptance; they avoid situations that might lead to criticism. Their primary defense mechanism is fantasy. *Dependent personality disorder* is characterized by an extreme lack of self-confidence, reliance on others for decisions, and an ingrained assumption that they are inadequate and must be cared for by others. *Obsessive-compulsive personality disorder* is marked by excessive perfectionism, devotion to details, an inability to express warmth, and indecisiveness.

5. **Antisocial personality disorder** (pp. 265–267) Cleckley's (1976) classic description of *antisocial personality disorder* includes superficial charm, shallow emotions and lack of guilt,

unplanned actions, failure to learn from experiences, absence of anxiety, and irresponsibility. DSM-IV criteria do not include lack of anxiety, shallow emotions, failure to learn, and superficial charm. They do include being at least 18 years old, a history of breaking laws since age 15, aggressiveness, and impulsivity. People with antisocial personality are also called sociopaths and psychopaths. Criminals are not necessarily antisocial personalities; they often have a sense of loyalty to others and feelings of guilt, which are missing in antisocial personalities. Primary psychopaths feel no guilt over antisocial behaviors, secondary psychopaths do.

The incidence of antisocial personality disorder is estimated at 3 percent for American men and 1 percent for American women.

6. **Explanations of antisocial personality disorder** (Focus 9.2; pp. 267–274) Psychoanalytic theory stresses a lack of parental identification and consequent superego deficiency. Family/socialization theories stress parental rejection and modeling of antisocial behavior by fathers. Poor parental supervision predicts delinquency better than poverty. Genetic theory is supported by evidence of MZ twin concordance and greater likelihood of the disorder in the adoptees of antisocial parents. Central nervous system theory maintains that antisocial personalities have abnormal EEGs. Autonomic nervous system theory stresses the low anxiety level and thrill-seeking of antisocial personalities to counteract general underarousal. Eysenck and Lykken have done research to support these ideas. Lykken and Farley suggest that psychopaths and heroes have traits of fearlessness or thrill seeking in common (they are called "Big T's"). "Little t's" prefer certainty and low conflict. Antisocial personalities are also influenced by the kind and timing of punishment.

7. **Treatment of antisocial personality disorder** (pp. 274–275) Due to their lack of anxiety, antisocial personalities are poorly motivated to change. Behavior modification and cognitive therapies have been somewhat helpful, but effective treatments for antisocial personality are rare.

8. **Etiological and treatment considerations for personality disorders in general** (pp. 275–278) There has been little empirical research on the causes of personality disorders. Women are more likely to be diagnosed histrionic; men are more likely to be diagnosed obsessive-compulsive, antisocial, and paranoid. Gender differences may be due to bias in clinicians, the assessment instruments used, or sampling (oversampling men in Veterans Administration hospitals). Because diagnosis is unreliable, research is hampered. Personality in general is due to both genetic and environmental factors. Effective treatment is hard to find.

9. **Disorders of impulse control** (pp. 278–282) *Impulse control disorders* are unrelated to personality disorders and are included in this chapter for the sake of convenience. These disorders involve an inability to resist the temptation to perform some act, a feeling of tension before the act, and a sense of excitement, release, and sometimes guilt afterwards. *Intermittent explosive disorder* is marked by brief episodes of losing control, leading to destruction of property or assaults on other people. *Kleptomania* involves stealing, even when the article is not needed. *Pathological gambling* involves an inability to resist impulses to gamble and afflicts 2 to 3 percent of American adults. *Pyromaniacs* repeatedly and deliberately set fires without the motive of revenge. Children who are fire-setters are more often boys than girls and have problems with impulsivity and hostility. *Trichotillomania* is the inability to refrain from pulling out one's hair.

10. **Etiology and treatment of impulse control disorders** (pp. 282–283) Little research has been done on the causes of these disorders. In some ways, impulse control disorders are similar to obsessive-compulsive, substance abuse, and sexual disorders. Psychoanalytic theory stresses sexual symbolism, behavioral theory focuses on reinforcement and modeling, and biogenic theory points out greater thrill-seeking in pathological gamblers. Lesieur (1989) notes two schools of thought: Impulse control problems range on a continuum, or they are disease-like (one either has it or not). Behavioral and cognitive treatments have had some success, as have insight therapies and self-help groups such as Gamblers Anonymous.

KEY TERMS

Fill-in-the-Blanks Quiz

1. The personality disorder characterized by intense fluctuations in mood, self-image, and interpersonal relationships is called ___________.

2. The personality disorder characterized by failure to conform to social rules, lack of guilt feelings for wrongdoing, and superficial relationships is called ___________.

3. The impulse control disorder in which there is a recurrent failure to resist impulses to steal objects is called ___________.

4. The personality disorder characterized by self-dramatization, exaggerated emotions, and attention-seeking behavior is called ___________.

5. The group of maladaptive behavior patterns that stem from immature or distorted personality structure are called ___________.

6. The personality disorder characterized by unwarranted suspiciousness, hypersensitivity, and a reluctance to confide in others is called ___________.

7. The disorders characterized by a failure to resist the temptation to perform an act that is harmful to oneself or others are called ___________.

8. The personality disorder characterized by such oddities of thinking and behavior as frequent digressions in speech or a belief in personal magical powers is called ___________.

9. The impulse control disorder that is marked mainly by deliberate fire setting is called ___________.

10. The impulse control disorder characterized by an inability to resist pulling out one's hair is called ___________.

11. The personality disorder characterized by a fear of rejection and humiliation, and, as a result, reluctance to enter into social relationships, is called ___________.

12. The personality disorder characterized by extreme reliance on others and an unwillingness to assume responsibility is called ___________.

13. The impulse control disorder characterized by an inability to refrain from gambling is called ___________.

14. The personality disorder characterized by social isolation and emotional coldness is called ___________.

15. The personality disorder characterized by perfectionism, indecision, devotion to details, and lack of personal warmth is called ___________.

16. The personality disorder characterized by an exaggerated sense of self-importance is called ___________.

17. The impulse control disorder marked by loss of control over aggressive impulses is called ___________.

Answers to Fill-in-the Blanks Quiz

1. borderline personality disorder
2. antisocial personality disorder
3. kleptomania
4. histrionic personality disorder
5. personality disorders
6. paranoid personality disorder
7. impulse control disorders
8. schizotypal personality disorder
9. pyromania
10. trichotillomania
11. avoidant personality disorder
12. dependent personality disorder
13. pathological gambling
14. schizoid personality disorder
15. obsessive-compulsive personality disorder
16. narcissistic personality disorder
17. intermittent explosive disorder

FACT AND CONCEPT QUESTIONS

1. Which statement below is *true* concerning the personality disorders?
   a. They are recorded on Axis I of the DSM-IV.
   b. They have symptoms that can overlap with those of other disorders.
   c. Symptoms first appear in young adulthood.
   d. They are characterized by an inability to resist temptation.

2. Which proposed personality disorder in the DSM-IV has been criticized because it might be unfairly applied to battered women?
   a. Negativistic personality disorder
   b. Sadistic personality disorder
   c. Dependent personality disorder
   d. Self-defeating personality disorder

3. The principal feature of paranoid personality disorder is
   a. excessive attention to details and general perfectionism.
   b. wide fluctuations in mood and self-image.
   c. unwarranted suspiciousness.
   d. a desire to be alone.

4. Schizoid personality disorder differs from schizotypal personality disorder in that in schizoid personality disorder there
   a. is a withdrawal from other people.
   b. are psychotic mood swings.
   c. is unwarranted suspiciousness of other people.
   d. are odd thoughts that border on delusions.

5. Which of the following statements about histrionic personality disorder is *true*?
   a. It is more commonly reported in women than in men.
   b. It is characterized by withdrawal from other people.
   c. It is related to abnormally low levels of arousal.
   d. It can mimic the symptoms of paranoid schizophrenia.

6. How do narcissistic personalities relate to other people?
   a. Narcissistic personalities do not trust others.
   b. Narcissistic personalities rely on others' opinions.
   c. Narcissistic personalities feel superior to others.
   d. Narcissistic personalities avoid other people.

7. Extreme fluctuations in mood, a sense of being empty, and intense interpersonal relationships are characteristics of
   a. borderline personality disorder.
   b. antisocial personality disorder.
   c. histrionic personality disorder.
   d. dependent personality disorder.

8. In this personality disorder, people believe they are innately inadequate and must rely on others for protection and information. They rarely have or express their own opinions. What is being described?
   a. Borderline personality disorder
   b. Dependent personality disorder
   c. Narcissistic personality disorder
   d. Obsessive-compulsive personality disorder

9. Perfectionism is to ___________ personality disorder as attention-seeking is to ___________ personality disorder.
   a. borderline; obsessive-compulsive
   b. obsessive-compulsive; avoidant
   c. narcissistic; histrionic
   d. obsessive-compulsive; histrionic

10. In general, there are few effective treatments for antisocial personality disorder because
   a. there are so few people with the disorder.
   b. antisocial personalities suffer from extreme anxiety.
   c. the neurotransmitter imbalance of antisocial personalities cannot be offset by medication.
   d. antisocial personalities are unmotivated for treatment.

11. Which description of antisocial personality is accurate?
    a. It is three times more common in women than in men.
    b. It is characterized by marked irresponsibility and lack of empathy.
    c. Attention to details and lack of expressed warmth are common symptoms.
    d. Development of symptoms usually occurs after the age of 21.

12. Cleckley's indicators include lack of anxiety and superficial charm; the DSM-IV criteria include breaking social norms and acting impulsively. What is being described?
    a. Narcissistic personality disorder
    b. Histrionic personality disorder
    c. Antisocial personality disorder
    d. Secondary impulse control disorder

13. What is the incidence of antisocial personality in males in the United States?
    a. 1 percent
    b. 3 percent
    c. 20 percent
    d. 45 percent

14. Which of the following is a problem when criminal psychopaths are used in research on antisocial personality disorder?
    a. Very few antisocial personalities engage in criminal behavior.
    b. Criminals, unlike antisocial personalities, tend to request treatment for psychological problems.
    c. Criminals may not be representative of nonprison psychopaths.
    d. Criminals tend to be male, whereas noncriminal psychopaths tend to be female.

15. ___________ psychologists would explain the cause of antisocial personality in terms of inadequate superego development.
    a. Behavioral
    b. Physiological
    c. Humanistic
    d. Psychoanalytic

16. Twin and adoption studies of antisocial personalities tend to
    a. support the idea that the disorder is inherited.
    b. reject the idea that the disorder is inherited.
    c. explain why females are especially likely to develop the disorder.
    d. highlight the role of the superego in the disorder.

17. Both Lykken and Farley assume that psychopaths are
    a. fearless.
    b. similar to heroes in their thrill seeking.
    c. both a and b.
    d. neither a nor b.

18. Research on antisocial personalities shows that they make fewer errors in avoiding punishment when
    a. they are given tranquilizers.
    b. punishment means losing money.
    c. punishment is highly uncertain.
    d. any of the above is true.

19. What do pyromania, kleptomania, and trichotillomania have in common?
    a. They all affect women more than men.
    b. They are all personality disorders.
    c. They all involve lower than normal levels of arousal.
    d. They are all impulse control disorders.

20. According to psychoanalytic theory, the irresistible actions and feelings of excitement and guilt related to them in the impulse control disorders are evidence of
    a. traumatic experiences in early childhood.
    b. the sexual symbolism in these disorders.
    c. excessive superego development.
    d. anal fixation.

APPLICATION QUESTIONS

1. Irma, 29, spends her days alone in her room playing records and looking at magazines. She has no desire to talk with others, and has had no intimate relationships in her life. Irma illustrates which personality disorder?
    a. Avoidant
    b. Obsessive-compulsive
    c. Schizoid
    d. Antisocial

2. Dr. Clopper says, "Georgette is an unusual case of histrionic personality. She constantly seeks attention, dramatically 'performs' emotions, and demands perfection of herself and others." What is unusual about the case?
    a. Most histrionics are shy and withdrawn.
    b. Most histrionics are not perfectionistic.
    c. Most histrionics are unable to express emotions.
    d. Most histrionics are men.

3. "The incompetence of my subordinates upsets me. If I didn't have ignorant people holding me down, I'd get the promotions I deserve." People with which personality disorder are most likely to make such statements?
    a. Narcissistic
    b. Dependent
    c. Obsessive-compulsive
    d. Avoidant

4. A psychologist says, "Because of early childhood experiences, these people see others as either all good or all bad. That accounts for their tremendous swings in mood and self-image." The psychologist is giving a ___________ explanation for ___________ personality disorder.
   a. behavioral; antisocial
   b. psychoanalytic; borderline
   c. psychoanalytic; avoidant
   d. behavioral; borderline

5. Shandra is an accountant with a passion for details. She is so perfectionistic, she drives everyone else crazy. These behaviors best illustrate the ___________ personality disorder.
   a. schizotypal
   b. avoidant
   c. narcissistic
   d. obsessive-compulsive

6. Juan is diagnosed as a primary psychopath. He exploits other people and feels no guilt about it. Intensely loyal to his criminal friends, he has been imprisoned repeatedly for small crimes because he acts impulsively and fails to learn from his mistakes. What is unusual about this case?
   a. Most antisocial personalities are women.
   b. Most antisocial personalities learn from mistakes.
   c. Most antisocial personalities experience intense guilt.
   d. Most antisocial personalities aren't loyal to anyone.

7. While interviewing a client whom he suspects should be diagnosed with ___________, Dr. Hill asks many questions about whether the client's father was an impulsive criminal, a hostile and rejecting parent, or physically abusive.
   a. borderline personality disorder
   b. kleptomania
   c. antisocial personality disorder
   d. pathological gambling

8. Tom is diagnosed as an antisocial personality. He takes several psychological tests and is measured for physiological arousal when under stress. What ought to be the results of the tests and physiological measures?
   a. He is highly fearful, but has a low arousal level.
   b. He is a "Big T" and has a low arousal level.
   c. He is a "little t" and has a high arousal level.
   d. He is fearless and has a high arousal level.

9. A psychologist says, "Unlike pyromania and kleptomania, this impulse control disorder does not involve an action that is harmful to others. Indeed, the irresistible response in this disorder is physically painful to the person with the disorder." What disorder is being discussed?
   a. Trichotillomania
   b. Intermittent explosive disorder
   c. Antisocial personality disorder
   d. Pathological gambling

10. A student goes to the library to study about impulse control disorders. The student is likely to find that
    a. there is little research on their cause.
    b. they are very similar to anxiety disorders.
    c. behavioral and cognitive behavioral therapies are totally ineffective.
    d. the cause of these disorders is neurological.

ANSWERS TO FACT AND CONCEPT QUESTIONS

1. a. The major clinical syndrome is recorded on Axis I; personality disorders are listed on Axis II.
   *b. One problem with diagnosing personality disorders is that symptoms, such as suspiciousness, overlap with those of other disorders, such as paranoia or paranoid schizophrenia. (p. 254)
   c. Personality disorders usually become evident during adolescence or earlier.
   d. An inability to resist temptation is associated with the impulse control disorders.

2. a. Negativistic personality disorder is a proposed addition that involves a critical attitude toward others and passive resistance to performing expected social and occupational obligations. It does not have anything to do with feminist thinking.
   b. Sadistic personality disorder is also a proposed category, but it would be more applicable to the batterer than to the battered woman.
   c. Dependent personality disorder is a well-established category.
   *d. Self-defeating personality disorder would apply to people who put themselves in punitive situations, much like the plight of the battered woman. (Focus 9.1; pp. 256–257)

3. a. Excessive attention to details is a feature of obsessive-compulsive personality disorder.
   b. Wide fluctuations in mood and self-image are related to borderline personality disorder.
   *c. Paranoid personality disorder is characterized by suspiciousness without cause and emotional distance from others. (p. 255)
   d. A desire to be alone can be associated with the schizoid personality disorder and with complete normality.

4. *a. Although both personality disorders have some symptoms in common with schizophrenia, schizoid personality disorder is marked by the social withdrawal (autism) that is seen in schizophrenia. (p. 256)
   b. Psychotic mood swings are not related to any personality disorder (except perhaps borderline).
   c. Unwarranted suspiciousness is most important in paranoid personality disorder.
   d. Odd thoughts are the key symptom of schizotypal personality disorder; social withdrawal is seen as secondary to cognitive difficulties.

5. *a. Histrionic personality disorder is something of a caricature of traditional femininity; it is more commonly reported in women. (p. 258)
   b. Histrionics need the attention of others; they seek out people rather than withdrawing from them.
   c. There is no evidence that low arousal is related to histrionic personality disorder.
   d. Paranoid personality may mimic paranoid schizophrenia, but not histrionic personality.

6. a. Paranoid personalities do not trust other people.
   b. Dependent personalities rely on others' opinions.
   *c. Narcissistic personalities feature inflated self-importance, which is propped up by devaluing others. (p. 259)
   d. Schizoid personalities tend to avoid other people.

7. *a. Extreme fluctuations in mood and self-image, impulsivity, and underlying feelings of purposelessness are key symptoms of borderline personality disorder. (p. 261)
   b. Antisocial personalities use other people and do little self-evaluation, so there is rarely a time of low self-image.
   c. Histrionic personalities can have mood swings, but this is coupled with attention seeking, seductiveness, and shallowness.
   d. Dependent personalities rely on others for advice and information.

8. a. Borderline personalities have mood swings; they have no trouble expressing opinions.
   *b. Dependent personalities rely on others for their ideas because they have low self-confidence. (p. 263)
   c. Narcissistic personalities devalue others to inflate their own self-concept and feel superior to others.
   d. Obsessive-compulsives take on many responsibilities and attempt to execute them perfectly.

9. a. Perfectionism is a characteristic of obsessive-compulsives, not borderlines.
   b. Avoidant personalities fear criticism from and embarrassment before others; they shy away from center stage.
   c. Narcissistic personalities do not strive for perfectionism; if they are sloppy, they blame others.
   *d. Perfectionism and devotion to details are key symptoms of obsessive-compulsive personality disorder; histrionic personalities seek attention by dramatizing their lives and emotions. (pp. 258, 264)

10. a. With an incidence of 3 percent among males in the United States, antisocial personality disorder is fairly common.
    b. Antisocial personalities experience abnormally low levels of anxiety.
    c. There is no clear neurotransmitter imbalance.
    *d. Because of underarousal, antisocial personalities are not motivated for treatment; they usually consider therapy a joke. (p. 274)

11. a. Antisocial personality is three times more likely in men than in women.
    *b. Irresponsibility, impulsivity, lack of empathy, and lack of remorse are key features of antisocial personality. (p. 267)
    c. Attention to details is a sign of obsessive-compulsive personality disorder.
    d. All personality disorders show symptoms in adolescence or earlier.

12. a. Narcissistic personality involves a inflated self-concept; there is no alternative diagnostic criteria.
    b. Histrionics are attention-seekers who have exaggerated emotional displays.
    *c. Antisocial personality disorder has these two sets of symptoms, which overlap somewhat. (pp. 266–267)
    d. There is no such term as *secondary impulse control disorder*.

13. a. 1 percent or less is the incidence for females in the United States.
*b. Although this may be an underestimate, 3 percent is the approximate rate of new cases in males. (p. 267)
c. Twenty percent is roughly seven times the U.S. male incidence rate.
d. Forty-five percent is roughly fifteen times the U.S. male incidence rate.

14. a. Research with nonprison populations shows that antisocials engage in a great deal of criminal behavior.
b. Antisocials both inside and outside of prison do not feel there is anything wrong with them.
*c. Imprisoned psychopaths have been studied because they are clearly a captive audience, but it is unclear whether they are representative; they might be more impulsive than others, since they got caught. (p. 267)
d. There is no evidence that nonprison psychopaths are any more likely to be female, but even if there is this bias, c is a more general answer.

15. a. Behaviorists would stress modeling and inconsistent reinforcement.
b. Physiological psychologists would stress nervous system abnormalities.
c. Humanistic psychologists are not typically concerned with antisocial personalities but might stress social conditions.
*d. Psychoanalysts see morality and self-control as stemming from the superego; lack of parental identification produces a faulty superego. (p. 268)

16. *a. Both kinds of studies find that the greater the genetic similarity of one person to an antisocial personality, the greater the likelihood that that person is antisocial, too. (p. 269)
b. Twin and adoption studies support genetic theory.
c. Females are less likely to develop the disorder.
d. The superego is related to psychoanalysis.

17. a. Lykken and Farley report that psychopaths enjoy taking risks and showing their fearlessness. (Focus 9.2; p. 272)
b. Lykken and Farley suggest that psychopaths are like heroes in their thrill seeking; the main difference is the way they get their thrills. (p. 272)
*c. Because both a and b are correct, this is the best answer.
d. Because both a and b are correct, this cannot be the best answer.

18. a. Tranquilizers would further reduce the already low arousal level of antisocial personalities.
*b. When punishment was defined as losing money (rather than electric shock), antisocial personalities learned the avoidance task better. (p. 274)
c. Antisocial personalities learn less well when there is high uncertainty about when punishment will occur.
d. Because a and c were incorrect answers, this cannot be the best choice.

19. a. There is no evidence for a sex difference in these disorders.
b. None of them is a personality disorder.
c. Antisocial personality involves abnormally low levels of arousal; there is no evidence for such a deficit in these disorders.
*d. Since all these disorders involve an inability to resist some behavior and excitement or guilt when engaged in that behavior, they are impulse control disorders. (p. 278)

20. a. Early traumatic experiences are not necessarily associated with these disorders.
    *b. Psychoanalysts see each forbidden behavior as linked to sex; for instance, gambling and masturbation or stealing and sexual gratification. (p. 282)
    c. Excessive superego concern is expressed in perfectionism and a need to obey all rules.
    d. Anal fixation is associated with stinginess and stubbornness.

ANSWERS TO APPLICATION QUESTIONS

1. a. Although avoidant personalities may spend time alone, they crave attention and uncritical acceptance.
   b. Obsessive-compulsive personality disorder is marked by attention to detail and perfectionism.
   *c. Social isolation is the key symptom of schizoid personality disorder. (p. 255)
   d. Antisocial personalities seek others out so that they can exploit them.

2. a. Histrionics seek attention, so they are rarely withdrawn.
   *b. Histrionics are impressionistic and vague; they are not perfectionists. (p. 259)
   c. Histrionics are constantly expressing emotions that appear, after a while, to be superficial.
   d. More women are diagnosed with histrionic personality disorder than men, perhaps because it is a caricature of traditional femininity.

3. *a. The central feature of narcissistic personality disorder is inflated self-importance, which is demonstrated by devaluing others. (p. 259)
   b. Dependent personalities would not make a statement like this; they have very low self-confidence.
   c. Obsessive-compulsive personality disorder is marked by perfectionism and a lack of warmth.
   d. Avoidant personality disorder involves hypersensitivity to criticism by others.

4. a. Behaviorists would stress the reinforcements for exploiting others (antisocial personality).
   *b. Psychoanalysts believe that the borderline person has split the world into "good objects" and "bad objects," which accounts for the extreme mood swings seen in the disorder. (p. 261)
   c. Avoidant personality disorder does not involve such wide fluctuations of mood.
   d. Behaviorists would stress the reinforcements for being changeable.

5. a. Schizotypal personalities have odd thoughts and ways of speaking.
   b. Avoidant personality disorder involves hypersensitivity to criticism and fantasies of being loved.
   c. Inflated self-importance is the hallmark of narcissistic personality disorder.
   *d. Obsessive-compulsives are devoted to details and insist that everything be done perfectly. (p. 264)

6. a. Most antisocial personalities are men.
   b. Most antisocial personalities fail to learn from mistakes.
   c. Most antisocial personalities exploit others without any remorse or guilt.
   *d. Most antisocial personalities show no loyalty or love, even toward family. (p. 261)

7. a. Borderline personality disorder may be related to splitting the world into "all good" and "all bad."
   b. There is no evidence that kleptomania stems from parental rejection or the modeling of impulsivity.
   *c. Family/socialization theory suggests that antisocial personality develops in families where fathers model antisocial behavior and parents are hostile and rejecting. (p. 268)
   d. Pathological gambling is too little understood to suggest this pattern of development.

8. a. Research shows that antisocial personality is associated with fearlessness.
   *b. Farley has coined the term "Big T" for thrill seekers such as psychopaths; Lykken's and other research show psychopaths to be low in autonomic arousal. (p. 272)
   c. "Little t's" avoid reckless activity, making them the opposite of antisocial personalities.
   d. High arousal during stress is true of nonpsychopaths; psychopaths keep their cool when everyone else would be emotional.

9. *a. Trichotillomania—uncontrolled hair pulling—harms only oneself, not others. (p. 282)
   b. The physical and verbal aggression of intermittent explosive disorder certainly hurts others.
   c. Antisocial personality disorder involves the exploitation of others and invariably produces harmful consequences for others.
   d. Pathological gambling may be harmful to one's self, but cannot be seen as *physically* damaging.

10. *a. There is very little research on the cause of impulse control disorders. (p. 282)
   b. Impulse control disorders have more similarities with substance abuse disorders and sexual deviations.
   c. Booth's (1988) review shows that behavioral and cognitive behavioral methods can be helpful.
   d. There is no evidence that impulse control disorders are caused by neurological factors.

CHAPTER 10
Substance-Related Disorders

LEARNING OBJECTIVES

When you have mastered the material in Chapter 10, you should be able to:

1. Describe the nature and scope of substance use in our society. Distinguish substance-related disorders from substance-induced cognitive disorders. Define substance abuse, substance dependence, intoxication, and withdrawal. Discuss the overlap in criteria for dependence and abuse. (pp. 287–289)
2. Describe the characteristics typical of problem drinking. Discuss the nature and magnitude of drinking problems in the United States. Describe the position and impact of Mothers Against Drunk Driving. (Focus 10.1; pp. 289–292)
3. Indicate how alcoholism can be exhibited. Describe and differentiate between the short- and long-term physiological and psychological effects of alcohol. Describe the progression of alcohol problems. (pp. 292–294)
4. Describe the level of consumption of drugs other than alcohol. Describe and discuss the problems related to depressants or sedatives, including opiates (narcotics) and barbiturates. Define polysubstance dependence. Discuss benzodiazepine abuse. (pp. 294–297)
5. Describe and discuss the problems of stimulant-use disorders, including amphetamines, caffeine, nicotine, cocaine, and crack. Evaluate the controversy concerning nicotine addiction and its treatment. (Focus 10.2; pp. 297–300)
6. Describe and discuss the problems of hallucinogen use disorders, including marijuana, LSD, and phencylidine (PCP). Evaluate evidence concerning marijuana's harmful effects. Describe substances included in the category "other substance use disorders." (Focus 10.3; pp. 300–302)
7. Describe the two general types of etiological theories of substance-related disorders. Describe and evaluate the biological explanations for alcohol and other substance dependence. (pp. 302–304)
8. Describe and discuss the psychodynamic and personality explanations for alcoholism and other substance-related disorders. Evaluate research evidence on the relation between drug use and maladjustment. (pp. 304–309; Critical Thinking 10.1)
9. Describe evidence that alcoholism and other substance-related disorders are influenced by sociocultural factors. (p. 305)
10. Describe and discuss behavioral explanations for alcohol abuse and dependence, including challenges to the disease concept, problems with the tension reduction hypothesis, and the role of expectancies. (pp. 305–308)

11. Discuss explanations for relapse among alcoholics and people who are dependent on other substances. Describe and distinguish three overall theories of the addiction process. (pp. 308–310).
12. Describe the two phases of most alcohol and drug treatment programs. Describe the nature and effectiveness of self-help groups and chemical agents as means of treating substance-related disorders. (pp. 310–312)
13. Describe and compare the cognitive and behavioral approaches to treating substance-related disorders, including aversion therapy, covert sensitization, rapid smoking, nicotine fading, relaxation and social learning methods, and cognitive change treatments. Evaluate the controlled drinking controversy. (pp. 312–314; Focus 10.4)
14. Discuss what is meant by multimodal treatment. (pp. 314–315)
15. Describe and evaluate the evidence concerning treatment effectiveness for alcohol and other substance-related disorders. (pp. 315–316)

CHAPTER OUTLINE

1. **Substance-related disorders** (pp. 287–289) In the United States, large minorities of the population have used illicit drugs, over 83 percent have used alcohol, and 73 percent have smoked cigarettes. Interestingly, use of most drugs has declined since the late 1970s. *Substance-related disorders* involve drug use that alters one's psychological state and causes impaired functioning and an inability to abstain despite harmful effects. DSM-IV distinguishes substance-related disorders from cognitive disorders, where central nervous system effects are due to acute or chronic drug ingestion.

   DSM-IV defines *substance abuse* as excessive and uncontrolled use that causes impairment or distress; *substance dependence* adds the concepts of tolerance (needing increased dosages) and *withdrawal* (physical or emotional symptoms after reduced intake). Further, *intoxication* refers to central nervous system effects following ingestion of a drug that involve maladaptive behaviors or thinking.

2. **Alcohol-related disorders and consumption in the United States** (Focus 10.1; pp. 289–292) Problem drinking often begins as a way to reduce anxiety and expands to heavier drinking. About 35 percent of Americans abstain from alcohol, but 10 percent of the drinkers consume 50 percent of all alcohol consumed in this country. Men drink two to five times as much as women; adults between the ages of 21 and 34 drink more than those in other age groups. About 90 percent of high school seniors report having used alcohol at least once. An estimated 10 to 15 million Americans have serious problems with alcohol; another 35 million are indirectly affected. Drinking is associated with lowered work productivity, reduced life expectancy, increased suicide, violence, traffic fatalities, and many other problems. However, an estimated 85 percent of alcoholics receive no treatment.

3. **The effects of alcohol** (pp. 292–294) People who have either alcohol abuse or alcohol dependence are considered *alcoholics* and are said to have *alcoholism*. Alcohol has short-term physiological effects, such as impaired speech and motor coordination, because it is a central nervous system depressant. Its short-term psychological effects include poor judgment, feelings of happiness, and reduced concentration, but the precise effects are influenced by the situational context. The long-term effects are serious: Some drinkers become preoccupied with thoughts of alcohol, experience blackouts, loss of control, and deterioration. However, most research has been based on male alcoholics, and effects may be different for females. Physiological effects can include liver damage, heart disease, and cancers of the mouth and throat.

4. **Drug-related disorders: Depressants or sedatives** (pp. 294–297) Substance-related disorders are most prevalent among youths and young adults. The drugs described below are illicit or may be used legally only under medical supervision.

   Among the depressants or sedatives are organic *narcotics,* including opium derivatives such as heroin, morphine, and codeine. They depress the nervous system and are highly addicting. *Barbiturates* are used mostly by middle-aged and older people to induce sleep and relaxation. Combined with alcohol, barbiturates can lead to fatal overdoses. DSM-IV lists a diagnosis of polysubstance dependence in which three or more substances (not including nicotine and caffeine) are abused for at least six months. Benzodiazepines, including Valium, a widely prescribed drug, are overused to deal with stress.

5. **Stimulants** (Focus 10.2; pp. 297–300) A *stimulant* energizes the central nervous system. One example is *amphetamine,* which increases alertness and inhibits both appetite and sleep. Tolerance builds quickly, and chronic high doses can lead to aggressive behavior. Caffeine and nicotine are both legal and widely used stimulants. Caffeine has mild effects; nicotine is associated with many life-threatening diseases. Smoking is believed to be hard to stop (and stay stopped) because individuals are addicted to nicotine and because many environmental cues are associated with smoking. Crack, a rock-like, purified form of *cocaine*, is smoked, resulting in rapid euphoria followed by depression. Cocaine and amphetamine alter moods by increasing brain dopamine levels. Crack is a major social concern because it is inexpensive, easy to acquire, produces an intense high, leads to rapid addiction, and is associated with crime.

6. **Hallucinogens** (Focus 10.3; pp. 300–302) *Hallucinogens* are not believed to be physically addicting, although psychological dependence may occur. Over 33 percent of the U.S. population has used *marijuana* although it is illegal. Marijuana is a mild hallucinogen that produces euphoria, passivity, and memory impairment. There is considerable controversy concerning its short- and long-term physical and psychological effects. *Lysergic acid diethylamide (LSD)* is a psychotomimetic drug that alters visual and auditory perceptions and can produce flashbacks. *Phencyclidine (PCP)* is an extremely dangerous hallucinogen because it often leads to assaultive and suicidal behavior. Other DSM-IV categories for substance-related disorders include anabolic steroids and nitrous oxide ("laughing gas").

7. **Etiology of substance-related disorders** (pp. 302–310) There are two major perspectives on substance-related disorders, biogenic and cultural, although integration of the two is growing. The genetic transmission of alcoholism is supported by evidence with children of alcoholics adopted by nonalcoholics and twin research. Biological markers for alcoholism have been found in the form of neurotransmitter differences and insensitivity to alcohol. There is less research on the hereditary basis for other substances. Psychodynamic and personality explanations stress childhood traumas, dependency needs, and low frustration tolerance. Research identifies antisocial behavior and depression as personality characteristics associated with drinking problems. It is highly unlikely that a single personality type predicts addiction. In fact, children who experiment with drugs seem to be more adaptive than either those who abstain completely or become heavy users.

   Sociocultural explanations note differences in consumption based on sex, age, social class, ethnicity, and religion. France and Italy both have high alcohol consumption, but only France has high rates of alcoholism. In the United States, European Americans are less likely to use heroin than African Americans or Latinos, a probable reflection of sociocultural influences.

   Behavioral explanations originally focused on the tension-reducing properties of alcohol. However, the Marlatt et al. (1973) study, in which alcoholics and social drinkers were led to believe they were drinking alcohol when they actually got tonic, showed that expectation has a strong influence on use. Alcohol seems either to increase or decrease anxiety, depending on whether there is a distraction to divert the drinker's attention from his or her anxiety.

Relapse is a crucial topic for substance-related disorders. Certain feelings and situations increase the risk for relapse, although recent research found that relapse was least likely when users set goals of absolute abstinence and had positive moods rather than when they were in stress-free environments. Relapse is not merely caused by physiological withdrawal effects; cognitive, behavioral, and biological factors interact.

8. **Overall theories of the addiction process** (pp. 309–310) Solomon (1977) argues that addiction is an acquired motivation. His opponent process theory says that chronic use decreases the initial effects of a drug but increases the intensity of withdrawal reactions. Wise (1988) believes that positive and negative reinforcement combine to explain addiction. Finally, Tiffany (1990) suggests that drug use is largely an automatic process, where urges and plans play little role.

9. **Treatment of substance-related disorders** (pp. 310–316) A first step in most treatment programs is *detoxification*, the elimination of the chemical from the body. Self-help groups, such as Alcoholics Anonymous, which stresses support, spiritual awareness, and public self-revelations, are often helpful, but less so than its members assert. Chemicals such as Antabuse for alcohol and methadone for heroin treatment can be useful but have the problem of individuals ceasing to take the medication. However, in smoking cessation, nicotine patches hold promise. Cognitive and behavioral therapies include aversion therapy, *covert sensitization*, rapid smoking, nicotine fading, relaxation training, and coping skills training. There is considerable controversy about treatment for *controlled drinking* for alcoholics. In addition to the problem of retraining patients to drink socially, the researchers themselves have been attacked. Most treatment uses a multimodal effort, including inpatient individual and group therapy followed by outpatient treatment and support groups. Treatment effectiveness ranges between one-third and one-half improved, but 10 to 20 percent of alcohol abusers improve on their own. Relapse is a major problem, and recovery is greatly affected by life-context variables. Premature termination by drug abusers is quite common, but can be reduced with convenient, highly individualized treatment.

KEY TERMS

Fill-in-the-Blanks Quiz

1. The treatment aimed at removing all alcohol (or other substance) from a user's body is called ___________.

2. Excessive use of a substance leading to lack of control over use and impaired functioning is called ___________.

3. Substance abuse or dependence in which the substance being used is alcohol is called ___________.

4. The physical or emotional symptoms, such as shaking and irritability, that appear when intake of a regularly used substance is halted are called ___________.

5. The hallucinogenic drug that gained notoriety in the mid-1960s and occasionally leads to recurring hallucinations long after the person ceases taking the drug is called ___________.

6. The pathological pattern of excessive use of a substance that results in impaired social and occupational functioning but not tolerance or withdrawal is called ___________.

7. When a substance is ingested and causes central nervous system effects involving maladpative behaviors or thinking, this state is called ___________.

8. The pathological pattern of excessive use of a substance involving psychological and physical (tolerance and/or withdrawal symptoms) dependence is called ___________.

9. People who abuse and depend on alcohol are called ___________.

10. Substances known as "uppers" that speed up central nervous system activity, produce increased alertness and euphoria, and, in chronic users, paranoia are called ___________.

11. Substances known as "downers" that are powerful depressants of the central nervous system and are capable of inducing physical dependency and lethal overdose are called ___________.

12. A drug that induces feelings of euphoria and self-confidence in users and is usually inhaled is called ___________.

13. An aversive conditioning technique in which the individual imagines a noxious stimulus in the presence of a behavior is called ___________.

14. The controversial concept of teaching alcoholics to drink socially is called ___________.

15. A substance that produces hallucinations, vivid sensory awareness, or increased insight is called a(n) ___________.

16. The mildest and most commonly used hallucinogen is called ___________.

17. An addictive substance that depresses the central nervous system, provides relief from pain and anxiety, and is derived from opium is called a(n) ___________.

18. A psychoactive substance that energizes the central nervous system and causes elation, hyperactivity, and appetite suppression is called a(n) ___________.

19. A hallucinogen sometimes called "angel dust" that can cause aggressive behavior is officially called ___________.

Answers to Fill-in-the-Blanks Quiz

1. detoxification
2. substance-related disorder
3. alcoholism
4. withdrawal symptoms
5. LSD
6. substance abuse
7. intoxication
8. substance dependence
9. alcoholics
10. amphetamines
11. barbiturates
12. cocaine

13. covert sensitization
14. controlled drinking
15. hallucinogen
16. marijuana
17. narcotic
18. stimulant
19. phencylcidine (PCP)

FACT AND CONCEPT QUESTIONS

1. When repeated use of a substance has produced brain damage, the resulting mental disorders are considered
   a. on Axis II of the DSM-IV.
   b. cognitive disorders, not substance-related disorders.
   c. forms of substance abuse.
   d. symptoms of substance dependence.

2. The major difference between substance abuse and substance dependence is that, in substance dependence,
   a. the problem has lasted one month or more.
   b. social functioning has been affected.
   c. there are signs of tolerance or withdrawal symptoms.
   d. the person shows other signs of mental disorder.

3. Which statement about alcohol consumption is *true*?
   a. Roughly 50 percent of the alcohol consumed in the United States is consumed by 10 percent of the drinkers.
   b. Women drink more frequently than men.
   c. About 50 million Americans have been problem drinkers at some time in their lives.
   d. Less than 10 percent of American adults abstain from drinking.

4. Which of the following is a physiological effect of chronic alcohol use?
   a. Intoxication
   b. Absorption into the blood without digestion
   c. Liver cirrhosis
   d. Lung disease

5. Heroin, barbiturates, and benzodiazepines have what in common?
   a. They are all depressants or sedatives.
   b. They are all illegal.
   c. None of them produces tolerance.
   d. None of them can be lethal.

6. ___________ are a category of drug that is widely prescribed for reduction of anxiety and muscle tension.
   a. Hallucinogens
   b. Opiates
   c. Amphetamines
   d. Benzodiazepines

7. Which drugs have their stimulant effect by increasing dopamine levels?
   a. Amphetamine and cocaine
   b. Alcohol and narcotics
   c. Marijuana and LSD
   d. Barbiturates and cocaine

8. According to Schachter, most smokers have difficulty quitting because of
   a. expectation, since nicotine cannot be physically addicting.
   b. the drug's ability to produce hallucinations.
   c. physical addiction to nicotine.
   d. the social pressures that smokers feel to fit in with their peers.

9. Which statement about marijuana is *true*?
   a. It is the least commonly used hallucinogen.
   b. More high school students use it than drink alcohol.
   c. All its supposed effects on memory and perception are really under voluntary control.
   d. It does not lead to physical addiction.

10. The hallucinogen that is most related to uncontrolled aggression and delusional states is called
    a. PCP.
    b. marijuana.
    c. heroin.
    d. crack cocaine.

11. There are two general explanations for substance-related disorders: ___________ and ___________.
    a. personality; environment
    b. biology; psychological/cultural factors
    c. social class; education
    d. learning; psychoanalytic factors

12. Results of twin and adoption studies tend to
    a. support the idea that alcoholism is due to preexisting personality characteristics.
    b. reject the idea that alcoholism is due to heredity.
    c. support the idea that alcoholism is a sociocultural phenomenon.
    d. support the idea that alcoholism is due to heredity.

13. Which of the following is a biological marker related to alcoholism?
    a. Neurotransmitter differences
    b. Central nervous system functioning differences
    c. Differences in sensitivity to alcohol
    d. All of the above

14. Research by Shedler and Block compared the psychological adjustment of adolescents who abstained from drugs, experimented with drugs, or used drugs heavily. The results showed that
    a. heavy drug use caused maladjustment.
    b. abstainers were the least likely to have adjustment problems.
    c. those who experimented with drugs were best adjusted.
    d. all the "experimenters" became maladjusted, heavy users.

15. Which of the following statements strengthens the belief that cultural values play an important role in drinking patterns?
    a. Alcohol is a central nervous system depressant in all races.
    b. Although France and Italy have high rates of consumption, the rate of alcoholism is high only in France.
    c. When pregnant women drink, they increase the risk that their babies will have fetal alcohol syndrome.
    d. Antisocial behavior and depression are frequently associated with alcoholism.

16. Early behavioral explanations for alcoholism emphasized findings that
    a. cats placed in approach-avoidance conflicts learn to prefer milk mixed with alcohol over regular milk.
    b. rats will refuse to drink alcohol-spiked water when they are under stress.
    c. in conditioning experiments, rats' responses indicate that alcohol is a more aversive stimulus than electric shocks.
    d. responses to alcohol in stress-producing situations are more a function of our expectations than of the chemical's effect.

17. Results from the study in which alcoholics and social drinkers drank either tonic or alcohol indicate that
    a. alcoholism is a disease in which one loses control over drinking.
    b. a subject's expectations have little effect on how much he or she drinks.
    c. expectations are important only for social drinkers.
    d. the disease concept of loss of control is inaccurate.

18. Recent research indicates that relapse among alcoholics, smokers, and cocaine users is
    a. not related to stress or negative moods.
    b. directly related to the user's unconscious conflicts.
    c. best predicted by biological markers.
    d. caused by a motive to avoid withdrawal effects.

19. The problem with methadone treatment is that
    a. it is part of an aversive behavior therapy that clients drop out of before completing treatment.
    b. it substitues one addiction for another.
    c. it relies heavily on the Alcoholics Anonymous requirement of spiritual awareness.
    d. it intensifies the experience of narcotic withdrawal.

20. Multimodal treatment for substance-related disorders entails
    a. working with people who are addicted to several different chemicals.
    b. extinguishing behaviors to many different cues and situations.
    c. detoxifying people before they become involved with Alcoholics or Narcotics Anonymous.
    d. inpatient treatment group therapy, individual psychotherapy, self-help groups, and behavior therapy.

APPLICATION QUESTIONS

1. Karen has been using marijuana for several months. Using the drug has led to several minor traffic accidents and a marked drop in her school grades. Her friends find her uninvolved and unhappy. She can go for several days without using pot and feels no craving. What diagnosis is appropriate for Karen?
   a. Substance use without abuse
   b. Substance abuse
   c. Substance dependence
   d. Addiction to stimulants

2. James is the son of an alcoholic. On the basis of research studies, if James is at high risk for alcoholism, what biological marker is most likely to be seen?
   a. Flashbacks
   b. Insensitivity to alcohol (he can consume large amounts without effect)
   c. Hypersensitivity to alcohol (he becomes intoxicated after ingesting small amounts)
   d. High levels of optimism and high tolerance for frustration

3. Dr. Enberg says, "Alcoholism is caused by frustration of oral dependency needs in infancy. Alcohol allows the expression of repressed feelings and gratification of oral needs." These remarks reflect the ____________ perspective.
   a. behavioral
   b. family systems
   c. biological-physical
   d. psychoanalytic

4. Dr. Gomez says, "There are two personality factors that are associated with drinking problems: low intelligence and a tendency to become depressed." Is anything wrong with the doctor's statement?
   a. Yes; the personality factors associated with alcoholism are repression and antisocial behavior.
   b. No; the doctor's statement is accurate.
   c. Yes; *no* personality factors are associated with drinking problems.
   d. Yes; the personality factors associated with alcoholism are antisocial behavior and depression.

5. Jane quit smoking cigarettes in July and promised not to smoke another one. Now, in August, having had one cigarette, she feels guilty. Losing all sense of personal control, she smokes two packs of cigarettes the same day. According to behavioral explanations, what happened?
   a. Nicotine sets up a physiological chain reaction that no one can stop.
   b. She fell victim to the abstinence violation effect.
   c. She experienced what is called covert sensitization.
   d. She had stopped taking her Antabuse tablets.

6. Alvin says, "My treatment was successful because I became a part of a fellowship that provides support and increases spiritual awareness. That group saved my life!" What kind of treatment is Alvin describing?
   a. Methadone maintenance
   b. Systematic desensitization
   c. Alcoholics Anonymous
   d. Group behavior therapy

7. Dr. Richmond says, "Although 32 to 53 percent of treated alcoholics improve, a good 10 to 20 percent recover without any formal treatment. Unfortunately, relapse rates during the first year after treatment may be as high as 60 percent." What is incorrect in Dr. Richmond's statement?
   a. The improvement rate with treatment is closer to 90 percent.
   b. No alcohol abuser has ever recovered without formal treatment.
   c. Relapse rates are closer to 10 percent in the first year.
   d. Nothing in the statement is incorrect.

8. Stanley is being treated for a substance-related disorder with a patch of medication he wears on his arm. The patch slowly helps him over the withdrawal effects of the substance he is trying to stop using. What is Stanley's problem?
   a. LSD
   b. Marijuana
   c. Nicotine
   d. Caffeine

9. Fran looks back on her days of drug use and says, "The good trips were filled with startling hallucinations and feelings of ecstasy. But weeks later, I'd have 'flashbacks' at truly inopportune times, like when I was driving on the freeway." What drug did Fran use?
   a. Heroin
   b. Marijuana
   c. LSD
   d. Crack cocaine

10. Dr. Swartz says, "Drug addiction is a habit that is so automatic, there is no role for urges or plans. Once you are an addict, certain situations trigger certain responses. Treatment must demand the addict's attention; that's what makes treatment effectiveness so poor." These remarks reflect
    a. the Alcoholics Anonymous point of view.
    b. a psychoanalyst's explanation of addiction.
    c. Solomon's opponent process theory.
    d. Tiffany's explanation of drug addiction.

ANSWERS TO FACT AND CONCEPT QUESTIONS

1. a. Substance-related disorders are recorded on Axis I.
   *b. In DSM-IV, all forms of brain damage are considered cognitive disorders regardless of whether substances were the cause. (pp. 288–289)
   c. Substance abuse involves pathological chemical use without indications of physical addiction or brain damage.
   d. Symptoms of tolerance and withdrawal are signs of substance dependence.

2. a. Both substance abuse and substance dependence are associated with use over a period of at least one month.
   b. Substance abuse and substance dependence both impair social functioning.
   *c. The key feature of substance dependence is tolerance or withdrawal symptoms. (p. 289)
   d. Mental disorders may or may not be associated with abuse or dependence.

3. *a. Statistics show that a small number of drinkers (10 percent) account for half of all alcohol consumed. (p. 290)
   b. Men drink two to five times as much as women.
   c. The estimate is closer to 10 to 15 million; about 13 percent of the adults in the United States have drinking problems.
   d. Roughly one-third of Americans do not drink at all.

4. a. Intoxication is the physical and psychological effect of acute doses of a substance.
   b. Alcohol is absorbed directly into the bloodstream in first-time drinkers as well as chronic heavy users.
   *c. Liver cirrhosis is one of the many serious physiological effects of chronic alcohol use; heart failure and cancers of the mouth and throat are others. (p. 294)
   d. Lung disease is an outcome of smoking, not drinking.

5. *a. All three are depressants or sedatives—they slow down the working of the brain. (p. 295)
   b. Barbiturates are prescribed drugs, but are often obtained illegally; benzodiazepines (such as Valium) are widely available from doctors.
   c. All three produce tolerance.
   d. All three can be lethal, particularly barbiturates.

6. a. Hallucinogens are all illegal drugs, so they are not prescribed.
   b. Opiates are narcotics; they are not prescribed for anxiety reduction.
   c. Amphetamines are stimulants; they increase muscle tension.
   *d. Benzodiazepines, such as Valium, are prescribed frequently for anxiety and tension reduction. (p. 297)

7. *a. Amphetamine and cocaine are central nervous stimulants that prevent the reuptake of dopamine and therefore increase its concentration in certain brain synapses. (pp. 297–298)
   b. Alcohol and narcotics are depressants.
   c. Marijuana and LSD are hallucinogens, not stimulants.
   d. Barbiburates are depressants.

8. a. Schachter's work suggests that nicotine is strongly addicting.
   b. Nicotine is not a hallucinogen.
   *c. Schachter's work suggests that the body craves nicotine, and that continued smoking is an attempt to avoid withdrawal. (Focus 10.2; pp. 298–299)
   d. Schachter's work stresses the physiological needs of smokers, not their psychological needs.

9. a. Marijuana is the most commonly used hallucinogen.
   b. About 90 percent of high school seniors report having used alcohol, whereas less than 40 percent report having used marijuana.
   c. Although some effects can be altered by "willing" them to change, memory effects cannot.
   *d. There is no evidence that marijuana produces a withdrawal effect when chronic users stop consumption. (Focus 10.3; p. 301)

10. *a. Phencyclidine (PCP or "angel dust") is a hallucinogen that can produce homicidal aggression and delusions of such invincibility that people jump out of windows expecting to fly. (p. 302)
    b. Marijuana is a mild hallucinogen that causes passivity, not aggressiveness.
    c. Heroin is not a hallucinogen; it usually promotes relaxation rather than aggression.
    d. Crack is a stimulant, not a hallucinogen.

11. a. Both personality and environment are part of the psychological/cultural viewpoint.
    *b. Causes are usually seen as internal and biogenic (especially genetics) or psychological/cultural (personality and social factors); however, an integration of the two schools of thought is quite common. (p. 302)
    c. Social class and education are both cultural factors.
    d. Learning and psychoanalytic perspectives are both psychological; biogenic factors are important in understanding substance-related disorders.

12. a. Support for personality factors comes from longitudinal studies, which find that impulsive and antisocial youths are more likely than others to develop drinking problems.
    b. Evidence from this work tends to support the genetic position.
    c. Support for the sociocultural position comes from evidence that different cultures have different rates of consumption and alcoholism.
    *d. Concordance ratios of MZ twins are higher than those of DZ twins, and children of alcoholics who are adopted by nonalcoholics have higher rates of drinking problems—both support the role of heredity. (p. 303)

13. a. Research shows that neurotransmitters are biological markers for alcoholism.
    b. Research shows that central nervous system functioning is a biological marker for alcoholism.
    c. Research shows that insensitivity to alcohol is a biological marker of some who develop alcoholism.
    *d. Because a, b, and c are all correct, this is the best answer. (p. 303)

14. a. Shedler and Block found that maladjustment preceded heavy drug use in adolescents.
    b. Abstainers had more adjustment problems than experimenters; they tended to be inflexible and had poorer social skills.
    *c. Much to the surprise of many, those who experimented with drugs but did not use heavily had the best social adjustment. (p. 307)
    d. Experimenters did not become heavy users.

15. a. If alcohol has the same physiological effect on all people, culture is irrelevant.
    *b. If cultures differ in their rates of alcoholism, it *may* be because the cultures teach different values concerning what is deviant drinking. (p. 305)
    c. Fetal alcohol syndrome is a physiological effect that appears to be unrelated to cultural values.
    d. The fact that antisocial behavior and depression are related to drinking is support for a personality explanation.

16. *a. Early behaviorists stressed the role of alcohol as an anxiety-reducing chemical, which was supported by the research with cats. (p. 305)
    b. If rats did this (and they don't), it would undercut the early behaviorist position, which stressed anxiety reduction.
    c. Such a finding would undercut the behaviorist position.
    d. The importance of expectation is a *recent* behavioral explanation for why alcohol sometimes has anxiety-reducing properties and sometimes doesn't.

17. a. If alcoholism were a disease involving loss of control, the only thing that would have influenced drinking would have been drinking alcohol, not expectation.
    b. The subjects' expectations had a great impact on the amount they drank.
    c. Expectations were important for both groups.
    *d. The fact that alcoholics primed with alcohol did *not* drink more alcohol when they thought it was tonic undercuts the disease notion of loss of control. (p. 307)

18. *a. Neither physical symptoms, negative moods, nor stress predicted relapse. What predicted a *lack* of relapse was having a goal of abstinence and expectations of being successful. (p. 308)
    b. Unconscious conflicts have not been found to predict relapse.
    c. Biological markers may help predict who will develop an addiction; they have not been used to predict who relapses.
    d. The motive to avoid withdrawal was *expected* to predict relapse but failed to.

19. a. Methadone treatment is unrelated to behavior therapy and is far from aversive since it produces a euphoria.
    *b. Because methadone produces a euphoria and is addictive, it substitutes one substance-related problem for another. (p. 312)
    c. Methadone treatment is unrelated to Alcoholics Anonymous.
    d. The goal of methadone is to do the opposite—to reduce the impact of heroin withdrawal.

20. a. The term for people who are addicted to several substances is *polyaddicted.*
    b. Extinction connotes only behavior therapy; multimodal treatment may use behavior therapy and several others.
    c. Detoxification is not a form of treatment per se; Alcoholics Anonymous is only one method of treatment.
    *d. Multimodal treatment uses a wide range of individual, group, and self-help measures to stop substance abuse and find alternative behaviors. (p. 314)

ANSWERS TO APPLICATION QUESTIONS

1. a. Karen's drug use has led to social and occupational (school) impairments; this cannot be considered nonabusive use.
   *b. Karen's use is clearly pathological and has lasted for more than one month, but there are no signs of dependence, so the diagnosis is substance abuse. (p. 289)
   c. Without signs of tolerance or withdrawal, one cannot diagnose this as substance dependence.
   d. Marijuana is not a stimulant; it is a mild hallucinogen.

2. a. Flashbacks are recurrences of hallucinations long after one stops taking LSD.
 *b. Children of alcoholics who are insensitive to the effects of alcohol have a higher risk of becoming alcoholics; this is a biological marker. (p. 303)
 c. One biological marker for alcoholism is *not* responding to alcohol; hypersensitivity (getting drunk or nauseated) does not predict alcoholism.
 d. Neither of these is a biological marker; if anything, the opposite of these (low frustration tolerance and depression) are predictors of alcoholism.

3. a. The behavioral perspective stresses modeling, anxiety reduction, and expectations.
 b. The family systems perspective stresses the adaptive role of drunkenness in the family.
 c. The biological-physical perspective emphasizes the role of genetic vulnerability.
 *d. The psychoanalytic perspective emphasizes early childhood influences and the symbolic nature of adult drinking. (p. 304)

4. a. This is inaccurate because, although psychoanalysts focus on repression, no empirical relationship between it and alcoholism has been documented.
 b. This is inaccurate because intelligence has no relationship to alcoholism.
 c. This is inaccurate; two personality factors *have* been related to alcoholism.
 *d. Peter Nathan (1988) has shown that antisocial behavior and depression are the two factors most related to drinking problems. (p. 304)

5. a. Behaviorists do not believe that physiological loss of control occurs when people relapse.
 *b. The abstinence violation effect is the feeling of having "blown it" when one gives in to temptation once; according to Marlatt, it is a principal reason for relapses. (p. 308)
 c. Covert sensitization is a treatment method using imagery.
 d. Antabuse is used in the treatment of alcoholism.

6. a. Methadone maintenance is not done in groups; it is administered individually on a daily basis to offset the craving for heroin.
 b. Systematic desensitization is an individual treatment that uses classical conditioning principles.
 *c. Alcoholics Anonymous is a group treatment that uses self-revelation, support, and spiritual involvement. (p. 311)
 d. Behavior therapy, if done in groups, would not focus on the spiritual, but would teach coping skills.

7. a. The improvement rate varies depending on how "improvement" is defined, but no treatment can make a claim of 90 percent success.
 b. Since 80 percent or more of alcoholics get no treatment, it is fortunate that 10 to 20 percent do improve on their own.
 c. Relapse is a major problem for alcoholics; the relapse rate is often 50 to 60 percent after one year.
 *d. Everything the psychologist says is based on research evidence reported by Moos and Finney. (p. 315)

8. a. LSD does not produce withdrawal effects.
 b. Marijuana does not produce withdrawal effects.
 *c. Transdermal nicotine patches have proven to be useful in weaning cigarette smokers from their addiction to nicotine. (p. 312)
 d. Caffeine does not produce serious withdrawal effects and is not treated with transdermal patches.

9. a. Heroin does not produce hallucinations, and there is no evidence of it producing flashbacks.
   b. Marijuana produces only the mildest of hallucinations and no flashbacks.
   *c. One of LSD's unique properties is that hallucinations can occur weeks after use has stopped; these are called flashbacks. (p. 301)
   d. Crack cocaine produces a strong and rapid high, but there is no evidence of hallucinations or flashbacks.

10. a. Alcoholics Anonymous stresses the disease aspects of addiction and the need for spiritual awareness and self-revelation.
   b. Psychoanalytic explanations involve unconscious conflicts, especially concerning dependency needs.
   c. Solomon's opponent process theory suggests that addiction is maintained to offset the negative effects of withdrawal.
   *d. Tiffany (1990) argues that addiction is an automatic process where situational cues trigger responses and where urges, thoughts, and plans are short-circuited. (p. 310)

CHAPTER 11
Sexual and Gender Identity Disorders

LEARNING OBJECTIVES

When you have mastered the material in Chapter 11, you should be able to:

1. Describe the three major categories of disorders covered in the chapter. Discuss the definition problems and controversies associated with these disorders. (pp. 319–320)
2. Define and describe the gender identity disorders. Describe and discuss the psychoanalytic, behavioral, and biogenic explanations for gender identity disorders. (pp. 320–323)
3. Describe the treatments available for gender identity disorders and their effectiveness. (pp. 323–324)
4. Define the paraphilias and describe the characteristics of the person likely to be diagnosed with a paraphilia. Describe fetishism, transvestic fetishism, exhibitionism, voyeurism, and frotteurism. (pp. 324–328)
5. Describe pedophilia and the characteristics of pedophiles. Discuss the problems of people who were childhood victims of sexual abuse. Describe sadism and masochism. (pp. 328–332)
6. Discuss the etiology and treatment of the paraphilias from the psychoanalytic, behavioral, and biogenic perspectives. (pp. 332–334)
7. Appreciate the prevalence of rape, including date rape. Explain the wide range of estimates on data rape frequency. Describe and discuss the effects of rape. (pp. 334–336)
8. Describe the three motivational types of rapists and research on the personalities of potential rapists. Discuss the relationship between cultural acceptance of violence and rape as well as the social and biological reasons for rape. (pp. 336–337; Critical Thinking, p. 338)
9. Define incest and understand the types of incest as well as the types of incestuous fathers. Describe and discuss treatments for incest offenders and rapists, including surgical castration and chemical therapy. (pp. 337, 340–341)
10. Describe the phases of normal sexual response. Discuss how HIV leads to AIDS and how the virus is transmitted sexually. (pp. 341–344; Focus 11.2)
11. Describe and differentiate sexual desire disorders in men and women, sexual arousal disorder in men and women, and male and female orgasmic disorder. Discuss the controversies over criteria for female orgasmic disorder. (pp. 344–348; Focus 11.3)
12. Describe and differentiate inhibited sexual orgasm in females, inhibited male orgasm, premature ejaculation, and functional vaginismus. Discuss the problems with defining "normal" female orgasmic functioning. Describe and discuss premature ejaculation and sexual pain disorders. (Focus 11.3; pp. 348–349)
13. Discuss the biological causes and treatments for psychosexual dysfunctions. (pp. 349–351)

14. Discuss the psychological causes of and general treatment approaches for sexual dysfunctions. Describe specific treatments for the four psychosexual dysfunctions. Evaluate the effectiveness of behavior therapy. (pp. 351–352)
15. Explain why homosexuality is not a psychological disorder. Discuss research on children of gay parents. (pp. 353–354; Focus 11.4)
16. Discuss research on aging and sexual activity. (pp. 354–355)

CHAPTER OUTLINE

1. **Problems in defining sexual and gender identity disorders** (pp. 319–320) Sexual disorders are the hardest to distinguish from "normal" sexual behavior because of cultural differences as well as moral and legal judgments. Normal sexual behavior is poorly understood and in flux.

2. **Gender identity disorders** (pp. 320–324) *Gender identity disorders*, often called "transsexualism," involve a conflict between anatomical sex and gender self-identification. Transsexuals have a lifelong conviction that they are in the body of the wrong sex. Sex role conflicts start at an early age; they are more common in boys than in girls. Prevalence estimates range from 1 in 100,000 to 1 in 37,000 among males and about one-quarter that rate among females.

   Because it is rare, we do not know much about the disorder's cause. Psychoanalysts suggest that sexual deviations symbolize unconscious conflicts involving separation from the mother. Behaviorists note that parental encouragement to act like the opposite sex and cross-dress may lead to gender identity disorder. The biogenic perspective emphasizes research showing abnormal testosterone levels in female transsexuals, but such research is not always replicated.

   Most treatment programs with children having gender identity disorder assign boys to male therapists to facilitate identification with a male and teach behavior modification skills to the parents. Sex conversion treatment involving hormones and surgery can alter the apparent sex of transsexuals; woman-to-man changes seem to have more positive outcomes. Behavior therapy reinforcing heterosexual fantasies has had some success, too.

3. **Paraphilias** (pp. 324–327) *Paraphilias* are sexual disorders in which repeated intense sexual urges exist for nonhuman objects, real or simulated suffering, or nonconsenting others. Sex offenders often have multiple paraphilias. They are overwhelmingly male problems. DSM-IV makes a diagnosis of paraphilia when the person has acted on urges or is markedly distressed by them.

   Fetishism is a strong sexual attraction to inanimate objects, such as shoes or underwear. As a group, fetishists are not dangerous. In *transvestic fetishism*, the person obtains sexual arousal by dressing in the clothes of the opposite sex. Most transvestites are heterosexual males who use cross-dressing to facilitate sexual intercourse, but many transvestites feel they have both male and female personalities.

4. **Paraphilias involving nonconsenting others** (pp. 327–328) Exhibitionists derive gratification from the reaction they get when they expose their genitals to strangers. Women commonly report being victims of *exhibitionism*. Most exhibitionists are young married men who want no further contact with the women to whom they expose themselves. Most have fantasies of being admired by female observers. *Voyeurism* is sexual gratification obtained primarily from observing others' genitals or others engaged in sex. Acts are repetitive and

premeditated. *Frotteurism* involves intense sexual urges to touch and rub against nonconsenting individuals.

5. **Pedophilia and paraphilias involving pain or humiliation** (pp. 328–332) *Pedophilia* is characterized by adults obtaining erotic gratification from fantasies or sexual contact with children. DSM-IV criteria include being at least 16 years old and 5 or more years older than the victim. The disorder is not rare; 20 to 30 percent of women report having had a childhood sexual encounter with an adult man. Victims often have long-term psychological difficulties. Molesters tend to be impulsive, passive, and alcoholic. Social skill deficits and below-average intelligence are also reported.

   Sadism and *masochism* involve associations between pain or humiliation and sex. Sadists inflict pain; masochists receive it. Often people engage in both roles. Some cases develop from early experiences with pain, but causal explanations are currently weak.

6. **Etiology and treatment of paraphilias** (pp. 332–334) Psychoanalytic theory links paraphilias to unresolved oedipal conflicts, particularly castration anxiety. Treatment involves making these unconscious conflicts conscious. Learning theory stresses early conditioning experiences, masturbation fantasies, and a lack of social skills. Conditioning must overcome the process of preparedness—the fact that some stimuli become associated more readily than others because of evolutionary pressures. Treatment seeks to extinguish inappropriate behaviors and reinforce appropriate ones. One example is aversive behavior rehearsal, in which the exhibitionist exposes himself to a prepared female audience and must explain his fantasies. Biological treatments are not available.

7. **Other deviations involving sex: Rape and incest** (Focus 11.1; pp. 334–340) *Rape* is forced intercourse by a male with a female. It can be seen as either a sexual act, a violent act, or both. Rape is common: An estimated one-fourth of all U.S. women will be raped in their lifetime. Many rapists are friends or acquaintances of the victims. Many young men who do not rape try to coerce women into intercourse. Both rapists and their victims tend to be young. Victims may experience prolonged distress and sexual dysfunction. Flashbacks during sex are common. Rapists are most often motivated by power and anger, not by sex. Nonrapists report being aroused by aggressive sex; a significant proportion of university men report some likelihood they would rape if they could get away with it. Where there is general acceptance of violence, there is a spillover effect on rape. The cause of rape can be seen as sociocultural (male sex roles and general social violence) or sociobiological (innate sex differences in sexual motivation).

   Incest is sexual relations between close relatives. Most common is father-daughter incest. Estimates of incidence rates range from 48,000 to 250,000 cases per year. Incestuous fathers are more likely than nonincestuous fathers to have been victims of childhood sexual abuse, although this is not common. Survivors have a range of difficulties, continuing into adulthood.

8. **Treatment for incest offenders and rapists** (p. 340) Imprisonment, behavioral therapy, surgical castration, and drug therapies have all been used. Results are mixed, with more success treating child molesters and exhibitionists than rapists. Biological treatments, in particular, have been very controversial.

9. **Sexual dysfunctions** (Focus 11.2; pp. 341–347) *Sexual dysfunctions* involve a disruption of the normal sexual response (see below). The human immunodeficiency virus (HIV) and the disease it causes, Acquired Immune Deficiency Syndrome (AIDS), have generated great public concern because the virus can be transmitted sexually.

Research on normal sexual function began with Kinsey's survey research and was strengthened by Masters and Johnson's laboratory work. Recently, the Janus Report surveyed thousands of men and women, including those over age 65. The sexual response cycle has an *appetitive phase* when fantasies about sex increase. The *excitement phase* occurs when direct sexual stimulation (not necessarily physical) increases blood flow to the genitals. The *orgasm phase* produces involuntary contractions and the release of sexual tension. Men ejaculate; women are capable of multiple orgasms. The body then returns to relaxation during the *resolution phase.* Decreased functioning in any of these phases can be criteria for a sexual dysfunction. In addition, pain associated with intercourse may indicate a sexual pain disorder. DSM-IV also notes sexual dysfunction due to a general medical condition and substance-induced sexual dysfunction. Diagnosis requires that the problem be "recurrent and persistent"; subjective distress, frequency, and effects on other areas of functioning are also factored into the diagnosis.

Psychosexual dysfunction disorders are considered to be common. *Sexual desire disorders* involve a lack of interest in or aversion to sex. These are more common in women than in men, and there are many questions about what "normal" sexual interest is (about 20 percent of the adult population is believed to suffer from this disorder).

Erectile dysfunction is the inability to maintain an erection sufficient for intercourse. Physical conditions may account for a large minority of cases. Distinguishing biogenic erectile dysfunction from psychogenic cases is difficult. Primary dysfunction is when a man has never been successful in intercourse; secondary dysfunction means the problem is situational.

Female sexual arousal disorder involves lack of vaginal lubrication or erection of the nipples. This disorder, too, can be primary or secondary.

10. **Female orgasmic disorder, male orgasmic disorder, premature ejaculation, and sexual pain disorders** (Focus 11.3; pp. 347–349) In *inhibited orgasm*, the woman is unable to achieve orgasm. Many questions arise about whether the lack of an orgasm is a normal variant of sexual behavior or a disorder. Some argue the disorder should not be diagnosed until all experiences conducive to orgasm have proven ineffective. Inhibited male orgasm is the inability to ejaculate intravaginally. *Premature ejaculation* is a common disorder involving an inability to delay ejaculation during intercourse, but definitions of "premature" vary. *Sexual pain disorders* include vaginismus (involuntary muscular contraction of the outer vagina) and genital pain (dyspareunia).

11. **Etiology and treatment of sexual dysfunctions** (pp. 349–352) Many dysfunctions are due to a combination of biological and psychological factors. Organic factors include sex hormone levels, blood flow in the genitals, hypersensitivity to physical stimulation, and the side effects of medications. Medical treatments include exercise, surgery, and injections into the penis of substances that induce erections. Psychological factors include predisposing causes, such as early experiences and upbringing, and current concerns, such as poor marital relations and performance anxiety. Research shows that anxiety and self-focus impair performance.

    Treatment often includes education, anxiety reduction, structured behavioral exercises, and improved communications. Specific treatments for dysfunctions include masturbation as treatment for female orgasmic disorder, the "squeeze technique" for premature ejaculation, and relaxation and insertion of dilators for vaginismus. The glowing reports of success for these methods have been called into question recently. Long-term success requires relapse prevention.

12. **Homosexuality** (Focus 11.4; pp. 353–354) Homosexuality is not a mental disorder. There are no physiological differences in sexual arousal, no differences in psychological disturbance, no gender identity distortions that differentiate homosexuals and heterosexuals. Two small-scale

studies of children reared by homosexual parents show no differences in play or sexual behavior compared to those with children reared by heterosexual parents.

13. **Aging and sexual activity** (pp. 354–355) Sexuality continues into old age, although sexual dysfunction increases. Patterns of sexuality during middle age are maintained. The recent (1993) Janus survey suggests that sexual activity and enjoyment remain high among those 65 and older.

KEY TERMS

Fill-in-the-Blanks Quiz

1. The disorder characterized by an extremely strong sexual attraction for a particular nongenital part of the anatomy or an inanimate object is called ___________.

2. The disorder in which an adult obtains erotic gratification through fantasies about or sexual contact with children is called ___________.

3. The paraphilia characterized by the sexual desire to rub against, or act of rubbing against, the body of a nonconsenting individual is called ___________.

4. The disorder characterized by conflict between an individual's anatomical sex and his or her sexual identity is called ___________.

5. The conditions where there is pain caused by vaginismus or dyspareunia are called ___________.

6. The sexual disorder in which erotic or sexual gratification is obtained by receiving pain or punishment is called ___________.

7. An act of intercourse accomplished through force or the threat of force is called ___________.

8. Sexual relations between close relatives is called ___________.

9. The sexual dysfunctions characterized by a lack of interest in or aversion to sexual arousal are called ___________.

10. The disorder in which sexual gratification is obtained by inflicting pain or punishment on others is called ___________.

11. Disruptions in any part of the normal sexual response cycle that cause distress are called ___________.

12. Sexual disorders in which unusual or bizarre acts or objects are required for sexual arousal or where such urges are distressing are called ___________.

13. The sexual dysfunction in which an individual is unable to achieve orgasm during coitus despite adequate stimulation is called ___________.

14. The inability of a male to attain or maintain an erection that is sufficient for sexual intercourse is called ___________.

15. The dysfunction characterized by ejaculation before penile entry into the vagina or so soon after entry that sexual relations are unsatisfactory is called ___________.

16. The disorder in which sexual gratification is obtained by secretly observing strangers disrobe or engage in sex is called ___________.

17. The disorder in which sexual gratification is obtained by exposing the genitals to strangers or in which distress is caused by the urge to do this is called ___________.

18. The paraphilia in which a person derives sexual gratification from cross-dressing is called ___________.

Answers to Fill-in-the-Blanks Quiz

1. fetishism
2. pedophilia
3. frotteurism
4. gender identity disorder
5. sexual pain disorders
6. masochism
7. rape
8. incest
9. sexual desire disorders
10. sadism
11. sexual dysfunctions
12. paraphilias
13. inhibited orgasm
14. erectile dysfunction
15. premature ejaculation
16. voyeurism
17. exhibitionism
18. transvestic fetishism

FACT AND CONCEPT QUESTIONS

1. Sexual deviation disorders
   a. are unaffected by legal or moral judgments.
   b. can be reliably diagnosed because they all entail personal distress.
   c. are difficult to define because they involve legal and moral judgments.
   d. involve an inability to perform at some stage in the normal sexual response cycle.

2. Transsexuals tend to
   a. show sex role conflicts at an early age.
   b. be women.
   c. outgrow their gender identity disorder.
   d. engage in gender-inappropriate behavior, but have no desire to change their physical characteristics.

3. Absence of a male role model, lack of male playmates, and parental encouragement of cross-dressing are psychological factors in the development of
   a. pedophilia.
   b. premature ejaculation.
   c. sexual desire disorders.
   d. gender identity disorders.

4. The inability to obtain sexual arousal unless one is wearing the clothes of the opposite sex indicates
   a. transvestic fetishism.
   b. gender identity disorder.
   c. exhibitionism.
   d. fetishism.

5. Rubbing against a nonconsenting person is to ___________ as observing others in sexual activity is to ___________.
   a. transvestic fetishism; exhibitionism
   b. frotteurism; voyeurism
   c. transvestic fetishism; voyeurism
   d. frotteurism; exhibitionism

6. Contrary to popular belief, most ___________ tend to be people who are relatives or friends of their victims.
   a. exhibitionists
   b. pedophiles
   c. masochists
   d. transvestites

7. Which of the following is a paraphilia that involves intentional pain or humiliation?
   a. Transvestic fetishism
   b. Premature ejaculation
   c. Voyeurism
   d. Sadomasochism

8. According to psychoanalytic theory, sadomasochism and other sexual deviations are caused by
   a. the pairing of certain stimuli with sexual arousal in early childhood.
   b. cultural requirements of males and females.
   c. unconscious conflicts related to castration anxiety.
   d. a lack of superego controls.

9. Learning approaches to treating pedophilia would focus on
   a. strengthening the association between sexual arousal and children.
   b. bringing to consciousness unconscious fears and conflicts.
   c. both a and b.
   d. neither a nor b.

10. The behavioral treatment called aversive behavior rehearsal involves shame and is most appropriate for treating
    a. gender identity disorder.
    b. exhibitionism.
    c. premature ejaculation.
    d. homosexualism.

11. Anger and power are two of the more common motivations for
    a. sadomasochists.
    b. rapists.
    c. transvestic fetishists.
    d. exhibitionists.

12. "Cultural spillover" theory suggests that a culture where violence is encouraged or condoned will have
    a. very few incidents of sexually deviant behavior.
    b. a high rate of sexually dysfunctional men.
    c. a high rate of exhibitionism, voyeurism, and other paraphilias.
    d. more rapes than in other cultures.

13. Which statement about the treatment of sex offenders is *true*?
    a. Imprisonment is the main form of "treatment."
    b. Controlled research shows that psychotherapy is more effective than biological treatments.
    c. Treatment for rapists is far more successful than for any other type of offender.
    d. Surgical castration has been found to have no effect on sexual fantasies or recidivism rates.

14. Which statement about AIDS is true?
    a. People develop physical symptoms immediately after they are infected with HIV, the virus that causes AIDS.
    b. AIDS kills by attacking the genitals and weakening the heart.
    c. HIV infection is most often caused by kissing.
    d. Ten years after being infected, most people die of AIDS because "opportunistic diseases" cannot be fought off.

15. The recent Janus Report gathered data on the sexual beliefs and behaviors of over 2500 individuals over a 9-year period. The results show that
    a. AIDS has drastically reduced the frequency of sexual behavior.
    b. sexual behavior among people over 65 is virtually nonexistent.
    c. the normal sexual response cycle consists of four stages.
    d. belief in lowered sexual satisfaction among people over 50 is incorrect.

16. Which sexual dysfunction, believed to affect 20 percent of the adult population, is difficult to diagnose because we know little about the "normal" frequency of sexual fantasies and activities?
    a. Paraphilia
    b. Premature ejaculation
    c. Sexual desire disorder
    d. Primary erectile dysfunction

17. A woman who has experienced orgasm in the past but currently cannot be brought to orgasm should be diagnosed as having
    a. a sexual desire disorder.
    b. primary vaginismus.
    c. secondary female orgasmic disorder.
    d. a secondary paraphilia.

18. Which of the following are related to sexual pain disorders?
    a. Lack of sexual desire and lack of orgasm
    b. Vaginismus and dyspareunia
    c. Premature ejaculation and erectile dysfunction
    d. Hypoactive sexual desire and erectile dysfunction

19. Which of the following is a current psychological factor that increases the likelihood of erectile dysfunction?
    a. Excessive levels of testosterone
    b. A strict moral upbringing
    c. Unresolved castration anxiety
    d. Pressure to perform sexually

20. Research with nonclinical samples of homosexuals suggests that
    a. they are more inclined to develop psychoses than are heterosexuals.
    b. lesbians are far more disturbed than male homosexuals.
    c. distress over being homosexual rarely, if ever, occurs.
    d. there is no more psychopathology in homosexuals than in heterosexuals.

APPLICATION QUESTIONS

1. At an early age, Albert avoided all traditionally male activities and felt that he was a girl trapped in the body of a boy. As an adult, he had a sex change operation and is now called Alberta. This case illustrates
   a. gender identity disorder.
   b. sexual desire disorder.
   c. pedophilia.
   d. transvestic fetishism.

2. Doris derives sexual gratification from fondling men's underwear. She is a shy, married woman who also must dress in men's clothes to have satisfactory intercourse with her husband. What is unusual about Doris's case?
   a. Men are more likely to have paraphilias than women.
   b. People rarely have more than one paraphilia.
   c. Transvestites are almost always homosexuals.
   d. People with paraphilias are rarely shy or married.

3. Todd, 26, responds to attractive women in public by fantasizing about exposing his genitals, then returning to the same place and actually exposing himself. Todd would probably be diagnosed with
   a. gender identity disorder.
   b. sexual dysfunction of the arousal stage.
   c. voyeurism.
   d. exhibitionism.

4. Donald, who likes to look at attractive women, wonders whether he is really a voyeur. Which incident below would indicate that he is?
   a. He drove fifty miles to see bottomless dancers.
   b. He bought ten copies of nudist magazines.
   c. He prefers "peeping" to having sex with his wife.
   d. He spends the summer at a swimming pool so that he can watch women in swimsuits.

5. Harold is in behavior therapy for exhibitionism. His therapist is helping him learn appropriate ways of deriving sexual gratification and is modeling improved social skills. What component of Harold's therapy, common in a learning approach, is missing?
   a. Harold is not examining unconscious castration anxieties.
   b. Harold is not receiving medical treatment to reduce his sex drive.
   c. Harold is not receiving the "squeeze technique."
   d. Harold's inappropriate behaviors are not receiving aversive conditioning.

6. Gina has become intensely fearful of the dark. Since a particular incident occurred, she has little desire for sex, and, when she has sex, there are flashbacks of that incident. It's a good bet that Gina
   a. has survived a rape.
   b. has a husband with erectile dysfunction.
   c. was a victim of an exhibitionist.
   d. has a paraphilia.

7. Kara has inhibited sexual desire, whereas Fred occasionally has problems maintaining an erection. Kara's problem is an example of a disorder in the ____________ stage of the sexual response cycle; Fred's problem is in the ____________ stage.
   a. excitement; orgasm
   b. appetitive; excitement
   c. appetitive; resolution
   d. excitement; appetitive

8. Dr. Knowlton says, "If women masturbate, this common problem can be completely eliminated. However, there is good reason to believe that, without manual stimulation, the problem will continue during normal intercourse." What problem is Dr. Knowlton discussing?
   a. Functional vaginismus
   b. Transvestic fetishism
   c. Primary inhibited sexual orgasm
   d. Gender identity disorder in women

9. John received a penile implant as treatment for a sexual problem. It is likely that the problem was
   a. premature ejaculation.
   b. low sexual desire.
   c. pedophilia.
   d. erectile dysfunction.

10. Mrs. Johnson is instructed by a therapist to stimulate her husband's penis while it is outside the vagina until he senses an ejaculation about to occur. She is then to stop stimulation and continue only after a short time has gone by. What sexual dysfunction is probably being treated?
    a. Mrs. Johnson's sexual pain disorder
    b. Mr. Johnson's premature ejaculation
    c. Mr. Johnson's erectile dysfunction
    d. Mrs. Johnson's sexual desire disorder

ANSWERS TO FACT AND CONCEPT QUESTIONS

1. a. Religious and legal authorities have made many pronouncements about which sexual acts are moral or illegal, and these color definitions of sexual deviation.
   b. Not all sexual deviations involve personal distress; for example, fetishists can be quite content with their behavior.
   *c. Because there are many conflicting legal and moral perspectives on acceptable sex, definitions of deviance are difficult. (p. 320)
   d. Only the sexual dysfunctions involve an inability to perform; gender identity disorders and paraphilias involve no such problem.

2. *a. Transsexuals show gender identity abnormalities at a young age. (p. 322)
   b. Most transsexuals are men.
   c. Transsexuals maintain their gender identity disorder throughout adulthood.
   d. Transsexuals feel trapped in the wrong body and desire a change in physical characteristics.

3. a. Pedophilia, sexual involvement with children, is unrelated to cross-dressing.
   b. Premature ejaculation is a sexual dysfunction unrelated to male role models or cross-dressing.
   c. Sexual desire disorders are unrelated to cross-dressing.
   *d. Lack of male role models and cross-dressing are early experiences in many cases of gender identity disorder. (p. 323)

4. *a. Transvestic fetishism involves sexual arousal when cross-dressing, but not as a function of gender identity disorder. (p. 326)
   b. Cross-dressing related to gender identity disorder is not done for sexual arousal; the person feels he or she is trapped in the body of the wrong sex.
   c. Exhibitionism is revealing one's genitals in order to shock someone else.
   d. Fetishism involves extremely strong attraction to an inanimate object (bras, shoes, etc.).

5. a. Rubbing against a nonconsenting person is the core symptom of frotteurism.
 *b. Rubbing against a nonconsenting person is the core symptom of frotteurism; voyeurism involves watching others engage in sexual actitivity or observing unsuspecting undressed people. (p. 328)
 c. Transvestic fetishism is deriving sexual arousal from cross-dressing.
 d. Exhibitionism involves exposing one's genitals to unsuspecting individuals for shock value.

6. a. Exhibitionists almost always expose themselves to strangers.
 *b. Pedophiles tend to be fathers, stepfathers, or friends of the children they abuse. (p. 329)
 c. Masochists receive pain and humiliation; they do not victimize others.
 d. Transvestites do not victimize others; they merely cross-dress to obtain sexual gratification.

7. a. Transvestites do not victimize others.
 b. Premature ejaculation, a sexual dysfunction, causes anguish to the premature ejaculator.
 c. Voyeurs tend to be harmless; they want only to "peep," not to have sex.
 *d. Sadomasochism may be scripted and mutual, but pain, humiliation, and helplessness are its goals. (p. 330)

8. a. Classical conditioning proposes that certain stimuli are paired.
 b. Sociocultural theory would stress the roles of men and women.
 *c. Psychoanalytic theory asserts that all sexual deviations stem from unconscious fears of castration that go back to the oedipal stage of development. (p. 332)
 d. Masochism would not involve too *few* superego controls, but excessively harsh controls.

9. a. Learning approaches would want to weaken and eliminate any association between children and sexual arousal.
 b. Only in psychoanalytic therapy would raising unconscious issues be important.
 c. Because neither a nor b is correct, this cannot be true.
 *d. Because both a and b are false, this is the best answer. (p. 333)

10. a. ABR involves getting the patient to see his effect on a victim; those with gender identity disorder have no victims.
 *b. ABR helps exhibitionists see the impact they have on victims and controls compulsive exposing. (p. 334)
 c. Premature ejaculation is shaming enough without additional "treatment."
 d. Homosexuality is a life lived in an atmosphere of unacceptance; there are no intended victims in this lifestyle.

11. a. The motivation behind most sadomasochism is helplessness.
 *b. Three common motives for rapists are power, anger, and sadism. (p. 336)
 c. Transvestic fetishism is motivated by sexual arousal, not power.
 d. Exhibitionists may want to impress and shock women, but anger is not a common motive.

12. a. Cultural spillover theory is associated with increased rates of one sexually deviant behavior: rape.
 b. Cultural spillover theory is unrelated to sexual dysfunction.
 c. Cultural spillover theory is unrelated to the paraphilias.
 *d. Research indicates that where violence is condoned there is a "spillover effect" and rape is more common. (p. 337)

13. *a. Imprisonment is the "treatment" most sex offenders get; it does not usually change their behavior. (p. 340)
    b. There has been no controlled research comparing psychotherapy and biological treatment.
    c. Rapists have *not* been found to be effectively treated; child molesters and exhibitionists seem to be treated more effectively.
    d. In one study, surgical castration led to reduced sexual activity and fantasy; results from Europe indicate low recidivism rates after castration.

14. a. AIDS symptoms take a very long time to show after a person is infected; this is why spread of the virus is so common.
    b. AIDS kills by attacking the immune system and allowing infections that ordinarily would be repelled to advance into such diseases as pneumonia and Kaposi's sarcoma (a form of cancer).
    c. There is no evidence that HIV is transmitted through kissing.
    *d. Roughly 95 percent of people infected with HIV are dead ten years later; their immune systems are so destroyed that they die of infections that ordinarily the body would be able to repel. (p. 342)

15. a. The Janus Report indicates that, despite worries about AIDS, sexual activity is the same or more frequent than before.
    b. On the contrary, the Janus Report indicates that sexual frequency for those over 65 is not much less than for those in their 30s and 40s.
    c. Research on the sexual response cycle was conducted by Masters and Johnson in laboratory settings.
    *d. The Janus Report shows that sexual behavior and satisfaction are unexpectedly high for those over 50 years old. (p. 355)

16. a. Paraphilias are relatively rare, occur in men more than in women, and are not sexual dysfunctions.
    b. Premature ejaculation is a dysfunction that occurs exclusively in men.
    *c. Perhaps the most common of the sexual dysfunctions, sexual desire disorders are more common in women, but, without knowing what is "normal," the diagnosis is difficult. (p. 346)
    d. Females do not achieve erections.

17. a. Sexual desire disorders involve a lack of interest in sexual behavior.
    b. Vaginismus involves uncontrolled spasms.
    *c. A secondary disorder is one that is currently a problem but was not at some previous time. (p. 348)
    d. A paraphilia is arousal associated with a bizarre object or situation; inhibited orgasm is not a paraphilia but a dysfunction.

18. a. Lack of sexual desire is a problem in the appetitive stage, not during excitement and orgasm, as is true with vaginismus.
    *b. Vaginismus (spasms in the vagina) and dyspareunia (pain on intercourse) are forms of sexual pain disorders. (p. 349)
    c. Premature ejaculation and erectile dysfunction are male dysfunctions unrelated to pain.
    d. Erectile dysfunction is unrelated to pain.

19. a. Excessive levels of testosterone would increase masculine behavior.
    b. Childhood upbringing is an example of a predisposing factor.
    c. Unresolved castration anxiety is an example of a predisposing factor.
    *d. Pressure and anxiety over performance are current factors that are particularly important causes of erectile dysfunction. (p. 347)

20. a. Comparisons of nonclinical samples of homosexuals with heterosexuals show no significant difference in psychological adjustment.
    b. If anything, lesbians show better psychological adjustment than male homosexuals.
    c. Most psychologists agree that ego dystonicity (distress) over one's homosexual orientation affects every homosexual at some point.
    *d. Nonclinical homosexual samples are no more disturbed than nonclinical heterosexual samples. (p. 354)

ANSWERS TO APPLICATION QUESTIONS

1. *a. Gender identity disorder involves the feeling of being trapped in the body of the wrong sex. (p. 322)
   b. Sexual desire disorder is reserved for adults who have no interest in sexual activity or who avoid it.
   c. Pedophiles do not feel trapped; they sexually abuse children.
   d. Transvestites cross-dress, but they do so for sexual arousal, not because they identify with the opposite sex.

2. *a. Paraphilias are quite rare in females. (p. 325)
   b. In most cases, people have more than one paraphilia; for example, child molesters often commit rape or expose themselves.
   c. Most transvestites are married heterosexual males.
   d. Most people with paraphilias are socially unskilled.

3. a. Gender identity disorders involve a conflict between genetic sex and preferred sex-appropriate dress and behavior.
   b. Exposing one's genitals constitutes a paraphilia, not a sexual dysfunction.
   c. Voyeurism involves observing sexual behavior in unsuspecting individuals or looking at disrobed people who do not consent to being observed.
   *d. The key symptom of exhibitionism is fantasizing about and actually exposing one's genitals in the manner Todd illustrates. (p. 327)

4. a. This does not illustrate the risk taking and exclusive preference shown in the disorder.
   b. This does not illustrate the risk taking and exclusive preference shown in the disorder.
   *c. When observing is preferred over sex, the disorder can be diagnosed. (p. 328)
   d. This does not illustrate the risk taking and exclusive preference shown in the disorder.

5. a. Psychoanalytic, not behavior, therapy would emphasize unconscious castration anxieties.
   b. Behavior therapists do not rely on medicine to alter this behavior.
   c. The "squeeze technique" is used to treat premature ejaculation.
   *d. Behavior therapists would first ensure that the problem behavior had been extinguished before moving on to more appropriate alternatives. (p. 333)

6. *a. The common psychological consequences of rape are fears related to rape, reduced desire for or aversion to sex, and flashbacks of the rape during sex. (p. 335)
   b. Erectile dysfunction may be upsetting, but fears and flashbacks in women are unheard of.
   c. Victims of exhibitionism may be distressed, but there are no reports of effects on the desire for sex or the production of flashbacks.
   d. Few women have paraphilias.

7. a. Erectile dysfunctions are associated with the excitement stage.
   *b. Sexual desire is part of the appetitive stage and erections are part of the excitement stage in the normal sexual response cycle. (p. 342)
   c. Erectile dysfunctions are associated with the excitement stage.
   d. Sexual desire is part of the appetitive stage, not the excitement stage.

8. a. Functional vaginismus usually stems from partners suffering from impotence, strict upbringing, sexual trauma, or dyspareunia.
   b. Transvestic fetishism is a male problem.
   *c. Inhibited sexual orgasm is often seen as a problem of insufficient stimulation, but a great deal of controversy exists over the "normal" response of women during intercourse. (Focus 11.3; p. 347)
   d. Gender identity disorders in women would stem from very early childhood upbringing or biological differences, not from masturbatory practices.

9. a. Premature ejaculation is treated with the "squeeze technique."
   b. Low sexual desire is a problem caused by relationship stress or medication, not physical equipment.
   c. Pedophilia is not a sexual dysfunction.
   *d. Penile implants are frequently a successful treatment for erectile dysfunction when psychological treatments have failed. (p. 350)

10. a. A sexual pain disorder (vaginismus) would be treated by relaxation and insertion of successively larger dilators.
   *b. Premature ejaculation is treated by increasing the time during which stimulation occurs prior to ejaculation. (p. 352)
   c. Treatment of erectile dysfunction would increase stimulation, not stop it.
   d. Sexual desire disorder is treated with education, relaxation, and couples therapy.

PART 4
Severe Disorders of Mood and Thought

CHAPTER 12
Mood Disorders

LEARNING OBJECTIVES

When you have mastered the material in Chapter 12, you should be able to:

1. Describe the mood disorders and distinguish them from normal mood changes. Recall prevalence rates for these disorders. (pp. 359–360)
2. Describe the clinical symptoms of depression, including the affective, cognitive, behavioral, and physiological domains. (pp. 360–362)
3. Describe the clinical symptoms of mania. Differentiate the two levels of manic intensity. (pp. 362–363)
4. Describe and differentiate among the following mood disorders: major depressive disorder, dysthymic disorder, the bipolar disorders, cyclothymic disorder, and mood disorders associated with a medical condition or substance use. (pp. 363–365)
5. List and differentiate the symptom features that may accompany mood disorders. Describe and differentiate course specifiers, including cycling type, seasonal, postpartum, and longitudinal patterns of mood disorders. Compare unipolar and bipolar disorders. (pp. 365–366)
6. Appreciate cross-cultural differences in depression. Explain how stress is related to depression and how symptoms of depression may make the disorder self-perpetuating. Discuss the role of social support on stress and depression. (pp. 366–369; Focus 12.1)
7. Describe what is known about sex differences and depression and explanations for any differences. (pp. 369–370).
8. Describe, compare, and contrast the psychoanalytic and behavioral theories of depression. Describe Lewinsohn's comprehensive view of depression. (pp. 370–372)
9. Describe Beck's cognitive theory of depression, including the "primary triad" and four errors of logic typical of negative schemas. Define the personality patterns called sociotropy and autonomy and explain how they influence depression. (pp. 372–374)
10. Describe Seligman's original learned helplessness formulation of depression. Describe the attributional style of depressives and the strengths and limits of using this idea to explain depression. (pp. 374–376)
11. Describe the genetic and biochemical theories of depression, discussing the strengths and limits of these ideas. Discuss the role of REM and cortisol in depression. (pp. 376–379)
12. Evaluate the strengths and weaknesses of the various theories of depression. (p. 379)
13. Indicate the kinds of medications that have been used to treat depression, the reasons they are effective, and their side effects. Describe what occurs during electroconvulsive therapy (ECT), its effectiveness, and side effects. (Focus 12.2; pp. 379–381)

14. Describe cognitive behavioral therapy for depression, its effectiveness, and evidence for its superiority over medication. Explain why treatment outcome research is so difficult. (Critical Thinking 12.1; pp. 381–385)
15. Describe the use of lithium and its problems in treating bipolar disorders. (pp. 385–387)

CHAPTER OUTLINE

1. **Mood disorders** (pp. 359–360) *Mood disorders* are disturbances in emotions that cause discomfort or hinder functioning. *Depression* is by far the most common mood disorder and is characterized by sadness, feelings of worthlessness, and social withdrawal. *Mania* is characterized by elevated mood, expansiveness, and irritability. Depression and mania are different from normal mood changes because they are more intense, last longer, and may occur for no apparent reason. Depression, more common in women, does not respect socioeconomic status, educational achievements, or personal characteristics.

2. **The symptoms of depression and mania** (pp. 360–363) The affective (emotional) symptoms of depression are sadness, dejection, crying spells, and feelings of worthlessness. Cognitive symptoms include profound pessimism, loss of interest, and suicidal thoughts. The cognitive triad (negativism about self, others, and the future) is found in depressives. Behavioral symptoms include poor personal hygiene, slowed speech and movement, and social withdrawal. Physiological symptoms of depression include disturbances of eating, sleeping, sexual activity, and menstruation.

   The affective symptoms of mania are elation or irritability and grandiosity. Cognitive symptoms include accelerated and disjointed speech. Behaviorally, at the level of hypomania, people are overactive but not delusional. Mania involves increased levels of activity, incoherence, and sleeplessness. In severe forms, hallucinations and delusions appear and the person is uncontrollable.

3. **Classification of mood disorders** (Focus 12.1; pp. 363–366, 368) Depressive disorders are considered *unipolar,* whereas disorders with manic and depressive episodes are *bipolar disorders*. Depressive disorders include major depressive disorder, *dysthymic disorder,* and depressive disorders not otherwise specified. Symptoms must be present for at least two weeks and must represent a change from typical functioning to be considered signs of a mood disorder. About half of those who have a depressive episode have another. Some depressions have psychotic features such as hallucinations and delusions. Dysthymic disorder is a chronic condition involving depressed mood, low self-esteem, fatigue, and apathy. Bipolar disorders are identified when manic episodes last one week or four days (in the case of hypomania). Depression almost always follows a manic period. If hypomanic and depressed mood swings do not meet the criteria for bipolar disorder, the diagnosis is *cyclothymic disorder*, a disorder more common than bipolar and less common than dysthymic disorder.

   Mood disorders due to general medical conditions and substance-induced mood disorders are also categories in the DSM-IV. DSM-IV also lists *symptom features*—characteristics that accompany mood disorders but are not criteria for diagnosis. These include *melancholia* (lost of pleasure, depression worse in the morning) and *catatonia* (immobility and negativism). *Course specifiers* in DSM-IV indicate whether the mood disorder is *cyclic* (how quickly moods shift from manic to depression), *seasonal, postpartum* (after giving birth), or *longitudinal* (length between relapses).

   Unipolar and bipolar disorders are distinguished from one another because, in bipolar, inheritance plays a bigger role, the age of onset is earlier, depressive episodes involve greater motor retardation, and lithium provides effective relief. Lifetime prevalence of bipolar disorder is between 0.4 and 1.2 percent; for major depressive disorder, it is between 7 and 18 percent. Finally, there is no sex difference for bipolar disorder, but major depression is far more common in women.

4. **The etiology of mood disorders** (pp. 366–379) There are few theories explaining the cause of bipolar disorders. For depression, differences in prevalence rates and symptom pictures across cultures suggest that culture and psychosocial stressors are important. Stress theory argues that individuals have a vulnerability to depression (diathesis), exposure to stressors, and limited resources such as social supports. Gender differences in depression may not be real because women are more likely to be seen in treatment and may report their symptoms more readily than men. Diagnostic bias and misdiagnosis of male depression are other explanations. Differences in how men and women respond to depressed moods may also account for the sex difference.

   Psychoanalysts suggest that separation and anger are potent factors in depression. Separation can be real or symbolic, but is different from normal mourning. Guilt can account for some depressive symptoms, and anger (at the lost person) turned against the self accounts for others. Behaviorists suggest that reduced reinforcements lead to reduced reinforceable activity, thus producing a downward spiral. A lack of self-reinforcement, social skills, and a tendency to create more stressors are also associated with depression.

   Lewinsohn and his colleagues have developed a comprehensive view of depression: Stress disrupts established behavior patterns, positive reinforcement declines, self-critical and low-confidence thoughts produce depressed affect, which makes functioning more difficult.

   Cognitive theorists suggest that depressives' *schemas* for interpreting events produce low self-esteem. According to Beck, depressives operate from a primary triad involving negative expectations about self, others, and the future. Four errors in logic typify this schema: arbitrary inference, selected abstraction, overgeneralization, and magnification and minimization. Beck has added *sociotropy* and *autonomy* (positive interchange with other people and independence from others, respectively) to the theory. *Learned helplessness* theory argues that depression occurs when, after experiencing uncontrollable stressors, a person comes to believe that he or she has no effect on the environment. Coupled with a certain attributional style, learned helplessness leads to the passivity that characterizes depression. The pessimistic attributional style sees the causes of bad events as internal, global (true for many situations), and stable (a permanent condition).

   Biological explanations of the causes of mood disorders emphasize evidence that genetic factors play a role, particularly in bipolar disorder. Genetic factors may predispose people to a deficit of activity in certain neurotransmitters called catecholamines. The *catecholamine hypothesis* proposes that low levels of norepinephrine, dopamine, or serotonin make individuals vulnerable to depression. Different neurotransmitter imbalances may be associated with different subtypes of mood disorders. Other biological factors related to depression are REM sleep patterns and responses to the dexamethasone suppression test (DST).

5. **Evaluating the causation theories** (p. 379) Our knowledge has been increased by using longitudinal research designs, advanced technologies, and an awareness that there are subtypes of mood disorders. All current causation theories have weaknesses. Some seem oversimplistic, whereas others are unable to explain all forms of depression. It is likely that at the mild end of the continuum, psychological factors explain many disorders, but, as severity increases, the influence of biological factors increases, too.

6. **The treatment of mood disorders** (pp. 379–387) The principal medications used to treat depression are *tricyclic antidepressants* and *monoamine oxidase (MAO) inhibitors*. About 65 percent of moderately to severely depressed patients improve on tricyclics; however, clinicians give more favorable ratings about the effectiveness of medication than do patients. *Prozac* is a widely used medication; it blocks the reuptake of serotonin.

   Electroconvulsive therapy (ECT) is usually reserved for severe depressives who do not respond to medications. Combinations of these two treatments are sometimes used. Cognitive therapy is growing in popularity. In the first stage of this therapy, the client monitors all thoughts and discovers how thinking is related to negative moods. Irrational beliefs are challenged and replaced. In the second stage, the client engages in more pleasurable activities and learns better social skills. Cognitive-behavioral therapy reduces risk of relapses and is as effective as medication. There are many problems in doing treatment outcome research.

   Drugs such as lithium are often used in the treatment of bipolar disorder, although there are disturbing side effects. Patient compliance with lithium treatment is another impediment.

KEY TERMS

Fill-in-the-Blanks Quiz

1. A pattern of thinking or a cognitive set that determines an individual's reactions and responses is called a(n) ___________.

2. In Beck's cognitive theory of depression, the tendency to be independent of other people is called ___________.

3. The emotional state characterized by great elation, seemingly boundless energy, and irritability is called ___________.

4. Severe disturbances of mood or affect involving depression, mania, or both are called ___________.

5. The disorders in which both depression and mania are exhibited and those in which only mania has been exhibited are called ___________.

6. The idea that neurotransmitters such as norepinephrine, serotonin, and dopamine are implicated in mood disorders is called the ___________.

7. The emotional state characterized by intense dysphoria, sadness, feelings of futility and worthlessness, and withdrawal from others is called ___________.

8. A mild, chronic mood disorder characterized by nonpsychotic mood swings is called ___________.

9. A mild, chronic mood disorder characterized by nonpsychotic depression is called ___________.

10. Acquiring the belief that one is helpless and cannot control the outcomes in one's life is called ___________.

11. A major mood disorder in which depressive symptoms are exhibited but not mania is called ___________.

12. In Beck's theory of depression, the tendency to be involved with other people is called ___________.

13. The medication for depression that works by impeding serotonin reuptake is called ___________.

14. Diagnostic characteristics of mood disorders that indicate whether the disorder occurs during specific seasons of the year, after a woman gives birth, or cycles rapidly between mania and depression are called ___________.

15. The medications for depression that work by preventing an enzyme from breaking down norepinephrine are called ___________.

16. The characteristics of mood disorders that indicate such things as whether an individual experiences catatonia or melancholia are called ___________.

17. The medications for depression that work by impeding the reuptake of norepinephrine are called ___________.

Answers to Fill-in-the-Blanks Quiz

1. schema
2. autonomy
3. mania
4. mood disorders
5. bipolar disorders
6. catecholamine hypothesis
7. depression
8. cyclothymic disorder
9. dysthymic disorder
10. learned helplessness
11. unipolar disorder
12. sociotropy
13. Prozac
14. course specifiers
15. monoamine oxidase (MAO) inhibitors
16. symptom features
17. tricyclic antidepressants

FACT AND CONCEPT QUESTIONS

1. When a person's mood disturbance involves hyperactivity, irritability, and expansiveness, the problem is considered
   a. depression.
   b. dysthymia.
   c. mania.
   d. schizophrenia.

2. The prevalence of mania is ___________ that of major depression.
   a. about one-half
   b. about the same as
   c. more than two times
   d. about one-tenth

3. Difficulty in concentration, suicidal thoughts, and loss of motivation are
   a. physiological signs of depression.
   b. cognitive signs of depression.
   c. elements of the cognitive triad.
   d. affective signs of hypomania.

4. Which of the following symptoms is characteristic of hypomania?
   a. Slowed movements and speech
   b. Wild ranting, sleeplessness, and hallucinations
   c. "High" mood, poor judgment, and grand ideas
   d. Weight loss, feelings of worthlessness, and apathy

5. When a mild depression continues for many months or years and depression seems to be part of a person's personality, the appropriate diagnosis is
   a. dysthymic disorder.
   b. exogenous depression.
   c. cyclothymic disorder.
   d. major depression.

6. Mood disorders that occur during certain seasons of the year or after a woman gives birth are considered disorders
   a. that are endogenous.
   b. with certain symptom features.
   c. that are bipolar.
   d. with course specifiers.

7. The gender difference in ____________ may be either "real" and due to hormonal differences or caused by ____________.
   a. bipolar disorder; diagnosticians' expectations about women
   b. major depression; women's greater likelihood to ask for help
   c. major depression; men's tendency to ruminate about their symptoms
   d. bipolar disorder; women's greater likelihood to ask for help

8. Symbolic loss, grief work, and anger turned inward are central concepts in the ____________ theory of depression.
   a. psychoanalytic
   b. cognitive
   c. learned helplessness
   d. operant conditioning

9. When family and friends are sympathetic toward a depressed person, according to behavioral psychologists,
   a. the person develops a negative cognitive schema.
   b. the family shows a negative attributional style.
   c. the depression will deepen.
   d. this will challenge the depressive's irrational beliefs.

10. According to ___________, the cure for depression requires increased activity levels and improved social skills; according to ___________, the cure for depression is changed schemas and improved self-esteem.
    a. Beck; Seligman
    b. Seligman; Lewinsohn
    c. Freud; Beck
    d. Lewinsohn; Beck

11. In Weiss's research, helplessness in laboratory animals stemmed from
    a. experiencing electric shocks.
    b. being given drugs that reduced their norepinephrine levels.
    c. being raised without their mothers.
    d. the experience of having no control over electric shocks.

12. When things are going poorly, depressives make attributions that are
    a. external, unstable, and global.
    b. internal, stable, and global.
    c. internal, unstable, and specific.
    d. external, stable, and global.

13. Studies to determine the biological factors that cause mood disorders have shown that
    a. concordance rates for MZ and DZ twins are about the same for bipolar disorder.
    b. the incidence of major depression is higher in individuals' adoptive families than in their biological families.
    c. concordance rates for bipolar disorder are higher for MZ twins than for DZ twins.
    d. biological factors are more potent predictors of major depression than of bipolar disorder.

14. Low levels of ___________ are most commonly found in people suffering from major depression.
    a. REM sleep
    b. norepinephrine
    c. dexamethasone
    d. Prozac and lithium carbonate

15. What does the dexamethasone suppression test measure?
    a. Degree of norepinephrine reuptake
    b. The degree of "high" and depth of "low" in bipolar patients
    c. The cortisol levels of depressives
    d. The contribution of genetic factors to chronic depression

16. One type of drug used to treat unipolar depression has a number of serious side effects related to diet. These drugs are known as
    a. MAO inhibitors.
    b. catecholamines.
    c. tricyclics.
    d. Prozac.

17. Electroconvulsive therapy (ECT) is usually used for treating ___________, but it causes serious side effects, such as ___________.
    a. bipolar disorder; gastrointestinal difficulties
    b. severely depressed patients; confusion and memory loss
    c. dysthymic individuals; increased REM sleep and decreased norepinephrine
    d. mildly depressed individuals; dependency on the therapist and increasing apathy

18. The client monitors his or her thoughts and emotions, then increases pleasurable activities and social skills. These processes are components of
    a. psychoanalytic therapy for depression.
    b. psychoanalytic therapy for bipolar disorder.
    c. cognitive-behavioral therapy for bipolar disorder.
    d. cognitive-behavioral therapy for depression.

19. Which of the following is a desirable feature in a study to evaluate the effectiveness of treatment for depression?
    a. Identifying clients high in sociotropy or autonomy
    b. Allowing therapists to adopt procedures that are individualized for each client
    c. Protecting the privacy of clients by not revealing the demographic characteristics of the sample
    d. Using only one measure of outcome

20. Lithium carbonate is usually used in the treatment of
    a. dysthymic disorder.
    b. bipolar disorder.
    c. unipolar depression.
    d. melancholia.

APPLICATION QUESTIONS

1. Jon is so depressed that if he thinks about himself or the future, all he can imagine is failure. He does not believe that anyone else can help him, either. Jon's symptoms illustrate
    a. the physiological symptoms of depression.
    b. the affective symptoms of depression.
    c. what Beck calls the cognitive triad of depression.
    d. what Freud calls learned helplessness.

2. Frank is diagnosed with bipolar disorder. His symptoms are elevated mood, disjointed talk, excessive sleep, and irritability at others. Which aspect of Frank's case is unusual?
    a. Most people with bipolar disorder are female.
    b. Most people with bipolar disorder remain awake for long periods.
    c. Most people with bipolar disorder are calm rather than irritable.
    d. Disjointed talk never occurs in bipolar disorder.

3. Sarah has been mildly depressed for almost three years. Depression is virtually a part of her personality, but she gets neither much better nor much worse. What is a likely diagnosis for Sarah?
   a. Dysthymic disorder
   b. Cyclothymic disorder
   c. Psychotic depression
   d. Bipolar disorder, depressed

4. Dr. Nathan says, "If there is a sex difference, it is probably because women tend to present themselves to helping professionals more often than men do." Dr. Nathan's remarks indicate
   a. a belief that the sex difference is real, not apparent.
   b. a belief that the sex difference is apparent, not real.
   c. both a and b are true.
   d. neither a nor b is true.

5. Richard is depressed, and his therapist says, "The best way to feel better is to do more. Doing more increases your chances of being rewarded and finding pleasure in your activities." Richard's therapist illustrates
   a. the psychoanalytic approach to treatment.
   b. Lewinsohn's learning approach to treatment.
   c. Beck's cognitive approach to treatment.
   d. the humanistic-existential approach to treatment.

6. Cathy throws a party one evening, but it rains so hard that the party must be cancelled. Cathy concludes that she is worthless. According to Beck's cognitive theory, this error in logic is called
   a. magnification and minimization.
   b. undergeneralization.
   c. the cognitive triad.
   d. arbitrary inference.

7. Seligman suggests that depressives make a certain type of attribution for failure. Which statement below best illustrates that attributional style?
   a. "I didn't work hard enough, but tomorrow I will work harder."
   b. "The job was too hard for anyone to do; I can't blame myself."
   c. "I am stupid and I always will be stupid; it shows in everything I do."
   d. "Just because I fail in one area of life doesn't mean I'll fail in others."

8. Verne suffers from major depression. What can we predict about his sleep habits?
   a. He may have trouble getting to sleep or awaken earlier than he wants.
   b. He may have slower onset and less frequent REM sleep than others.
   c. Both a and b are true.
   d. Neither a nor b is true.

9. Kim was severely depressed and was given a certain kind of biological treatment. One evening, at a wine and cheese party, she became terribly ill. What kind of treatment was Kim probably receiving?
   a. Prozac
   b. Electroconvulsive therapy (ECT)
   c. Tricyclic medication
   d. MAO inhibitors

10. Martha has major depressive disorder. She was treated with tricyclics and MAO inhibitors without success. Her therapist tells her, "The only effective treatment left is ECT." What is incorrect about this advice?
    a. ECT is only effective with people suffering from bipolar disorder.
    b. ECT is ineffective if tricyclic medication has been ineffective.
    c. Cognitive therapy is as successful as drug therapy.
    d. Lithium is the most successful treatment for major depressive disorder.

ANSWERS TO FACT AND CONCEPT QUESTIONS

1. a. Depression is characterized by sadness, feelings of worthlessness, and reduced activity.
   b. Dysthymia is a mild depression that goes on for long periods.
   *c. Mania involves uncontrollably "high" moods that include excessive activity, sleeplessness, and irritability because others cannot keep up. (p. 363)
   d. Schizophrenia is a thought disorder rather than a mood disorder.

2. a. Mania occurs with a prevalence of about 0.6 percent, whereas the prevalence of depression is about 5 percent or more, about 10 times the difference.
   b. Mania is much less common than depression.
   c. Mania is much less common than depression.
   *d. Mania occurs with a prevalence of about 0.6 percent, whereas the prevalence of depression is about 5 percent or more, about 10 times the difference. (pp. 359–360)

3. a. Physiological (bodily) symptoms of depression include gastrointestinal problems, weight loss, and sleep problems.
   *b. Cognitive (thought) symptoms of depression include poor concentration, thoughts of suicide and worthlessness, and negative self-statements. (p. 361)
   c. The cognitive triad involves illogical ways of viewing one's self.
   d. The affective signs of hypomania are hyperactivity and grandiosity.

4. a. Hypomania is a form of bipolar disorder involving excessive and rapid activity.
   b. Mania is the more severe form of bipolar disorder where people are delusional, stay up for long hours, and speak wildly.
   *c. Hypomania, a milder form of mania, is marked by hyperactivity and poor judgment. (p. 363)
   d. Feelings of worthlessness and apathy are key symptoms of depression.

5. *a. Dysthymic disorder is a mild depression that goes on for so long (years, in many cases) that it seems congruent with the person's personality. (p. 365)
   b. An exogenous depression is triggered by outside events and usually ends when the stressor does.
   c. Cyclothymic disorder involves mild, but chronic, mood swings.
   d. Major depression has more severe symptoms than those described here and must elicit behaviors foreign to the person's personality.

6. a. Endogenous mood disorders are ones that are unrelated to environmental changes.
   b. Symptom features include catatonia (lack of movement) and melancholia (lack of motivation) and focus on the behaviors of the individual, not the circumstances under which the disorders occur.
   c. Bipolar disorders involve mood swings.
   *d. Course specifiers describe the circumstances under which the disorders occur: seasonal, postpartum, cycling, and longitudinal patterns are examples. (p. 363)

7. a. There is no sex difference in rates of bipolar disorder.
   *b. There is a considerable sex difference in reported rates of major depression, but this may only be an illusory difference because women are more likely to request help. (p. 369)
   c. The sex difference in major depression is that women have a higher rate than men; women tend to ruminate about their symptoms more than men.
   d. There is no sex difference in rates of bipolar disorder.

8. *a. Psychoanalysts believe that early childhood losses, incomplete grieving, and angry feelings turned toward oneself are important in depression. (p. 370)
   b. The cognitive perspective emphasizes illogical thinking, negative schemas, and inappropriate attributions.
   c. Learned helplessness argues that depression occurs when individuals mistakenly generalize the belief they have no control over the events in their lives from a circumstance when inescapable negative consequences occurred.
   d. The operant conditioning approach to depression highlights poor social skills, lack of reinforcement for actions, and reinforcement for inaction.

9. a. Negative cognitive schemas are persistent thoughts that cause depression; kindness will not help one develop.
   b. The depressive has a negative attributional style (gives internal and stable [trait] reasons for any failure), not the family or friends.
   *c. According to operant theorists, when depressive behavior is rewarded through sympathetic attention, the depressed person will probably withdraw further and get worse. (p. 371)
   d. Sympathy does not challenge irrational beliefs; in fact, it may strengthen them.

10. a. Increases in social skills are more the concern of an operant therapist than of a cognitive therapist like Beck.
    b. Lewinsohn is a believer in operant conditioning and puts less emphasis on cognitive issues like schemas and self-esteem.
    c. Freud stressed the symbolic, not the social skills or activity levels of patients.
    *d. Lewinsohn is an operant theorist and emphasizes what people do; Beck is a cognitive theorist concerned with what they think. (pp. 371–373)

11. a. Weiss's animals did receive electric shocks, but as long as they were able to attempt to escape, they did not become depressed.
    b. Weiss's animals were given electric shocks, not drugs.
    c. Weiss's animals were not separated from their mothers.
    *d. Learned helplessness theory suggests that it is the uncontrollability of shocks that produces passivity, not the shocks themselves. (p. 378)

12. a. Depressives tend to blame themselves (make internal attributions) when things go poorly.
 *b. Depressives are depressed because they blame themselves (internal) for everything (global) and assume that their inability is unchanging (stable). (pp. 375–376)
 c. If people say that they are at fault (internal) but that the fault is specific to one situation and may change, they are less apt to become depressed.
 d. Depressives tend to blame themselves, not outside factors.

13. a. Higher concordance rates for MZ (70+ percent) than for DZ twins (10+ percent) indicate a strong genetic contribution.
 b. Rates are higher in biological families than in adoptive ones.
 *c. Higher concordance rates for MZ (70+ percent) than for DZ twins (10+ percent) indicate a strong genetic contribution. (p. 377)
 d. Biological factors appear to be better predictors of bipolar disorder than of major depression.

14. a. In major depression, REM sleep appears to be excessive.
 *b. Supporting the catecholamine hypothesis, low levels of norepinephrine activity are found in major depression and are changed by antidepressant drugs. (p. 378)
 c. Dexamethasone usually suppresses cortisol levels, but only in certain kinds of depression.
 d. Prozac is an antidepressant medication; lithium carbonate is a treatment for bipolar disorder.

15. a. There is no test for norepinephrine reuptake; tricyclic antidepressants work by decreasing such reuptake.
 b. Mood swings are evaluated by observation of behavior.
 *c. The dexamethasone suppression test detects abnormally high levels of cortisol in some kinds of depression. (p. 379)
 d. The dexamethasone suppression test cannot assess genetic influence.

16. *a. MAO inhibitors are antidepressants that interact with tyramine (an amino acid found in many foods) and cause side effects that can be lethal. (p. 380)
 b. Biogenic amines are neurotransmitters that are associated with mood disorders; they are not drugs.
 c. Tricyclics are antidepressants, but they have no known side effects resulting from food interactions.
 d. Prozac is an antidepressant that does not, as far as we know, have any interaction with chemicals in the diet.

17. a. Electroconvulsive therapy is reserved almost exclusively for treating severe unipolar depression.
 *b. ECT is used when drugs have not helped seriously depressed people. Common side effects include memory loss, and in about 1 in every 1,000 cases there are serious medical complications. (p. 381)
 c. Dysthymic disorder is too mild a depression for ECT to be used.
 d. ECT's major side effect is memory loss, not dependency.

18. a. Psychoanalysts would be interested in dreams and the symbolic meaning of depression, not in activities and social skills.
    b. Psychoanalysts would be interested in dreams and the symbolic meaning of bipolar disorder, not in activities and social skills.
    c. Bipolar disorder is usually treated with drugs, particularly lithium carbonate, since it appears to be an endogenous mood disorder.
    *d. Cognitive-behavioral therapy stresses irrational thoughts and the need to change both those thoughts and the behaviors that typically reduce opportunities for pleasure. (p. 381)

19. *a. Research shows that certain forms of treatment are more effective with depressives who are high in autonomy while others are better for depressives high in sociotropy. (Critical Thinking, pp. 384–385; pp. 386–387)
    b. If therapists alter their procedures for each client, comparisons become impossible.
    c. Demographic characteristics are important for understanding which treatments are effective and generalizing results to other, untreated populations.
    d. The validity of results is improved if several measures of outcome are used.

20. a. Dysthymic disorder is a mild, chronic depression; medical treatment would probably involve antidepressants.
    *b. Lithium carbonate is used almost exclusively to treat bipolar disorder; it brings down the highs and lifts the lows. (p. 385)
    c. Unipolar depression is most often treated with antidepressants.
    d. Melancholia is a symptom feature of depressive disorders.

ANSWERS TO APPLICATION QUESTIONS

1. a. Physiological symptoms include weight loss, sleeplessness, and gastrointestinal problems.
   b. Affective symptoms include sadness and crying, slumped posture, and a sense of defeat.
   *c. Beck stresses the cognitive aspects of depression; the cognitive triad consists of negative views of others, of oneself, and of the future. (p. 373)
   d. Seligman, not Freud, is associated with learned helplessness.

2. a. There is no sex difference in rates of bipolar disorder.
   *b. When in the midst of a manic episode, bipolar patients can stay awake for days on end. (p. 365)
   c. When people experience mania, they speed up activity and become irritable with others who cannot keep up.
   d. As mania becomes more severe, the speed of speech increases and its coherence decreases.

3. *a. Dysthymic disorder is a mild form of depression that can last for years and that becomes a natural part of the person's personality. (p. 365)
   b. Cyclothymic disorder is a mild form of bipolar disorder, with repeated mood swings, but without loss of reality contact.
   c. Psychotic depression is so severe that hallucinations and delusions occur.
   d. Bipolar disorder, depressed, requires the experience of at least one manic episode; the depression is more acute than chronic.

4. a. The doctor's remarks suggest that the difference is based on help seeking, not on real differences in depressive behavior.
   *b. The doctor's remarks suggest that the difference is based on help seeking, not on real differences in depressive behavior (p. 369)
   c. Because a is incorrect, this cannot be the best choice.
   d. Because b is correct, this cannot be the best choice.

5. a. Psychoanalysts would see depression as symbolic loss and anger turned inward.
   *b. Lewinsohn takes an operant approach to depression: a lack of reinforcement leads to a lack of action. (pp. 371–372)
   c. Beck's theory would stress how Richard thinks.
   d. Humanistic-existentialists say little about mood disorders.

6. a. Magnification is an exaggeration of limitations, and minimization is a diminution of achievements.
   b. The logical error is *over*generalization.
   c. The cognitive triad is a negative schema for self, others, and the future.
   *d. Arbitrary inference occurs when a depressive draws a conclusion without evidence (for example, a rainy day does not indicate that one is worthless). (p. 373)

7. a. How hard one works is an internal attribution, but suggesting the possibility for change makes it unstable.
   b. Blaming an external factor (task difficulty) for failure contradicts the depressive's attributional tendency.
   *c. The depressive attributional style involves making internal and stable attributions for failure. (pp. 374–375)
   d. Specific attributions are unlike the global attributions of the depressive attributional style.

8. *a. Insomnia and early waking are classic symptoms of depression. (p. 362)
   b. Depressives demonstrate more rapid onset and more frequent REM sleep.
   c. Because b is incorrect, this cannot be the best answer.
   d. Because a is correct, this cannot be the best answer.

9. a. Prozac does not interact with food to cause a negative side effect.
   b. ECT has the side effects of memory loss and confusion, not dangerous interactions with foods.
   c. Tricyclic medications do not interact with tyramine.
   *d. MAO inhibitors interact with the tyramine in certain foods such as wine and cheese and cause serious illness. (p. 380)

10. a. ECT is used with severely depressed people and is much less effective with bipolar disorder.
   b. ECT is often successfully used when antidepressant medication is ineffective.
   *c. Research shows that cognitive therapy is as effective as medication; the two together are no more effective than either separately. (pp. 384–385)
   d. Lithium is only effective in treating bipolar disorder.

CHAPTER 13
Suicide

LEARNING OBJECTIVES

When you have mastered the material in Chapter 13, you should be able to:

1. Identify some of the possible reasons for suicide. Explain why suicide deserves a chapter in the text despite not being classified in the DSM-IV. Discuss why it is difficult to study suicide. Define psychological autopsy. Describe the prevalence, methods, and trends of suicide. (Focus 13.1; pp. 391–393, 394–395)
2. Discuss the relationship between hopelessness, depression, and suicide. Describe and differentiate assessment instruments for suicidality. (pp. 393–396)
3. Discuss the relationship between suicide and other psychological factors, especially alcohol abuse. Explain why alcohol and suicide are closely linked. (pp. 396–397)
4. Describe the sociocultural factors in suicide, including egoistic, altruistic, and anomic suicide. (pp. 397–398)
5. Describe the intrapsychic and biochemical factors related to suicide and the different types of suicide notes. (Focus 13.2; pp. 398–400)
6. Describe and discuss research on child and adolescent suicide, including characteristics of suicidal children, family issues, imitative suicides, and school-based programs. (pp. 400–402)
7. Describe and discuss research on college student suicide, including the characteristics of the victims and reasons for student suicide. (pp. 402–404)
8. Describe and discuss suicide among the elderly and among Asian Americans. (pp. 404–405)
9. Describe Kübler-Ross's stages of reaction by family and friends to a suicide. Discuss how a family member or friend can be effective with a suicidal individual. Discuss the response of mental health professionals to suicide by former clients. (Focus 13.3; pp. 405–407)
10. Describe clues to suicide and crisis intervention efforts to prevent it. (pp. 407–409)
11. Describe the methods used by workers in suicide prevention centers. Discuss the effectiveness of suicide prevention centers. (pp. 409–412)
12. Describe how community prevention programs may help to reduce the stress of suicide on survivors, with a focus on school-based interventions. (pp. 412–413)
13. Discuss the moral, ethical, and legal implications of the right to suicide. Clarify your own position on the legality of doctor-assisted suicide. (Critical Thinking, pp. 406–407; pp. 413–416)

CHAPTER OUTLINE

1. **Problems in the study of suicide** (Focus 13.1; pp. 391–393) People may commit suicide if they feel depressed, like a failure, as though the quality of their life is poor, unwanted, as though their death is for a greater good, and for many other reasons. Suicide is not a disorder in DSM-IV, but is important in abnormal psychology. As a topic, it has been hidden, but is now emerging as a focus of research and social discussion.

   Those who complete suicide attempts cannot be asked their reasons. Patterned after medical autopsies, a psychological autopsy attempts to make psychological sense of suicide by examining the person's case history, interviewing family and friends, and analyzing suicide notes. However, these sources of information are often unavailable or unreliable.

   More than 30,000 people in the United States kill themselves each year, but the real number may be 25 to 30 percent higher. In addition, eight to ten people make an attempt for each completed suicide. Suicides among the young have increased dramatically in the past decade. Suicide is twice as common among college students as among those of the same age who are not in college. One in five students think about suicide sometime during their college career. Men complete suicide three times as often as women, but women attempt suicide three times as often. High-risk people are unmarried, professionals, and those living in countries where religious authority is weak. The rate is 12.2 per 100,000 in the United States; Hungary's rate is highest at 40.7 per 100,000. Most people communicate their intent to kill themselves within three months of the suicide.

2. **Hopelessness, depression, and suicide** (pp. 393–396) Depression and suicide are strongly correlated. The suicide rate for depressives is thirty-six times that of the general population. However, most depressives do not commit suicide, and the risk of suicide increases after a depression has lifted. Negative expectations about the future—hopelessness—may be the major catalyst for suicide. It predicts suicidal behavior better than depression, and better than thoughts about suicide *(suicidal ideation)*.

3. **Other psychological factors and suicide** (pp. 396–397) Those who commit suicide are more likely than others to suffer from mood disorders, schizophrenia, or substance abuse. A variety of stressors are associated with suicide. There is a strong correlation between alcohol consumption and suicide: intoxication may lower inhibitions or constrict thought and make negative moods or thoughts more intense.

4. **The dynamics of suicide** (Focus 13.2; pp. 397–400) Emile Durkheim, a sociologist, proposed that suicide was related to sociocultural influences. He concluded that three categories of suicide exist: *egoistic* (when the person is unable to integrate with society), *altruistic* (when self-destruction is for the culture's greater good), and *anomic* (when a major life event leaves a person unable to cope).

   Intrapsychic explanations stress the idea of anger turned inward on the self. However, psychological autopsies show this to be a cause of suicide in only a minority of cases.

   The chemical 5HIAA, a metabolite of the neurotransmitter serotonin, is found to be at abnormally low levels in people who commit suicide. This raises the possibility that suicides have a biological basis. Low 5HIAA levels occur in suicidal individuals who were not depressed.

   Edwin Shneidman's research on *suicide notes* has produced a three-part categorization of such notes: *egoistic* (where inner turmoil is expressed), *dyadic* (where interpersonal conflicts are described), and *ageneratic* (where the person is alienated from the flow of human life).

5. **The victims of suicide** (pp. 400–405) Children and adolescents take their lives at an alarming rate. There was a 200 percent increase in adolescent suicide from 1960 to 1988. Recent polls indicate that 8 or 9 percent of teens have engaged in self-harm behavior. Those who attempt suicide tend to show clinical symptoms of psychological disturbance, use drug overdose as the method, make their attempt at home, and come from families with high levels of stress as a result of economic instability, substance abuse, or other life events. Copycat suicides, when adolescents imitate media portrayals of other adolescents' suicides, are less common than the media suggests and tend to affect those already contemplating suicide. However, highly publicized suicides can increase the chances of attempts. Fortunately, 41 percent of schools report having programs aimed at suicide prevention.

   Seiden's research at the University of California at Berkeley has helped to clarify which college students are at greatest risk for suicide. They appear to be older students, foreign-born students, undergraduates with extremely good grades but many self-doubts, and postgraduates with poor grades. Reasons for college student suicides include shifting sex roles, unrealistic standards for excellence, shame and disgrace, and emotional disturbance.

   The many stresses of life among the elderly place them at high risk for suicide. Suicide rates are particularly high for white males and first-generation Asian Americans. Native Americans and African Americans show low rates of suicide among older adults, although both groups are at high risk during young adulthood.

6. **The other victims of suicide** (pp. 405–407) The relatives and friends left behind after a suicide experience great psychological pain. Survivors have an especially difficult grieving process. Elisabeth Kübler-Ross speculates that survivors of suicides go through a three-stage process of recovery. The first stage involves shock, denial, and emotional withdrawal. In the second stage, anger and guilt are dominant emotions. At this point, the survivor needs social support to face the reality of the death. In the last stage, letting go, the survivor takes care of "unfinished business" and says goodbye to the suicidal individual.

   About one in five psychologists have worked with a client who committed suicide. While it is an occupational hazard, the effects on mental health professionals are often like those of posttraumatic stress syndrome.

7. **Preventing suicide** (pp. 407–413) People who attempt suicide have a wish to live along with a wish to die. They usually leave verbal or behavioral clues of their intentions, although these may be subtle. A clinical approach to suicide intervention stresses the fact that most individuals are ambivalent about ending their lives, counselors must be comfortable discussing the subject, and that taking action such as signing a behavioral contract to reduce suicide risk is a top priority. Crisis intervention strategies are used to abort suicide attempts by offering intensive counseling to the individual and stabilizing him or her in a hospital environment while clarifying ways to deal with the crisis. Suicide prevention centers usually use paraprofessionals to take telephone calls from potentially suicidal individuals. These paraprofessionals are trained to establish rapport with the caller, evaluate suicidal potential, clarify the nature of the problem and the caller's ability to cope, and recommend a plan of action. There is no conclusive evidence for the effectiveness of suicide prevention centers. Little research has been conducted, and alternative explanations for results are possible. Community prevention efforts can involve going into a school where a suicide has occurred and educating and providing counseling to survivors. Such an institutional response serves to minimize the mental health problems of survivors and can prevent future suicides.

8. **The right to suicide: moral, ethical, and legal implications** (pp. 413–416) The Catholic religion sees suicide as a sin. On the other hand, Thomas Szasz criticizes suicide

prevention programs because they limit individual options and personal responsibility. Some people contend that the elderly have the right to end their lives when they suffer terminal illness or an incapacitating illness that causes others misery. The quality of life is a significant moral and ethical issue that has led to right-to-die legislation and "living wills" that are recognized in fifteen states. Dr. Jack Kevorkian, a physician in Michigan, has assisted patients to commit suicide, an act which a new law states is illegal. In 1992, Californians voted on a bill to allow physicians to help terminally ill patients die. Students are challenged to build cases for and against suicide prevention. Mental health professionals, like their medical colleagues, must face the issue of treating people who want to die. Practicing therapists must consider their responsibility to keep someone alive who wants to die and the legal consequences of allowing someone to die. The Constitution appears to provide a basis for the right to refuse treatment, but therapists who fail to prevent suicides can anticipate that they will be sued.

KEY TERMS

Fill-in-the-Blanks Quiz

1. Suicide that results from a maladaptive relation to society is called ___________.
2. A systematic examination of information in order to explain the behavior of a person prior to his or her death is called a(n) ___________.
3. Suicide that is motivated by a desire to further group goals or to achieve some greater good is called ___________.
4. Suicide that results from an inability to integrate oneself with society is called ___________.
5. Thoughts about suicide are called ___________.
6. The taking of one's own life is called ___________.

Answers to Fill-in-the-Blanks Quiz

1. anomic suicide
2. psychological autopsy
3. altruistic suicide
4. egoistic suicide
5. suicidal ideation
6. suicide

FACT AND CONCEPT QUESTIONS

1. Why is it difficult to answer the question, "Are people who commit suicide always mentally disturbed?"
   a. Because it is impossible to do psychological autopsies on suicide victims
   b. Because it is impossible to do medical autopsies on suicide victims
   c. Because no single explanation is sufficient to account for all types of suicide
   d. Because suicide is so rare that it is difficult to find enough cases to study

2. Which statistic below is accurate?
   a. Roughly 2 million people commit suicide in the United States each year.
   b. Men are six times as likely to attempt suicide as women.
   c. Suicides among people aged 15 to 24 have stayed about the same over the past ten years.
   d. The suicide rate for men is three times that for women.

3. Which of the following increases the risk of suicide?
   a. Heavy alcohol consumption
   b. Living is a highly religious country
   c. Being married
   d. Having an antisocial personality

4. What mental state seems to increase one's risk of suicide?
   a. Dwelling on the past
   b. Negative expectations about the future
   c. An inflated sense of self-importance
   d. Cognitive slippage

5. According to Durkheim's sociological perspective on suicide, when a person is unable to integrate himself or herself with society, the result may be an ____________ suicide.
   a. anomic
   b. altruistic
   c. existential
   d. egoistic

6. When explaining suicidal behavior, Freud stresses ____________ , whereas Durkheim stresses ____________.
   a. lack of social support; economic influences
   b. genetic factors; environmental factors
   c. anger turned inward; economic influences
   d. sexual symbolism; discrimination and prejudice

7. Abnormally low amounts of ____________ have been found in the spinal fluid of patients who are at high risk for killing themselves.
   a. 5HIAA
   b. phenylalanine
   c. Thorazine
   d. dopamine

8. Research on adolescent suicide attempters indicates that
   a. they are unlikely to show any symptoms of psychological disturbance.
   b. most attempts occur at home.
   c. they represent fewer than 1 percent of all adolescents.
   d. almost all attempts occur during spring and summer.

9. Which statement about adolescent suicide attempters is *true*?
   a. Most use methods that are low in lethality.
   b. The majority are determined to end their lives.
   c. Most come from economically well-off families.
   d. Most use firearms or hanging.

10. According to Seiden's research on college student suicide, which category of student is most likely to take his or her own life?
    a. Math and science majors
    b. Black students
    c. Students who commute to school
    d. Very high achieving students at large universities

11. Which of the following reasons for college student suicide is most plausible?
    a. As final examinations approach, stress levels become unbearable.
    b. Highly successful students are filled with doubt about their ability to succeed.
    c. Men are confused about the new roles society has pressured them to adopt.
    d. Foreign students are discriminated against by teachers and administrators.

12. Among the elderly in the United States, which group has the *highest* rate of suicide?
    a. Black females
    b. Black males
    c. First-generation Asian Americans
    d. Males of Northern European backgrounds

13. Who developed a three-stage model of recovery experienced by family members after a person commits suicide?
    a. Edwin Shneidman
    b. Elisabeth Kübler-Ross
    c. Hans Selye
    d. Doris Portwood

14. When a person is in the second stage of recovery from a family member's suicide,
    a. it is important for friends to prevent the grieving person from expressing anger or guilt.
    b. the principal mental state is shock and denial.
    c. he or she must face the truth that a suicide occurred.
    d. the normal response is to let go of the loved one without much emotion.

15. Mental health professionals are optimistic that suicide prevention is possible
    a. because they assume that a wish to live coexists with a wish to die.
    b. despite the fact that very few suicidal individuals give hints of their self-destructive intentions.
    c. despite the knowledge that suicidal individuals are determined to die.
    d. because suicide is such a rare event.

16. Making or rewriting a will and giving away one's record collection are examples of
    a. verbal clues to suicide.
    b. lethality of suicide intent.
    c. learned helplessness.
    d. behavioral clues to suicide.

17. The main difference between crisis intervention and suicide prevention centers is that
    a. crisis intervention centers do not deal with suicidal people.
    b. crisis intervention stresses the need to educate the whole community.
    c. suicide prevention centers do not deal with distressed individuals.
    d. suicide prevention centers are available around the clock through through telephone hotlines.

18. Studies of the effectiveness of suicide prevention centers have shown that
    a. callers feel that the service is far more helpful than discussions with friends.
    b. few suicidal people use the centers and those who do call only once.
    c. cities with centers have one-half the suicide rate of those without centers.
    d. approximately one-half of the callers do commit suicide.

19. Community suicide prevention programs might include
    a. individual counseling sessions with people affected by a suicide.
    b. school classroom discussions in which suicide is considered a rational response to stress.
    c. both a and b.
    d. neither a nor b.

20. Which of the following statements regarding health professionals and the law is *correct*?
    a. Therapists have a responsibility to prevent suicide if they anticipate it.
    b. Lawsuits cannot be brought against a psychologist who fails to treat a person who threatens to commit suicide.
    c. "Living wills" are not recognized as valid in any state in the United States.
    d. The Constitution specifically states that professionals must save people's lives, even if the person wants to die.

APPLICATION QUESTIONS

1. Dr. Ortman is interviewing the friends and family of a college student who committed suicide. She is also analyzing the student's suicide note and diary. Dr. Ortman is engaged in
    a. a form of treatment called "crisis intervention."
    b. a psychological autopsy.
    c. an assessment called "anomic evaluation."
    d. a medical autopsy.

2. On the basis of research evidence, Dr. Fellini is better able to predict potential suicides by examining not only evidence of depression in her patients, but also
    a. paranoid ideas.
    b. sexual symbolism in their dreams.
    c. evidence of introjected anger.
    d. hopelessness.

3. A psychologist who made use of Durkheim's explanation for suicide would stress the
    a. early childhood experiences that led to anger turned inward.
    b. genetics of neurotransmitter imbalance.
    c. social factors that influence individuals.
    d. attention-seeking nature of suicide.

4. Karen leaves this suicide note: "Life is too hard for a weak person like me. The struggle is pointless; there is no escape from my pain. Goodbye." This note illustrates a(n) ___________ suicide.
    a. egoistic
    b. altruistic
    c. psychotic
    d. dyadic

5. Dr. Wilton says, "The suicide rate for children under 14 is rapidly decreasing, but it is increasing for those aged 14 to 25. Suicide is second only to automobile accidents as a cause of death among teens. Girls are three times as likely as boys to attempt it." What part of Dr. Wilton's statement is *inaccurate*?
   a. It is inaccurate to say that that suicide is decreasing among those under 14.
   b. It is inaccurate to say that suicide is increasing among those 14 to 25.
   c. It is inaccurate to say that suicide is the second leading cause of death among teens.
   d. It is inaccurate to say that that girls are more likely to attempt suicide.

6. Which adolescent is most likely to attempt suicide?
   a. George, whose parents are wealthy
   b. Paula, whose parents are alcoholics
   c. Jonathan, who is depressed during the summertime
   d. Nathan, who shows little hostility or anger

7. After a television news episode showing dramatic scenes of a tenth grader's suicide is broadcast, a second tenth grader at the same school kills herself. This kind of suicide is
   a. much more common than the news media have suggested.
   b. called an altruistic suicide.
   c. especially unfortunate because such depictions influence well-adjusted teens to kill themselves.
   d. called a copycat suicide.

8. Which of the following examples is most consistent with the results of Seiden's research on college suicide at the University of California at Berkeley?
   a. A graduate student with poor grades committed suicide.
   b. An undergraduate with below-average grades committed suicide during final examinations.
   c. A foreign student, younger than the average student, committed suicide.
   d. A freshman, male, science major committed suicide at home.

9. At an elementary school where a suicide occurred, a psychologist meets with the teachers so they can share their feelings and learn how to respond to their students' concerns. Parents are informed of their children's likely reactions. This best illustrates
   a. what Durkheim called an "altruistic reaction."
   b. a community prevention intervention.
   c. a traditional crisis treatment program.
   d. what Szasz considers the right way to respond to suicide.

10. Dr. Lin says, "In one survey of psychologists, about 22 percent had worked with a client who committed suicide. The suicide made these professionals more sensitive to suicidal clues and had a strong emotional impact, but all of them were 'over it' within a month." What part of Dr. Lin's statement is *inaccurate*?
   a. The idea that only 22 percent have suicidal clients
   b. The idea that it altered professionals' sensitivity
   c. The idea that it had an emotional impact
   d. The idea that effects lasted less than six months

ANSWERS TO FACT AND CONCEPT QUESTIONS

1. a. Psychological autopsies are done on suicide victims by looking at information they left behind and by interviewing survivors.
   b. Medical autopsies are routinely done on suicide victims.
   *c. There are many reasons for suicide, some of which are rational and some of which are not. (p. 392)
   d. Suicide is rather common; a minimum of 30,000 cases occur each year.

2. a. Although the figure of 30,000 cases per year is an underestimate, it is highly *unlikely* that the true incidence is forty times greater.
   b. Women are three times as likely as men to attempt suicide.
   c. The suicide rate among teens and young adults has risen dramatically.
   *d. The completed suicide rate is three times greater among men, although women are three times as likely to attempt suicide. (Focus 13.1; p. 394)

3. *a. Alcohol consumption is consistently associated with suicide: the alcohol-implicated suicide rate is 27 times the rate in the general population. (p. 396)
   b. Suicide rates are highest in countries where there is low religious influence; lowest in countries where religion is powerful.
   c. Suicide is more likely when a person is divorced or single.
   d. Antisocial personality disorder is not associated with suicidal behavior.

4. a. Although dwelling on past difficulties may increase a sense of hopelessness, it does not necessarily have this effect.
   *b. Negative expectations—or hopelessness—seem to be even more predictive of suicide than depression. (p. 395)
   c. People contemplating suicide often have a reduced sense of self-worth.
   d. Cognitive slippage is a characteristic of schizophrenia and is unrelated to suicide.

5. a. Anomic suicide occurs when a dramatic event overwhelms the person's capacity to cope.
   b. Altruistic suicide occurs when the person is concerned with the group's greater good (for example, a suicide in protest of injustice).
   c. *Existential suicide* is a made-up term, not one defined by Durkheim.
   *d. Egoistic suicide occurs in social isolates, people who are not integrated into the cultural fabric. (p. 397)

6. a. Although Durkheim is interested in economic conditions, Freud never discusses social supports.
   b. Freud stresses unconscious conflicts, not genetics.
   *c. Freud sees suicide as a self-destructive act that originates in rage at another person; Durkheim emphasizes social conditions, including economic ones. (pp. 397–398)
   d. Freud's theory of suicide emphasizes the *thanatos* (death instinct) rather than the *libido* (sexual, id instinct).

7. *a. 5HIAA is a metabolite of the neurotransmitter serotonin, and is abnormally low in people who commit suicide, even those who are not depressed. (p. 399)
   b. Phenylalanine is an amino acid unrelated to suicide.
   c. Thorazine is the brand name of a chemical used to treat schizophrenia.
   d. Dopamine is a neurotransmitter; too much dopamine activity is associated with schizophrenia.

8. a. Suicide attempters are likely to have a past history of psychological disturbance.
   *b. Suicide attempts tend to take place in the home. (p. 401)
   c. Recent polls indicate that 6 percent of teens admit to a suicide attempt; probably 8 and 9 percent of teens engage in self-harmful behavior.
   d. Winter is the most typical time for adolescents to make suicide attempts.

9. *a. Adolescents usually make attempts with low-lethality methods such as drug overdoses; this indicates that, probably, a large part of them wants to live. (p. 401)
   b. Most adolescents are not really sure they want to die.
   c. Adolescents with economically stressed families are at higher risk.
   d. Firearms and hanging, highly lethal methods, are rarely used in *attempts*.

10. a. Language and literature majors are more prone to suicide than others.
   b. Black students were not found to be at high risk.
   c. Most suicides take place at campus residences.
   *d. High-achieving undergraduates were among the most likely suicide victims; suicide is more prevalent at large universities than at small colleges. (p. 403)

11. a. Suicidal behavior peaks at the beginning of semesters, not at final examination time.
   *b. Suicide risk is high for the strongest students because they appear to have unrealistically high standards of performance. (p. 403)
   c. Women may be more inclined to commit suicide because of role confusion.
   d. Foreign students may be more inclined to commit suicide because of shame and fear of letting down their parents.

12. a. Black females have a relatively low suicide rate.
   b. Elderly black males have a relatively low suicide rate.
   *c. First-generation Asian Americans have a high rate of suicide, perhaps because of their cultural dislocation. (p. 405)
   d. White males have a suicide rate lower than that of Asian Americans.

13. a. Edwin Shneidman developed the first suicide prevention center, in Los Angeles.
   *b. Elisabeth Kübler-Ross has developed extensive theories of death, grieving, and responses to suicide. (p. 405)
   c. Hans Selye developed a three-stage theory of stress reaction called the "general adaptation syndrome."
   d. Doris Portwood is an activist for the right to commit suicide.

14. a. Kübler-Ross argues that friends should help suicide survivors express their negative feelings.
   b. The first stage is characterized by shock and denial.
   *c. According to Kübler-Ross, despite angry feelings and self-blame, people must confront the reality of the death during the second stage. (p. 405)
   d. Letting go is a part of the third stage, according to Kübler-Ross.

15. *a. Mental health professionals operate under the assumption that most (if not all) people who are suicidal also have a desire to live. (pp. 407–408)
   b. Most suicidal people leave clues to their intentions, although some are rather subtle.
   c. Mental health professionals do *not* believe that suicidal people have shut the door on living.
   d. Suicide is all too common.

16. a. An example of a verbal clue might be, "Everyone would be happier if I just shot myself."
    b. Lethality is determined by a person's plan to take his or her life and his or her access to the means of doing it.
    c. Learned helplessness has more to do with believing that one has no control over the consequences of one's actions.
    *d. Making a will is a physical action; therefore it is a behavioral clue. (p. 408)

17. a. Suicide is certainly a crisis and is a part of crisis intervention work.
    b. Crisis intervention focuses on direct care for the suicidal person rather than on community education.
    c. Suicide prevention centers take telephone calls from people in acute distress.
    *d. Suicide prevention centers have paraprofessionals who take telephone calls twenty-four hours per day; crisis intervention involves direct care after the person presents himself or herself to the counseling center. (p. 409)

18. a. Unfortunately, callers who were included in such evaluation studies saw no more benefit from calling the center than from discussing the problem with friends.
    *b. Only 2 percent of suicidal individuals use suicide prevention hotlines; about 95 percent of those who call once never call again. (p. 411)
    c. No clear difference in community suicide rates has been found; those with hotlines can have higher, lower, and similar rates of suicide compared with communities not having a hotline.
    d. Because there is no way to trace callers, we do not know how many actually commit suicide.

19. *a. The program described in the text offered students and teachers the chance to talk individually with a counselor. (p. 412)
    b. It would be inappropriate to suggest to impressionable youngsters that suicide is a legitimate coping mechanism.
    c. Because b is incorrect, this cannot be the best answer.
    d. Because a is correct, this cannot be the best answer.

20. *a. Although laws are not clear on all points, therapists have an ethical duty to preserve life when they can. (p. 416)
    b. Therapists can be sued for refusing to offer life-protective treatment.
    c. "Living wills" are recognized as valid in fifteen states.
    d. The Constitution implies that people can refuse treatment that will save their lives (as in cases when those who believe in faith healing refuse medical treatment).

ANSWERS TO APPLICATION QUESTIONS

1. a. Crisis intervention involves assisting a person who may be contemplating suicide.
   *b. A psychological autopsy involves looking at material about the suicide victim to help us understand the person's motives. (p. 393)
   c. *Anomic evaluation* is a made-up term.
   d. Although medical autopsies are performed on suicide victims, they do not involve interviewing friends or family or analyzing suicide notes.

2. a. Paranoid ideas are not clearly associated with risk of suicide.
   b. Psychoanalytic thinking on suicide focuses on anger turned inward, not on sexual symbolism.
   c. Although psychoanalysts focus on introjected anger, there is little research supporting the idea that such anger predicts suicide.
   *d. Research shows that hopelessness is the component of depression most related to suicidal behavior. (p. 393)

3. a. Durkheim was a sociologist, not a psychoanalytic thinker.
   b. Durkheim was a sociologist, not a physiological psychologist.
   *c. Durkheim was a sociologist; his interests included social integration, economic change, and individuals' responses to these factors. (p. 397)
   d. Attention seeking might be a behavioral conceptualization of suicidal behavior; Durkheim was not a behaviorist.

4. *a. Edwin Shneidman's research on suicide notes illustrates that an egoistic suicide stems from inner torment that produces a sense of defeat. (Focus 13.2; pp. 398–399)
   b. Durkheim's altruistic suicide concept is applied to cases in which death is seen as a means of achieving a greater good for the group.
   c. There is no such category as "psychotic suicide"; if one existed, we would expect more scattered or paranoid thinking than is found in Karen's note.
   d. Shneidman's concept of dyadic suicide involves self-destruction out of anger or frustration with another person.

5. *a. The suicide rate has been increasing in the preteenage population. (p. 400)
   b. The suicide rate among those 15–24 has tripled in the past 30 years.
   c. Automobile accidents are the leading cause of death; suicide is second.
   d. Girls are more likely to attempt suicide, although boys are more likely to be "successful."

6. a. Children whose parents are in financial stress are more likely to commit suicide than those whose parents are well off.
   *b. Suicide among teens is higher when their parents suffer from alcohol or other chemical dependencies. (p. 401)
   c. Suicide among teens tends to be most common during the winter months.
   d. Hostility and aggressiveness are strongly associated with suicide.

7. a. Copycat suicides are far less common than the media indicate.
   b. Altruistic suicide is when one kills oneself for the group's greater good, such as *kamikaze* pilots in World War II.
   c. Depictions of suicide do not seem to influence well-adjusted adolescents; they *do* have an impact on those with suicidal tendencies.
   *d. Copycat suicides are more likely to occur when media portrayals of suicide influence those with suicidal tendencies to take their own lives. (p. 402)

8. *a. Seiden found that graduate students who were doing poorly were a high-risk group for suicide. (pp. 402–403)
   b. When undergraduates were superb students, the risk of suicide increased.
   c. Foreign students were at high risk, but older students were far more likely to commit suicide than younger ones.
   d. Older students were more likely to commit suicide; literature and language majors were more likely than science majors.

9. a. Durkheim categorized reasons for suicide; an altruistic suicide is one committed for the greater good of a cause or community.
   *b. What is being described matches the illustration of a community prevention intervention given in the text. (pp. 412–413)
   c. Traditional crisis intervention requires an individual to come to a clinic for counseling.
   d. Szasz is vehemently against all suicide prevention because he claims it interferes with individual, moral decisions.

10. a. It is accurate to say that 22 percent of surveyed psychologists have had a client who committed suicide.
   b. Psychologists report becoming more sensitive to client suicidal clues after one of their clients commits suicide.
   c. The emotional aftereffects of a client's suicide are intense and long-lasting.
   *d. Many psychologists who had a client who committed suicide experienced a kind of posttraumatic stress disorder for six months or longer. (p. 407)

CHAPTER 14
Schizophrenia: Diagnosis and Symptoms

LEARNING OBJECTIVES

When you have mastered the material in Chapter 14, you should be able to:

1. Discuss the history of the diagnostic category known as schizophrenia. (pp. 419–421)
2. Describe the DSM-IV criteria for schizophrenia and discuss research into current psychiatrists' uses or misuses of these criteria. (pp. 421–423)
3. Describe the attention problems of schizophrenics. Describe the types and dimensions of delusions that occur in schizophrenia. Discuss how schizophrenics may respond to their delusions. Describe the perceptual distortions seen in schizophrenia and the degree to which those who suffer from the disorder can control their symptoms. (Focus 14.1; pp. 428–429)
4. Discuss the differences between positive and negative symptoms of schizophrenia. Describe research results from a cross-cultural study of symptoms used to diagnose schizophrenia. Describe the thought disturbances, association problems, and neologisms characteristic of schizophrenia. (Focus 14.2; pp. 423–428)
5. Describe the motoric disturbances in schizophrenia. Discuss what is meant by "negative" symptoms, including flat affect and the identity symptoms of schizophrenia. (pp. 429–430)
6. Describe the paranoid and disorganized types of schizophrenia. Differentiate between delusional (paranoid) disorder and paranoid schizophrenia. (Focus 14.3; pp. 430–432)
7. Describe the catatonic, undifferentiated, and residual types of schizophrenia. (pp. 432–434)
8. Describe the nonschizophrenic disorders called brief reactive psychosis and schizophreniform disorder, and differentiate them from schizophrenia. (p. 434)
9. Describe the three phases of schizophrenia. (pp. 435–436)
10. Discuss research on the long-term outcome of schizophrenia, including studies of schizophrenia in developing and developed countries and concern about discrimination against the mentally ill. (Critical Thinking, Focus 14.4; pp. 436–438)

CHAPTER OUTLINE

1. **Schizophrenia: diagnosis and symptoms** (pp. 419–420) Schizophrenia is a group of disorders characterized by cognitive distortions, personality disintegration, and social withdrawal. It receives a great deal of attention because it is so disabling, the prevalence rate is 1 percent (and therefore millions of people are affected), and its symptoms and causes are diverse.

2. **History of the diagnostic category** (pp. 420–423) Emil Kraepelin first named the disorder *dementia praecox* (meaning "early insanity"), defining it as an early occurring, incurable organic disorder involving progressive mental deterioration. Eugen Bleuler objected to this, arguing that the disorder did not necessarily occur early in life. Bleuler proposed that four A's defined the disorder: autism (self-focus), associations (unconnected ideas), affect (inappropriate emotions), and ambivalence (uncertainty over actions). He also suggested that schizophrenia was caused by a combination of genetic and environmental factors with different possibilities for recovery of functioning. In early editions of the diagnostic manual, schizophrenia was broadly defined, using Bleuler's four A's. With the DSM-III, DSM-III-R, and DSM-IV the definition became quite restrictive. The current category in the DSM-IV has aspects of both. A diagnosis of schizophrenia should be given only if delusions, hallucinations, or disturbed thinking and emotional expression have impaired functioning for at least six months at some point in the person's life and for at least one month currently. However, psychiatrists often make inconsistent use of the DSM-IV criteria and substitute subjective impressions.

3. **The symptoms of schizophrenia: perceptual distortion, disorganized speech and thought disturbances, disorganized motoric disturbances, and negative symptoms** (Focus 14.1; pp. 425–430) Schizophrenics often report *hallucinations,* although these are not distinctive to schizophrenia. Research indicates that auditory hallucinations may stem from subvocal speech, and are phenomena people with schizophrenia can cope with in a variety of ways. During times when symptoms are prominent, hallucinations and delusions are so strong they are treated as real; in other situations, people with schizophrenia can ward them off. *Loosening of associations*, shifting of thoughts from topic to topic, is a major symptom of schizophrenia. So too are *neologisms*, made-up words, although this occurs rarely. Schizophrenics have trouble maintaining attention.

   Bizarre gestures and movements or lack of movement also characterize the schizophrenias. In many cases, bizarre movements are related to delusions. The catatonic schizophrenic often holds odd postures and is unresponsive to others.

   Negative symptoms are associated with poor prognosis and include flat affect (expressionless face), an inability to feel pleasure, a lack of motivation, and lack of meaningful speech.

4. **The symptoms of schizophrenia: delusions** (Focus 14.2; pp. 423–425) In DSM-IV, symptoms are divided into positive symptoms (delusions, hallucinations, and bizarre behavior) and negative symptoms (flat affect, apathy, and lack of speech). Prognosis is better for positive symptoms than negative symptoms. Schizophrenics suffer from *delusions*, false beliefs that are held despite disconfirming evidence. Types of delusions include grandeur, persecution, reference, and thought withdrawal, among others. There seem to be four qualities of delusions: conviction, extension, disorganization, and pressure. Unlike nonschizophrenics, schizophrenics reach delusional conclusions on the basis of little information; they can, however, be treated to challenge their delusions.The most common symptom of schizophrenia is lack of insight, an inability to recognize one's own disturbance. Attempts are being made to find pathognomonic symptoms—those only found in schizophrenia.

5. **Types of schizophrenia** (pp. 430–434) *Paranoid schizophrenia* is the most common form of schizophrenia and is characterized by delusions or hallucinations, usually involving persecution or grandiosity. It is possible to differentiate this disorder from *delusional* (paranoid) *disorder* because delusional disorder involves less bizarre beliefs and is free from other dysfunctional behaviors. *Disorganized schizophrenia* features severe regression to a childish state without delusions. Behavior and speech tend to be bizarre. *Catatonic schizophrenia* is divided into an excited form marked by hyperactivity and a withdrawn form in which immobility

and waxy flexibility are seen. Often patients swing from one state to the other. *Undifferentiated schizophrenia* is a form marked by a mix of symptoms; *residual schizophrenics* are those people whose symptoms are in remission.

6. **Psychotic disorders once considered schizophrenia** (p. 434) In DSM-IV, the term *schizophrenia* is reserved for psychotic episodes lasting six months or more. Brief psychotic reaction is diagnosed when symptoms have lasted less than one month; the disorder where symptoms last between one and six months is called *schizophreniform disorder.* DSM-IV recommends these disorders be "provisional."

7. **The course of schizophrenia** (Focus 14.4; pp. 435–438) Most people with schizophrenia show poor premorbid personality before the onset of the disorder. The typical course of schizophrenia consists of three phases. The *prodromal phase* includes social withdrawal and peculiar speech or actions. In the *active phase,* symptoms are in full evidence, and, by the *residual phase,* symptoms are no longer prominent. International studies show that return to work and reduction in symptoms is more common in developing countries than in the United States, the former USSR, or Western Europe.

   It is unclear what the long-term outcome of schizophrenia tends to be. In one study, 78 percent of schizophrenics suffered a relapse; in another, long-term prognosis was favorable in half of the cases. Differences in outcome may be due to criteria used to define schizophrenia.

KEY TERMS

Fill-in-the-Blanks Quiz

1. A group of disorders characterized by severe impairment of cognitive processes, personality disintegration, and social withdrawal is collectively called ____________.

2. A schizophrenic disorder in which the individual regresses to a childlike state but does not exhibit delusions is called ____________.

3. A schizophrenic disorder characterized by persistent and systematized delusions is called ____________.

4. A schizophrenic disorder characterized by extreme excitement or extreme withdrawal is called ____________.

5. A schizophrenic disorder characterized by a mix of symptoms that does not clearly fit any other type of the disorder is called ____________.

6. A disorder characterized by persistent but nonbizarre delusions not accompanied by any other unusual behaviors is called ____________.

7. A false belief that is firmly held despite disconfirming evidence is called a(n) ____________.

8. A category of schizophrenic disorder reserved for individuals who, in the past, manifested symptoms but now no longer show prominent signs of the disorder is called ____________.

9. Sensory perceptions that are not directly attributable to environmental stimuli are called ____________.

10. Continual shifting from topic to topic without logical or meaningful connections is called ____________.

11. New words that are typically formed by combining words in common usage are called ____________.

Answers to Fill-in-the-Blanks Quiz

1. schizophrenia
2. disorganized schizophrenia
3. paranoid schizophrenia
4. catatonic schizophrenia
5. undifferentiated schizophrenia
6. delusional disorder
7. delusion
8. residual schizophrenia
9. hallucinations
10. loosening of associations
11. neologisms

FACT AND CONCEPT QUESTIONS

1. Which of the following symptoms are considered to be central to schizophrenia?
   a. Changing from one personality style to another
   b. Severely impaired thinking and social withdrawal
   c. Compulsive rituals and extreme anxiety
   d. An inability to feel loyalty towards others

2. He called the disorder *dementia praecox* and thought that it was an organic problem with no possibility for recovery. Who is being described?
   a. Emil Kraepelin
   b. Sigmund Freud
   c. Eugen Bleuler
   d. David Rosenhan

3. Which statement is *true* of DSM-IV's criteria for diagnosing schizophrenia?
   a. The patient is assumed to have an organic disorder.
   b. The disorder lasts for less than six months.
   c. The patient must show insight into his or her disorder.
   d. The disorder may involve positive or negative symptoms.

4. When psychiatrists were recently surveyed to learn which clinical symptoms they used to diagnose schizophrenia, it was found that
   a. almost all of them used the new DSM-IV criteria.
   b. almost all of them saw schizophrenia as lasting less than one month.
   c. about half used only one of the diagnostic criteria.
   d. about half used all findings necessary for diagnosis, according to the DSM-IV.

5. According to the World Health Organization study of schizophrenia, the most common symptom used in making such a diagnosis is
   a. mood swings.
   b. visual hallucinations.
   c. lack of insight.
   d. psychomotor disturbances.

6. Unchangeable false beliefs are to ___________ as perceptions in the absence of stimuli are to ___________.
   a. paranoid schizophrenia; catatonic schizophrenia
   b. delusions; hallucinations
   c. hallucinations; loose associations
   d. loose associations; hallucinations

7. A false belief that others are plotting to embarrass or harm you is called a
   a. delusion of persecution.
   b. delusion of grandeur.
   c. psychomotor disturbance.
   d. neologism.

8. A schizophrenic who engages in neologisms is
   a. failing to display emotions that are appropriate for a situation.
   b. making up words that only he or she understands.
   c. standing in awkward postures but allowing others to move him or her like a mannequin.
   d. unable to concentrate and organize incoming information.

9. People with schizophrenia have problems with attention. What problems, exactly?
   a. They crave the attention of others but withdraw from social attention.
   b. They focus their attention so narrowly that they are unaware of other people.
   c. They choose to focus their attention on fantasy instead of reality.
   d. They find it difficult to concentrate and organize incoming information.

10. A delusion that involves many other people is considered ___________; a delusion that a person is absolutely convinced of is considered ___________.
    a. high in pressure; low in disorganization
    b. a delusion of reference; high in extension
    c. high in extension; high in conviction
    d. high in conviction; a delusion of persecution

11. Which statement about auditory hallucinations is *true*?
    a. Auditory hallucinations are extremely rare in schizophrenia.
    b. People with schizophrenia have no control over their auditory hallucinations.
    c. Some evidence suggests that auditory hallucinations stem from subvocal speech.
    d. People with schizophrenia have complete control over their auditory hallucinations.

12. Which form of schizophrenia is associated with poor prognosis and must be diagnosed with care because the symptoms may develop in response to medication and institutionalization?
    a. Schizophrenia with negative symptoms
    b. Paranoid schizophrenia
    c. Schizophrenia with positive symptoms
    d. Capgras's syndrome

13. ____________ schizophrenia is the most common form of the disorder and is characterized by illogical and contradictory delusions.
    a. Paranoid
    b. Catatonic
    c. Disorganized
    d. Undifferentiated

14. In what kind of schizophrenia do patients stand in awkward positions for hours at a time?
    a. Paranoid
    b. Catatonic
    c. Disorganized
    d. Undifferentiated

15. Which of the following is a criterion for diagnosing residual schizophrenia?
    a. The presence of auditory or visual hallucinations
    b. Early onset of the disorder and extremely bizarre speech
    c. The presence of many severe schizophrenic symptoms at the same time
    d. The absence of prominent symptoms after an episode of full-blown schizophrenia

16. When the sole symptom is a delusion that does not affect functioning in other spheres of a person's life, the best diagnosis is
    a. paranoid schizophrenia.
    b. brief reactive psychosis.
    c. delusional (paranoid) disorder.
    d. paranoid schizophreniform disorder.

17. In what way is schizophreniform disorder different from schizophrenia?
    a. It involves thought disturbances that the patient can control; in schizophrenia, there is no control.
    b. It begins at an early age; in schizophrenia, the onset is in middle age.
    c. It involves no thought disturbances; in schizophrenia, thought disturbances are critical symptoms.
    d. It has not lasted six months or more; in schizophrenia, psychosis must have lasted at least that long.

18. The active phase of schizophrenia
    a. follows the residual phase.
    b. includes symptoms at their early stages of development.
    c. continues throughout the schizophrenic's life.
    d. follows the prodromal phase.

19. Long-term outcome studies of schizophrenia indicate that
    a. Emil Kraepelin was wrong: In many cases, people recover.
    b. Eugen Bleuler was wrong: Treatment rarely produces recovery.
    c. Sigmund Freud was right: Unconscious conflicts continue throughout life.
    d. Emil Kraepelin was right: Schizophrenia is a progressive illness.

20. International research seems to show that recovery from schizophrenia is
    a. more rapid in developed countries such as the United States.
    b. more rapid in developing countries such as India.
    c. virtually impossible no matter where it occurs.
    d. more dependent on good diet than on good therapy.

APPLICATION QUESTIONS

1. "In my opinion, there are a variety of disorders that we lump together under 'schizophrenia.' They have different causes that may include environmental factors, and different chances of recovery." These remarks best reflect the beliefs of
    a. Philippe Pinel.
    b. Eugen Bleuler.
    c. Emil Kraepelin.
    d. Dorothea Dix.

2. Don talks incoherently and uses words that no one else understands, yet he is unable to recognize that his thinking is bizarre. This shows the most common symptom of schizophrenia:
    a. lack of insight.
    b. delusions.
    c. waxy flexibility.
    d. auditory hallucinations.

3. Kristin, a schizophrenic patient, believes that all events revolve around her. Whatever anyone says, it is about her. All news broadcasts contain hidden messages for her. Kristin's thinking illustrates
    a. a delusion of persecution.
    b. a delusion of grandeur.
    c. Capgras's syndrome.
    d. a delusion of reference.

4. Justin was diagnosed with schizophrenia. He shows little emotional expression and has no motivation. He seems unable to feel pleasure. Justin's form of schizophrenia
    a. involves positive symptoms.
    b. is usually considered "disorganized schizophrenia."
    c. usually has a very good prognosis.
    d. involves negative symptoms.

5. Dr. Ortlieb says, "In schizophrenia, the person has no control over his or her symptoms. These symptoms can involve the production of unique words called neologisms, an absence of emotion called flat affect, or false beliefs called delusions." What part of Dr. Ortlieb's statement is *incorrect*?
    a. The idea that schizophrenics have no control over their symptoms
    b. The idea that unique words are called neologisms
    c. The idea that schizophrenics do not show emotion
    d. The idea that false beliefs are called delusions

6. Jonathan has shown thought disturbances since he was 8 years old. He is now 27 and still acts in bizarre and silly ways. When most people would laugh, he cries. He shows no consistent delusions. Jonathan would most likely receive a diagnosis of
   a. schizophreniform disorder.
   b. catatonic schizophrenia.
   c. undifferentiated schizophrenia.
   d. disorganized schizophrenia.

7. When Tina is totally withdrawn, she shows waxy flexibility. When she is out of that state, she is extremely active and hypertalkative. Tina would most likely receive a diagnosis of ___________ schizophrenia.
   a. paranoid
   b. catatonic
   c. undifferentiated
   d. residual

8. Barney believes that his office phone is monitored and that his boss is trying to poison the air in his office. Other than these unfounded suspicions, Barney shows no thought disturbance or functioning problems. Barney would most likely receive a diagnosis of
   a. paranoid schizophrenia.
   b. undifferentiated schizophrenia.
   c. brief reactive psychosis.
   d. delusional (paranoid) disorder.

9. Chuck responds to his father's death with a two-week psychotic episode during which he hears voices, is delusional, and shows bizarre affect. What diagnosis should Chuck receive?
   a. Paranoid schizophrenia
   b. Catatonic schizophrenia
   c. Brief psychotic disorder
   d. Prodromal schizophrenia

10. Dr. Jenkins says, "More than one-half of schizophrenics show moderate to complete recovery, although recovery rates differ depending on whether the country is developed or developing. Developing countries have very poor recovery rates." What part of Dr. Jenkins's statement is *inaccurate*?
    a. The idea that one-half of schizophrenics recover
    b. The idea that recovery can be complete for any schizophrenic
    c. The idea that the type of country affects recovery
    d. The idea that developing countries have very poor recovery rates

ANSWERS TO FACT AND CONCEPT QUESTIONS

1. a. Changes in personality style are associated with multiple personality disorder, not schizophrenia.
   *b. Schizophrenia is fundamentally a thought disorder in which coherent speech is impaired and a retreat into a private reality occurs. (p. 420)
   c. Compulsive rituals are associated with obsessive-compulsive disorder, a nonpsychotic anxiety disorder.
   d. An inability to feel loyalty is a sign of antisocial personality disorder.

2. *a. Emil Kraepelin used the term *dementia praecox* to describe what we now call schizophrenia; he saw the illness as organic and irreversible. (p. 420)
   b. Sigmund Freud had little to say about schizophrenia; most of his work was on neurotic conditions.
   c. Eugen Bleuler objected to Kraepelin's view that schizophrenia was a single entity without possibility of recovery.
   d. David Rosenhan is a modern psychologist who tested psychiatry's ability to detect psychosis in a famous study done in 1973.

3. a. The DSM-IV rules out schizophrenia if symptoms are due to organic causes.
   b. Psychoses that last less than six months are considered psychotic disorders other than schizophrenia (up to one month's duration is "brief reactive psychosis"; between one and six months is "schizophreniform disorder").
   c. Lack of insight is the symptom most commonly used in diagnosing schizophrenia.
   *d. DSM-IV includes both positive symptoms (hallucinations, delusions, and disorganized thought) and negative symptoms (flat affect and lack of motivation). (p. 422)

4. a. Many of the psychiatrists used idiosyncratic symptoms, such as, "It just doesn't add up."
   b. No data were reported on duration; DSM-IV requires six months' duration.
   *c. Of 301 surveyed psychiatrists, 49 percent relied on a single sign to diagnose the disorder. (p. 422)
   d. Only 1 of 301 surveyed psychiatrists used all of the DSM-III-R's criteria.

5. a. Mood swings are associated with bipolar disorder; they were not listed among the top twelve symptoms used.
   b. Visual hallucinations are relatively rare, although auditory hallucinations ranked second on the list of symptoms used.
   *c. Lack of insight, an inability to recognize the abnormality of one's actions, was found in 97 percent of schizophrenics. (Focus 14.2; p. 428)
   d. Psychomotor disturbances are associated with the rare, catatonic form of the disorder; they were not listed among the top twelve symptoms used.

6. a. Although paranoid schizophrenia is characterized by false beliefs, catatonic schizophrenia involves motor disturbances, not hallucinations.
   *b. False beliefs are delusions; false sensory perceptions are hallucinations. (pp. 423, 425)
   c. False sensory perceptions are hallucinations, not delusions.
   d. Loose associations involve incoherent thoughts, not consistent ones that defy evidence (delusions).

7. *a. Delusions of persecution involve suspicions that others will harm or humiliate you. (p. 424)
   b. Delusions of grandeur involve a belief in self-importance (such as, "I am the king of the world").
   c. Psychomotor disturbances involve wild activity or extreme immobility.
   d. A neologism is a made-up word, not a false belief.

8. a. Failure to display emotions appropriate for a situation is an example of a negative symptom. (p. 429)
   *b. Neologisms are new words formed by combining words in common usage. (p. 428)
   c. Standing in awkward postures is typical of a catatonic schizophrenic. (p. 429)
   d. Difficulty with attention is a separate symptom of schizophrenia. (p. 428)

9. a. People with schizophrenia are often socially withdrawn; they do not seek attention from others.
   b. They have the opposite problem—they cannot focus their attention narrowly.
   c. While people with schizophrenia have trouble distinguishing fantasy and reality, it is untrue that the problem of attention is a choice they make.
   *d. People with schizophrenia are easily distracted, and their ability to organize incoming information is severely impaired. (p. 428)

10. a. A delusion that is high in pressure is one that completely preoccupies the individual; delusions with low disorganization are consistent across time.
   b. A delusion of reference is one where coincidental events or information targeted at the general public is considered to be a personal message.
   *c. Delusions high in extension involve many other people; those that are high in conviction are believed thoroughly by the person with the delusion. (p. 424)
   d. A delusion high in conviction is one that is believed thoroughly; a delusion of persecution is when one believes that others are out to embarrass or otherwise threaten him or her.

11. a. Auditory hallucinations are a common symptom of schizophrenia.
   b. Under certain conditions (humming), people with schizophrenia can reduce their experience of auditory hallucinations.
   *c. Some researchers report a good deal of control over auditory hallucinations while others show that only humming reduces self-report of hearing voices. (p. 426).
   d. Because some conditions designed to reduce subvocal speech (biting one's tongue) do *not* reduce the experience of auditory hallucinations, this is not the best answer.

12. *a. Schizophrenia with negative symptoms (apathy, remaining mute, showing little emotion) is associated with poor prognosis, but these symptoms may be brought on by medication or institutionalization. (p. 429)
   b. Paranoid schizophrenia is marked by positive symptoms and does not necessarily warrant a poor prognosis.
   c. Schizophrenia with positive symptoms (delusions and hallucinations) has a more promising prognosis than the disorder with negative symptoms.
   d. Capgras's syndrome is a delusion (positive symptom) in which people think there are doubles for oneself and others.

13. *a. The hallmark of paranoid schizophrenia is delusions; it is the most common subtype of schizophrenia. (pp. 430–431)
   b. Catatonic schizophrenia is characterized by psychomotor disturbances.
   c. Disorganized schizophrenia features very regressive behavior without delusions.
   d. Undifferentiated schizophrenia has no particular symptom picture. It may include delusions, but is not the most common subtype.

14. a. Paranoid schizophrenia features consistent delusions.
   *b. Psychomotor disturbances such as extreme activity and complete immobility are the fundamental signs of catatonic schizophrenia. (p. 432)
   c. Disorganized schizophrenia is marked by extremely bizarre and childish behavior from an early age.
   d. Undifferentiated schizophrenia is the label given when no particular symptom stands out.

15. a. Auditory or visual hallucinations are found in a variety of schizophrenic subtypes.
    b. Early onset and bizarre behavior are signs of disorganized schizophrenia.
    c. When many symptoms are simultaneously present, the diagnosis is usually undifferentiated schizophrenia.
    *d. Residual schizophrenia is the diagnosis given to schizophrenics when they are in remission. (p. 434)

16. a. In paranoid schizophrenia, delusions and other thought disturbances affect a wide range of functioning; there is a deterioration in functioning in all the schizophrenias.
    b. Brief reactive psychosis is diagnosed if symptoms last one month or less.
    *c. Delusional disorder is reserved for highly compartmentalized delusions that do not have a broad effect on functioning. (Focus 14.3; p. 432)
    d. There is no such subtype.

17. a. Schizophrenic patients report being able to control or modify their symptoms.
    b. Schizophrenia does not usually begin in middle age; age of onset does not differentiate these disorders.
    c. There are thought disturbances in schizophreniform disorder.
    *d. Duration is the only means of differentiating these disorders. (p. 434)

18. a. The active phase follows the prodromal phase.
    b. During the active phase, symptoms are at their peak.
    c. Schizophrenia includes three phases; the active phase may not last very long or may occur intermittently over a lifetime.
    *d. The three phases are the prodromal, the active, and the residual. (pp. 435–436)

19. *a. Conservative estimates indicate that one-half of schizophrenics will show moderate or complete recovery by the end of their lives. (p. 436)
    b. Long-term outcomes are fairly positive for one-half or more of cases.
    c. Although Freud assumed that unconscious conflicts occur throughout life, this is unrelated to the research finding that in one-half of cases, schizophrenic symptoms improve or disappear.
    d. This was Kraepelin's position, but research rejects this idea.

20. a. Recovery was slower in developed countries such as the United States and the former Soviet Union.
    *b. Recovery, including return to employment, was quicker in developing countries. (Critical Thinking, p. 437)
    c. Many studies indicate that moderation or elimination of symptoms is likely in one-half of cases.
    d. If diet were important, we would expect better recovery in developed countries than in developing ones, where food may be scarce.

ANSWERS TO APPLICATION QUESTIONS

1. a. Philippe Pinel's contributions were made around the turn of the nineteenth century, almost 100 years before writings on schizophrenia began.
   *b. Bleuler disputed Kraepelin's view that *dementia praecox* was a unitary organic illness; he argued that a range of symptoms developed from a range of causes. (pp. 420–421)
   c. Emil Kraepelin took the opposite position to this statement.
   d. Dorothea Dix established state mental hospitals in the United States; she was not a theorist about schizophrenia.

2. *a. Lack of insight, not recognizing that one's bizarre behavior is just that, is the most common symptom of schizophrenia. (Focus 14.2; p. 428)
   b. Although delusions are common symptoms of schizophrenia, there is no information indicating that Don suffers from them.
   c. Waxy flexibility is a symptom of a rare form of schizophrenia, the catatonic subtype.
   d. Auditory hallucinations are common in schizophrenia, but there is no information indicating that Don suffers from them.

3. a. A delusion of persecution would involve threats of harm or humiliation.
   b. Delusions of grandeur involve a belief in one's special status or ability ("I can see through walls").
   c. Capgras's syndrome is a delusion that oneself and others have been replaced by identical doubles.
   *d. Delusions of reference involve beliefs that external events have personal meaning ("When police sirens are sounded, they are signaling me"). (p. 424)

4. a. Positive symptoms include activity such as bizarre gestures, as well as delusions, hallucinations, and disorganized thought.
   b. Disorganized schizophrenia is characterized by bizarre actions, fragmented thinking, and emotional expression that can include silly smiles or giggles.
   c. Schizophrenia involving an absence of emotion and motivation involves negative symptoms; these are associated with poor prognosis.
   *d. Negative symptoms such as the ones Justin shows are associated with poor prognosis. (p. 429)

5. *a. Schizophrenic patients report that they can take actions to reduce their symptoms. (Focus 14.1; p. 427)
   b. Neologism is the term for the made-up words that schizophrenics use in their disturbed speech.
   c. Flat affect, an absence of emotional expression, is an important symptom of schizophrenia.
   d. False beliefs that are unswayed by evidence are called delusions.

6. a. Schizophreniform disorder is diagnosed when symptoms last less than six months.
   b. Catatonic schizophrenia is characterized by psychomotor disturbances, which Jonathan does not display.
   c. In undifferentiated schizophrenia, symptoms are more diffuse than Jonathan's and are not so regressive.
   *d. Disorganized schizophrenia involves bizarre symptoms that have an early onset, as in Jonathan's case. (p. 431)

7. a. Paranoid schizophrenia is characterized by delusions.
   *b. Catatonic schizophrenia involves the psychomotor disturbances and social withdrawal seen in Tina's case. (p. 432)
   c. Undifferentiated schizophrenia does not involve such bizarre behaviors as are described in Tina's case.
   d. Residual schizophrenia is diagnosed when a person has had an episode of full-blown schizophrenia and now shows some symptoms but not prominently enough to get another diagnosis.

8. a. In paranoid schizophrenia, delusions are part of a more general cognitive impairment that leads to deteriorated functioning.
   b. In undifferentiated schizophrenia, delusions are not predominant.
   c. Brief reactive psychoses are acute conditions that impair functioning; they last less than one month.
   *d. In delusional disorders, paranoid ideas are highly organized, but no other thought disturbance is seen. (Focus 14.3; p. 432)

9. a. Paranoid schizophrenia is diagnosed only after symptoms have lasted for six months or more.
   b. Catatonic schizophrenia is diagnosed after symptoms of psychomotor disturbance have lasted for six months or more.
   *c. Brief psychotic disorder is diagnosed in cases like Chuck's, where symptoms of thought disturbance last less than one month. (p. 434)
   d. *Prodromal schizophrenia* is not an official label in DSM-IV.

10. a. Long-term outcomes show that one-half of schizophrenic patients make moderate or complete recoveries.
   b. Some schizophrenics make complete recoveries.
   c. Recovery seems to be more rapid in developing countries than in developed ones such as the United States.
   *d. Although misdiagnosis may be the reason, higher recovery rates have been found in developing countries (Nigeria and India) than in developed countries (the United States and Great Britain). (Critical Thinking, p. 437)

CHAPTER 15
Schizophrenia: Etiology and Treatment

LEARNING OBJECTIVES

When you have mastered the material in Chapter 15, you should be able to:

1. Discuss the need for combining hereditary and environmental influences to understand the origins of schizophrenia. Discuss problems with interpreting genetic studies on schizophrenia. (pp. 441–443)
2. Describe the results of research using blood relatives and twins to investigate the genetics of schizophrenia. Evaluate the methodological problems of these types of research. (pp. 443–446)
3. Describe the results of adoption studies as well as those with high-risk populations. Evaluate the methodological problems of these types of research. (pp. 446 – 450)
4. Describe the dopamine hypothesis of schizophrenia and research results that strengthen and weaken this hypothesis. (pp. 451–452)
5. Describe research linking neurological impairments to Type I and Type II schizophrenia. Describe the evidence that schizophrenics have information-processing deficits. List the three types of factors that Nuechterlein and his colleagues suggest will separate the causes and effects of schizophrenia. (pp. 452–454)
6. Discuss the role of stress in the development of schizophrenic symptoms. Describe the family environment theories of schizophrenia and the methodological problems with earlier research. (pp. 454 – 456)
7. Describe the importance of expressed emotion in schizophrenia. (pp. 456 – 457)
8. Discuss the social class and cross-cultural aspects of schizophrenia. (pp. 457–458)
9. Describe and evaluate the diathesis-stress model of schizophrenia. (pp. 459–460)
10. Discuss the use of antipsychotic medication in the treatment of schizophrenia and its side effects problems. Discuss changes in patients' rights to refuse medication. (Critical Thinking; pp. 460–461, 462)
11. Describe the psychosocial therapies (institutional approaches, social skills training, and cognitive therapy). Describe Integrated Psychological Therapy (IPT). Discuss the effectiveness of these treatments. (pp. 461–464)
12. Describe interventions targeted at relapse prevention by reducing expressed emotion. (p. 465)

CHAPTER OUTLINE

1. **Etiology of schizophrenia** (pp. 441–442) The causes of schizophrenia may involve genetic, physiological, psychological, and environmental factors. Therapies include antipsychotic medication and psychotherapy, but relapse rates remain too high. Researchers disagree on the impact of social and genetic factors in the cause and development of this disorder.

2. **Heredity and schizophrenia: problems in interpreting genetic studies, studies involving blood relatives** (pp. 442–444) The highest probability of selecting a schizophrenic from the general population would be reached by finding an individual with an identical twin who has the disorder. However, genetic studies are limited by the variety of subtypes of the disorder, as well as by sampling and definitional problems.

   We might assume that the closer the blood relationship between a person and a diagnosed schizophrenic, the higher the probability of the disorder in that person. However, relatedness and risk are not always linked because of problems in defining *schizophrenic,* in reliably diagnosing individuals, and in biased selection and analysis. Furthermore, such studies confound genetics and environment.

3. **Heredity and schizophrenia: twin studies and adoption studies** (pp. 444–448) Since their genes are identical, we would assume that there would be stronger *concordance rates* among MZ twins than among DZ twins (who share about 50 percent of their genes) if schizophrenia is genetically transmitted. Concordance rates are usually two to four times higher in MZ twins than in DZ twins, but method problems, including definitions along the schizophrenia spectrum, account for the wide range in these findings.

   Adoption studies screen out the effects of family environment. Heston (1966) found that five of forty-seven adoptees of schizophrenic mothers (at-risk children) later became schizophrenics themselves, but none of the control adoptees did. However, many at-risk children also became creative, successful adults. Other adoption studies also support the idea that heredity plays a major role in the transmission of schizophrenia.

4. **Heredity and schizophrenia: studies of high-risk populations** (pp. 448–450) High-risk studies are developmental comparisons between children with schizophrenic parents and those with nonschizophrenic parents. Results of Mednick et al.'s research show that children who became sick had mothers with more severe schizophrenic symptoms and birth complications. They were also more disruptive as children and had a slower autonomic recovery rate. An Israeli *prospective study* indicates that schizophrenia is most common when high-risk children are raised in a kibbutz or in a highly stressful family environment. None of the high-risk children receiving adequate parenting developed schizophrenia or a schizophrenia-like disorder.

   Although high-risk studies are a promising line of research, they have no control groups with other forms of psychopathology, generalizations may be difficult, and relevant variables and appropriate definitions of disorder may be missing.

5. **Physiological factors in schizophrenia** (pp. 451–454) After previous dead ends, the idea that a chemical imbalance exists in schizophrenics shows promise. The effects of phenothiazine drugs, L-dopa, and amphetamine support the *dopamine hypothesis,* which suggests that dopamine activity in certain areas of the brain is excessive in schizophrenics. However, some schizophrenics do not respond to phenothiazines or L-dopa in ways predicted by this biochemical theory. This could be due to there being varieties of schizophrenia.

   Research supports the view that, especially in schizophrenics who show such negative symptoms as flat affect (Type II schizophrenics), there are neurological abnormalities, including cerebral atrophy and low cerebral glucose metabolism. Schizophrenics show poorer sustained attention and eye movement coordination than nonschizophrenics. Nuechterlein and his colleagues suggest that some neurological factors in schizophrenia predate the disorder and are unchanged during a psychotic episode, some are present beforehand but are worsened during the disorder, and some are short-term indicators that are the result of the disorder. However, neurological abnormalities are not specific to schizophrenia, and some treatment effects run counter to prediction.

6. **Environmental factors in schizophrenia: family influences** (pp. 454–456) Environmental factors act as stressors and thereby help produce psychopathology. In a large minority of schizophrenics, onset of the disorder and relapse are associated with increased frequency of stressful life events. The family is an important source of stress. Psychodynamic theory focused on the personality of the *schizophrenogenic* mother, whereas family systems theory stresses the *double-bind theory* of communication patterns. Research on family influence has been hampered both by observations after the child has been diagnosed and by the lack of control groups.

7. **Environmental factors in schizophrenia: expressed emotion** (pp. 456–457) Expressed emotion—highly critical, hostile, and overinvolved parenting—is related to increased relapse among schizophrenics, especially those who have stopped taking medication. However, as with other environmental factors, it is not clear whether these problems are the effect of schizophrenia or its cause; neither does it appear to be pathognomonic for the disorder.

8. **Environmental factors in schizophrenia: effect of social class, cross-cultural comparisons** (pp. 457–458) Schizophrenia is more common in the lower social classes than in the upper ones. Theories attribute this to the stress of poverty or the downward drift of impaired people. Research evidence can support both positions.

   The incidence of schizophrenia in ten countries studied ranged from 1.5 per 10,000 in Denmark to 4.2 per 10,000 in India, but symptoms appear to reflect cultural norms and current concerns specific to the culture. Racial differences exist within the United States: Blacks exhibit more severe, angry, and antisocial symptoms than do whites. Misdiagnosis based on race may be one explanation.

9. **The diathesis-stress model of schizophrenia** (pp. 459–460) Lacking evidence for a single cause of schizophrenia, the growing consensus is that schizophrenia develops out of a genetic or acquired predisposition coupled with a stressful environment. The vulnerability may include impaired information processing, overreactivity, and poor social skills. The stressors may include an overstimulating environment where EE is present. Such a model implies that intervention should involve medication, individual coping skills, and family support.

10. **The treatment of schizophrenia** (Critical Thinking; pp. 460–465) Antipsychotic medication *(neuroleptics)* is the principal means of treating schizophrenia today. A new drug, clozapine, may be effective in cases not previously helped by neuroleptics. Although effective in many cases, medications can produce neurological conditions, including *tardive dyskinesia*, a disorder of involuntary movements for which there is no cure. Other side effects have led to legal action to provide patients with the right to refuse such medical treatment. Clinicians often misinterpret or ignore the symptoms of drug side effects. The need for maintenance dosages for schizophrenics is currently in question.

    Psychosocial therapy is now often paired with drug treatment. In inpatient settings, *milieu therapy* and behavioral treatment have been shown to be more effective than traditional treatment. Milieu allows patients to take more responsibility for decision making. In behavior therapy, the client is taught social skills so that interactions are not avoided. Cognitive approaches have been useful in reducing delusions and hallucinations. *Integrated Psychological Therapy (IPT)* teaches patients to use information appropriately, respond to social cues, make conversation, and interact appropriately. Interventions to reduce expressed emotion in families has also proven useful in reducing relapse rates. Combining various treatments gives hope for even more successful therapy for schizophrenia in the future.

KEY TERMS

Fill-in-the-Blanks Quiz

1. The suggestion that schizophrenia results from an excess of dopamine activity at certain brain synapses is called the ___________.

2. The suggestion that schizophrenia develops in an individual because, as a child, that person continually received contradictory messages from parents is called the ___________.

3. A theoretical model postulating that innate vulnerability and the effect of environmental stressors combine to produce schizophrenic episodes is called the ___________.

4. Antipsychotic medications that can produce symptoms that mimic neurological disorders are called ___________.

5. The likelihood that family members will exhibit the disorder being studied is called the ___________.

6. A therapy program in which the hospital environment operates as a community and patients have decision-making responsibilities is called ___________.

7. An adjective describing a parent who is simultaneously or alternately cold and overprotecting, rejecting and dominating, and who may produce schizophrenia is ___________.

8. A study that is performed before the symptoms of an illness have been identified is called a(n)___________.

9. The disorder involving involuntary lip-smacking, protruding of the tongue, and jerking of the limbs caused by long-term use of neuroleptic medication is called ___________.

10. The cognitive-behavior therapy for schizophrenia that focuses on information processing, verbal communication, social perceptions, and social skills is called ___________.

Answers to Fill-in-the-Blanks Quiz

1. dopamine hypothesis
2. double-bind theory
3. diathesis-stress model
4. neuroleptics
5. concordance rate
6. milieu therapy
7. schizophrenogenic
8. prospective study
9. tardive dyskinesia
10. Integrated Psychological Therapy

FACT AND CONCEPT QUESTIONS

1. Because ____________ studies of schizophrenics often use chronically ill patients and adopt very narrow definitions of the disorder, evidence of ____________ may be inaccurate.
   a. sociological; the inheritance of the disorder
   b. genetic; the inheritance of the disorder
   c. psychoanalytic; the unconscious conflicts in the disorder
   d. genetic; cross-cultural differences in the disorder

2. Research on the relationship between the risk of developing schizophrenia and the degree of blood relatedness indicates
   a. a wide range of results.
   b. that schizophrenia is clearly a genetically caused disorder.
   c. that social class and stressors are more important than genetic factors.
   d. the greater the relatedness, the greater the risk of developing the disorder.

3. Why is it impossible to demonstrate the inheritance of schizophrenia on the basis of blood relative studies?
   a. There are many different blood groups.
   b. There are many different kinds of schizophrenia.
   c. There are no probands in a blood relative study.
   d. There are environmental factors that are uncontrolled.

4. The likelihood that two members of a family will both develop a disorder is called the
   a. proband index.
   b. vulnerability index.
   c. concordance rate.
   d. MZ or DZ rate.

5. Heston's (1966) research examining the rate of schizophrenia among adopted children born to schizophrenic parents found
   a. no difference between the rate of the disorder in the control and at-risk groups.
   b. no cases of the disorder among control children.
   c. that 100 percent of the at-risk children developed the disorder.
   d. that at-risk children tended to be duller and less spontaneous than the controls.

6. The value of a high-risk study of schizophrenia over an adoption study is that it
   a. separates the effects of genetic factors from those of the environment.
   b. includes a control group.
   c. allows for the use of concordance rates.
   d. allows the investigator to see how the disorder develops.

7. Mednick et al.'s high-risk research indicates that children who develop schizophrenia are
   a. more likely to be identical twins than fraternal twins.
   b. extremely aggressive and slower to habituate to certain stimuli.
   c. extremely intelligent and had less severely disordered mothers.
   d. all identified as "sick" as young children.

8. High-risk research studies on schizophrenia
   a. show reasonably strong evidence that heredity is involved in schizophrenia.
   b. show that 80 to 90 percent of diagnosed schizophrenics have a schizophrenic parent.
   c. indicate that family environment plays no meaningful role in the development of symptoms.
   d. have failed to show that heredity plays a major role in schizophrenia.

9. Because phenothiazines reduce schizophrenic symptoms and amphetamine overdoses can mimic schizophrenic symptoms, it is believed that the neurotransmitter _______________ is involved in schizophrenia.
   a. L-dopa
   b. 5HIAA
   c. dopamine
   d. acetylcholine

10. One problem with the dopamine hypothesis is that it fails to explain why
    a. people who take large doses of phenothiazines develop symptoms much like Parkinson's disease.
    b. more than 75 percent of those who take antipsychotic medications remain unimproved.
    c. both a and b are true.
    d. neither a nor b is true.

11. Type II schizophrenia involves such negative symptoms as flat affect and lack of drive. This type of schizophrenia has been found to correlate with
    a. abnormally low levels of dopamine.
    b. tardive dyskinesia.
    c. neurological abnormalities such as cerebral atrophy.
    d. high levels of expressed emotion in the family environment.

12. The theory that schizophrenia develops out of family environments in which there are contradictory messages and in which no responses go unpunished is called the
    a. double-bind communication theory.
    b. diathesis-stress model.
    c. neurological deficit theory.
    d. schizophrenogenic mother theory.

13. The most common flaws with earlier research on the families of schizophrenics were
    a. too few subjects and too narrow a definition of schizophrenia.
    b. analysis of interactions after one family member was diagnosed and a lack of control groups.
    c. a lack of control groups and overreliance on MZ and DZ twins.
    d. too few subjects and the use of a developmental method.

14. When the parents of schizophrenics engage in heated criticism and become overinvolved in the lives of their children, they engage in
    a. double-bind communications.
    b. social skill training.
    c. expressed emotion.
    d. tardive dyskinesia.

15. When low socioeconomic status results from schizophrenia, a ___________ explanation of the relationship between the two is supported.
    a. genetic
    b. biochemical
    c. stressful life events
    d. downward drift

16. Evidence from international research indicates that schizophrenia
    a. shows the same symptoms in every culture in the world.
    b. shows different symptoms depending on the culture in which it occurs.
    c. occurs with widely varying frequency, depending on the culture in which it occurs.
    d. has a slower onset in third-world countries.

17. According to the diathesis-stress model,
    a. the vulnerability to schizophrenia can be inherited or acquired.
    b. all people have about the same vulnerability to the disorder.
    c. once the disorder begins, stressful life events play no role.
    d. the presence of social supports has no effect on the outcome of a schizophrenic episode.

18. Which side effect is a well-established problem with antipsychotic medication?
    a. The development of phobias
    b. Paranoid delusions
    c. Expressed emotion
    d. Tardive dyskinesia

19. The Paul and Lentz (1977) study comparing traditional institutional treatment with social learning and milieu therapy found that
    a. milieu therapy was superior to both social learning and traditional approaches.
    b. traditional approaches were superior to both milieu and social learning therapies.
    c. all three were roughly equally effective.
    d. the milieu and social learning approaches were superior to traditional treatment.

20. To reduce expressed emotion in families, Falloon et al. (1984) suggest that interventions include
    a. high doses of antipsychotic medication.
    b. a careful analysis of communication patterns.
    c. a psychoanalytically oriented investigation of unconscious conflicts.
    d. increased decision-making responsibility in the treatment ward.

APPLICATION QUESTIONS

1. Don and Ron are identical twins. Tim and Harry are fraternal twins. Don and Tim are both diagnosed as schizophrenics. According to the results of most research studies on twins,
    a. Ron has a greater chance of being schizophrenic than Harry.
    b. Ron and Harry have equal chances of being schizophrenic.
    c. Harry has a greater chance of being schizophrenic than Ron.
    d. there is little chance that either Harry or Ron will have schizophrenia.

2. Dr. Arensky says, "Adoption studies such as Heston's (1966) show that few or none of the control group children develop schizophrenia and that those in the at-risk condition either develop the disorder or are socially dysfunctional. However, environmental factors play a major causal role." What idea here is *inaccurate*?
   a. The idea that control group children are free of the disorder
   b. The idea that at-risk children are more prone to the disorder
   c. The idea that at-risk children are socially dysfunctional even if they do not develop schizophrenia
   d. The idea that environmental factors are major influences

3. A psychologist investigating the genetics of schizophrenia is most likely to find a high concordance rate for the disorder if
   a. she uses a broad definition of schizophrenia.
   b. the subjects are fraternal twins, rather than identical twins.
   c. she uses a narrow definition of schizophrenia.
   d. the subjects are distant relatives.

4. Brenda is a chronic schizophrenic who is being treated with antipsychotic medication. She goes to a party where someone gives her an amphetamine. What is likely to happen to Brenda?
   a. The amphetamine will combine with the medication and reduce her symptoms.
   b. The amphetamine will increase her dopamine levels and worsen her symptoms.
   c. The amphetamine will greatly lower her dopamine levels and produce tardive dyskinesia.
   d. The amphetamine will increase dopamine and induce the symptoms of Parkinson's disease.

5. Irma has Type II schizophrenia: She shows no emotional expression and is passive and withdrawn. On the basis of research evidence, if she has a neurological abnormality, it is probably
   a. a low level of dopamine.
   b. extremely small ventricles in the brain.
   c. excessive activity in the medulla and cerebellum.
   d. cerebral atrophy and reduced glucose metabolism.

6. Marvin is diagnosed as a schizophrenic. His mother is overprotective, rejecting, cold, and dominating. According to psychoanalytic thinkers, Marvin's mother
   a. became this way in response to his disorder.
   b. could be considered schizophrenogenic.
   c. is probably an antisocial personality.
   d. is responding to castration anxieties.

7. Dr. Earl says, "The problem with these studies is that there were no control groups and the family's interactions were studied *after* a family member was diagnosed with schizophrenia." What kind of study is Dr. Earl discussing?
   a. Recent high-risk studies
   b. Recent studies examining expressed emotion and relapse
   c. Earlier studies of double-bind communications
   d. Kraepelin's early twin studies

8. Cindy says, "I don't think that poverty causes schizophrenia; I think being so dysfunctional makes schizophrenics poor." Cindy's ideas illustrate the
   a. downward drift hypothesis.
   b. diathesis-stress model of schizophrenia.
   c. schizophrenogenic theory.
   d. poverty-as-stressor hypothesis.

9. An elderly schizophrenic patient who has been taking phenothiazines for twenty years shows involuntary thrusting of her tongue, lip smacking, and jerking movements of the neck. What is wrong with this patient?
   a. She has cerebral atrophy as a result of Type II schizophrenia.
   b. She has symptoms of the disorder that are still not controlled through medication.
   c. She has developed Parkinson's disease because of her medication.
   d. She has developed tardive dyskinesia because of her medication.

10. Harold has been diagnosed with schizophrenia and is currently in treatment. His counselor teaches him to recognize and respond to social cues. He also learns to retrieve appropriate information so he can make conversation with others. What kind of treatment is Harold receiving?
    a. Integrated Psychological Therapy (IPT)
    b. Milieu therapy
    c. Traditional institutional care
    d. Intervention to reduce expressed emotion

ANSWERS TO FACT AND CONCEPT QUESTIONS

1. a. Sociological research would not reveal anything about the inheritance of the disorder.
   *b. Chronically ill subjects probably have a higher genetic component than other subjects; broad definitions of *schizophrenia* increase the chances of concordance and would inflate estimates of genetic contribution. (p. 443)
   c. Psychoanalytic research rarely uses schizophrenics, and the use of chronically ill patients is even rarer.
   d. Genetic research would not reveal anything about cross-cultural differences.

2. *a. The range of risk for first-degree relatives is very wide due mostly to methodological differences. (pp. 443–444)
   b. Because environmental influences are strong in family studies, such a statement is improper.
   c. Family studies have not controlled for the effects of social class or other environmental effects.
   d. Although the relationship is weak, in general, as relatedness gets closer, the risk of the disorder increases.

3. a. Although there are different blood groups, blood relative studies are interested only in the similarity of genes in the people being researched.
   b. Although there are different kinds of schizophrenia, this is not a problem specific to blood relative research.
   c. There must be a proband, a person with the disorder in question, in any genetic research study.
   *d. Because people are raised by their family members, it is always impossible to separate the effects of genetics from those of learning in this type of research. (p. 444)

4. a. The proband is the index case, the person who has the disorder.
   b. *Vulnerability index* is a made-up term.
   *c. When all the co-twins in a twin study have the disorder, the concordance rate is 100 percent; when none of the co-twins has the disorder, the rate is 0 percent. (p. 444)
   d. MZ and DZ are terms for types of twins (monozygotic and dizygotic), and neither represents a likelihood of developing a disorder.

5. a. There was a considerable difference in the rate of schizophrenia between at-risk and control children.
   *b. None of the control group children developed schizophrenia, compared with five of forty-seven in the at-risk group. (p. 447)
   c. More than forty of forty-seven at-risk children did not develop the disorder.
   d. The at-risk children who were free of schizophrenia were highly successful adults and were unusually creative.

6. a. High-risk children are raised by their biological parents, so such a separation is not possible.
   b. Control groups are a part of both research designs, so this does not represent a specific advantage of high-risk studies.
   c. Concordance rates are used in any study that compares a proband and someone else; they are used in twin, adoption, and other genetic research designs.
   *d. High-risk studies begin observations before the onset of symptoms; they have the advantage of being developmental studies. (p. 448)

7. a. High-risk research does not involve twins of any kind.
   *b. Mednick et al. found that children who developed schizophrenia were aggressive, disruptive, slow to habituate, and had mothers who were more severely disturbed and who had had pregnancy complications. (p. 448)
   c. No difference in intelligence was reported, and the mothers were more disturbed.
   d. Many of the "sick" children did not develop the disorder.

8. *a. High-risk studies show that children who have a schizophrenic parent and who are raised in stressful situations have a greater likelihood of developing the disorder; this is evidence that genetics is a partial cause. (p. 449)
   b. The reverse is true: Only 10 to 20 percent of those with a schizophrenic parent develop the disorder.
   c. Stressors play a major role, as can be seen in the Israeli studies comparing kibbutz- and family-reared children.
   d. Because more children in high-risk groups develop the disorder, genetic factors must play an important role.

9. a. L-dopa is a drug used to treat Parkinson's disease because it is used by the body to manufacture dopamine.
   b. 5HIAA is a metabolite of the neurotransmitter serotonin and is involved in affective disorders.
   *c. Dopamine activity has been found to be excessive in certain areas of the brains of schizophrenics, and it is reduced by phenothiazines and increased by amphetamines. (p. 451)
   d. Acetylcholine is a neurotransmitter, but it is not implicated in schizophrenia.

10. a. Phenothiazine use can lead to Parkinsonian symptoms because it reduces dopamine activity; these findings support the dopamine hypothesis.
   b. This statistic is inaccurate; only about 25 percent are unaffected.
   c. Because both a and b are incorrect, this cannot be the best answer.
   *d. Because both a and b are incorrect, this is the best answer. (p. 451)

11. a. Abnormally high levels of dopamine activity are a general finding in schizophrenia.
   b. Tardive dyskinesia is a serious side effect of heavy phenothiazine use.
   *c. Cerebral atrophy, ventricular enlargement (caused by the shrinkage of cerebral tissue), and low glucose metabolism are neurological signs of Type II schizophrenia. (pp. 452–453)
   d. Expressed emotion is not correlated with Type II schizophrenia.

12. *a. Double-bind communications involve contradictory messages that punish the child; the outcome is believed by some to be schizophrenia. (p. 455)
   b. The diathesis-stress model involves a predisposition to a disorder and environmental stresses that trigger symptoms.
   c. Neurological deficits involve Type II schizophrenia, not communications issues.
   d. Schizophrenogenic mothers are central to psychoanalytic theory.

13. a. One of the problems with earlier research was that the definition of the disorder was too broad.
   *b. Both of these problems characterized earlier work and made its results suspect. (p. 456)
   c. MZ and DZ twins were never used in family studies.
   d. One of the problems with earlier research was the failure to use a developmental method.

14. a. Double-bind communications involve contradictory messages, but do not necessarily involve heated criticism.
   b. Social skill training is something professionals do when they teach clients to speak and act assertively.
   *c. Expressed emotion is defined in terms of overinvolvement and excessive criticism of family members. (p. 456)
   d. Tardive dyskinesia is a neurological problem brought on by chronic, heavy use of antipsychotic medications.

15. a. Genetic explanations are supported by high-risk, twin, or adoption studies.
   b. Biochemical explanations are supported by neurotransmitter imbalances or drug effects.
   c. Stressful life events are seen as the cause of the disorder: Poverty so overwhelms the person that he or she becomes schizophrenic.
   *d. Downward drift suggests that poverty is the effect of schizophrenia; people cannot work well and become poorer. (p. 457)

16. a. Research shows that symptoms are influenced by cultural values and concerns.
  *b. Symptoms differ among cultures; for example, Japanese schizophrenics are more passive than Italian schizophrenics. (p. 458)
  c. The incidence of schizophrenia is very stable across cultures.
  d. If anything, abrupt onset is more common in third-world countries.

17. *a. The diathesis-stress model involves the predisposition to be vulnerable; this can be inherited or acquired at an early age. (p. 459)
  b. Differences in vulnerability account for the very different rates of the disorder in different segments of the population.
  c. Stress is a part of the entire course of schizophrenia, from onset to recovery.
  d. Social supports appear to be an important way of preventing the predisposition from producing symptoms.

18. a. There is no evidence that antipsychotic medication produces phobias.
  b. Antipsychotic medication reduces paranoid thinking.
  c. Expressed emotion is a family factor that seems to increase the chances of relapse in schizophrenia.
  *d. Tardive dyskinesia, involuntary tongue thrusting and lip smacking, is a sometimes irreversible side effect of antipsychotic medication. (Critical Thinking; p. 462)

19. a. Milieu therapy was not found to be superior to the social learning approach.
  b. Traditional approaches were less successful than either of the other methods.
  c. Traditional approaches were less successful than either of the other methods.
  *d. Patients who were treated with milieu and social learning therapy were more likely to live independently after discharge. (p. 461)

20. a. High doses of medication may reduce relapse rates, but it is not clear whether they have a direct effect on expressed emotion.
  *b. Falloon et al. suggest that, after a family makes a careful analysis of how it communicates, it can improve its clarity of speaking and quality of listening to reduce expressed emotion. (p. 465)
  c. Falloon et al.'s intervention is behaviorally oriented and avoids psychoanalytic concepts.
  d. Increased decision-making responsibility is part of milieu therapy.

ANSWERS TO APPLICATION QUESTIONS

1. *a. Identical twins have a higher concordance rate than fraternal twins because all of their genes are the same. (p. 444)
  b. Because there is one-half the similarity of genes in fraternal twins, there should be a reduced likelihood for Harry.
  c. Being a fraternal twin, Harry's likelihood is lower.
  d. It is true that schizophrenia is rare, but, as Meehl points out, an identical twin has about a 50 percent chance of developing the disorder if the other twin is so diagnosed.

2. a. This is accurate because past research reports that control group children have 0 percent chance of developing the disorder.
   b. At-risk children are more likely to develop schizophrenia, so this is accurate.
   *c. This is inaccurate because the at-risk children who did not develop schizophrenia turned out to be creative and successful. (p. 447)
   d. Environmental factors, as in the Israeli kibbutz study, play a major role in the development of schizophrenia.

3. *a. Broad definitions of schizophrenia increase the chances that both people being compared have the disorder, thereby inflating estimates of schizophrenia's heritability. (p. 444)
   b. Since fraternals share only 25 percent of their genes (compared to 100 percent for identicals), using them would reduce concordance rates.
   c. A narrow definition would exclude people who otherwise might be considered sharing the disorder (being concordant).
   d. The more distant the relatives, the fewer the genes in common.

4. a. Only antipsychotic medication is known to reduce psychotic symptoms.
   *b. Amphetamine in very large doses produces a psychosis that mimics schizophrenia; even in small doses, it creates and exaggerates symptoms in chronic schizophrenics. (p. 451)
   c. Only antipsychotic medication is known to produce tardive dyskinesia.
   d. A lack of dopamine produces Parkinson's disease; L-dopa is prescribed for this condition, not amphetamine.

5. a. Abnormally low dopamine levels are associated with Parkinson's disease, not with schizophrenia.
   b. Ventricles (spaces in the brain) become enlarged in Type II schizophrenia because cerebral tissue has shrunk.
   c. Cerebral activity is reduced in Type II schizophrenia; no studies have implicated the medulla and cerebellum (sites regulating basic body processes and coordination, respectively).
   *d. Type II schizophrenia is associated with the wasting away of cerebral tissue and a reduced metabolism. (p. 452)

6. a. Psychoanalysts call this woman schizophreno*genic;* the suffix *genic* means "causing."
   *b. The schizophrenogenic mother was thought by analysts to be cold and intrusive, rejecting and dominating. (p. 455)
   c. Antisocial personality in parents is not associated with a likelihood of schizophrenia.
   d. Psychoanalysts attribute castration anxieties to men, not to mothers.

7. a. High-risk studies involve observations of people before the diagnosis is made.
   b. Recent research on expressed emotion has included control groups.
   *c. Early double-bind communication studies did not look for similar patterns in nonschizophrenic families or investigate whether the patterns were the result of having a schizophrenic child rather than the cause. (p. 455)
   d. Kraepelin did no twin research.

8. *a. In downward drift theory, the fact that schizophrenics cannot be gainfully employed is the explanation for the correlation between low social class and the disorder. (p. 457)
   b. Diathesis-stress theory states only that a combination of predisposition and environmental stress produces the disorder; it says nothing about social class.
   c. Schizophrenogenic theory stresses the role of a dominating and rejecting mother; it says nothing about social class.
   d. If Cindy thought that poverty caused the disorder, this would be the best answer.

9. a. The symptoms of Type II schizophrenia are flat affect and passivity.
   b. Although, in rare cases, lip smacking may be a psychotic behavior, it is far more commonly seen in tardive dyskinesia.
   c. The symptoms of Parkinson's disease are a shuffling gait and flat affect; medication can produce only similar symptoms, not the disease itself.
   *d. These are the classic signs of tardive dyskinesia, which is most likely in elderly individuals who have taken neuroleptic medications for some years. (Critical Thinking; p. 462)

10. *a. Integrated Psychological Therapy (IPT) has four components: cognitive differentiation, social perception (including responding to social cues), verbal communication, and social skills. (p. 464).
   b. Milieu therapy is an inpatient treatment where patients are given responsibility for decision making.
   c. Traditional institutional care involves medication and "warehousing" patients.
   d. Interventions to reduce expressed emotion focus on the communication patterns and problem-solving abilities of family members who must deal with a schizophrenic.

PART 5
Organic and Developmental Problems

CHAPTER 16
Cognitive Disorders

LEARNING OBJECTIVES

When you have mastered the material in Chapter 16, you should be able to:

1. Define cognitive disorders and their possible causes. Explain why the cause and treatment of cognitive disorders is usually complex. List the DSM-IV categories of cognitive disorders and when a disorder involving cognitive problems is *not* listed with the cognitive disorders. (pp. 469 – 470)
2. Describe the methods for assessing brain damage and the problem of linking functional loss to a specific brain location. (pp. 470 – 474)
3. Describe the dimensions by which brain damage is categorized. (p. 474)
4. Describe the problems of diagnosing organic brain disorders. (pp. 474 – 475)
5. Describe how cognitive disorders are categorized by cause. Describe and differentiate dementia and delirium. Describe aphasia. Discuss the possible causes of dementia and delirium. (Focus 16.1; pp. 475 – 477)
6. Describe the amnestic disorders and differentiate them from dementia and delirium. (p. 478)
7. Discuss the Case of Phineas Gage as an illustration of the cause and effect of brain damage. List and differentiate the types of head injuries. (pp. 478 – 479)
8. Describe the characteristics of the aging population. Describe the mental changes that accompany old age. Describe the nature and effects of strokes and multi-infarct dementia. (Critical Thinking; pp. 479 – 481)
9. Discuss the extent and reasons for memory loss in the elderly. Describe the effects of Alzheimer's disease and what is known about its cause. (Focus 16.2; pp. 481– 484)
10. Describe and differentiate among the following: Parkinson's disease, AIDS and the cognitive impairments it causes, neurosyphilis (general paresis), encephalitis, meningitis, Huntington's chorea, and cerebral tumors. (pp. 484 – 487)
11. Define epilepsy. Discuss the extent and nature of epilepsy and its treatment. Describe and differentiate the following forms of epilepsy: petit mal, Jacksonian, psychomotor, and grand mal. (pp. 487–490)
12. Discuss the causes of epilepsy. (p. 490)
13. Describe the relationship between psychoactive substance use and cognitive disorders. (p. 490)
14. Describe methods of treating cognitive disorders, including medication and cognitive and behavioral approaches. (pp. 490 – 493)
15. Discuss the need for environmental interventions and methods of supporting the caregivers of individuals with cognitive disorders. (pp. 493 – 494)

CHAPTER OUTLINE

1. **Cognitive disorders and the assessment of brain damage** (pp. 469–472) *Cognitive disorders* are those affecting thinking, memory, consciousness, and perception that are due to brain damage. These behavioral disturbances are affected by social and psychological factors such as coping ability and stress. The DSM-IV category of cognitive disorders includes what previous editions of DSM called *organic mental syndromes* and *organic disorders.* DSM-IV differentiates delirium, dementia, amnestic disorders, and other cognitive disorders.

   Brain damage can be assessed through neuropsychological testing and neurological tests. The first uses behavioral responses from the patient on memory or manual dexterity tasks. The second directly monitors the brain through *electroencephalography (EEG)*, *computerized axial tomography (CAT) scans*, *positron emission tomography (PET) scans*, and *magnetic resonance imaging (MRI)*. Each has its strengths and weaknesses.

2. **Localization and the dimensions of brain damage** (pp. 472–474) Neurological techniques can locate brain damage; however, there is extensive overlapping of functions in the brain. Localization is also complicated by diaschisis, where lesions in one area disrupt other intact areas, and by recovery of function after damage. Unused portions of the brain can take up functions of damaged areas, a process called plasticity. Brain damage ranges from mild to severe, and can be distinguished as endogenous or exogenous, diffuse or specific, acute or chronic.

3. **Diagnostic problems** (pp. 474–475) People without brain damage can be misdiagnosed as having a cognitive disorder. This is particularly likely for those suffering from severe depression or schizophrenia. The elderly are also vulnerable to misdiagnosis. Many older persons who function well score in the brain-damaged range on neuropsychological tests. The opposite is also true: Those with brain damage are misdiagnosed as having a psychological disorder. For this reason, follow-up testing at regular intervals is often recommended.

4. **Types of cognitive disorders: dementia, delirium, and amnestic disorders** (Focus 16.1; pp. 475–478) Cognitive disorders are classified by their cause, such as psychoactive substance-induced or general medical condition. The most prominent features of *dementia* are memory impairment; a decline in language, motor activities, and identification of faces or objects; and poor planning. It is found in a range of cognitive disorders, including AIDS. The onset of dementia is usually gradual and is often caused by general medical conditions (especially Alzheimer's disease), substance abuse, or combinations of the two.

   Delirium involves impairments in consciousness (disorientation, incoherent speech, perceptual distortions), and it usually develops rapidly.

   Amnestic disorders are usually caused by thiamine deficiency and entail an inability to retain new information or recall old information, or both.

   While the three conditions have overlapping symptoms, dementias are usually accompanied by language problems such as *aphasia* and come on gradually (as opposed to delirium). Memory loss is the primary symptom of amnestic disorders.

5. **Etiology of cognitive disorders: brain trauma** (pp. 478–479) *Brain trauma*—a physical wound to the brain—is one cause of cognitive disorders. Head injuries include *concussions*, when blood vessels are damaged by a blow to the head; *contusions*, when blood vessels rupture because of impact against the skull; and *lacerations*, when tissue is torn or pierced by an object penetrating the skull. More than eight million Americans suffer head injuries each year, and 20 percent of these result in serious head trauma. Personality changes as well as cognitive and

motor impairments are common. Only one-third of closed-head injury patients return to gainful employment after traditional rehabilitation. New treatments for head injury survivors, including cognitive retraining and coping skill training, hold promise.

6. **Aging and disorders associated with aging** (Critical Thinking, p. 481, Focus 16.2; pp. 479–484) The aging population of the United States is growing and has the following characteristics: There are more females than males, one-fifth are poor or near poor, and most have at least one chronic health problem. But most are able to live independently, and only 6 percent of those 60 to 85 and living in their own communities show signs of mild cognitive impairment.

   Stroke, the third major cause of death in the United States, is a common cognitive disorder in the elderly. Strokes (*cerebrovascular accidents*) occur when blood flow to an area of the brain is cut off, causing the death of that tissue (infarction). Common effects of stroke include loss of language function (various forms of aphasia), paralysis, and death. At least 25 percent of stroke victims develop major depression. Causes of stroke include bursting of blood vessels and narrowing or blockage of blood vessels due to buildup of fatty material on interior walls. A series of small strokes is known as *multi-infarct dementia*; it is characterized by uneven deterioration of intellectual abilities, including memory loss.

   Memory loss in the elderly may be due to brain cell deterioration, multi-infarct dementia, and the normal aging process. Another cause is intoxication from prescribed medication.

   Alzheimer's disease, involving atrophy of cortical tissue, leads to memory loss, irritability, and withdrawal. Death usually occurs within five years. The likelihood of developing Alzheimer's increases with age, affecting 5 to 10 percent of those over 65 but 20 percent of those over 80. Alzheimer's cause is unknown, but heredity may play a role in some subtypes; infection, head injury, exposure to aluminum, and reduced neurotransmitter levels may be related to others.

7. **Other diseases and infections of the brain** (pp. 484–487) *Parkinson's disease* has the following symptoms: muscle tremors; a stiff, shuffling gait; and an expressionless face. The disorder is associated with insufficient dopamine levels.

   The majority of AIDS patients also suffer from dementia. It is not clear whether the AIDS virus affects the brain, if AIDS-related infections cause neuropsychological problems, or if depression and anxiety about having AIDS causes cognitive symptoms.

   Neurosyphilis (*general paresis*) is brain damage caused by the delayed effect of a syphilis infection. It occurs in about 10 percent of syphilis cases. Symptoms include memory impairment, delusions, paralysis, and eventual death.

   Encephalitis (sleeping sickness) is a viral infection of the brain that produces long periods of sleep followed by agitation and seizures.

   Meningitis, an inflammation of the membrane around the brain, can be caused by bacteria, viruses, or fungi, and has a wide range of effects and potential residual disturbances.

   Huntington's chorea is a genetically transmitted disorder that first shows in early middle age. Symptoms begin with twitches and progress to uncontrollable jerking movements, irritability, and confusion. Death comes within thirteen to sixteen years after onset. A gene has been identified that causes the disorder.

8. **Cerebral tumors** (p. 487) A tumor is a mass of abnormal tissue. Fast-growing tumors in the brain produce severe mental symptoms, such as diminished attention, drowsiness, dementia, and mood changes.

9. **Epilepsy** (pp. 487–490) *Epilepsy* is a symptom, not a disorder. It involves brief periods of altered consciousness, often accompanied by seizures. About 2.5 million children and adults in

the United States have epilepsy or some other seizure disorder. The most common neurological problem, epilepsy is often diagnosed during childhood. Causes are genetic as well as environmental. Although epilepsy cannot be cured, it can be controlled with medication.

In *petit mal seizures,* brief (sometimes undetectable) dimming or loss of consciousness occurs. In *Jacksonian seizures,* the seizure starts in one part of the body and spreads to others. *Psychomotor seizures* involve spells during which people engage in normal behavior but have no recollection of their actions when the spell is over. *Grand mal seizures* are most dramatic and include an aura (a signal before seizures), tonic-clonic convulsions, and a coma (exhaustion) after the seizures are over. Causes ranging from tumors to illness to stress can account for epilepsy. Heredity may not be a necessary condition for onset; no personality type is associated with epilepsy.

10. **Etiology of cognitive disorders: psychoactive substances** (p. 490) Substances can cause cognitive disorders by having effects on the nervous system. The most common substances involved include alcohol, amphetamines, cocaine, hallucinogens, and opiates.

11. **Treatment considerations** (pp. 490 – 494) Treatment approaches include medical strategies such as surgery and medication, and psychological efforts such as skills training, cognitive preparation, and psychotherapy. Stress inoculation training is also useful, as is classical conditioning to reduce epileptic seizures.

    How family and friends can assist those with cognitive disorders is an important issue. Some suggestions are: preserving a sense of control, maintaining interpersonal contacts that do not overwhelm, providing tasks that increase self-worth, and ensuring that caregivers obtain social support for themselves.

KEY TERMS

Fill-in-the-Blanks Quiz

1. A sudden stoppage of blood flow to a portion of the brain that leads to a loss of brain function is called a(n) ____________ or ____________.

2. The syndrome that is characterized by a continuous decline in intellectual ability and judgment that often includes language problems and has a gradual onset is called ____________.

3. Disorders involving impairments of thinking, memory, perception, or consciousness caused by brain damage are called ____________.

4. The progressively worsening cognitive disorder characterized by muscle tremors, stiff and shuffling gait, lack of facial expression, and social withdrawal is called ____________.

5. The cognitive disorder in which there is reduced ability to attend to stimuli, difficulty in shifting attention, and disorganized thinking, and which usually has a sudden onset, is called ____________.

6. The cognitive disorder that involves atrophy of the brain and leads to marked deterioration in memory and emotional functioning is called ____________.

7. Any disorder that is characterized by intermittent and brief periods of altered consciousness and is often accompanied by seizures is called ___________.

8. The cognitive disorder that is an outcome of a syphilitic infection is called ___________ or ___________.

9. A physical wound or injury to the brain is called a(n) ___________.

10. Cognitive disorders in which the primary symptom is an inability to learn new information or a failure to retain old information are called ___________.

11. The cognitive disorder characterized by uneven deterioration of intellectual abilities (dementia) that results from a number of cerebral infarctions is called ___________.

12. The form of brain trauma where blood vessels rupture because of the brain's impact against the skull is called a(n) ___________.

13. The form of brain trauma where tissue is torn or pierced because an object penetrates the skull is called a(n) ___________.

14. A neurological test that uses x-rays and computer technology to assess brain damage is called ___________.

15. A neurological test for the assessment of brain damage that measures the electrical activity of the brain is called a(n) ___________.

16. The technique that uses radio waves and a magnetic field to produce an image of the brain and to assess brain functioning is called ___________.

17. The technique for assessing brain damage that involves the injection of radioactive glucose and the monitoring of glucose metabolism is called ___________.

18. A symptom of cognitive disorders in which language is impaired either because the individual cannot gain access to words and their meanings or cannot retain words is called ___________.

19. A mild form of brain trauma involving brief loss of consciousness due to a blow to the head is called ___________.

Answers to Fill-in-the-Blanks Quiz

1. cerebrovascular accident; stroke
2. dementia
3. cognitive disorders
4. Parkinson's disease
5. delirium
6. Alzheimer's disease
7. epilepsy
8. neurosyphilis; general paresis
9. brain trauma
10. amnestic disorders
11. multi-infarct dementia
12. contusion
13. laceration
14. computerized axial tomography (CAT scan)
15. electroencephalograph (EEG)
16. magnetic resonance imaging (MRI)
17. positron emission tomography (PET scan)
18. aphasia
19. concussion

FACT AND CONCEPT QUESTIONS

1. A person showing behavioral disturbances that are caused by brain damage is considered to have a ____________ disorder.
   a. cognitive
   b. general medical
   c. delirium
   d. psychotic

2. Treatment for cognitive disorders
   a. is always medical, never psychological.
   b. is always psychological, never medical.
   c. is often a combination of medical and psychological.
   d. is never psychological if the brain damage is irreversible.

3. Neuropsychological testing relies on
   a. electroencephalographs.
   b. CAT scans.
   c. radioactive chemicals.
   d. assessments of memory and manual dexterity.

4. Plasticity is one explanation of why it is difficult to identify specific areas of the brain and their function. *Plasticity* refers to the fact that
   a. undeveloped portions of the brain can take up the functions of damaged portions.
   b. lesions in one area of the brain can disrupt function in distant, undamaged areas.
   c. no two brains are identical.
   d. one hemisphere of the brain controls behavior on the opposite side of the body.

5. When brain damage leads to permanent and irreversible loss of function, the disorder is considered
   a. chronic.
   b. diffuse.
   c. acute.
   d. endogenous.

6. Dementia is characterized by
   a. the inability to either comprehend or produce speech.
   b. fever, disorganized thinking, and an inability to concentrate on a particular stimulus.
   c. rapid onset and rapid recovery.
   d. slow-onset impairment of memory and judgment that interferes with functioning.

7. Why is it important to know that dementia can be caused by factors other than aging?
   a. Because it makes psychotherapy unnecessary
   b. Because other causative problems can be corrected
   c. Because nearly 50 percent of the elderly are demented
   d. Because it used to be thought of as a functional disorder

8. When the primary symptoms are an inability to learn new information or recall past events and the probable cause is a thiamine deficiency, the diagnosis should be
   a. delirium caused by substance use.
   b. amnestic disorder.
   c. dementia caused by nutrition deficit.
   d. aphasia.

9. When portions of the brain are torn or pierced, survivors may have very serious symptoms, including intellectual impairment and personality changes. The cause is a
   a. concussion.
   b. form of epilepsy.
   c. brain laceration.
   d. cerebral tumor.

10. Young adults who survive severe head injuries typically
    a. make full recoveries.
    b. completely recover their mental functioning, but continue to have emotional disturbances.
    c. have continuing mental and emotional disturbances that make return to full employment unlikely.
    d. have continuing physical problems, but rarely emotional disturbances.

11. This organic mental disorder represents the third major cause of death in the United States. It can occur when blood vessels burst or when blocked blood flow causes brain tissue to die. What is this disorder?
    a. Aphasia
    b. Stroke (cerebrovascular accident)
    c. Senile dementia
    d. Alzheimer's disease

12. What one symptom is found in Alzheimer's disease, senile dementia, and multi-infarct dementia?
    a. Brain trauma
    b. Brief periods of unconsciousness
    c. Restlessness and irritability followed by excessive sleep
    d. Memory loss

13. Difficulty in forming words and an inability to retain their meanings are central problems in
    a. aphasia.
    b. delirium.
    c. Parkinson's disease.
    d. strokes that affect the right side of the brain.

14. Which statement about Alzheimer's disease is *true*?
    a. Alzheimer's is usually caused by people taking too many prescription medications.
    b. Memory loss is the last symptom to appear in the disorder.
    c. Although a disabling disorder, Alzheimer's does not lead to early death.
    d. Alzheimer's accounts for almost 80 percent of dementia in older persons.

15. Which of the following is associated with Parkinson's disease?
    a. Stiff, shuffling walk
    b. Onset in adolescence
    c. Atrophy of large portions of the brain as a result of aging
    d. Excessive emotionality

16. What do encephalitis, meningitis, and neurosyphilis have in common?
    a. They are all associated with aging.
    b. They are all caused by viral or bacterial infections.
    c. They are all incurable and caused by genetic factors.
    d. They are all effectively treated with the neurotransmitter L-dopa.

17. Which statement below is *true* concerning epilepsy?
    a. It is the third leading cause of death in the United States.
    b. It is most frequently diagnosed during childhood.
    c. It can be caused only by a genetic defect.
    d. It is an organic mental disorder that affects the limbic system.

18. Auras and comas are symptoms of ____________ epilepsy, whereas momentary dimming or loss of conconsciousness that others might not even notice is a symptom of ____________.
    a. grand mal; petit mal epilepsy
    b. grand mal; Jacksonian seizures
    c. petit mal; Jacksonian seizures
    d. petit mal; psychomotor epilepsy

19. Which of the following represents the appropriate use of medication for a cognitive disorder?
    a. Antidepressant medication for people with epilepsy
    b. L-dopa for people with closed head injuries
    c. Anti-seizure medications for people with epilepsy
    d. Central nervous stimulants for people with strokes

20. Family and friends who are caregivers for people with irreversible cognitive disorders are advised to
    a. prevent the patient from taking on tasks unless they can be completed perfectly.
    b. prevent the patient from making personal decisions.
    c. maintain social contacts that are brief and without pressure.
    d. keep their anxieties and concerns private, and refrain from using outside help.

APPLICATION QUESTIONS

1. Which person below is *most* likely to be misdiagnosed as having a cognitive disorder when he or she does not actually have one?
    a. A teenager who has severe anxiety symptoms
    b. An energetic middle-aged man with excellent memory
    c. A young mother who has difficulty falling asleep
    d. An elderly woman who is is quite depressed

2. Larry has AIDS. He has trouble remembering where he has put things, and occasionally is frightened when he cannot concentrate or keep track of simple conversations. Larry's behavior illustrates
   a. early signs of delirium, a rare symptom in AIDS.
   b. Parkinson's disease, a common result of AIDS.
   c. dementia, a common symptom of AIDS.
   d. multi-infarct dementia, a rare symptom in AIDS.

3. Dr. Elsberg says, "Neuropsychological tests such as the Halstead-Reitan pinpoint cognitive disorders so accurately that there are rarely cases in which organic causes are confused with functional ones." What is *inaccurate* about Dr. Elsberg's statement?
   a. It is inaccurate to say that the Halstead-Reitan is a neuropsychological test.
   b. It is inaccurate to say that organic causes are rarely confused with functional ones.
   c. It is inaccurate to say that neuropsychological tests are used to pinpoint cognitive disorders.
   d. It is inaccurate to say that cognitive disorders can have an organic cause.

4. John was not wearing his seat belt, and his head struck the windshield when he was in a car accident. He was dazed and had a headache for several days after the accident, but soon he recovered completely. John's problem would most likely be diagnosed as a
   a. cerebrovascular accident.
   b. cerebral infarction.
   c. laceration.
   d. concussion.

5. A community that is trying to meet the needs of its elderly should provide
   a. many places for older men to congregate, since elderly men outnumber elderly women by two to one.
   b. many full-time institutions, since 75 percent of the elderly cannot live independently.
   c. drug treatment for dementia, since more than 50 percent of those over age 65 have a serious organic mental disorder.
   d. affordable health care, since the majority of the elderly have health complaints and one-fifth are poor or near poor.

6. Hilda was fine when she went to sleep but died the next morning when a large portion of her brain died from lack of blood caused by a buildup of fatty material inside her brain arteries. Hilda suffered from
   a. atherosclerosis.
   b. multi-infarct dementia.
   c. both a and b.
   d. neither a nor b.

7. Roger shows increasing muscle tremors, a shuffling walk, and an expressionless face. He also has delusions that people are poisoning him, and he is frequently depressed. Which of Roger's symptoms are *uncommon* in cases of Parkinson's disease?
   a. The delusions of persecution
   b. The expressionless face
   c. The muscle tremors
   d. The shuffling walk

8. A doctor says, "It is caused by bacterial, viral, or sometimes fungal infectious agents that attack and inflame the membrane surrounding the brain and spinal cord." What is the doctor describing?
   a. Neurosyphilis (general paresis)
   b. Meningitis
   c. Cerebral tumor
   d. Cerebrovascular accident (stroke)

9. Jane developed twitches in her fingers at age 30, just as her father did. The twitches got worse, until her arms and legs jerked in a dance-like fashion. Her personality changed, too, so that sometimes she seemed psychotic. She died at age 38. Jane probably suffered from
   a. Huntington's chorea.
   b. Parkinson's disease.
   c. Jacksonian seizures.
   d. Alzheimer's disease.

10. As a child, Sharon would often stop what she was doing, stare blankly, and flutter her eyelids involuntarily. She had no recollection of these spells. She "grew out of them" by the time she was 18. Sharon probably suffered from
   a. Jacksonian seizures.
   b. substance-induced delirium.
   c. petit mal epilepsy.
   d. psychomotor epilepsy.

ANSWERS TO FACT AND CONCEPT QUESTIONS

1. *a. Cognitive disorders involve behavioral disturbances such as memory loss or speech impairment due to brain damage. (p. 470)
   b. Some disorders (including cognitive disorders) can be caused by general medical conditions such as brain tumors or Alzheimer's disease; "general medical" is a cause, not a category.
   c. Delirium is one of four subtypes of cognitive disorders, it does not describe the whole category.
   d. Psychotic disorders involve delusions, hallucinations, and disorientation—all of which may occur in some cognitive disorders, but also in disorders *not* associated with brain damage (functional disorders).

2. a. Social skills training and other psychological treatments are useful in the treatment of many cognitive disorders.
   b. Such medical procedures as surgery and medication can be very effective in treating many cognitive disorders.
   *c. Medical treatments are often helpful for controlling symptoms; psychological treatments can help patients master their emotions and relearn functional behaviors. (p. 491)
   d. When brain damage is irreversible, social skills and other rehabilitative treatments that are psychological are often the only treatments available.

3. a. Electroencephalographs record brain activity and are neurological tests.
   b. CAT scans are computer-composite pictures of the brain using x-rays; they are neurological tests.
   c. Radioactive chemicals are used in blood flow and positron emission tomography, both of which are neurological tests.
   *d. Neuropsychological tests such as the Halstead-Reitan use measurements of memory, cognitive flexibility, and manual dexterity to determine organic damage. (p. 475)

4. *a. Plasticity is the brain's ability to use undeveloped portions as substitutes for damaged areas; children born without an entire hemisphere can have the remaining hemisphere perform functions usually found in the missing one. (p. 473)
   b. When damage in one portion of the brain disrupts functioning in other, intact portions, the phenomenon is called diaschisis.
   c. While it is true that no two brains are the same, this is unrelated to plasticity.
   d. The fact that one hemisphere controls specific functions underscores structure-function specificity, the opposite of plasticity.

5. *a. *Chronic* means a continuing problem. (p. 474)
   b. *Diffuse* means that damage occurs in a broad region of the brain.
   c. *Acute* is the opposite of chronic; it means temporary.
   d. *Endogenous* means that damage is caused from within.

6. a. An inability to comprehend or produce speech is a definition of aphasia.
   b. Disorganized thinking and lack of concentration are characteristics of delirium.
   c. Rapid onset and recovery are characteristics of delirium.
   *d. Dementia is a cognitive deterioration in memory and judgment that makes living difficult; it usually has a gradual onset. (p. 476)

7. a. Dementia and most of the other organic mental syndromes produce emotional problems that can be helped through psychotherapy.
   *b. Not much can be done to treat aging, but, for example, brain tumors can be surgically removed. (p. 476)
   c. Probably less than 15 percent of the elderly are demented.
   d. Dementia has always been seen as an organic symptom.

8. a. Delirium involves disorganized thinking rather than failure to learn or recall; it is not associated with a thiamine deficiency.
   *b. Amnestic cognitive disorder involves memory and learning problems and little else; Wernicke's encephalopathy, which is probably caused by thiamine deficiency, is the most common form of amnestic disorder. (p. 478)
   c. Dementia is not caused by nutrition deficit: the leading causes are Alzheimer's disease, stroke, and hydrocephalus. Dementias have other symptoms besides amnesia—delusions, hallucinations, and speech problems.
   d. Aphasias are speech impairments involving either the comprehension or expression of words and their meanings.

9. a. Aphasia is impairment of language comprehension or production.
   b. Epilepsy involves uncontrolled electrical activity in the brain.
   *c. A laceration is defined as a cut or tear caused by an external object such as a gunshot. (p. 479)
   d. Tumors are abnormal masses of tissue.

10. a. Full recoveries from severe head injury are fairly rare.
    b. Continuing problems of memory loss, inattention, and speech are common in severe head injury.
    *c. In the majority of cases, recovery includes a combination of difficulties that make gainful employment quite difficult. (p. 479)
    d. Those who recover from severe head injury often show irritability and depression, although they are unaware of it.

11. a. Aphasia is impairment of language comprehension or production; it is a symptom, not a disorder.
    *b. Stroke is the third major cause of death (400,000 or more cases annually) and is defined as tissue death (infarction) caused by insufficient blood flow. (p. 480)
    c. Senile dementia is caused by the aging process.
    d. Alzheimer's disease is caused by a general atrophy of brain tissue and is unrelated to a sudden shut-off of blood.

12. a. Brain traumas are sudden-onset causes and rarely produce dementias.
    b. Brief periods of unconsciousness are characteristics of petit mal epilepsy and concussions, not dementias.
    c. Restlessness and irritability followed by excessive sleep are prominent symptoms in encephalitis, not dementias.
    *d. All three are forms of dementia, and the chief symptom of dementia is memory loss. (p. 476)

13. *a. Aphasia involves the loss of the ability to speak or to comprehend speech. (Focus 16.1; p. 477)
    b. Delirium occurs when thinking is disorganized and attention and concentration cannot be maintained.
    c. Parkinson's disease affects motor control, not language.
    d. Strokes that affect the right hemisphere are less likely to produce language impairment (aphasia) than those that affect the left.

14. a. Excessive medication is a reason for misdiagnosing cognitive disorders, but Alzheimer's is not caused by medication.
    b. Memory loss is the first symptom to appear.
    c. Alzheimer's has a prolonged deterioration that leads to death in an average of five years.
    *d. Alzheimer's accounts for about 80 percent of older people with dementias. (p. 482)

15. *a. Together with muscle tremors and an expressionless face, a stiff, shuffling gait is a fundamental sign of Parkinson's disease. (p. 484)
    b. Parkinson's disease rarely develops until a person is in his or her forties or fifties.
    c. Atrophy of large brain areas as a result of aging is associated with senile dementia.
    d. Lack of emotional expression is a symptom of Parkinson's disease.

16. a. The disorders associated with aging are stroke, Alzheimer's disease, and senile dementia.
    *b. All three are caused by infectious agents that produce damage to the brain or its surrounding membranes. (pp. 485–486)
    c. None of these disorders has a genetic link.
    d. Parkinson's disease is treated with L-dopa, since that disorder is associated with reduced amounts of dopamine.

17. a. The third leading cause of death is stroke.
 *b. Epilepsy is usually diagnosed early in life. (p. 488)
 c. Although there may be a genetic component in the cause of epilepsy, environmental factors such as drug use and head injury can cause the disorder as well.
 d. Epilepsy is not a disorder, but a symptom that involves uncontrolled electrical activity in many portions of the brain.

18. *a. Grand mal epilepsy involves an aura (anticipatory experience), tonic and clonic phases, and a coma (sleep); petit mal epilepsy involves minor alterations of consciousness. (pp. 488, 490)
 b. Jacksonian seizures are seizures that start in one body part and spread to others.
 c. Petit mal epilepsy involves minor alterations in consciousness, and does not show auras or comas.
 d. Psychomotor epilepsy involves behavior, often in anger, that is not remembered when the person is out of the "spell."

19. a. Antidepressant medication would not stop or control the seizures of epilepsy.
 b. L-dopa is prescribed for Parkinson's disease.
 *c. Since the problem of epilepsy involves seizures, anti-seizure medication is appropriate. (p. 491)
 d. Stimulants would not be helpful to people recovering from strokes.

20. a. If tasks must be performed to perfection, patients with cognitive disorders lose confidence and give up trying.
 b. Allowing patients to have control in their lives increases their cognitive functioning and prolongs the quality of their lives.
 *c. Social contacts that are brief and do not overwhelm the patient counteract the social withdrawal that often occurs in cognitive disorders. (p. 494)
 d. Caregivers can become overwhelmed, emotionally drained, and physically ill; they need to vent their emotions and make use of such resources as self-help groups.

ANSWERS TO APPLICATION QUESTIONS

1. a. Youngsters are not expected to have cognitive disorders; anxiety is an uncommon symptom of most cognitive disorders.
 b. Cognitive disorders often involve a lack of energy and almost always involve memory deficits.
 c. Young people are not expected to have cognitive disorders.
 *d. Elderly individuals are expected to have cognitive disorders, and symptoms of depression (lethargy, poor decision making) can be confused with cognitive disorders. (p. 481)

2. a. Memory loss is associated with dementia, not delirium.
 b. Parkinson's disease cannot be acquired from AIDS and does not involve memory loss.
 *c. Memory loss is a key symptom of dementia, a problem that occurs frequently in people with AIDS. (p. 485)
 d. Multi-infarct dementia is caused by a series of small strokes, not by AIDS.

3. a. The Halstead-Reitan is the cornerstone of neuropsychological testing.
   *b. Poor scores on the Halstead-Reitan may stem from causes including such functional disorders as schizophrenia and depression; such confusions are all too common. (p. 475)
   c. Neuropsychological tests are frequently used to detect organic disorders, but do so imperfectly.
   d. By definition, cognitive disorders have organic causes.

4. a. A cerebrovascular accident (stroke) is caused by internal problems such as atherosclerosis, not external ones like a car accident.
   b. A cerebral infarction occurs when tissue dies because, for example, the blood supply for that area was cut off.
   c. Such minor problems and rapid recovery would not be likely in a laceration, where areas of the brain are cut or ripped.
   *d. A concussion causes relatively minor problems and usually leads to a full recovery. (p. 478)

5. a. Elderly women far outnumber elderly men.
   b. The vast majority of elderly people can take care of themselves, and most of the rest need less than full-time assistance.
   c. Something less than 15 percent of the elderly show signs of dementia.
   *d. More than half of the elderly have physical infirmities, and 20 percent are poor or near poor. (p. 480)

6. *a. Atherosclerosis is the buildup of fatty material such as cholesterol that chokes off the free flow of blood and which can produce infarction (tissue death) to areas of the brain. (p. 480)
   b. Alzheimer's disease comes on gradually and is not associated with the buildup of fatty material in blood vessels.
   c. Since b is inaccurate, this answer cannot be the best choice.
   d. Since a is correct, this answer cannot be the best choice.

7. *a. Delusions of persecution are more commonly found in Alzheimer's disease or Huntington's chorea than in Parkinson's disease. (p. 484)
   b. An expressionless face is a symptom of Parkinson's disease.
   c. Muscle tremors are a fundamental symptom of Parkinson's disease.
   d. A stiff, shuffling walk is a central feature of Parkinson's disease.

8. a. Neurosyphilis is caused by an infection, but damage is done to the cerebral cortex, not the membrane around the brain.
   *b. Meningitis is an infection of the meninges (membrane around the brain and spinal cord) that can be caused by viruses, bacteria, or sometimes fungi. (p. 486)
   c. Cerebral tumors are abnormal masses that are not due to infections.
   d. Cerebrovascular accidents (strokes) occur when brain tissue dies because of a blood vessel rupturing or because of a blockage in blood flow through a blood vessel.

9. *a. Huntington's chorea is a genetic organic disorder that first shows itself in early middle age and involves jerky movements and cognitive deterioration. (pp. 486–487)
   b. Parkinson's disease is an organic disorder characterized by stiff movements, muscle tremors, and an expressionless face; it is associated with low levels of dopamine.
   c. Jacksonian seizures, a kind of epilepsy, are characterized by starting in one area of the body and spreading to others.
   d. The primary early symptoms of Alzheimer's disease are memory loss and irritability.

10. a. Jacksonian seizures, a kind of epilepsy, are characterized by starting in one area of the body and spreading to others.
   b. Substance-induced delirium involves disorganized thinking related to known psychoactive drugs such as amphetamine or LSD.
   *c. Petit mal epilepsy involves mild dimming or loss of consciousness for short periods of time; it is more common in children than in adults. (p. 488)
   d. Psychomotor epilepsy features long spells during which people may act "normally" but have no recollection of their actions when the spell is over.

CHAPTER 17
Disorders of Childhood and Adolescence and Mental Retardation

---

LEARNING OBJECTIVES

When you have mastered the material in Chapter 17, you should be able to:

1. Describe the prevalence of behavior problems in children and adolescence. Discuss the changes in childhood disorders in the DSM-IV. Define and list the pervasive developmental disorders. Describe the main symptoms of autistic disorder, including social, communications, and intellectual problems. Discuss the term *autistic savant.* (Focus 17.1; pp. 497–501)
2. Describe diagnostic difficulties and research findings related to autism. Describe Rett's disorder, childhood disintegrative disorder, and Asperger's disorder. (pp. 501–503)
3. Discuss the etiological theories concerning autism, including psychoanalytic, family and genetics, central nervous system impairment, and biochemical studies. (pp. 503–505)
4. Describe the prognosis and treatment for children with pervasive developmental disorders. Discuss drug therapy and behavior modification done with these children. (pp. 505–507)
5. Discuss the problems with the diagnosis and classification of other developmental disorders. (pp. 507–508)
6. Describe the symptoms, etiology, and treatment of the attention deficit disorders. (pp. 508–513; Focus 17.2)
7. Define and differentiate oppositional defiant disorder and conduct disorder. Describe the two subtypes of conduct disorder. Discuss the prevalence of conduct disorder, its etiology, and treatment. (pp. 513–516)
8. Describe changes in the classification of childhood anxiety-related disorders. Describe separation anxiety disorder. Explain what causes school phobia; discuss how it can be treated. (pp. 516–518; Focus 17.3)
9. Describe the prevalence, symptoms, and treatment of childhood depression. (pp. 518–519)
10. Describe the symptoms, etiology, and treatment of tic disorders, including Tourette's syndrome. (pp. 519–520)
11. Describe the prevalence and symptoms of anorexia nervosa and bulimia nervosa. (pp. 521–524)
12. Discuss the etiology of eating disorders. Clarify your thinking about the role of culture in eating disorders. (pp. 524–525; Critical Thinking)
13. Describe treatment approaches to eating disorders. (pp. 525–527)
14. Describe changes in how mental retardation is perceived. Discuss how mental retardation is diagnosed, including the levels of retardation. (pp. 527–529)

15. Explain how environmental factors can cause mental retardation. Describe the genetic factors that account for mental retardation, including Down syndrome—its characteristics, prevalence, and prenatal detection. (pp. 529–531)
16. Describe and discuss the nongenetic biogenic factors involved in mental retardation. (pp. 531–532)
17. Describe and discuss early intervention and employment programs for people with mental retardation. (pp. 532–534)

CHAPTER OUTLINE

1. **Disorders of childhood and adolescence and mental retardation** (pp. 497–498) Between 11 and 14 percent of children and adolescents in the United States have a serious behavioral problem, costing more than 1.5 billion dollars in treatment. DSM-IV has eliminated two childhood disorders—avoidant disorder (now classified as a social phobia) and overanxious disorder (now considered a childhood form of generalized anxiety disorder). The category "pervasive developmental disorders" now includes three specific disorders plus autistic disorder.

2. **Pervasive developmental disorders** (pp. 498–503) *Pervasive developmental disorders* are severe disturbances affecting language, social relations, and emotions, distortions that would be abnormal at any developmental stage. Prevalence of autistic disorder is about 4 to 7 cases per 10,000 children; the other three pervasive developmental disorders occur at a rate of about 22 in 10,000.

   Autistic disorder was first described by Kanner in 1943 and is characterized by an unusual lack of interest in others as well as by communication problems and bizarre, repetitive movements. Autistic children interact with others as though people were unimportant objects. Half do not speak; the other half often show *echolalia*—echoing whatever was just said. Most autistic children are mentally retarded, although *splinter skills* (special abilities) are found, most dramatically in *autistic savants.* Misdiagnosis as mental retardation only or as a different disorder or condition is common. Research shows that autistic children are less able than matched children to identify human characteristics. It is also possible that bizarre speech is a way of communicating frustration or need for attention.

   A new set of pervasive developmental disorders that do not meet the criteria for autistic disorders are *pervasive developmental disorder not otherwise specified, Rett's disorder, childhood disintegrative disorder,* and *Asperger's disorder*. Because they are new, little research on the causes of these is available.

3. **Etiology** (pp. 503–507) One early theory about the cause of autism was a psychoanalytic view that parent-child interactions produce withdrawal. Current knowledge gives no justification for this idea. Most research points to a biological cause: Studies show high concordance ratios for MZ twins (36 percent), central nervous system impairment, and elevated serotonin levels. The prognosis for children with pervasive developmental disorders is mixed. Those with severe retardation have worse outcomes. On the other hand, one person with autistic disorder went on to earn a doctorate degree. Treatment has involved intensive behavior modification, antipsychotic and other medications, and language education programs.

4. **Other developmental disorders** (pp. 507–508) The definition of less severe childhood disorders often depends on the tolerance of the referring agent. Cultural norms also influence what behaviors are considered problems. Diagnosis using the DSM-IV involves counting

symptoms, but judgment is necessary in deciding if symptoms such as "often easily distracted" exist.

5. **Disruptive behavior disorder and attention deficit hyperactive disorder** (pp. 508–516) *Attention deficit hyperactive disorder (ADHD)* is characterized by attention problems and may involve heightened motor activity. Children may show distractibility and lack of attention to detail without being impulsive and restless. ADHD is a relatively common disorder, far more common in boys than in girls. In some cases, ADHD children continue to have antisocial or psychiatric problems as adults; those with attention problems but not hyperactivity have better outcomes. Theories on the cause of ADHD cite a delay in the maturation of the central nervous system (although findings are inconsistent) and genetic and psychological factors. Food additives and sugar are not significant factors.

   Children with ADHD are typically treated with stimulant medication, but there is considerable controversy about the overmedication of children and the poorly supervised prescription of drugs. Self-instructional procedures in which children talk themselves through tasks have proven useful.

   Oppositional defiant disorder is characterized by negativistic and hostile behavior. DSM-IV criteria include "significant impairment in social and academic functioning," a raising of the threshold for diagnosis.

   Conduct disorder involves a persistent pattern of antisocial behavior. It is relatively common, particularly in boys, and can be subtyped according to age of onset (prior to age 10 and after age 10). Oppositional defiant disorder often precedes conduct disorders and is coexistent with ADHD. Violence is a quite likely among these children. Prognosis is poor, particularly if there is sexual aggression. Theories of cause include psychoanalytic ideas concerning underlying anxiety, genetic factors, and inadequate parental behavior. Cognitive behavioral treatment that combines social skills and parent management training holds the most promise for treating conduct disorder.

6. **Anxiety disorders: separation anxiety disorder** (pp. 516–518) *Separation anxiety disorder* is marked by excessive anxiety when the child is separated from parents or home. Somatic symptoms are prominent. This and other childhood anxiety disorders are probably caused by an interaction between the child's temperament (very early personality style) and the home environment that parents establish. School phobia is one result of such anxiety, but may be a separate syndrome. The causes of separation anxiety disorder may include overdependence on the mother (psychoanalytic) and parental reinforcement of avoiding fears (learning). Prognosis is better when separation anxiety disorder is treated in childhood rather than in adolescence.

7. **Childhood depression** (pp. 518–519) Childhood depression is not listed under childhood disorders in the DSM-IV, but depression can occur in children as early as infancy. In one study, 5 to 11 percent of children scored at a "serious" level of depression. Depression in adolescence is common, particularly among girls. The symptoms are much the same as in adults; treatment requires support and cognitive and social skill training.

8. **Tic disorders** (pp. 519–520) *Tics* are involuntary, repetitive movements or vocalizations. Many children have a single, transient tic such as eye blinking. *Tourette's syndrome* is a puzzling disorder in which childhood tics evolve into grunting and barking, and finally *coprolalia* (the compulsion to shout obscenities). Stress appears to be a factor in causing these disorders, although multiple tics and Tourette's syndrome appear to be transmitted in families, and may be

related to obsessive-compulsive disorder or ADHD. Treatment can involve negative practice or haloperidol.

9. **Eating disorders** (pp. 521–527) Eating problems are becoming more prevalent among young people in the United States. In *anorexia nervosa*, a disorder found almost exclusively in women, fear of weight gain leads to self-starvation or eating and purging, with such consequences as low blood pressure and heart disease. About 75 percent show a distorted body image. The criteria for *bulimia nervosa* include eating large quantities of high-caloric foods at least twice weekly for three months, feeling a loss of control over eating, and following eating with self-induced vomiting, purging, or fasting. Much more prevalent than anorexia, bulimia is unrelated to an individual's weight. Binges tend to be related to negative emotions.

10. **Eating disorders: etiology and treatment** (pp. 524–527) The social desirability of thinness in women in western culture plays a major role in causing eating disorders. Eating disorders are rare in Asia. In addition, those with these disorders tend to suffer from poor self-esteem, depression, and perceived lack of control. Initial treatment for anorexia focuses on weight gain (by feeding tube, contingent reinforcement for weight gain, or both). Cognitive-behavioral and family therapy sessions are common after weight gain, but relapse and continued obsession with weight are common. Bulimia has been successfully treated with psychotherapy and behavior therapy that uses response prevention and self-control.

11. **Mental retardation** (pp. 527–528) Until recently, people with *mental retardation* were considered incapable of benefiting from schooling and were institutionalized. Public Law 94-142 (enacted 1975) mandated education for all handicapped people and provided an opportunity for learning. About 75 percent of people with mental retardation can be completely self-supporting; the number of institutionalized people with mental handicaps has decreased from over 200,000 in 1967 to 110,000 in 1984.

12. **Diagnosing mental retardation** (pp. 528–529) About 7 million people in the United States have mental retardation based on IQ scores below 70 and deficiencies in adaptive behavior. IQ scores are particularly problematic with Hispanics and African Americans. Levels of retardation based on Wechsler IQ scores are: Mild (IQ 50–55 to 70); Moderate (IQ 35–40 to 50–55); Severe (IQ 20–25 to 35–40); and Profound (IQ 0 to 20–25). The American Association on Mental Retardation no longer relies on IQ scores to classify those with retardation.

13. **Etiology of mental retardation** (pp. 529–531) Environmental factors such as poor nutrition and substandard school or home environments are associated with retardation. Genetics may account for the low end of intelligence where appearance and health are normal. Genetic abnormalities result in severe forms of retardation such as *Down syndrome,* whose characteristics include short stature, slanted eyes, and protruding tongue. Although risk of Down syndrome increases with mothers giving birth after age 38, two-thirds of Down syndrome babies are born to women under 37. Down syndrome stems from having an extra chromosome, something that can be identified during pregnancy through amniocentesis.

14. **Nongenetic biogenic factors** (pp. 531–532) Retardation can be caused by environmental mishaps before birth (prenatal), during birth (perinatal), or after birth (postnatal). Important prenatal causes are rubella (German measles) during pregnancy and *fetal alcohol syndrome*, which causes small body and brain size and may cause retardation and hyperactivity. Important perinatal factors are prematurity, low birth weight, and trauma. Postnatal causes, which seem to be on the rise, include head injury sustained in auto accidents or child abuse.

15. **Programs for people with mental retardation** (pp. 532–534) Programs such as Head Start have had positive long-term results. Employment programs such as Structured Training and Employment Transitional Services (STETS) have helped moderately and mildly retarded individuals secure regular employment in competitive jobs.

    Institutionalization of people with mental retardation has been declining, but alternative settings (group homes) are not getting uniformly better. Behavioral approaches are usually used to teach independent living skills.

KEY TERMS

Fill-in-the-Blanks Quiz

1. Disorders of childhood and adolescence that involve persistent patterns of antisocial behavior that violate the rights of others are called ___________.

2. Stereotyped and repetitive, but involuntary, twitchings or spasms of the voluntary muscles are called ___________.

3. An eating disorder in which the person is intensely fearful of becoming obese and engages in either self-starvation or purging after eating is called ___________.

4. A childhood disorder characterized by excessive anxiety concerning separation from parents and home is called ___________.

5. A childhood disorder characterized by multiple motor and verbal tics that develop into a compulsion to shout obscenities is called ___________.

6. A severe childhood disorder characterized by early onset, an extreme lack of interest in interpersonal relationships, and impairment in verbal and nonverbal communication is called ___________.

7. An eating disorder characterized by the consumption of large quantities of food, usually followed by self-induced vomiting, is called ___________.

8. A disorder of childhood and adolescence characterized by short attention span, impulsiveness, constant activity, and lack of self-control is called ___________.

9. Severe disorders of childhood that affect language, social relationships, attention, and affect, and that include autistic disorder, are called ___________.

10. A childhood disorder characterized by negativistic, argumentative, and hostile behavior that impairs social or academic functioning is called ___________.

11. Disorders with onset in childhood that are characterized by involuntary and repetitive movements or vocalizations, including transient and chronic tic disorders and Tourette's syndrome, are called ___________.

12. A group of symptoms including mental retardation and physical defects in infancy caused by alcohol consumption by a pregnant woman is called ___________.

13. Substandard intellectual functioning accompanied by deficiencies in adaptive behavior, with onset before age 18, is called ___________.

14. A condition produced by the presence of an extra chromosome that results in mental retardation and physical abnormalities is called ___________.

15. The pervasive developmental disorder in which children show normal development for at least two years and then display severe deterioration is called ___________.

16. The pervasive developmental disorder in which children show normal development for six months and then display severe deterioration is called ___________.

17. The pervasive developmental disorder that has most, but not all, of the symptoms of autistic disorder is called ___________.

18. The pervasive developmental disorder that involves severely impaired social relationships and lack of emotional reciprocity but *not* impaired language development is called ___________.

19. The screening procedure performed during pregnancy that can determine the presence of Down syndrome is called ___________.

Answers to Fill-in-the-Blanks Quiz

1. conduct disorders
2. tics
3. anorexia nervosa
4. separation anxiety disorder
5. Tourette's syndrome
6. autistic disorder
7. bulimia nervosa (or bulimia)
8. attention deficit hyperactive disorder (ADHD)
9. pervasive developmental disorders
10. oppositional defiant disorder (ODD)
11. tic disorders
12. fetal alcohol syndrome
13. mental retardation
14. Down syndrome
15. childhood disintegrative disorder
16. Rett's disorder
17. Pervasive developmental disorder not otherwise specified
18. Asperger's disorder
19. amniocentesis

FACT AND CONCEPT QUESTIONS

1. Pervasive developmental disorders are childhood disorders that
   a. are quite common, with 4 to 5 cases per 100 births.
   b. are presently considered forms of schizophrenia.
   c. usually have their onset after age 10.
   d. involve behavior that is abnormal for any developmental stage.

2. In the majority of cases, autistic children are
   a. autistic savants.
   b. mentally retarded.
   c. able to speak like normal children.
   d. overly attached to their parents.

3. Diagnosis of autism is deceptively difficult because
   a. symptoms are not noticeable until age 6 or later.
   b. most of the symptoms of autism are internalized and not observable.
   c. symptoms can vary widely among such children.
   d. parents are unwilling to accept that something is wrong with the child.

4. Research indicates that autistic speech disturbances such as ____________ may be the child's way of communicating ____________.
   a. echolalia; delusional ideas
   b. echolalia; stressful feelings
   c. coprolalia; need for attention
   d. pronoun reversal; empathy for parents

5. What do Rett's disorder and Asperger's disorder have in common?
   a. They are pervasive developmental disorders other than autistic disorder.
   b. Children with these disorders fail to develop any language skills.
   c. They are both successfully treated with antipsychotic medications.
   d. They are forms of anxiety disorder that have been eliminated from the list of DSM-IV childhood disorders.

6. Which statement about the causes of autism is *most accurate*?
   a. Recent research strengthens the belief that there is one cause for all its forms.
   b. The only research on genetic influence was weak methodologically and showed no difference in concordance rates for MZ and DZ twins.
   c. Nearly all autistic children have abnormally low levels of serotonin, a pathognomonic sign for the disorder.
   d. Organic causes are likely although research findings are inconsistent.

7. Treatment of children with pervasive developmental disorders
   a. usually includes psychodynamic approaches.
   b. involves humanistic and family systems approaches.
   c. is, in general, very difficult.
   d. has excellent long-term outcomes.

8. Some clinical psychologists are quite upset with the childhood and adolescent section of DSM-IV. Why?
   a. Because significant categories of disorders, such as tic disorders and eating disorders, have been eliminated
   b. Because conduct disorders have been separated from pervasive developmental disorders
   c. Because bothersome childhood behaviors that may be normal are now considered disorders
   d. Because all subjective judgments have been taken out of the diagnostic criteria

9. Heightened motor activity, impulsiveness, and school problems because of distractibility are all symptoms of
   a. attention deficit hyperactive disorder (ADHD).
   b. school phobia.
   c. conduct disorder.
   d. pervasive developmental disorder not otherwise specified.

10. The type of drug most often prescribed for attention deficit hyperactivity disorder is
    a. the tranquilizer haloperidol.
    b. the anti-manic drug lithium carbonate.
    c. the stimulant Ritalin.
    d. the anti-depressant Ritalin.

11. Which disorder does not belong with the others?
    a. Separation anxiety disorder
    b. Oppositional defiant disorder
    c. Conduct disorder
    d. Attention deficit hyperactive disorder

12. Psychodynamic theory suggests that conduct disorder is caused by ____________, whereas learning theory suggests it is caused by ____________.
    a. underlying anxiety and emotional deprivation; central nervous system damage
    b. conflict over sexuality; parental reinforcement
    c. double-bind communication patterns; inconsistent discipline
    d. underlying anxiety and emotional deprivation; inconsistent discipline

13. Which type of treatment has been most effective with adolescents with conduct disorders?
    a. Tranquilizers and central nervous stimulants
    b. Psychotherapy and incarceration
    c. Negative practice and relaxation skills
    d. Cognitive social skills and parent training

14. It is much more likely in children from broken homes and is particularly apparent in adolescent girls. It is associated with low self-esteem and self-blame. What is being described?
    a. Childhood depression
    b. Tic disorders
    c. Separation anxiety disorder
    d. Conduct disorders

15. What behaviors differentiate anorexia nervosa from bulimia nervosa?
    a. Only anorexics are afraid of gaining weight.
    b. Only bulimics occasionally binge and purge.
    c. Only anorexics look like skeletons.
    d. Only bulimics tend to be women.

16. Which of the following has occurred in the field of mental retardation in the past twenty-five years?
    a. The number of people with mental retardation who reside in public institutions has increased.
    b. A law was passed mandating that IQ tests could not be used to determine the educational needs of African American children.
    c. Forms of mental retardation that were once believed to be treatable are now known to be hopeless.
    d. Research has shown that there is only one cause of mental retardation.

17. Based on DSM-IV criteria, a diagnosis of mental retardation requires
    a. IQ below 70, deficiencies in adaptive behavior, and onset before age 18.
    b. IQ below 50, inability to speak, and signs that the cause is biological.
    c. IQ below 100, inability to succeed in a school environment, and low self-esteem.
    d. none of the above.

18. Generally speaking, mental retardation caused by genetic abnormalities tends to be
    a. more severe than retardation caused by environmental factors.
    b. more prevalent in African Americans than in European Americans.
    c. less likely in women who have children after age 40.
    d. less likely to produce deformities in physical appearance.

19. Amniocentesis is valuable in detecting
    a. mental retardation caused by the normal variation in intelligence.
    b. postnatal forms of mental retardation.
    c. deficiencies in adaptive behavior.
    d. cases of Down syndrome.

20. The STETS employment training program for people with moderate to mild levels of mental retardation showed that
    a. successful placement in jobs is only possible for those with environmentally caused retardation.
    b. some "graduates" were regularly employed in competitive jobs.
    c. most people in the program required no job training prior to getting competitive jobs.
    d. competitive jobs are not a reasonable objective for people with mental retardation.

APPLICATION QUESTIONS

1. Warren is mentally retarded and autistic, yet he can calculate, in his head, the square root of any number and give the answer to three decimal points. This remarkable feat illustrates
    a. the autistic's superior ability to empathize.
    b. the term *echolalia.*
    c. the attention deficit that is found in autistics.
    d. the abilities of autistic savants.

2. An autistic child is in an inpatient treatment facility. What form of therapy is *most* likely to be offered?
    a. Central nervous system stimulants such as Ritalin
    b. Group therapy
    c. Self-instructional procedures and role playing
    d. Intensive behavior modification

3. Chuck was diagnosed with attention deficit *without* hyperactive disorder when he was 7 years old. He has difficulty concentrating, so he does poorly in school. As an adolescent, he was frequently arrested for criminal activity. What aspect of Chuck's case is unusual?
    a. It is unusual for boys to have attention deficits.
    b. It is unusual for attention deficit to be diagnosed at 7.
    c. It is unusual for attention deficit children to have school difficulties.
    d. It is unusual for children without hyperactive disorder to become criminals.

4. A child is in therapy and is taught to say out loud how she should work on an academic task. She says things like this: "Okay, what is the problem? I have to stay on the task. Good. Slow down, you're doing fine." This child probably has the disorder called
   a. attention deficit hyperactive disorder.
   b. separation anxiety disorder.
   c. Tourette's syndrome.
   d. pervasive developmental disorder.

5. Dr. Chess says, "Childhood disorders are partly caused by the personality of the infant, but they are also strongly influenced by the parents' style of life. Furthermore, these two factors influence each other." Dr. Chess's point of view
   a. is not supported by the majority of research evidence.
   b. applies only to the pervasive developmental disorders.
   c. mirrors the thinking of most psychoanalysts.
   d. supports the temperament-environment fit model.

6. Terry is in outpatient treatment and is being taught relaxation skills and social skills so she is less dependent on her mother. What disorder is probably being treated?
   a. Rett's disorder
   b. Oppositional defiant disorder
   c. School phobia
   d. Bulimia

7. Nathan is 8 years old and has had a repetitive, involuntary eye blink for seven months. What should the wise diagnostician say?
   a. Nathan has a chronic tic disorder.
   b. Nathan's tic disorder could be transient, chronic, or an early form of Tourette's syndrome.
   c. Nathan has no disorder at all.
   d. Nathan has an early form of Tourette's syndrome.

8. Cheryl, a high school student, sometimes eats in binges. Should she be diagnosed as having an eating disorder?
   a. No, many high school students binge.
   b. Yes, it is a pathognomonic sign of anorexia nervosa.
   c. No, eating disorders are diagnosed on the basis of preoccupations about weight, not behavior.
   d. Yes, it is a pathognomonic sign of bulimia.

9. Greg says, "There are more than 7 million people in the United States with mental retardation. They have IQs less than 80, and most are able to support themselves. That is why there has been a big drop in the number of such people in public institutions." What part of Greg's statement is *incorrect*?
   a. It is inaccurate to say that there are 7 million people with retardation.
   b. It is inaccurate to say that retardation involves IQs under 80.
   c. It is inaccurate to say that people with retardation can be self-supporting.
   d. It is inaccurate to say that there has been a drop in the number of people with retardation in public institutions.

10. A public health department wants to reduce the rate of mental retardation. What is the single most important condition to eliminate in order to accomplish this?
    a. Premature infants (and their accompanying low birth weight)
    b. Mothers having children after the age of 40
    c. Children involved in car accidents
    d. Amniocentesis

ANSWERS TO FACT AND CONCEPT QUESTIONS

1. a. The prevalence rate of autistic disorder is closer to 4 to 7 per 10,000; the other pervasive developmental disorders are 22 per 10,000.
   b. Pervasive developmental disorders are sufficiently different from schizophrenia to warrant their own category.
   c. Pervasive developmental disorders are usually evident in the first several years of life.
   *d. Pervasive developmental disorders involve bizarre behaviors or severe deficits, such as an absence of language, that are abnormal at any developmental stage. (p. 498)

2. a. Only about 10 percent of autistics show the savant phenomenon.
   *b. Up to 75 percent of autistic children have IQs below 70. (p. 501)
   c. One of the key symptoms of autism is lack of speech or its dysfunctional quality.
   d. Autistic children fail to show affection for anyone, even their parents.

3. a. Autistic symptoms are noticeable at a very early age, even in infancy.
   b. Almost all autistic behaviors, from echolalia to wild tantrums to spectacular feats of memory, are observable.
   *c. Symptoms can vary widely, particularly with regard to level of functioning and developmental delay. (p. 502)
   d. There is no reason to believe that parents of autistic children are dysfunctional.

4. a. Autistics do not show delusions.
   *b. Echolalia—meaningless repeating of phrases—is a symptom of autism; research indicates that it may be induced by stress. (p. 502)
   c. Coprolalia—the compulsion to shout obscenities—is a symptom of Tourette's syndrome.
   d. Pronoun reversal is a symptom of autism, but autistic children show no empathy for others.

5. *a. Four new pervasive developmental disorders have been added to DSM-IV: Rett's disorder, Asperger's disorder, childhood disintegrative disorder, and pervasive developmental disorder not otherwise specified. (p. 503)
   b. Children with Asperger's disorder have major impairments but normal language.
   c. These disorders are too new for us to know what treatments are effective.
   d. The childhood anxiety disorders eliminated from DSM-IV are avoidant disorder and overanxious disorder.

6. a. Research shows a multitude of causal factors, so it is unlikely that a single cause exists.
   b. A very strong study found that 36 percent of MZ twins were concordant while 0 percent of DZ twins were concordant.
   c. There is no pathognomonic sign for autism; when serotonin levels are abnormal in the disorder, they are high.
   *d. Many central nervous system abnormalities have been found, but research results are inconsistent and inconclusive. (p. 505)

7. a. Psychoanalytic thinking about pervasive developmental disorders is largely discredited.
   b. Humanistic approaches are both uncommon and unlikely to be successful.
   *c. Because there are such profound impairments, the treatment of children with these disorders has had limited success. (p. 506)
   d. In one study, even among high-functioning patients with good verbal skills, only 6 of 22 were competitively employed.

8. a. Both tic and eating disorders remain in DSM-IV.
   b. Pervasive developmental disorders involve psychotic, thoroughly dysfunctional behaviors; conduct disorders involve neither psychosis nor interpersonal dysfunction. They deserve to be separated.
   *c. Temper tantrums, argumentativeness, and problems doing arithmetic are now included as disorders; many clinicians see this as wrongly characterizing ordinary childhood difficulties as psychopathological. (p. 508)
   d. There are many subjective decisions such as deciding if "often does not finish tasks" is abnormal given the child's developmental level and cultural norms.

9. *a. ADHD is characterized by short attention span, high motor activity, impulsivity, and poor self-control. (p. 509)
   b. School phobia is a subcategory of separation anxiety disorder and does not include these symptoms.
   c. Conduct disorder overlaps somewhat with ADHD but is characterized by repeated violations of the rights of others.
   d. This disorder is diagnosed when a child acts in a bizarre fashion at an early age, but this behavior does not match the criteria for autism.

10. a. Haloperidol is not used with ADHD; it has been somewhat effective with autistic children.
    b. Mania is not a problem for ADHD children.
    c. Stimulants such as Ritalin and Dexadrine are frequently prescribed for children with ADHD. (pp. 511–512)
    d. Ritalin is a stimulant, not an anti-depressant.

11. *a. Oppositional defiant disorder, ADHD, and conduct disorder are all problems with excessive, defiant behavior and have little to do with anxiety. (p. 516)
    b. Oppositional defiant disorder, ADHD, and conduct disorder are all problems with excessive, defiant behavior.
    c. Oppositional defiant disorder, ADHD, and conduct disorder are all problems with excessive, defiant behavior.
    d. Oppositional defiant disorder, ADHD, and conduct disorder are all problems with excessive, defiant behavior.

12. a. Learning theory does not speculate on CNS damage.
 b. For this disorder, conflicts over sexuality are not important in the psychoanalytic explanation of cause.
 c. Double-bind communications are important in explaining schizophrenic disorder.
 *d. Psychoanalysts believe such children are neglected and have underlying anxiety; behaviorists think they have learned to be antisocial because their parents failed to control them. (pp. 514, 515)

13. a. Psychoactive drugs have not been successful in treating conduct disorders.
 b. These children are not motivated to use psychotherapy; incarceration does not effectively "treat" them.
 c. Negative practice—the repetition of a behavior until it becomes aversive—is useful in eliminating tics; anxiety is not a problem for those with conduct disorders.
 *d. Cognitive social skills programs and Patterson's parent training groups have shown both short- and long-term effectiveness. (p. 515)

14 *a. Childhood depression is much more common when there is a broken home than when the family is intact, it is more prominent in adolescent girls, and, as with adults, it involves cognitive distortions of self-blame. (p. 519)
 b. Tic disorders are most common in childhood, not adolescence; they are unrelated to divorce.
 c. Separation anxiety disorder is much more common in childhood than adolescence.
 d. Conduct disorders are far more common in boys than girls and involve problems of blaming others.

15. a. Both anorexics and bulimics are afraid of gaining weight.
 b. One form of anorexia involves binging and purging.
 *c. Anorexics starve themselves and look that way; bulimia is unrelated to body size (most are of normal weight). (pp. 522, 523)
 d. Both forms of eating disorder are more common in women.

16. a. Fewer and fewer people with mental retardation are in institutions.
 *b. The *Larry P. v. Riles* case banned such testing for this purpose. (p. 529)
 c. The reverse is true: There is greater hope for people once thought to be untreatable.
 d. There are many causes for mental retardation, from poverty to genetic abnormalities to head injury.

17. *a. These are the three criteria for diagnosing mental retardation according to DSM-IV. (p. 528)
 b. Most people with mental retardation have IQs between 50 and 70, can speak, and have causes that are environmental.
 c. IQ must be below 70.
 d. Because a is the correct answer, this cannot be the best answer.

18. *a. Genetically caused retardation is associated with the more severe forms of cognitive and physical impairment, such as Down syndrome. (p. 530)
 b. There is no race difference in vulnerability to genetically caused retardation.
 c. If anything, being over 40 when having children increases vulnerability for Down syndrome, but more than two-thirds of cases are unrelated to mother's age.
 d. Genetically caused retardation is more likely to involve physical deformities.

19. a. Amniocentesis detects disorders in which there are an abnormal number of chromosomes, such as Down syndrome; normal variations in intelligence cannot be detected this way.
  b. Amniocentesis detects disorders that occur prenatally.
  c. Amniocentesis can detect genetically caused disorders, not behavior (since the child is still a fetus during the procedure).
  *d. Amniocentesis involves the culturing of fetal tissue so that abnormal chromosomal conditions such as Down syndrome can be identified before birth. (p. 531)

20. a. The most successful graduates of the STETS program had biologically caused and more severe forms of retardation.
  *b. About one-third of program graduates were employed in competitive jobs, far more than those in a control group. (p. 533)
  c. The STETS program involved three stages, two of which trained individuals for the world of work.
  d. The fact that one-third of graduates were regularly employed in competitive jobs argues that such jobs are a reasonable objective for adequately trained people.

ANSWERS TO APPLICATION QUESTIONS

1. a. Frith (1991) suggests that autistic individuals have no theory of mind—they are especially deficient at empathizing with others.
  b. Echolalia is the meaningless repetition of phrases spoken by others.
  c. Autistics do not have the attention deficits seen in children with ADHD.
  *d. Astounding memory and artistic feats performed by otherwise severely dysfunctional individuals characterize autistic savants. (p. 501)

2. a. Ritalin is a stimulant medication used for children with ADHD.
  b. Because they do not attend to others and one-half do not speak, group therapy would be useless.
  c. Self-instructional procedures and role playing are too advanced for autistics, many of whom do not speak.
  *d. Intensive behavior modification for learning language and attending to others has had modest success in treating children with autistic disorder. (p. 506)

3. a. Males outnumber females with ADHD by four or five to one.
  b. ADHD is often detected in the preschool or early elementary school years.
  c. Because of attention problems, most ADHD children have great difficulty completing academic work.
  *d. The prognosis for attention deficit without hyperactive disorder is quite good; criminal behavior is more likely if there is hyperactivity and sexual aggression. (p. 510)

4. *a. This self-instructional method, developed by Donald Meichenbaum, has had considerable success in teaching ADHD children to complete academic tasks and is as useful as drug therapy. (p. 512)
  b. Academic tasks and going too fast are not problems for the child with separation anxiety disorder.
  c. Tourette's syndrome involves uncontrolled tics, barking sounds, and inappropriate words.
  d. Pervasive developmental disorders involve so many speech and interpersonal problems that school performance would be irrelevant.

5. a. There is a good deal of evidence showing that temperament and environment interact to produce childhood problems.
   b. Pervasive developmental disorders are least likely to be caused by family environments.
   c. Psychoanalysts tend to stress parental actions over inherited temperaments.
   *d. Dr. Stella Chess is one developer of the temperament-environment fit model, which argues that children are born with a personality that may or may not agree with the parents' style. (Focus 17.3; p. 517)

6. a. Rett's disorder is a pervasive developmental disorder in which there is marked deterioration of social and language skills after at least six months of normal development.
   b. Oppositional defiant disorder involves defying parental rules and being hostile, not overly dependent.
   *c. School phobia is considered a problem of anxiety and poor social skills, but behaviorists would treat the disorder with relaxation and social skill training. (p. 518)
   d. Bulimia is not related to dependency on a parent.

7. a. Chronic tic disorder is not diagnosed until after the tic has continued for one year.
   *b. No one can tell whether a transient tic will go away by itself, become a chronic tic disorder, or develop into Tourette's syndrome; accurate "diagnosis" is possible only with hindsight. (p. 519)
   c. A repetitive eye blink that goes on for seven months is, at least, a transient tic disorder.
   d. An eye blink is very common; it is far too early to diagnose Tourette's syndrome.

8. *a. Approximately 20 percent of high school students report binging or overeating about once per week; a diagnosis of bulimia requires meeting other criteria. (p. 521)
   b. Binging is not a specific sign of anorexia; bulimics also purge after binging.
   c. Eating disorders are diagnosed on the basis of both preoccupations and observable behaviors.
   d. Binging and purging is a fundamental sign of bulimia, but also occurs in anorexia.

9. a. Approximately 7 million people in the United States have IQs under 70 and are potentially retarded.
   *b. IQ must be below 70 for a person to be considered having mental retardation; adaptive deficiencies and onset before 18 are also required. (p. 528)
   c. Most people with mild mental retardation (the majority of those diagnosed with retardation) can be self-supporting.
   d. There has been a dramatic decline in the number of people with mental retardation who reside in institutions.

10. *a. Prematurity and low birth weight are the single biggest reasons why children develop mental retardation. (p. 532)
   b. Although having children after age 40 increases the risks of Down syndrome, about two-thirds of cases occur in mothers younger than 37 and Down syndrome is a small minority of cases of mental retardation.
   c. Head trauma due to car accidents may be on the rise, but it represents a small fraction of the cases of retardation due to prematurity and low birth weight.
   d. Amniocentesis is a way of detecting prenatal conditions; it is not a cause of retardation.

PART 6
Individual, Group, and Community Intervention

CHAPTER 18
Individual and Group Therapy

LEARNING OBJECTIVES

When you have mastered the material in Chapter 18, you should be able to:

1. Describe and differentiate between electroconvulsive therapy (ECT) and psychosurgery. (pp. 537–538)
2. Define pharmacology. Describe and evaluate the use of antianxiety, antipsychotic, antidepressant, and antimanic medications. (pp. 540–545)
3. Define psychotherapy and describe its basic characteristics. Discuss why traditional psychotherapy may be inconsistent with nonwestern cultures. (Focus 18.1; pp. 545–547)
4. Describe the goals and techniques of psychoanalysis and post-Freudian psychoanalytic therapy. Evaluate the effectiveness of psychoanalytic therapy. (pp. 547–551)
5. Describe the goals and techniques of person-centered therapy, existential analysis, and gestalt therapy. (pp. 551–553)
6. Describe the goals and techniques of classical conditioning therapies, including systematic desensitization, flooding and implosion, and aversive conditioning. (pp. 553–556)
7. Describe the goals and techniques of the operant conditioning therapies of token economy and punishment, and observational learning techniques. Describe cognitive-behavioral therapy and both problem- and emotion-focused coping behaviors. (pp. 556–559)
8. Discuss the central ideas of behavioral medicine and describe the techniques used to promote lifestyle changes. Describe the guiding principles for resisting stress. (pp. 559–562)
9. Discuss research on the effectiveness of individual psychotherapy. (pp. 562–564)
10. Describe the common components and types of group therapy; evaluate the effectiveness of group therapy; describe the functions of marital and family therapy, and the different emphases of the communications and systems approaches. (Focus 18.2; pp. 562–569)
11. Define systematic eclecticism and discuss how this approach was illustrated in the Case of Steven V. (pp. 569–576)

CHAPTER OUTLINE

1. **Biology-based treatment techniques** (pp. 537–545) Biological treatment techniques have been used to alter patients' psychological states since ancient times. In our time, *electroconvulsive therapy (ECT)* was first used in the 1930s on the assumption that seizures would eliminate schizophrenic behavior. ECT has been found to be useful in treating severe

depression, but the reasons for this are unclear. There is considerable controversy over the use of ECT. *Psychosurgery*, particularly lesioning the frontal lobes, was once a common treatment for schizophrenia, but now it is used only as a last resort. Videolaserscopy now allows surgeons to make extremely small laser incisions, guided by a video camera.

The most common biology-based treatments are *psychopharmacology* (drug therapy) approaches. Antianxiety drugs, including propanediols (meprobamate compounds) and benzodiazepines (Librium and Valium) reduce tension, probably by blocking neural transmission, but they can be addictive and produce withdrawal effects. Antipsychotic drugs are used to treat schizophrenia and other psychotic conditions. Their effectiveness, not due to placebo effects, is superior to that of several forms of psychotherapy. Side effects include Parkinson-like symptoms, dry mouth, and tardive dyskinesia. Antidepressants include *tricyclics*, *MAO inhibitors*, and *fluoxetine (Prozac),* and are used to treat depression. Studies following assertions about Prozac's safety showed no credible link between the drug and increased suicidality. Lithium, the principal antimanic drug, is effective in the treatment of bipolar disorder.

Psychopharmacological considerations determine which drug in which amount should be prescribed for which condition and patient. Drugs are generally more effective for active symptoms like hallucinations than passive symptoms like social withdrawal.

2. **Psychotherapy** (Focus 18.1; pp. 545–547) *Psychotherapy* is defined as the systematic application of techniques derived from theory for the purpose of aiding psychologically troubled people. There are wide differences in strategies, but most psychotherapies agree that treatment is an opportunity for relearning, for developing new emotionally important experiences, for establishing therapeutic relationships, and for achieving hoped-for goals. However, traditional psychotherapy mirrors mainstream western culture, making it less effective for those from nonwestern cultures. Individual psychotherapy is usually subdivided into insight-oriented and action-oriented approaches.

3. **Insight-oriented approaches to individual psychotherapy** (pp. 547–553) Psychoanalysis, devised by Freud, stresses the resolution of unconscious conflicts through techniques such as free association and dream analysis, analysis of resistance, the transference relationship, and interpretation of events. Post-Freudian psychoanalysis is more flexible than traditional psychoanalysis, but still holds to the idea of symptom substitution if underlying factors are not analyzed and altered. Controlled research does not confirm the existence of symptom substitution.

   Humanistic-existential approaches stress the self and personal responsibility. Rogers's *person-centered therapy* emphasizes the relationship over any techniques. *Existential analysis* adheres to no single theory but takes a strongly philosophical approach, and Perls's *gestalt therapy* uses the person's here-and-now totality of experience to produce change. The humanistic-existential approach has had a major impact on therapy groups.

4. **Action-oriented approaches to individual psychotherapy: classical conditioning techniques, operant conditioning techniques, observational learning techniques, and cognitive-behavioral therapy approaches** (Focus 18.2; pp. 553–559) Classical conditioning principles guide the action-oriented therapies of *systematic desensitization, flooding* and *implosion,* and *aversive conditioning.* In systematic desensitization, relaxation is paired with anxiety-provoking scenes to reduce anxiety. In flooding, clients confront their fears in real situations, whereas, in implosion, the confrontation occurs in the imagination. In aversive conditioning, an undesirable behavior such as smoking is paired with a noxious stimulus.

Operant principles are at work in *token economies,* where desired behaviors are contingently reinforced with tokens that can be exchanged for privileges or other reinforcers. *Contingent punishment* may be used to suppress self-destructive behaviors, as in autism.

Modeling, based on observational learning theory, is effective in the treatment of phobias, delinquency, and other behavior problems. *Cognitive-behavioral therapies* focus on clients' thoughts as well as on their coping skills. Ellis's rational-emotive psychotherapy challenges the client's irrational beliefs; Beck's therapy is less confrontative, but uses similar themes to treat depression. Stress inoculation therapy is another form of cognitive-behavioral treatment. Lazarus has shown that denial can sometimes be an effective coping mechanism; both problem- and emotion-focused coping have value. For certain depressions, cognitive therapy may be more effective than drug treatment.

5. **Behavioral medicine and resisting stress: guiding principles** (pp. 559–562) Behavioral medicine links the biological and behavioral sciences for the purpose of changing people's lifestyles to prevent illness. *Biofeedback therapy* and counseling to reduce Type A behavior patterns have been useful in this effort. Most techniques for changing lifestyles involve establishing priorities, avoiding stressful situations, taking personal time, setting up an exercise schedule, proper diet, developing social supports, and learning to relax. In order to resist stress, individuals should practice and prepare for stressful circumstances, take concrete actions, reduce the ambiguity of the situation, and seek out social supports.

6. **Evaluating individual psychotherapy** (pp. 562–564) There are debates over the appropriateness of insight versus action therapies. In 1954, Eysenck created controversy by claiming that psychotherapy was ineffective. More recent studies have been methodologically cleaner, but Persons (1991) points out that therapy outcome studies fail to match the conditions of actual practice of assessment and psychotherapy. Use of meta-analysis to identify treatment effect size shows that those getting therapy show far more improvement than those untreated.

7. **Group, family, and marital therapy** (Focus 18.2; pp. 564–569) *Group therapy* has economic and therapeutic advantages over individual psychotherapy. There are many different forms of group therapy, including sensitivity and encounter groups, transactional analysis groups, assertiveness training groups, and psychodrama. The purposes and techniques of groups differ widely, but some common features are the experience of feedback on real-life social interactions, the opportunity for modeling, and the reduction of isolation through social support. There are advantages and disadvantages to group treatment. Measuring outcome for group therapy is more difficult than for individual treatment.

   Family therapy is a kind of group therapy seeking to modify family relationships to foster greater harmony. It is based on the assumption that the problems of the "identified patient" are symptoms of family distress. Two kinds of family therapy are the communications approach and the systems approach. *Marital therapy* also focuses on communications and system roles; it is not designed to save marriages, but to clarify understanding and options.

8. **Systematic integration and eclecticism: a systematic and eclectic approach to the case of Steven V.** (pp. 569–576) No one therapy has a monopoly on good ideas for producing behavior change. The majority of clinicians are eclectic and select methods that work from a variety of theories. During the initial meeting, the therapist used a person-centered approach to encourage Steven to express himself. When they failed to connect, he used a more direct approach. While learning about Steven, the therapist discovered information that had symbolic meaning from a psychoanalytic viewpoint. Formal testing (with the MMPI) helped clarify the level of Steven's disturbance. Assigning an autobiographical essay helped

the therapist enter Steven's subjective world (humanistic-existential perspective). Philosophically, the therapist took an existential viewpoint—suggesting that Steven was responsible for his actions—but he used rational-emotive therapy principles to help Steven look at his irrational beliefs, and other behavioral notions to help teach assertiveness skills.

KEY TERMS

Fill-in-the-Blanks Quiz

1. Brain surgery performed to correct a severe mental disorder is called ____________.
2. A form of therapy that involves the simultaneous treatment of two or more clients is called ____________.
3. The study of the effects of drugs on the mind and behavior is called ____________.
4. A humanistic-existential approach to therapy that emphasizes the client's awareness of the here-and-now and his or her totality of experience is called ____________.
5. A humanistic therapy emphasizing the kind of person the therapist should be in the therapeutic process, rather than the techniques that he or she should use, is called ____________.
6. Group therapy that is characterized by an attempt to modify relationships within the family is called ____________.
7. The systematic application of techniques based on psychological principles for the purpose of helping psychologically troubled individuals is called ____________.
8. A therapeutic approach in which a patient receives information about autonomic functions and is rewarded for influencing them in a desirable direction is called ____________.
9. The antidepressant medication that affects serotonin levels and has been the target of controversy about its side effects is called ____________.
10. The application of electric voltage to the brain to induce convulsions and reduce depression is called ____________.
11. A therapeutic approach that is concerned with the person's existence and involvement in the world and focuses on a complex encounter with the therapist is called ____________.
12. A behavioral technique aimed at extinguishing fear by having the client confront the real-life threat at full intensity is called ____________.
13. A behavioral technique aimed at extinguishing fear by having the client *imagine* the threat at full intensity is called ____________.
14. Antidepressant compounds believed to correct the balance of neurotransmitters in the brain and which can interact with certain foods to cause dangerous side effects are called ____________.

15. The treatment aimed at helping couples understand and clarify their communications, roles, and expectations is called ___________.

16. Antidepressant compounds that relieve symptoms of depression are called ___________.

Answers to Fill-in-the-Blanks Quiz

1. psychosurgery
2. group therapy
3. psychopharmacology
4. gestalt therapy
5. person-centered therapy (also client-centered therapy)
6. family therapy
7. psychotherapy
8. biofeedback therapy
9. fluoxetine (Prozac)
10. electroconvulsive therapy
11. existential analysis
12. flooding
13. implosion
14. monoamine oxidase (MAO) inhibitors
15. marital therapy
16. tricyclics

FACT AND CONCEPT QUESTIONS

1. This treatment was first used in the 1930s in the mistaken belief that epileptic seizures and schizophrenia could not both occur in the same person. Now it is used to treat severe depression. What form of therapy is this?
   a. Prefrontal lobotomy
   b. Electroconvulsive therapy (ECT)
   c. Phenothiazine medication
   d. Lithium carbonate

2. ___________ drugs are used to treat people who are extremely tense. However, they have the potential to be overused and for people to become psychologically dependent on them.
   a. Antidepressant
   b. Phenothiazine
   c. Antimanic
   d. Benzodiazepine

3. Symptoms like those of Parkinson's disease and the drug-induced disorder tardive dyskinesia are serious side effects of prolonged treatment with
   a. electroshock.
   b. psychosurgery.
   c. antipsychotic medication.
   d. antianxiety medication.

4. Which statement about drug treatment is *true?*
   a. In many cases, medication cures mental disorders because it can teach new ways of acting.
   b. Because antipsychotic drugs give people a "high," discharged patients almost always continue to take their medication.
   c. Antipsychotic medication is a principal reason why prolonged hospitalization is no longer needed in most cases.
   d. The greatest danger of drug treatment is that it may lead to permanent memory loss.

5. Having new, important emotional experiences and engaging in a therapeutic relationship are both components of
   a. basic methods of resisting stress.
   b. biology-based approaches to treatment.
   c. action-oriented therapies only.
   d. all forms of psychotherapy.

6. Asian Americans may find that traditional psychotherapy threatens their cultural values because
   a. psychotherapy puts a high value on individual responsibility.
   b. psychotherapy denies the importance of insight.
   c. Asian cultures encourage the uncontrolled expression of emotion.
   d. Asian cultures encourage children to separate from their parents.

7. Psychoanalysts who ask their clients to say whatever comes to their minds are using the technique
   a. that uncovers the manifest content of dreams.
   b. called "countertransference."
   c. that exaggerates feelings in the here-and-now.
   d. called "free association."

8. In what way is post-Freudian psychoanalysis different from traditional psychoanalysis?
   a. It no longer believes that interpersonal relations are important.
   b. It increases the number of sessions and places more emphasis on past situations.
   c. It loosens up previously rigid therapeutic techniques.
   d. It no longer believes in the unconscious motivation of behavior.

9. Person-centered and gestalt therapies are based on the ____________ orientation toward abnormal behavior.
   a. psychoanalytic
   b. humanistic-existential
   c. cognitive-behavioral
   d. family systems

10. In existential analysis, the therapist
   a. confronts the client with his or her irrational beliefs.
   b. fosters an encounter in which both people genuinely share each other's experiences.
   c. exaggerates the client's feelings, which stem from the latent content of dreams.
   d. takes over the client's responsibility for making choices.

11. Which of the following therapeutic techniques is *both* a form of classical conditioning and a means of reducing anxiety?
   a. Systematic desensitization
   b. Aversive conditioning
   c. Token economy
   d. Antianxiety medication

12. Typically, the goal of aversive conditioning is to
   a. decrease the frequency of undesirable behaviors.
   b. teach more adaptive coping skills.
   c. decrease the client's anxiety level.
   d. increase the client's level of self-understanding.

13. When certain behaviors are rewarded with coinlike objects or tally marks that can later be exchanged for privileges or desired activities, the treatment being used is
    a. an insight-oriented form of psychotherapy.
    b. a form of behavior therapy based on classical conditioning.
    c. called a "token economy."
    d. called "implosion" or "flooding."

14. The process of observing an adaptive individual and imitating this person's behaviors is called
    a. latent learning.
    b. modeling.
    c. rational-emotive learning.
    d. problem-focused coping.

15. In ___________, the client's irrational beliefs are identified and aggressively contradicted by the therapist.
    a. Beck's cognitive therapy
    b. token economies
    c. behavioral medicine
    d. Ellis's rational-emotive therapy

16. ___________ do not alter the relationship between the person and the environment, but they do make the person feel better.
    a. Lifestyle changes
    b. Problem-focused responses
    c. Countertransferences
    d. Emotion-focused responses

17. Instructions to establish priorities and avoid stressful situations are probably pieces of advice given by
    a. practitioners of behavioral medicine.
    b. psychoanalysts.
    c. nonwestern psychologists.
    d. psychologists who use observational learning principles.

18. Which statement about research on the effectiveness of psychotherapy is *true?*
    a. The best research indicates that people who receive therapy are no more improved than those who do not.
    b. In general, people who receive therapy show greater improvement than those who do not.
    c. Psychotherapy is too recent a phenomenon for there to be any adequate research on its effectiveness.
    d. Regardless of the problem, insight-oriented psychotherapy is more effective than action-oriented psychotherapy.

19. What do transactional analysis and system-oriented family therapy have in common?
    a. They are both based on psychoanalytic principles.
    b. They are both forms of group therapy.
    c. They are both based on aversive conditioning principles.
    d. They have both been found to be only minimally effective.

20. The application of a range of therapy techniques to fit the needs of an individual client is called
    a. action-oriented psychotherapy.
    b. insight-oriented psychotherapy.
    c. eclecticism.
    d. systems-oriented therapy.

APPLICATION QUESTIONS

1. Dr. Miller says, "I can't believe a schizophrenic patient received this form of treatment in the 1990s! It has little therapeutic effect, and the posttreatment effects can include permanent intellectual impairment or even death. The patient should have been given major tranquilizers." What kind of treatment is Dr. Miller upset about?
    a. Electroconvulsive therapy (ECT)
    b. Aversive conditioning
    c. Milieu therapy
    d. Prefrontal lobotomy

2. Ralph is first treated with tricyclic medications, but, when these do not alter his symptoms, he is given fluoxetine, which proves to be very effective. Ralph probably suffered from which disorder?
    a. Generalized anxiety disorder
    b. Schizophrenia
    c. Depression
    d. Bipolar disorder

3. Vera tells her therapist about one of her dreams in which she drives her car towards an evil-looking man, trying to kill him. Her therapist says, "The man represents your father. Unconsciously, you resent him." The therapist is
    a. interpreting the latent content of the dream.
    b. using person-centered therapy techniques.
    c. showing evidence of countertransference.
    d. using free association.

4. A therapist with an existential point of view would be most likely to say which of the following?
    a. "I am less concerned with the client's self-awareness than with the client's ability to cope with stress."
    b. "Unless the repressed conflicts of the past are uncovered and dealt with, any changes in behavior will only be temporary."
    c. "Everyone has a set of irrational beliefs that must be attacked and changed through cognitive restructuring."
    d. "Until people can accept the reality of death, they cannot grow and take personal responsibility for their lives."

5. Jim has a severe snake phobia. His therapist teaches him relaxation skills and then has him imagine, while remaining relaxed, situations that place him in increasing contact with snakes. This kind of therapy is called
    a. flooding.
    b. systematic desensitization.
    c. covert sensitization.
    d. modeling.

6. To treat Helen's cocaine addiction, her therapist instructs her to pair imagined scenes in which she is ready to use cocaine with images of her coughing, choking, and having a heart attack. What kind of therapy is this?
   a. Sadistic eclecticism
   b. Covert sensitization
   c. Observational learning
   d. Token economy

7. Bradley is an autistic boy who repeatedly bangs his head on the walls and floor. Reasoning, token economy programs, and drug treatment have not stopped the behavior. What would be the most sensible treatment to try next?
   a. Prefrontal lobotomy
   b. Electroconvulsive therapy (ECT)
   c. Operant punishment
   d. Insight-oriented psychotherapy

8. Dr. DiCarlo says, "The four most useful techniques are practice, preparation, reduction of ambiguity, and reliance on social supports." What are these techniques used for?
   a. Resisting stress
   b. Increasing emotion-focused coping skills
   c. Changing one's irrational belief system
   d. Convincing families that family therapy is appropriate

9. Which of the following is a critique that a research psychologist might reasonably have made of Eysenck's 1952 study of psychotherapy effectiveness?
   a. "Your statistics inflate the usefulness of psychotherapy."
   b. "You failed to include an untreated control group in your study."
   c. "It is inappropriate to compare people getting psychotherapy with those getting drug treatment."
   d. "The improvement criteria applied to the untreated patients were different from those used with the treated ones."

10. Dr. Adelson says, "Any attempt to treat a child individually is doomed to fail. Johnny may be the 'identified patient,' but his symptoms serve a greater function." What kind of therapist is Dr. Adelson?
    a. A family therapist
    b. An action-oriented psychoanalyst
    c. One who uses systematic eclecticism
    d. A humanistic-existential therapist

ANSWERS TO FACT AND CONCEPT QUESTIONS

1. a. Prefrontal lobotomies were used to treat schizophrenia; no assumption about the operation and epileptic seizures was made.
   *b. Meduna incorrectly connected schizophrenia and epilepsy, but ECT is now used for severe depression when drug treatment has been unsuccessful. (p. 538)
   c. Phenothiazines are antipsychotic drugs used to treat schizophrenia.
   d. Lithium carbonate is used almost exclusively to treat bipolar disorders.

2. a. There is little or no potential for overuse with antidepressants.
   b. Phenothiazines do not pose a threat of overuse and are prescribed for psychotic conditions, not anxiety.
   c. Lithium carbonate is the chief antimanic drug; it does not produce overdependence.
   *d. Benzodiazepines such as Valium and Librium are antianxiety drugs that have serious potential for psychological dependence. (p. 542)

3. a. The main side effects of ECT are memory loss and confusion.
   b. Psychosurgery produces cognitive impairments; it cannot produce a drug-induced disorder.
   *c. Antipsychotic medications such as the phenothiazines, when used for long periods to treat psychotic conditions, may produce symptoms of Parkinson's disease and the syndrome called tardive dyskinesia. (p. 544)
   d. Antianxiety medications may produce physical and psychological dependence, but not these side effects.

4. a. One thing drugs cannot do is teach new behaviors; they provide no cure.
   b. Antipsychotic drugs do not produce a "high"; if anything, the problem is that patients stop taking their medication because they don't like the side effects.
   *c. Because they can suppress psychotic symptoms and help people think straight, antipsychotic drugs have helped shorten the hospital stays of most psychotic patients. (p. 545)
   d. Drugs rarely, if ever, impair memory; the danger of this is from ECT.

5. a. Although these might not hurt one's chances of resisting stress, the components of stress resistance typically include preparation, ambiguity reduction, and social support.
   b. Biology-based treatment involves little, if any, therapeutic relationship.
   c. Action-oriented therapies value these components, but not as much as do insight-oriented approaches.
   *d. These are two of the common features of all forms of psychotherapy. (p. 546)

6. *a. Asian cultures are more likely than western culture to encourage adults to accede to the wishes of their parents; this might be seen as denying individual responsibility. (Focus 18.1; p. 548)
   b. Psychotherapy places greater emphasis on insight than those from Asian cultures may.
   c. People from Asian cultures are typically taught restraint in their emotional expression.
   d. Asian cultures encourage continuing ties between adult children and their parents.

7. a. The manifest content of dreams is the information one remembers after awakening.
   b. Countertransference is a therapist blunder; it occurs when the therapist reacts personally and emotionally to the patient's transferential responses.
   c. Gestalt therapists are far more likely to have clients exaggerate their feelings so that they can be aware of the here-and-now experience.
   *d. Free association involves the simple, but not very easy, request to "say whatever comes to mind." (p. 547)

8. a. Post-Freudian analysis places greater emphasis on interpersonal relations.
   b. Post-Freudian analysis usually requires fewer sessions and places more emphasis on current concerns.
   *c. The formal rules of therapy that Freud set down have been relaxed and modified in post-Freudian analysis. (p. 550)
   d. All psychoanalysts, Freudian and post-Freudian, assume that behavior is unconsciously motivated.

9. a. Psychoanalytic therapies emphasize the intrapsychic components of personality, not the holistic approach of these two.
   *b. Person-centered therapy and gestalt therapy emphasize the current feelings of people and treat them holistically. (pp. 551–552, 552–553)
   c. Cognitive-behavioral therapies stress the irrational beliefs and coping skills of people; neither of these two do.
   d. Family therapy includes communications and systems approaches, not client-centered and gestalt therapy.

10. a. Confronting a client's irrational beliefs is a feature of Ellis's rational-emotive therapy.
   *b. Existential therapists are philosophically oriented and encourage genuine encounters from which clients are expected to grow. (p. 552)
   c. The "exaggeration of feelings" notion is important in gestalt therapy; latent dream content comes from psychoanalysis.
   d. Humanistic-existential thinking emphasizes the need for personal responsibility for choices; therapists would not take over that responsibility.

11. *a. Systematic desensitization is a classical conditioning method because it pairs two stimuli; it is almost always used to eliminate anxiety symptoms. (p. 554)
   b. Aversive conditioning is often based on classical conditioning principles but is used to remove undesirable behaviors, such as excessive drinking or smoking.
   c. Token economies are based on operant conditioning because the consequences of behavior are altered.
   d. Antianxiety medication is certainly used to treat anxiety, but it represents a biology-based therapy.

12. *a. In aversive conditioning, noxious stimuli are paired with undesirable behaviors such as smoking or drinking in an attempt to decrease their frequency. (p. 555)
   b. Token economies, modeling, and cognitive-behavioral approaches stress the learning of new coping skills.
   c. Aversive conditioning would tend to increase one's anxiety; just imagine what the pairing of alcohol and vomiting would do for your tension level!
   d. Self-understanding is a high priority in insight-oriented therapies.

13. a. Insight-oriented approaches rely almost exclusively on speech as the mode of change.
   b. Classical conditioning involves the pairing of stimuli and a passive organism; when certain behaviors are rewarded, operant procedures are being used.
   *c. In token economies, coins, points, stamps, or other such devices are token reinforcers that are given contingent on appropriate behavior; they are traded in for valued activities or privileges. (p. 556)
   d. In implosion, fearful situations are imagined; in flooding, they are experienced for real.

14. a. Latent learning is any learning that occurs but is invisible until there is an incentive to demonstrate it.
   *b. In modeling, learning occurs when another's behavior is observed and then copied. (pp. 556–557)
   c. In rational-emotive learning (therapy), irrational beliefs are challenged and changed.
   d. Problem-focused coping involves taking direct action on the environment to reduce the threat of a situation.

15. a. Beck's cognitive therapy explores the client's illogical thinking but does so without aggressively challenging it.
 b. In token economies, appropriate behaviors are "paid off"; belief systems are not important.
 c. Behavioral medicine may examine beliefs, but far more emphasis is placed on healthy activities.
 *d. Ellis's rational-emotive therapy assumes that symptoms stem from irrational beliefs that must be aggressively attacked and changed. (p. 558)

16. a. Lifestyle changes are most related to behavioral medicine.
 b. Problem-focused responses change the person or the environment so that circumstances are less threatening.
 c. Countertransference is a therapist blunder in which the therapist's own emotions affect the therapy.
 *d. When people react to threats in such a way that they feel better, but the situation has not changed, they are using emotion-focused responses. (Critical Thinking 18.2; p. 558)

17. *a. The text gives seven steps for establishing a healthy lifestyle (a goal of behavioral medicine), two of which are establishing priorities and avoiding stressful situations when this is possible. (p. 561)
 b. Psychoanalysts tend not to give advice at all, but if they did, they would stress the examination of unconscious issues.
 c. The text does not examine the theories of nonwestern psychologists.
 d. Observational learning principles stress the imitation of effective individuals.

18. a. Only Eysenck's poorly executed research showed that treated people were no more improved than untreated people.
 *b. Meta-analysis of hundreds of studies (for example, work by Smith and Glass) shows that people treated with psychotherapy show far greater improvement than those who are untreated. (p. 563)
 c. Psychotherapy research has been done for more than thirty years; the research literature is quite extensive.
 d. Significant differences in effectiveness between insight- and action-oriented therapies are the exception rather than the rule; in those exceptions, action-oriented methods are superior.

19. a. Transactional analysis has some elements of similarity to psychoanalysis, but systems-oriented family therapy does not.
 *b. In transactional analysis, people meet in groups to become aware of their game playing; family therapy, by its nature, is group therapy. (Focus 18.2, p. 552; p. 567)
 c. Neither transactional analysis nor systems-oriented family therapy is based on learning principles.
 d. The text reports no information on their effectiveness.

20. a. Action-oriented psychotherapy tends to be based on behavioral principles.
 b. Insight-oriented therapies rely on emotional awareness to provide the impetus for change, regardless of the client.
 *c. Eclecticism selects the best methods from various theoretical perspectives and applies them to meet individual clients' needs. (p. 569)
 d. Systems-oriented therapy is strictly associated with family therapy.

ANSWERS TO APPLICATION QUESTIONS

1. a. Electroconvulsive therapy is still used in the 1990s (although not with schizophrenics) and does not lead to death.
   b. Aversive conditioning is used in the 1990s and does not have permanent side effects.
   c. Milieu therapy is a treatment for schizophrenia that involves self-government; it has no physiological side effects.
   *d. Psychosurgery such as prefrontal lobotomy has disappeared as a treatment for schizophrenia because of its serious side effects and its inferiority to drug therapy. (p. 539)

2. a. Antianxiety drugs, not tricyclics, would be given to a person with GAD.
   b. Antipsychotic drugs, not tricyclics, would be given to a person with schizophrenia.
   *c. Tricyclics and fluoxetine (Prozac) are both antidepressants. (p. 544)
   d. Lithium would be given to a person with bipolar disorder, although antidepressants might help during the depression phase.

3. *a. The latent content of dreams is the symbolic meaning that is disguised in our recollection (the manifest content); this therapist is being unusually active in the interpretation. (p. 548)
   b. Person-centered therapy places little emphasis on technique and even less on interpreting dreams.
   c. Countertransference occurs when the therapist's emotional life interferes with the therapeutic relationship.
   d. In free association, the patient says the first thing that comes to mind.

4. a. Existentialists emphasize self-understanding.
   b. Psychoanalysts, not existentialists, emphasize the uncovering of repressed material.
   c. Rational-emotive therapy, not existential therapy, emphasizes irrational beliefs.
   *d. Confronting the reality of death represents an existential crisis; existential analysts encourage genuine encounters with self and others. (p. 552)

5. a. In flooding, the feared stimulus is confronted in "real life."
   *b. Systematic desensitization has three stages: relaxation training, the development of an anxiety hierarchy, and the pairing of the images on the hierarchy with relaxation. (p. 554)
   c. In covert sensitization, disgusting scenes and undesirable behaviors are paired in the imagination.
   d. Modeling involves behavior change through the observation of people who demonstrate adequate behavior.

6. a. There is no such term as *sadistic eclecticism.*
   *b. In covert sensitization, undesirable behaviors are paired in the imagination with disgusting scenes as a way of reducing the likelihood of the behaviors. (p. 555)
   c. In observational learning, new skills are acquired by imitating others.
   d. In a token economy, desirable behaviors are rewarded with tokens that can be exchanged for reinforcing activities.

7. a. Prefrontal lobotomy may reduce negative behaviors, but it has the potential side effects of permanent intellectual impairment or even death.
   b. ECT, a treatment for depression, is never used as punishment.
   *c. Lovaas has used contingent punishment with electric shock as a method of suppressing self-destructive behavior in autistic children. (p. 556)
   d. Insight-oriented psychotherapy assumes verbal skills, which are nonexistent in autistic children.

8. *a. The text lists four strategies for resisting stress: practice, preparation, reduction of ambiguity, and reliance on others (social support). (pp. 561–562)
   b. Emotion-focused coping responses do not change the person-environmental relationship, and this relationship would be changed if one reduced the ambiguity in a situation.
   c. These actions are only tangentially related to rational-emotive therapy.
   d. These actions are unrelated to family therapy.

9. a. Eysenck's statistics underestimated the value of psychotherapy.
   b. Eysenck did compare treated people with untreated people.
   c. Drug therapy did not exist at the time of Eysenck's research.
   *d. A stiffer criterion for improvement was applied to treated people than to untreated ones. (p. 562)

10. *a. Family therapists argue that although children's symptoms frequently label only them as "identified patients," the whole family is hurting and in need of therapy. (p. 567)
   b. Action-oriented therapists tend to take a behavioral approach and may or may not include family members in treatment.
   c. Systematic eclectic therapists may include family therapy (if it seems appropriate), but no statements about "any attempt being doomed" would enter their vocabulary, since they tend to be flexible.
   d. Humanistic-existential therapists would focus on the subjective experience of an individual client.

CHAPTER 19
Community Psychology

LEARNING OBJECTIVES

When you have mastered the material in Chapter 19, you should be able to:

1. Describe the community psychology approach and differentiate its assumptions and methods from those of clinical psychology. (pp. 581–582)
2. Discuss how problems with traditional hospital care for mental patients and inequities in the delivery of services led to community psychology innovations. Describe culturally responsive psychological care. (Focus 19.1; pp. 582–586)
3. Describe the goals of community mental health centers and evaluate the criticisms of them. (pp. 586–588)
4. Define primary prevention and describe example programs for helping children and divorcing adults, and community-wide efforts to prevent depression and juvenile delinquency. Explain the resistance to prevention efforts. (Focus 19.2; pp. 588–590)
5. Define secondary prevention and discuss the problems in developing such programs. Describe and evaluate the Rochester, New York, primary-grade program. Describe suicide prevention efforts. (pp. 590–592)
6. Define tertiary prevention and describe halfway house programs. Evaluate prevention efforts. (Focus 19.2; pp. 592–593)
7. Describe the reasons and goals for the training of paraprofessionals. (pp. 593–595)
8. Explain the role of the community psychologist in social and political issues. Discuss the concept of empowerment and its implications. (pp. 595, 599)
9. Discuss the role of social supports in mental health and the value of self-help groups. Evaluate the impact of media self-help, including books and call-in radio shows. (Focus 19.3, Critical Thinking; pp. 596–598)
10. Discuss the roots of racism and its effects on self-esteem and mental health. Explain the contradictory results concerning racial differences in mental disorder. Describe methods of reducing racism. (pp. 598–602)
11. Discuss sex role stereotyping and the roots and effects of sexism on self-esteem and mental health. Discuss evidence that psychology contributes to sexism. Describe methods of reducing sexism. (pp. 602–605)

CHAPTER OUTLINE

1. **Why community psychology?** (Focus 19.1; pp. 581–586) With roughly 19 percent of U.S. citizens (more than 29 million people) suffering from some form of mental disorder, there will never be enough mental health professionals to provide direct service. *Community psychology* is an approach to this problem that emphasizes the use of community resources to offset the effects of environmental stresses. Unlike clinical psychology, it emphasizes *human ecology* (the interaction of humans and their environments), application as well as research, competencies, and prevention. It grew out of dissatisfaction with individual and medical models of disorders, the documented ineffectiveness of mental institutions in helping patients learn living skills, and inequity in service delivery.

   Alternative approaches include *therapeutic communities,* halfway houses, and the lodges (Fairweather), which give patients autonomy. Several factors account for the slow growth of these effective methods, but rising costs and negative side effects of hospitalization encourage the trend in deinstitutionalization. Culturally appropriate treatment approaches have been implemented and have been found to be helpful in increasing access to psychotherapy by minorities.

2. **Community mental health centers** (pp. 586–588) In 1963, the *community mental health center* system was established to improve the availability of mental health services. Each center was to provide inpatient and outpatient therapy, partial hospitalization, emergency services, and consultation and education. The system has not yet reached its goal for financial and conceptual reasons. Increasingly, health maintenance organizations (HMOs) provide psychotherapy and prevention services.

3. **Prevention programs** (Focus 19.2; pp. 588–593) Community prevention works to prevent psychopathology. In *primary prevention*, the goal is the elimination of new cases. Examples of primary prevention programs include interpersonal cognitive problem-solving programs with young children, an educational program for people going through divorce, and community-wide programs to prevent depression and juvenile delinquency. Despite the evidence that primary prevention can affect an immense range of social problems, there is controversy between some psychotherapists and some community psychologists over the value of treatment versus prevention.

   Secondary prevention involves the early identification and treatment of disorders to shorten their duration. Examples of this method include the Rochester, New York, primary-school project and suicide prevention programs.

   Tertiary prevention is designed to enhance the community integration of people discharged from institutional care. This can be done through halfway houses that assist individuals and through community education about mental disorders.

   The goals of prevention are difficult to attain. Early identification issues, funding difficulties, doubts about adequate knowledge, and fears about the invasion of privacy all present barriers.

4. **Paraprofessionals** (pp. 593–595) Most people who need help do not seek out mental health professionals. When psychologists train nonprofessionals, these people become *paraprofessional therapists*. They can increase the reach and effectiveness of one highly trained person. Paraprofessionals appear to be effective as therapeutic agents.

5. **Social and political action** (pp. 595–597) An important ethical decision for community psychologists is whether or not to become active in the social and political arena. Rappaport

(1981) suggests that, by empowering communities, psychologists can give people the power to solve their own problems, but this activity is itself value-laden.

6. **Social supports** (Focus 19.3; pp. 597–598) When people are under stress, interactions with friends and family can provide *social supports* that appear to reduce the likelihood of physical and psychological symptoms. Media aids such as self-help books may be helpful adjuncts to treatment, but little research has been done on their impact and they may raise expectations for change too high. How support works to reduce stress is not clearly understood. However, psychologists have begun to help establish and assist a wide range of self-help groups that provide support.

7. **Racism and sexism: two problems for community psychologists** (pp. 598–605) Members of minority groups often face *racism* and discrimination based on the assumption that minorities are inferior in some way. Such prejudice can have negative effects on self-esteem and mental health. However, some epidemiological research shows that poverty, not racism, may account for higher rates of treatment for African Americans than for European Americans. A wide range of methods for reducing racism exists, including *diversity training*, but evidence of long-lasting effectiveness is not available.

   Sexism is prejudice and discrimination directed against either sex, although women are its more frequent victims. Sex role stereotypes push men and women into confining patterns of behavior. Research from 1970 (Broverman & Broverman) found that therapists described psychologically healthy women differently than they did psychologically healthy adults, but there is reason to believe that these biases have been reduced. Women are more likely to seek help although, with the exception of depression, they are not more likely than men to have mental disorders. Efforts to reduce sexism include changing the image of women in the media, legal redress, and, in the mental health field, recommendations to help therapists confront their own sexism.

KEY TERMS

Fill-in-the-Blanks Quiz

1. The study of the interaction between human beings and their environments is called ___________.

2. The effort to lower the incidence of new cases of behavioral disorders by strengthening resources that promote mental health and by eliminating factors that threaten mental health is called ___________.

3. A hospital environment in which patients participate in activities so that these activities have a therapeutic function is called a(n) ___________.

4. People who are taught by professionals to provide some mental health services but who do not have formal mental health training are called ___________.

5. Centrally located mental health facilities that provide a more comprehensive range of services to individuals than do traditional hospitals are called ___________.

6. The effort to facilitate an individual's readjustment to community life after hospitalization for mental disturbances is called ___________.

7. The interpersonal resources that individuals can call on during times of stress are collectively called ___________.

8. An approach to mental health that takes into account the influence of environmental factors and stresses the use of community resources to eliminate various conditions that produce psychological problems is called ___________.

9. The effort to shorten the duration of mental disorders through early identification of cases and prompt treatment is called ___________.

10. Prejudice and discrimination directed against people of either sex because of their sex is called ___________.

11. Training intended to increase awareness of ethnic-related attitudes and behaviors and to promote cooperative human relationships is called ___________.

12. Discrimination and prejudice aimed at a culturally different group because it is considered to be inferior is called ___________.

Answers to Fill-in-the-Blanks Quiz

1. human ecology
2. primary prevention
3. therapeutic community
4. paraprofessional therapists
5. community mental health centers
6. tertiary prevention
7. social supports
8. community psychology
9. secondary prevention
10. sexism
11. diversity training
12. racism

FACT AND CONCEPT QUESTIONS

1. One major difference between traditional clinical psychology and community psychology is that, in community psychology,
   a. there is little interest in the interaction between person and environment.
   b. treatment is offered after the problem is in "full flower."
   c. the main goal is research rather than change.
   d. there is an effort to prevent new cases from arising.

2. Which of the following was a reason for the rise of community psychology?
   a. Outpatient therapy with YAVIS patients was usually ineffective.
   b. There were too many mental health professionals looking to treat too few patients.
   c. Psychiatric hospitalization cost a great deal and was dehumanizing.
   d. Therapeutic communities and token economies were found to discriminate against the poor.

3. Hospital environments in which activities are structured to be therapeutic and in which patients are encouraged to participate in their own treatment illustrate
   a. therapeutic communities.
   b. the need for paraprofessional training.
   c. primary prevention.
   d. deinstitutionalization.

4. Which statement about treating minority group patients is *true?*
   a. They tend to drop out of therapy early unless treatment is culturally appropriate.
   b. They have more trust in and dependency on their therapists than do European Americans.
   c. They are less likely than European American patients to be seen as distressed by their therapists.
   d. European American therapists usually consider them YAVIS-type clients.

5. Community mental health centers were designed to
   a. provide prevention services only.
   b. provide a range of services for communities of 75,000 to 200,000 individuals.
   c. provide psychotherapy services in the native language of clients.
   d. reduce the social stigma of discharged mental patients.

6. Which of the following accurately describes a reason why community mental health centers have not fulfilled their goals?
   a. They adhere to a model that emphasizes environmental factors.
   b. They often do not receive adequate funding.
   c. Although highly responsive to community needs, they are poorly organized.
   d. They rarely provide inpatient or outpatient forms of therapy.

7. Community psychology programs that seek to reduce the incidence of new cases of disorder by eliminating environmental factors that cause the disorder are considered a form of
   a. tertiary prevention.
   b. social support.
   c. social and political action.
   d. primary prevention.

8. Which statement about the community-wide program for the primary prevention of depression is *true?*
   a. It involved young children in schools.
   b. It turned into a form of self-help group.
   c. It might be considered secondary prevention because it benefited those with symptoms.
   d. It showed that exposure to certain television messages can have long-term effects on behavior.

9. The Rochester, New York "red-tag" program with first graders was
   a. an example of a therapeutic community.
   b. successful in eliminating the causes of disorder.
   c. successful because it turned into a self-help group.
   d. able to spot those children who later had problems.

10. Suicide prevention centers and crisis intervention services for rape victims are examples of
    a. primary prevention.
    b. secondary prevention.
    c. therapeutic communities.
    d. deinstitutionalization.

11. The goal of tertiary prevention is to
    a. eliminate the causes of mental disorder.
    b. change the attitudes, emotions, and behaviors of individuals.
    c. improve the readjustment of people discharged from institutions.
    d. secure adequate social supports for people who were formerly isolated.

12. There is ample evidence that paraprofessionals
    a. must be selected on the basis of their personality.
    b. usually trigger the same distrust of therapy in their patients as do professionals.
    c. can function only as buddies or friends.
    d. are effective as therapeutic agents.

13. What is the "mental health pyramid"?
    a. A model of needs that places physiological needs at the bottom and self-actualization at the top
    b. A way of seeing mental health centers as providers of primary, secondary, and tertiary prevention
    c. A model of helpers that puts professionals at the top and paraprofessionals at the bottom
    d. An explanation for the high concentration of mental patients in the lower socioeconomic classes

14. According to Rappaport's empowerment model, community psychologists should
    a. accept the fact that they do not know enough to assist community residents.
    b. enhance community residents' existing ability to shape their own lives.
    c. teach community residents their values through political action.
    d. take power away from government officials so that needed policy changes take place.

15. What can social supports provide?
    a. Positive interactions, guidance, feedback, and material aid
    b. Political and social empowerment
    c. A method of teaching nonprofessionals about mental health issues so that they can be effective therapists
    d. A therapeutic community in halfway houses

16. When individuals with a common problem come together for support so that they can cope with their problem more effectively, the group that forms can be considered a
    a. self-help group.
    b. form of tertiary prevention.
    c. paraprofessional group.
    d. community mental health center.

17. Discrimination on the basis of race has which of the following effects?
    a. A lower standard of living than that enjoyed by European Americans
    b. A higher rate of unemployment than that among European Americans
    c. The development of a negative self-image among minorities
    d. All of the above

18. Which statement about the incidence of mental disorder among ethnic minorities is *true*?
    a. Most studies show very low rates of disorder among African Americans based on who is treated.
    b. Immigrant ethnic groups are least likely to show mental disorders.
    c. When the effects of social class and age are removed, incidence rates are about the same as for whites.
    d. All research shows that minorities are less likely to be hospitalized, but no research shows that they have equal levels of disorder.

19. Which statement about sex role stereotyping is *correct*?
    a. There is a large sex difference in cognitive abilities.
    b. Similar behaviors are often evaluated differently if performed by men versus women.
    c. By age 5, most girls are more aggressive and independent than boys of the same age.
    d. In most situations women are thought to be more influential than men.

20. There is reason to believe that, since the Brovermans' study on therapists' views of women,
    a. therapists have become more bias-free in their interactions with women clients.
    b. therapists have been refusing to see women clients.
    c. therapists' perceptions have become more sex role stereotyped.
    d. therapists have come to rely heavily on paraprofessionals.

APPLICATION QUESTIONS

1. Dr. Milton considers herself a community psychologist. Which of the following statements would be most unusual for her to make?
   a. "I am interested in human ecology—in the interaction between people and their environments."
   b. "It is important to work to prevent disorders before they surface."
   c. "Genetic factors are the only really important cause of mental disorders."
   d. "I think competence and strength, not a preoccupation with defects and deviance, should be encouraged."

2. In the nation of Gwax, there is growing dissatisfaction with the traditional mental health system. Based on the experience in the United States, we can expect that, in Gwax,
   a. psychiatric hospitals are costly and understaffed.
   b. psychological services are equally available to all classes of people.
   c. there are more mental health professionals than are needed.
   d. people in their communities feel a sense of empowerment.

3. Dr. Hodges is an observer and critic of the community mental health center system. He is most likely to make which statement below?
   a. "Community mental health centers were given so much funding, they didn't know what to do with their money."
   b. "The centers were run by community residents who didn't know a thing about the needs of their community."
   c. "The centers were new packaging for an old product. The traditional way of offering treatment never changed."
   d. "The goal of relying solely on self-help groups never caught on in communities."

4. A community psychologist designs a program in which children of divorcing parents are given both information about what happens during the divorce process and an opportunity to express their emotions. The goal is to reduce symptoms in children after the divorce is over. This program illustrates
   a. a therapeutic community.
   b. social and political action.
   c. secondary prevention.
   d. primary prevention.

5. Dr. Mertz says, "Secondary prevention seeks to reduce the duration of disorders. It is done by educating people before symptoms surface. Suicide prevention centers and elementary school programs for slow learners are examples." Which idea is *inaccurate*?
   a. That secondary prevention seeks to reduce duration
   b. That secondary prevention is done before symptoms surface
   c. That suicide prevention centers illustrate secondary prevention
   d. That a school program illustrates secondary prevention

6. A center such as a halfway house or another agency in which ex-mental patients receive help in adjusting to community living is an example of ____________ prevention.
   a. primary
   b. secondary
   c. tertiary
   d. self-help

7. A community psychologist informs police officers who often deal with marital violence about how to reduce aggression and increase interpersonal communication. This program illustrates the
   a. value of social support.
   b. value of tertiary prevention.
   c. need for primary prevention.
   d. training of paraprofessionals.

8. A high school principal responds negatively to a plan for training senior students to counsel eighth graders who are having interpersonal problems. What is an appropriate response to the principal?
   a. "You have every right to be upset. Paraprofessionals often do more harm than good."
   b. "Given adequate training, paraprofessionals can be effective therapeutic agents."
   c. "You should stop the project. No one uses nonprofessionals as counselors."
   d. "The only way high school students should be involved is as researchers."

9. Julie is attending a seminar in which she learns about the attitudes and norms of people in ethnic minority cultures. She is given practice in interacting cooperatively with people from cultures other than her own. Julie is attending
   a. a diversity training seminar.
   b. a paraprofessional training seminar.
   c. a seminar on deinstitutionalization.
   d. a secondary prevention seminar.

10. Jessica is seeing a male therapist. According to recent research, what are the chances that she perceives herself as being treated in a sexist manner?
   a. They are much greater than if she were seen by a female therapist.
   b. They are extremely high: 90 percent of surveyed women reported sex bias.
   c. It is almost certain if Jessica is highly educated.
   d. It is unlikely, unless she was low in education or expressing anger during therapy.

ANSWERS TO FACT AND CONCEPT QUESTIONS

1. a. Human ecology, the study of the interaction between the person and the environment, is central to community psychology.
   b. Community psychology seeks to assist people early in the development of problems.
   c. Community psychologists use what they know to improve human welfare.
   *d. The hallmark of community psychology is an interest in the prevention of psychological problems. (p. 582)

2. a. YAVIS (young, attractive, verbal, intelligent, and successful) patients are most preferred by therapists and most helped by outpatient treatment.
   b. The opposite is true: With about 20 percent of the public suffering from a disorder, there are too few professionals.
   *c. Psychiatric hospitalization was expensive—both financially and in terms of human lives damaged. (p. 583)
   d. There is no evidence that either of these treatment methods is discriminatory.

3. *a. Therapeutic communities (an idea of Maxwell Jones) are found in mental hospitals; they provide activities that increase the patients' involvement and community living skills. (pp. 583–584)
   b. Paraprofessional training teaches helpers who are nonprofessionals and who are usually outside the hospital.
   c. Primary prevention does not involve treatment of disturbed individuals.
   d. Deinstitutionalization concerns the discharge of patients, not their care in the hospital.

4. *a. Dropout rates have been reduced and effective treatment increased when culturally sensitive treatment programs have been instituted. (p. 585)
   b. Minority clients have less trust in their European American therapists.
   c. European American therapists are more likely to misread as symptoms normal behaviors that may be appropriate for the minority culture.
   d. YAVIS stands for "young, attractive, verbal, intelligent, and successful." Most poor and minority clients are not seen this way.

5. a. Community mental health centers were designed to provide outpatient care, partial hospitalization, emergency services, and consultation services, too.
   *b. The goal was to link communities of between 75,000 and 200,000 to a centrally located facility that would provide all mental health services. (p. 586)
   c. Community mental health centers are only now (and in only a few regions) responding to the cultural needs of non-English speakers.
   d. Although this is a lofty goal, it was not part of the mission of the centers.

6. a. Part of the problem was that staff members did *not* embrace this aspect of the community psychology approach.
   *b. Funding was insufficient because of both federal cutbacks and economic difficulties in home communities. (p. 587)
   c. Centers have been criticized for being unresponsive to community needs.
   d. Inpatient and outpatient treatment were mandated (and traditional) services provided by centers.

7. a. Tertiary prevention is designed to help discharged patients readjust.
   b. Social support is the informal help received from friends and relatives.
   c. Although this goal may have political consequences, it is not necessary for community psychologists to take such action to effect prevention.
   *d. The goal of primary prevention is to reduce the incidence of new cases by strengthening people or by eliminating environmental causes of disorder. (p. 588)

8. a. The primary prevention program in the schools that is described in the text taught interpersonal cognitive problem-solving skills.
   b. The people in this study had no chance to meet with one another.
   *c. Only those who had symptoms of depression benefited from the televised messages; secondary prevention is aimed at helping those in the early stages of a problem. (p. 589)
   d. There was no assessment of the long-term effects of the program.

9. a. Therapeutic communities are in mental hospitals.
   b. The goal was not primary prevention, so elimination of causes was not addressed.
   c. The children did not form self-help groups.
   *d. First graders who were "red-tagged" were found to have more difficulty as third and seventh graders than other children did. (pp. 591–592)

10. a. Primary prevention works with people before symptoms have surfaced.
   *b. Secondary prevention catches people in the early stages of problems (when a crisis has arisen) and shortens the duration of their difficulties. (p. 590)
   c. Therapeutic communities are in mental hospitals.
   d. Deinstitutionalization is concerned with discharging people from institutions at the earliest possible time.

11. a. Primary prevention seeks to eliminate root causes.
   b. Psychotherapy is best defined as an attempt to change attitudes, emotions, and behaviors so that people can function better.
   *c. Tertiary prevention is designed to ease adjustment in the community—to make this the last inpatient treatment the person needs. (p. 592)
   d. Improvement in social supports can occur in all three forms of prevention.

12. a. Paraprofessionals have been chosen for many reasons, only one of which is personality.
 b. Because they are conversant with community norms, paraprofessionals usually trigger less resistance in clients.
 c. Paraprofessionals have served many roles, including that of therapist.
 *d. Paraprofessionals are effective, although we don't really know why. (p. 594)

13. a. Maslow's hierarchy of needs places self-actualization on the top and physiological needs at the bottom.
 b. Although it is hoped that centers will provide all three forms of prevention, there is no such pyramid model.
 *c. Seidman and Rappaport suggest that professionals (like faculty members) can train people (paraprofessionals) lower on the pyramid, who, in turn, provide service. (p. 594)
 d. There is no pyramid model for the inequities of service delivery.

14. a. Rappaport suggests that community psychologists can help, even though they do not have all the answers.
 *b. Empowerment means that people already have skills and solutions; they need only the methods to take control of their lives. (p. 595)
 c. Rappaport suggests that community psychologists *not* impose their values on community members.
 d. Power resides in the community; psychologists cannot and should not take it from officials.

15. *a. Social supports provide material aid, emotional and informational feedback, positive interactions, and many other functions that seem to reduce the impact of stress. (p. 597)
 b. Social supports tend to be informal help giving, not political action.
 c. Direct education is the method usually used for paraprofessional training.
 d. Supports would not hurt, but therapeutic communities require planned activities by professionals that are structured to help patients.

16. *a. Self-help groups are defined as meetings of individuals who share a common problem and seek mutual assistance. (Focus 19.3; p. 596)
 b. Tertiary prevention assists discharged mental patients with their adjustment.
 c. Paraprofessionals offer support to others; they are not involved in mutual assistance relationships.
 d. Community mental health centers are staffed by professionals; the help giving is one-way.

17. a. One piece of evidence to support this is the fact that the poverty rate of Native Americans is more than double that of the rest of the population of the United States. (p. 599)
 b. African Americans comprise 12 percent of the population of the United States but represent over 20 percent of the unemployed. (p. 598)
 c. Many case studies indicate that minorities adopt negative racial stereotypes and have lower levels of self-esteem. (p. 599)
 *d. Because a, b, and c are all true, this is the best answer.

18. a. Most research shows higher rates of hospitalization for African Americans.
    b. Immigrant ethnic groups, particularly Southeast Asians, seem to be at higher risk for mental disorder.
    *c. In one study of 1,000 African Americans and European Americans, once social class and age factors were removed from consideration, most of the racial differences in disorder incidence were removed, too. (p. 601)
    d. The reverse is true: Most research shows that incidence based on treatment is higher for African Americans; several studies show that mental disorders are at least as common in ethnic minorities as in whites.

19. a. Sex differences in cognitive ability are very, very small.
    *b. Whereas aging men become mature, women become unattractive; there is a long list of ways in which identical behaviors are evaluated differently because of gender. (p. 603)
    c. By age 5, most girls are socialized into stereotyped behaviors that include passivity and nurturing behaviors.
    d. In most situations, women are seen as less influential.

20. *a. A study by Sesan (1988) shows that the majority of women clients report that their therapists (male and female) are bias-free. (p. 604)
    b. More women than men are seen in psychotherapy.
    c. If anything, therapists' perceptions appear to be less sex-biased.
    d. Therapists do not make use of paraprofessionals; it is something community psychologists tend to advocate.

ANSWERS TO APPLICATION QUESTIONS

1. a. Most community psychologists value the notion of human ecology.
   b. Most community psychologists support the goal of preventing disorders before they surface (primary prevention).
   *c. Most community psychologists stress the impact of environmental factors over internal and biological ones. (p. 582)
   d. Most community psychologists object to the clinical viewpoint of fixing broken people; they try to strengthen existing coping skills.

2. *a. One of the dissatisfactions with mental health services in the United States that led to community psychology was the ineffectiveness of expensive hospital care. (p. 583)
   b. Inequity in service delivery based on class and race is a major reason for the rise in community psychology.
   c. If there were "too many" professionals, it is unlikely that such dissatisfaction would exist.
   d. A major source of dissatisfaction is the sense among community residents that they do not control their own destiny.

3. a. Community mental health centers did not receive adequate funding to implement their programs.
   b. Centers were run by professionals, who were not necessarily responsive to community needs.
   *c. Center staff members tended to rely on the medical or individual models of helping; some called the centers "old wine in new bottles." (p. 587)
   d. Centers never relied on self-help for treatment.

4. a. Therapeutic communities are solely methods of treating disturbed individuals in mental hospitals.
   b. Political action would be better illustrated by a program to change how the courts deal with divorcing families.
   c. Secondary prevention would focus on helping children who already showed signs of dysfunction.
   *d. Primary prevention involves strengthening individuals; this program would be the children's equivalent of Bloom's primary prevention effort for divorcing adults. (pp. 588–589)

5. a. The main purpose of secondary prevention is to reduce the duration of disorders.
   *b. Primary prevention, not secondary prevention, attacks the problem before it has made its appearance. (p. 588)
   c. Suicide prevention centers are a secondary prevention method in that they help people at the first signs of symptoms.
   d. Such a school program would be a secondary prevention method helping people at the early stages of problems.

6. a. Primary prevention helps people before they are mental patients.
   b. Secondary prevention helps people before they need full-blown treatment.
   *c. Tertiary prevention seeks to make the first hospitalization the last one. (p. 592)
   d. Self-help can involve ex-mental patients, but it is also used by a much wider range of people.

7. a. Support would involve understanding of the officer's stresses by spouse, friends, and co-workers.
   b. Tertiary prevention involves discharged patients.
   c. Primary prevention would examine the circumstances leading up to marital violence.
   *d. Police officers are often paraprofessionals who deal with mental health concerns although they have no formal training. (pp. 593–595)

8. a. Paraprofessionals are effective therapeutic agents.
   *b. From reviews of dozens of studies, it is now clear that paraprofessionals can be quite helpful. (pp. 593–594)
   c. Paraprofessionals have been used as counselors before.
   d. High school students (even dropouts) have been used as paraprofessional counselors.

9. *a. Diversity training involves teaching individuals about the attitudes and backgrounds of cultural minority members and facilitating more cooperative interactions between racially and ethnically different groups. (p. 602)
   b. A paraprofessional training seminar would teach her how to be a counselor or other form of treatment aide.
   c. Deinstitutionalization deals with the discharge of mental patients from hospitals.
   d. Secondary prevention involves the early identification and referral of people in the early stages of mental disorder.

10. a. Research on female clients' perceptions of therapy found no difference between those who saw male and female therapists.
    b. Less than half the respondents to Sesan's (1988) survey reported any evidence of sex bias.
    c. In Sesan's findings, women with low education and those with children were most likely to report sex bias.
    *d. A minority reported sex bias; of those who did, most were low in education or were dealing with anger issues in treatment. (p. 604)

CHAPTER 20
Legal and Ethical Issues in Abnormal Psychology

LEARNING OBJECTIVES

When you have mastered the material in Chapter 20, you should be able to:

1. Describe the range of abnormal behaviors that have legal and ethical implications. Define criminal commitment and discuss criminal law's position on free will. Describe the rationale for the insanity defense and how the Bianchi case indicates the psychologist's role. Discuss the legal precedents that have shaped the current standing of the insanity defense, including the M'Naghten rule, the irresistible impulse test, and diminished capacity. (pp. 609–614)
2. Discuss the arguments for and against the plea "guilty, but mentally ill." Understand Thomas Szasz's argument against the insanity defense and involuntary commitment. (p. 614)
3. Describe the criteria for finding a defendant competent to stand trial and the procedures involved in determining it. Discuss due process and *Jackson v. Indiana.* (pp. 614–615)
4. Describe the concept of civil commitment and the criteria by which individuals are committed. Explain why the assessment of dangerousness is difficult. Understand the personality profiles of serial killers and mass murderers. (Focus 20.1; pp. 615–617, 618)
5. Explain the rationale for civil commitment, the procedures involved, and the protections that exist against its abuse. Outline the criticisms of civil commitment. (pp. 617–618)
6. Discuss the key legal rulings concerning the rights of mental patients, including the level of proof necessary for commitment (*Addington v. Texas*), the least restrictive environment principle, and the right to treatment (*Wyatt v. Stickney* and *O'Connor v. Donaldson*). (pp. 618–620)
7. Discuss the legal rulings concerning the right to refuse treatment (*Rogers v. Okin*) and the arguments for and against this right. (p. 621)
8. Discuss the reasons for and the impact of the deinstitutionalization of mental patients. Explain the concept of mainstreaming. Discuss the present living conditions of many ex-mental hospital patients and the prospects for alternative community programs. (Focus 21.2; pp. 621–624)
9. Describe the concepts of confidential and privileged communications. Understand the American Psychological Association ethics code specifications for disclosure of confidential information. Discuss exemptions to privileged communications. (pp. 624–625)
10. Describe the duty-to-warn principle and the legal rulings related to it (*Tarasoff v. Board of Regents of the University of California, Hedlund v. Superior Court of Orange County*). Evaluate criticisms of the duty-to-warn principle, including the question of divulging a client's HIV-positive status to others. (Critical Thinking 20.1; pp. 625–627)

11. Discuss how mental health professionals need to accommodate the changes in the ethnic profile of Americans. Describe the ethical guidelines for working with culturally different clients and the information in DSM-IV that deals with multicultural influences. (pp. 627–629)
12. Identify the position of professional organizations on the issue of sexual intimacies between therapist and client. Discuss the research on the impact of therapists' sexual involvement with clients. (pp. 629–630)
13. Discuss the ethical issues related to nonerotic touching of clients by therapists. Appreciate the frequency of such behavior and the arguments for and against therapist-client physical contact. (pp. 630–631)

CHAPTER OUTLINE

1. **Legal and ethical issues in abnormal psychology** (pp. 609–611) Behaviors ranging from murder to public profanity to therapists touching their clients all have legal and ethical implications. Mental health decisions involve legal issues when psychologists consider a client or defendant's involuntary hospitalization, competence to stand trial, insanity defense, or rights as a mental patient. The *Tarasoff* case raises questions about therapists' responsibility to potential victims versus their oath not to breach confidentiality. Ethical questions also arise from the erotic implications of therapists touching their clients.

2. **Criminal commitment** (pp. 611–615) Criminal law assumes individual actions are based on free will. *Criminal commitment*—the incarceration of an individual for having committed a crime—is the consequence of criminal acts. The *insanity defense* recognizes that individuals may not always be held accountable for their criminal actions. Psychologists need to be on guard against those faking mental illness. The M'Naghten rule defines insanity as not knowing right from wrong. The *irresistible impulse test* says that insanity is also involved when a person could not have acted differently. The Durham standard argues that insanity must be a product of mental disease. The ALI standard (1962) combines earlier definitions. In some regions, the concept of diminished capacity has been added, allowing that a mental disease or defect may reduce a person's specific intent to commit a crime.

   After the successful insanity defense by John W. Hinckley, Jr., the man who attempted to assassinate President Reagan, the definition of insanity changed to the individual not understanding what he or she did. The plea of "guilty, but mentally ill" was developed as well to separate mental illness and criminal responsibility. Thomas Szasz argues against both the insanity defense and involuntary commitment as being contrary to individual liberty and responsibility.

   Competency to stand trial assesses the individual's mental state at the time of the trial. There are several criteria for competence. If individuals are found incompetent, they are committed but only for finite periods (*Jackson v. Indiana*, 1972), thereby protecting *due process*.

3. **Civil commitment** (Focus 20.1; pp. 615–618) Individuals can be hospitalized against their will although this should be avoided if possible. The criteria for commitment include danger to self or others, inability to care for self, inability to make responsible decisions, and unmanageable level of panic. Assessment of *dangerousness* is very difficult because it is rare, is influenced by specific situations, is best predicted by evidence inadmissible by courts, and is ill-defined. Serial killers and mass murderers have psychological profiles that are different from one another.

   Involuntary civil commitment occurs when a client does not consent to hospitalization and follows procedures that include professional testimony, formal hearings, and set periods of treatment. Controversy exists over the helpfulness of committing people for treatment against their will.

4. **Rights of mental patients** (pp. 618–621) Mental patients can be committed only with a level of proof that is "clear and convincing" (*Addington v. Texas*, 1979). Treatment should be provided in the *least restrictive environment*, confining people to hospitals only when they cannot care for themselves in less structured settings. *Wyatt v. Stickney* (1972) established the concept of *right to treatment* and stipulated minimal living conditions for care. *O'Connor v. Donaldson* (1975) also affirmed the right to treatment. Several cases have supported the patient's right to refuse treatment and for treatment to be the least intrusive form possible.

5. **Deinstitutionalization** (Focus 20.2; pp. 621–624) *Deinstitutionalization* involves the discharge of patients from mental hospitals. Reasons for this movement include the belief that living in institutions is harmful, that *mainstreaming* (integrating) patients back into the community can be accomplished, and that insufficient funds necessitate early discharge. Critics of deinstitutionalization point to the problem of dumping patients on city streets and to the related problem of homelessness. The lack of community resources for discharged patients is a primary reason for the problems with deinstitutionalization.

6. **The therapist-client relationship: confidentiality and privileged communication** (pp. 624–627) Ethics prohibit therapists from divulging information given by clients in much the same way that attorneys and doctors do not reveal information. However, there are a number of situations that call for breaking *confidentiality*, an ethical standard. A narrower legal concept is *privileged communication*, which prevents disclosure of information without the client's permission. There are at least five situations in which the therapist is obliged to disclose privileged commummincations. One of them is when a client is likely to carry out a threat to attack someone else. The *Tarasoff v. Board of Regents* case (1976) determined that therapists must warn potential victims of client aggression; *Hedlund v. Superior Court* (1983) ruled that those the victim might be with must be warned as well. It is unclear whether this principle applies to clients who are infected with the AIDS virus. There are several criticisms of the duty-to-warn principle.

7. **Cultural pluralism and the mental health profession** (pp. 627–629) The proportion of racial/ethnic minorities in the population of the United States is increasing. Mental health professionals need to be aware of biases, have adequate training, and adjust their methods to provide culturally appropriate services. DSM-IV includes information on culture-specific symptom patterns; the American Psychological Association has published guidelines for professionals serving culturally diverse populations.

8. **Social and personal relationships in therapy** (pp. 629–631) Sexual involvement of therapists with clients is condemned by virtually all professional organizations. Clients who become sexually involved with their therapists (almost always female clients with male therapists) are adversely affected. Professional organizations process ethical complaints against therapists who engage in misconduct.

   About one-third of therapists touch their clients in nonerotic ways (hugging or shaking hands) and over half believe such touching can be therapeutic. Critics suggest that this behavior is often misinterpreted by clients, that it has political overtones, and can lead to sexual intimacy, which is clearly unethical.

KEY TERMS

Fill-in-the-Blanks Quiz

1. The plea that defendants use if they have committed a crime but plead not guilty because of mental illness is called the ___________.

2. The shift of responsibility for the care of mental patients from large hospitals to agencies in local communities is called ___________.

3. The form of protective confinement when a person is judged to be dangerous to self or others even though no crime has been committed is called ___________.

4. The definition of insanity that states that a defendant is not responsible if he or she lacked the willpower to control his or her behavior is called the ___________.

5. The concept of judging whether a defendant's mental state at the time of trial is sufficient to enable him or her to assist in his or her own defense is called ___________.

6. The right of patients to be placed in an environment that gives maximum freedom considering the person's capacities is called ___________.

7. A mental patient's right to receive therapy to improve his or her emotional state is called the ___________.

8. The assessment of an individual's potential to harm self or others is the assessment of ___________.

9. The integration of mental patients back into the community as soon as possible after treatment is called ___________.

10. The legal concept that guarantees the right to a fair trial, to face accusers, and to present evidence (among other things) is called ___________.

11. The principle that prevents clients' confidential communications with their therapists from being disclosed in court without their permission is called ___________.

12. The incarceration of an individual on the basis of the committal of a crime is called ___________.

13. The ethical standard that protects clients from the disclosure of information without their consent is called ___________.

Answers to Fill-in-the-Blanks Quiz

1. insanity defense
2. deinstitutionalization
3. civil commitment
4. irresistible impulse test
5. competency to stand trial
6. least restrictive environment
7. right to treatment
8. dangerousness

9. mainstreaming
10. due process
11. privileged communication
12. criminal commitment
13. confidentiality

FACT AND CONCEPT QUESTIONS

1. According to the M'Naghten rule, defendants are insane if, at the time of
   a. their trial, they cannot assist in their own defense.
   b. the crime, they did not understand the wrongfulness of their actions.
   c. the crime, they were unable to act in any other way.
   d. their trial, they are severely mentally ill.

2. As a result of the successful insanity defense by John W. Hinckley, Jr.,
   a. defendants claim insanity in more than 20 percent of criminal cases today.
   b. the insanity defense has been abolished.
   c. some states have adopted alternative pleas, such as "guilty, but mentally ill."
   d. the criteria for defining "dangerousness" have been made more rigorous.

3. When psychologists assess a defendant to determine his or her competency to stand trial, they are interested in the
   a. person's mental state at present.
   b. person's dangerousness.
   c. availability and effectiveness of treatment alternatives.
   d. person's mental state at the time of the crime.

4. The *Jackson v. Indiana* ruling of 1972 protects committed patients in what way?
   a. It protects them from being committed indefinitely without review.
   b. It protects them from coercive or ineffective treatment.
   c. It protects them from inadequate living conditions.
   d. It assures that information about them will not be divulged by their therapists.

5. Being unable to care for oneself, being a dangerous threat to someone else, or being in a severe state of panic are
   a. ways of defining dangerousness.
   b. reasons for declaring someone insane.
   c. reasons for being allowed to refuse treatment.
   d. reasons for involuntary commitment.

6. Which statement about dangerousness in mental patients is *true?*
   a. Psychologists tend to underpredict dangerousness in patients.
   b. Dangerousness is rarely used as a criterion for civil commitment.
   c. Psychiatric patients are no more dangerous to others than the population at large.
   d. Among mental patients, the legal determination of dangerousness has little impact on whether or not violence will occur.

7. Which statement about involuntary civil commitment proceedings is *true?*
   a. Without relying on expert testimony, the judge decides whether the person needs to be in treatment.
   b. The person being examined can speak on his or her own behalf and is represented by counsel.
   c. In some states, a family physician can commit a person.
   d. A jury always decides whether a person needs to be committed.

8. *Addington v. Texas* (1979) has had its greatest impact on
   a. deinstitutionalization.
   b. the ethics of divulging confidential client information.
   c. the insanity defense.
   d. the standards used to determine civil commitment.

9. The principle of ___________ argues that patients should be confined to hospitals only when they are unable to care for themselves.
   a. deinstitutionalization
   b. most intrusive treatment
   c. least restrictive environment
   d. privileged communication

10. The right of patients to receive adequate care in a satisfactory living environment was based on rulings in which cases?
    a. *Wyatt v. Stickney* and *O'Connor v. Donaldson*
    b. *Tarasoff v. Board of Regents* and *Rouse v. Cameron*
    c. *Jackson v. Indiana* and *Tarasoff v. Board of Regents*
    d. *Rogers v. Okin* and *United States v. Hinckley*

11. According to a recent court ruling, who decides what constitutes "therapy"?
    a. Mental health professionals
    b. A jury
    c. The patient and his or her family
    d. No one; this has not been legally determined.

12. If, in the future, the use of ECT and psychosurgery to treat mildly disturbed patients is not permitted, this can be attributed to the
    a. principle of duty to warn.
    b. need for patients to be competent before being tried.
    c. concept of deinstitutionalization.
    d. principle of least intrusive treatment.

13. Which statement about deinstitutionalization is *accurate*?
    a. Despite thirty years of efforts to reduce the number of mental patients in hospitals, no decrease has occurred.
    b. The goal of deinstitutionalization was to eliminate the insanity defense.
    c. Generally speaking, deinstitutionalization has led to the successful reintegration of mental patients into their home communities.
    d. Deinstitutionalization has been very successful in reducing the number of patients in state mental hospitals.

14. Which problem is most directly related to deinstitutionalization?
    a. Therapists unethically engaging in sexual relations with their clients
    b. Large numbers of discharged patients becoming homeless
    c. A dramatic increase in the number of successful insanity defense cases
    d. Greater abuse and neglect of patients in mental hospitals

15. The need for trust and openness in psychotherapy is the reason for
    a. the principle of duty to warn.
    b. deinstitutionalization.
    c. confidentiality of client information.
    d. the principle of least restrictive environment.

16. The concept of privileged communication is
    a. a legal one, similar to the arrangement between husband and wife.
    b. an ethical one that involves no legal obligation.
    c. a recent "invention" stemming from the *Tarasoff v. Board of Regents* (1976) ruling.
    d. not as available to the therapist and client as it is to the attorney and client.

17. When can privileged communication be legally and ethically breached?
    a. When the therapist feels it would be helpful for therapy.
    b. When the client waives his or her privilege.
    c. Both a and b are true.
    d. Neither a nor b is true.

18. According to *Tarasoff v. Board of Regents* (1976) and *Hedlund v. Superior Court of Orange County* (1983), psychologists who suspect that a client might act violently
    a. must protect the privileged information and keep silent.
    b. are required to contact the police.
    c. must warn all potential victims.
    d. are expected to commit the client to a mental hospital.

19. Acccording to the American Psychological Association's ethical principles involving the treatment of culturally different clients,
    a. therapy is forbidden if the therapist and client come from different cultural backgrounds.
    b. therapists should have adequate training in multicultural psychology.
    c. it is the client's responsibility to conform to the cultural expectations of the therapist.
    d. it is assumed that psychological disorder and its treatment are consistent across different cultures.

20. Many humanistic psychologists argue that ____________ is ethical behavior between therapist and client.
    a. sexual intercourse
    b. nonerotic touching
    c. breaking confidentiality without cause
    d. sexual fondling

APPLICATION QUESTIONS

1. The Kenneth Bianchi (Hillside Strangler) case illustrates the issue of
   a. competency to stand trial.
   b. deinstitutionalization.
   c. faking insanity.
   d. privileged communication between therapist and client.

2. David T. is a defendant in a murder case. He claims that a mental disorder prevented him from acting in any way other than the way he did. David T.'s insanity defense is based on
   a. the principle of least restrictive treatment.
   b. the notion of irresistible impulse.
   c. the M'Naghten rule.
   d. the principle of competency to stand trial.

3. George is being examined by a psychiatrist to see whether he can assist his attorney in his own defense. In what kind of legal hearing is George engaged?
   a. Competency to stand trial
   b. Involuntary civil commitment
   c. Waiver of privileged communication
   d. An insanity defense trial

4. Judge Wallace says, "Thanks to *Jackson v. Indiana*, people are protected against the abuse of endless incarceration when they have committed no crime." The judge is talking about
   a. a ruling restricting deinstitutionalization.
   b. the new "guilty, but mentally ill" plea.
   c. the principle of least restrictive treatment environment.
   d. a ruling restricting confinement solely on the grounds of incompetency.

5. Dr. Roland says, "When people are so mentally ill that they cannot control their actions and may harm others, we cannot wait until they have become violent. We must treat them involuntarily." Dr. Roland's comments argue
   a. against the insanity defense.
   b. against deinstitutionalization.
   c. for the concept of duty to warn.
   d. for civil commitment.

6. Mr. Birch, an attorney, says, "If this person is going to be involuntarily committed, the judge needs to have 'clear and convincing evidence' that the person is mentally ill and potentially dangerous." Mr. Birch is using the ruling in
   a. *Tarasoff v. Board of Regents* (1976).
   b. *Addington v. Texas* (1979).
   c. *Wyatt v. Stickney* (1972).
   d. *United States v. Hinckley* (1982).

7. Dr. Poole, director of a state hospital, says, "Because of deinstitutionalization, we need to release patients quickly. But while they are here, they have the right to the treatment standards outlined in *Wyatt v. Stickney*." What part of Dr. Poole's statement is *incorrect*?
   a. The idea that deinstitutionalization might lead to quick discharge.
   b. The idea that *Wyatt v. Stickney* is linked to patients' rights.
   c. The idea that the right to treatment ends when a person is discharged.
   d. Nothing in Dr. Poole's statement is incorrect.

8. Dr. Luborsky says, "It has reduced the number of patients in state hospitals by more than 50 percent but has led to the criminalization of the mentally ill and has increased the problem of homelessness in the United States." Dr. Luborsky is commenting on
   a. deinstitutionalization.
   b. the insanity defense.
   c. the right to refuse treatment.
   d. the principle of duty to warn.

9. Dr. Judd's patient, Mike V., is threatening to blow up his father-in-law's store. Dr. Judd thinks the threat is legitimate. According to ____________, Dr. Judd must ____________.
   a. *Rogers v. Okin* (1979); not divulge this information to the police
   b. *Wyatt v. Stickney* (1972); have Mike V. committed
   c. *Tarasoff v. Board of Regents* (1976); warn Mike's father-in-law
   d. *Hedlund v. Superior Court of Orange County* (1983); not divulge this information to the police

10. Dr. Miller, a therapist, says, "It has political implications because it usually happens between male therapists and female clients. Furthermore, it can be misinterpreted, and it can put the relationship at risk." Dr. Miller is probably talking about
    a. nonerotic touching initiated by a therapist.
    b. a therapist assessing a client for competency.
    c. therapists who discharge patients to community settings.
    d. therapists who testify in insanity defense trials.

ANSWERS TO FACT AND CONCEPT QUESTIONS

1. a. The ability to assist in one's own defense is a criterion for competency to stand trial, not for insanity.
   *b. The M'Naghten rule defines insanity in terms of the inability to know right from wrong when the crime was committed. (p. 613)
   c. Irresistible impulse is the definition of insanity as an incapacity to act otherwise.
   d. The insanity defense pertains only to the person's mental state when the crime was committed.

2. a. The insanity defense is used in less than 2 percent of criminal cases.
   b. Although some would like to abolish the insanity defense, it still exists (in a somewhat more restricted form).
   *c. The furor after the verdict led to the American Bar and Medical Associations asking for changes in the law, and several states developing new pleas. (p. 614)
   d. Dangerousness is an issue in civil commitment cases, not in the insanity defense.

3. *a. Competency to stand trial is based on the defendant's current ability to understand the proceedings and to assist in his or her own defense. (p. 615)
   b. Dangerousness is most closely related to civil commitment cases, not competency.
   c. The availability of treatment does not pertain to competency to stand trial.
   d. The person's mental state at the time of the crime influences the validity of an insanity defense.

4. *a. Because of this ruling, people who are committed because they are incompetent to stand trial cannot be confined indefinitely without review. (p. 615)
   b. Relevant right to treatment rulings include *Wyatt v. Stickney* and *O'Connor v. Donaldson.*
   c. The relevant ruling here is *Wyatt v. Stickney.*
   d. This ruling deals with indefinite confinement, not privileged communication.

5. a. Although presenting a threat to someone else is a part of "dangerousness," the rest of the information suggests the broader category of concern, the need for commitment.
   b. Insanity is defined as being unable to appreciate the wrongfulness of an act or being incapable of resisting an impulse.
   c. Reasons for refusing treatment have more to do with delusional thinking than with dangerousness or a state of panic.
   *d. Dangerousness, an inability to care for oneself, and an extreme attack of anxiety are reasons for committing people to treatment against their will. (pp. 615-616)

6. a. The error that psychologists make is *over*predicting dangerousness.
   b. Dangerousness is the chief criterion for civil commitment.
   *c. Despite the popular myth, psychiatric patients are no more dangerous than is the population at large. (p. 617)
   d. Just as with other people, violent behavior among those with mental disorders is the result of both personality and situational factors.

7. a. Expert witnesses, such as psychologists and psychiatrists, testify to provide their assessments of the person's need for treatment.
   *b. Civil commitment proceedings include due process; the person can speak on his or her own behalf and get legal counsel. (p. 617)
   c. No longer can one person determine that another person should be committed; the legal proceedings provide greater protection of civil rights now.
   d. In most cases, commitment is decided by a judge, not a jury.

8. a. Deinstitutionalization is most affected by rulings involving the least restrictive environment principle.
   b. *Addington* had nothing to do with confidentiality.
   c. *Addington* had nothing to do with the placement of mental patients.
   *d. *Addington* raised the level of proof in civil commitment cases to "clear and convincing evidence" (75 percent certainty). (p. 619)

9. a. Deinstitutionalization is a related, but much broader, idea that considers all the reasons for using community agencies rather than large institutions.
   b. The legal principle is *least* intrusive treatment.
   *c. To ensure civil liberties, the principle of least restrictive environment allows for hospitalization only as a last resort. (p. 619)
   d. The principle of privileged communication is confined to therapist-client relationships.

10. *a. The *Wyatt* ruling of Judge Frank Johnson set the standards for mental treatment in institutions; *O'Connor* supported the right to treatment principle. (p. 620)
    b. *Tarasoff* dealt with duty to warn; *Rouse* did involve right to treatment.
    c. *Jackson* limited the duration for which people found incompetent can be confined; *Tarasoff* dealt with duty to warn.
    d. *Rogers* dealt with the right to refuse treatment; *Hinckley* was the insanity defense case involving the man who shot President Reagan.

11. *a. The case is *Youngberg v. Romeo* (1982), and the decision was that mental health professionals should define "therapy." (p. 620)
    b. *Youngberg* ruled that professionals decide.
    c. *Youngberg* ruled that professionals decide.
    d. Although the law in this area is new, the *Youngberg* case does give guidance.

12. a. Duty to warn defines a situation in which therapists must break confidentiality.
    b. Competency is unrelated to treatment issues.
    c. Deinstitutionalization is concerned with *where* treatment occurs, not so much with the matching of patients and therapy methods.
    *d. This principle suggests that ECT and surgery may be more intrusive therapies than insight or behavioral therapies and thus should not be used with mildly disturbed patients. (p. 621)

13. a. Deinstitutionalization has reduced hospital populations by more than one-half.
    b. The goal of deinstitutionalization was to dramatically reduce the reliance on hospitals for treatment.
    c. The great failure of deinstitutionalization is that discharged patients, lacking community support, return to the hospital.
    *d. The state hospital population of the United States dropped by more than 50 percent. (p. 621)

14. a. Deinstitutionalization is unrelated to therapist-client relationships.
    *b. In many cases, discharged patients have been "dumped" in urban areas, and have no homes or social supports. (p. 623)
    c. Deinstitutionalization is unrelated to criminal commitment.
    d. If anything, the reduced populations in mental hospitals have led to improvements in care.

15. a. Duty to warn puts greater emphasis on protecting victims than on assuring confidentiality; this reduces openness.
    b. Deinstitutionalization is unrelated to therapist-client relationships.
    *c. Confidentiality in therapy is necessary if clients are to believe that they can be open without fearing that they may be hurt. (p. 624)
    d. This principle considers only the location of treatment.

16. *a. Privileged communication between therapist and client is a legal concept. (p. 624)
    b. It is the wider concept of confidentiality that is an ethical concept unprotected by the law.
    c. *Tarasoff* defined when privileged communication must be breached.
    d. Therapists and clients have the same legal privilege as attorneys and their clients.

17. a. The privilege is in the hands of the client, not the therapist.
    *b. Only the client can waive the privilege. (p. 624)
    c. Because a is incorrect, this cannot be the best answer.
    d. Because b is correct, this cannot be the best answer.

18. a. *Tarasoff* ruled that duty to warn is stronger than privileged communication.
    b. Both *Tarasoff* and *Hedlund* ruled that the psychologist must warn potential victims, not just the police.
    *c. Both *Tarasoff* and *Hedlund* ruled that the psychologist must warn all potential victims. (pp. 625–626)
    d. Neither *Tarasoff* nor *Hedlund* considered civil commitment.

19. a. As long as therapists are aware of cultural differences and provide appropriate treatment, there is nothing to prohibit cross-cultural treatment.
    *b. Psychologists are expected to be aware of cultural differences, and their own biases, to be able to identify situations where specific therapeutic strategies must be modified to be culturally sensitive, and to obtain sufficient training to do these things. (p. 628)
    c. Ethical principles place responsibility for adjusting to cultural differences on the therapist, not the client.
    d. DSM-IV has an appendix that presents culture-bound syndromes; the APA ethical guidelines require psychologists to adjust treatment to be culturally appropriate.

20. a. Virtually no one, except perpetrators, believes that sexual intercourse with clients is ethical.
    *b. Humanistic psychologists are the most inclined to use nonerotic touching and to view it as ethical. (p. 631)
    c. Virtually no one believes that it is ethical to break confidentiality without cause.
    d. Any sexual intimacy between therapist and client is seen as unethical.

ANSWERS TO APPLICATION QUESTIONS

1. a. Bianchi's lawyers considered using the insanity defense.
   b. Bianchi was on trial for a series of murders; he was not a mental patient.
   *c. Until Martin Orne uncovered Bianchi's faking, it was believed that he was suffering from multiple personality disorder. (p. 611)
   d. Bianchi was not in therapy, so there was no such issue.

2. a. Treatment becomes an issue only after a person is found incompetent or insane.
   *b. Irresistible impulse is one definition of insanity; it is based on an inability to conform to the law because of a mental disease or defect. (p. 613)
   c. The M'Naghten rule is a definition of insanity based on the lack of appreciation that what one did was wrong.
   d. Competency is defined as mental capacity at the time of the trial, not at the time of the crime.

3. *a. Competency involves a defendant's capacity to understand the proceedings and to assist in his or her own defense. (pp. 614–615)
   b. Such an assessment assumes that a crime was committed; in civil commitment, no crime is presumed.
   c. Waiver of privileged communication is not based on a person's ability to act in his or her own defense.
   d. Insanity is concerned with a defendant's mental state at the time of the crime, not at the time of the trial.

4. a. *Jackson* protected people against indefinite confinement; this supports deinstitutionalization.
   b. *Jackson* (1972) occurred some ten years before the Hinckley case, which led to calls for more stringent definitions of insanity.
   c. *Jackson* dealt only with how long a person could be confined, not where.
   *d. The *Jackson* ruling held that those who were committed because they were not competent to stand trial could not be "forgotten" without either standing trial or being committed for treatment. (p. 615)

5. a. The insanity defense is unrelated to treatment.
   b. Although these comments have relevance to deinstitutionalization, that concept is much broader and deals with the need for community-based treatment.
   c. Duty to warn involves therapist-client relationships, not criminal cases.
   *d. Civil commitment deals with confining people for treatment before they have committed any crime. (pp. 617–618)

6. a. *Tarasoff* decided the therapist's role in protecting potential victims of his or her client.
   *b. *Addington* determined necessary levels of proof in commitment cases. (p. 619)
   c. *Wyatt* established the right to treatment and the conditions under which treatment should be offered.
   d. *Hinckley* dealt with the insanity defense.

7. a. Deinstitutionalization has led to earlier discharge.
   b. *Wyatt* was a major case supporting the patient's right to treatment.
   c. There is no court ruling that suggests that hospitals must provide treatment after discharge.
   *d. Because a, b, and c are all correct, there is nothing inaccurate in Dr. Poole's comments. (pp. 619–621)

8. *a. Deinstitutionalization has led to a reduction in hospital populations, but discharged patients often do not receive support in urban communities and wind up homeless or in jail. (pp. 621–622)
   b. The insanity defense has nothing to do with state hospital populations.
   c. The right to refuse treatment may lead to more untreated mental patients, but it does not as clearly lead to homelessness.
   d. Duty to warn is related to therapist-client relationships, not to hospitalization.

9. a. *Rogers* is a case involving the right to refuse treatment.
   b. *Wyatt* is a case involving the right to adequate treatment.
   *c. *Tarasoff* is the case that established the principle of duty to warn; Dr. Judd would be negligent if she did not warn. (p. 625)
   d. *Hedlund* expanded on *Tarasoff;* it widened the need to warn potential victims.

10. *a. Nonerotic touching may be seen as unethical because male therapists can use it to exercise dominance over female clients. (p. 631)
    b. Competency to stand trial is unrelated to male-female issues.
    c. Discharge is more closely related to deinstitutionalization.
    d. The insanity defense is unrelated to male-female issues.